The NEW HOUSE PLANT EXPERT

Dr. D.G. Hessayon

1st Impression	300,000

Previous Editions:
28 Impressions   8,160,000

Other books in the EXPERT Series:

THE GARDEN EXPERT
THE FLOWER EXPERT
THE TREE & SHRUB EXPERT
THE BEDDING PLANT EXPERT
THE ROSE EXPERT
THE LAWN EXPERT
THE VEGETABLE EXPERT
THE FRUIT EXPERT
THE HOME EXPERT

pbi
PUBLICATIONS

pbi PUBLICATIONS · BRITANNICA HOUSE · WALTHAM CROSS · HERTS · ENGLAND

Contents

		page
CHAPTER 1	**PLANTS IN THE HOME**	3–14
	Introduction	3
	The ten golden rules	4
	How to choose the right plant	4
	The naming of house plants	5
	The shape of house plants	6–7
	The growing conditions for house plants	8
	Buying a house plant	9
	Taking it home	9
	Housing your plant	10–11
	Repotting your plant	12–13
	Facts & figures	14
CHAPTER 2	**DISPLAYING INDOOR PLANTS**	15–48
	Introduction	15
	The Specimen Plant	16–17
	The Pot Group	18–19
	The Indoor Garden	20–25
	The Terrarium	26–28
	Positioning your plants	29–31
	A room-by-room guide to house plants	32–48
CHAPTER 3	**THE CLASSIFICATION OF HOUSE PLANTS**	49–59
	Introduction	49
	Foliage house plants	50–53
	Flowering house plants	54–55
	Flowering pot plants	56–57
	Cacti	58–59
CHAPTER 4	**HOUSE PLANTS A–Z**	60–225
	Introduction	60
	Varieties	61–225
CHAPTER 5	**PLANT CARE**	226–236
CHAPTER 6	**INCREASING YOUR STOCK**	237–240
CHAPTER 7	**PLANT TROUBLES**	241–246
CHAPTER 8	**HOUSE PLANT GROWER'S DICTIONARY**	247–250
CHAPTER 9	**PLANT INDEX**	251–255
	Acknowledgements	256

Printed and bound in Great Britain by Jarrold & Sons Ltd, Norwich

ISBN 0 903505 35 5

CHAPTER 1

PLANTS IN THE HOME

At first glance very little seems to have changed since the previous edition of this book appeared in 1980. Ivies, Tradescantias, Monsteras, Palms and Rubber Plants continue to provide the foliage background and African Violets continue to be popular for providing flowers throughout the year. Christmas remains a special time for indoor plants, and Poinsettia, Azalea, Winter Cherry and Cyclamen remain firm favourites.

In reality there have been all sorts of changes in the world of house plants. Orchids were regarded as specimens for the specialist grower in 1980 — now you can buy the easier varieties in garden centres everywhere. Kalanchoe, Pot Chrysanthemums, Air Plants, Weeping Figs and Boston Ferns are much more popular nowadays and many new types of house plants appeared in garden centres and department stores during the 1980s and early 1990s. Mikania, Radermachera, Leea and Lisianthus were all on the shelves before they appeared in the pages of the textbooks.

The popularity of house plants has continued to grow and the market is slowly changing. For the first time we are now buying more flowering plants than foliage ones and the purchaser is more likely to be 20–30 years old than 45–55. Our attitude towards indoor plants is also slowly changing — more and more people are willing to buy showy but short-lived specimens rather than always turning to evergreen varieties. Even the American Space Agency has brought about a change in our attitude towards plants — during the 1980s it was discovered that Scindapsus, Chlorophytum, Ivy, Spathiphyllum, Chrysanthemum and Aloe are extremely effective in removing pollutants from the air.

Things change and the fashion for certain plants will alter in the years to come. But the basic fascination for growing plants in the home will no doubt remain with us and will continue to increase. There are things to learn if you are a beginner but you don't need a book like this one in order to learn about the beauty, variety and popularity of house plants — just look around you. Everywhere you will find them, the impressive indoor gardens in public buildings .... tiny pots on windowsills .... scores of colourful varieties offered for sale in garden shops.

The charm of house plants may be universal, but many millions are allowed to die needlessly each year. You have to face the fact that your living room or hall is not a particularly good home for them — most plants would be much happier in the moist, bright air of a well-lit laundry. This means that you can't just leave them to look after themselves — each plant needs some care and each variety has its own particular requirements. It is the purpose of this book to tell you the secrets of success and the special problems you are likely to find.

Forget about green fingers. Anyone can grow the more popular varieties and make them look attractive. If you choose delicate or fussy types then green fingers won't help you but a conservatory will. If everything dies as soon as you take it home, then you are doing something seriously wrong and the answer is in these pages. If your plants look sickly and unattractive then it is a matter of poor choice, incorrect upkeep or lack of knowledge about house plant display. Once again the answers are here. Exciting displays are not difficult to make .... increasing your stock is surprisingly simple .... here you will find the key.

THE TEN GOLDEN RULES

● **DON'T DROWN THEM**
Roots need air as well as water — keeping the compost soaked at all times means certain death for most plants. Learn how to water properly — see pages 230-231.

● **GIVE THEM A REST**
Beginners are usually surprised to learn that nearly all plants need a rest in winter, which means less water, less feeding and less heat than in the active growing period. See page 234.

● **ACCEPT THE LOSS OF 'TEMPORARY' PLANTS**
Some popular gift plants, such as Cyclamen, Chrysanthemum and Gloxinia will die down in a matter of weeks. You've done nothing wrong — these types are flowering pot plants which are only temporary residents.

● **GIVE THEM EXTRA HUMIDITY**
The atmosphere of a centrally-heated room in winter is as dry as desert air. Learn how to increase the air humidity — see page 232.

● **TREAT TROUBLE PROMPTLY**
Expert or beginner, trouble will strike some time. One or two scale insects or mealy bugs are easily picked off; an infestation may be incurable. Overwatering is not fatal at first, but kills when prolonged. Learn to recognise the early signs of trouble.

● **GROUP THEM TOGETHER**
Nearly all plants look better and grow better when grouped together. Learn the how and why of plant grouping on pages 18-28.

● **LEARN TO REPOT**
After a year or two most plants begin to look sickly; in many cases the plant simply needs repotting into a larger container. Learn how on page 13.

● **CHOOSE WISELY**
The plant must be able to flourish in the home you provide for it. Even the expert can't make a shade-lover survive in a sunny window.

● **HAVE THE PROPER TOOLS**
Buy a watering can with a long, narrow spout and a mister for increasing humidity, reducing dust and controlling pests. You will need a reputable brand of compost and a collection of pots plus stakes and plant-ties or string. Drip trays will keep water off the furniture — a bottle of liquid fertilizer and a safe pest killer will keep the plants looking healthy. To complete your tool kit include a soft sponge, an old kitchen spoon and fork, a leaf gloss aerosol and a pair of small-sized secateurs.

● **CHECK THE PLANT'S SPECIFIC NEEDS**
Look up the secrets of success in the A–Z Guide for each plant (pages 61-225).

HOW TO CHOOSE THE RIGHT PLANT

A bewildering range of plants is now available, and it's all too easy to make a mistake. Look around the homes of your friends to see which plants appear to flourish, but don't be guided by the large specimens in public buildings. These plants are often rented and returned to the nursery when the poor conditions start to have an effect.

You want to buy a plant . . . ask yourself the following five questions and the answers will give you a short list of types which will suit your purpose. Then choose the one which really appeals to you, for that is the most important requirement of all.

QUESTION 1: DO I WANT THE PLANT TO BE ON DISPLAY ALL YEAR ROUND?
Practically all foliage plants keep their display value throughout the year. The situation with flowering plants is more complex. Some have a limited display life and have no place in the room after the flowers have faded. But there are other flowering ones which can be kept on display all year round. Read page 49 carefully.

QUESTION 2: HOW MUCH TIME AND SKILL DO I HAVE?
Some plants have the reputation of being almost indestructible — these 'cast-iron' plants include Sansevieria, Fatsia, Aspidistra, popular Succulents (if kept dry) and Cyperus (if kept wet). The 'easy' group is much larger. These plants tolerate a wide range of conditions — look for Asparagus, Bromeliads, Chlorophytum, Coleus, Hedera, Monstera, Neanthe, Philodendron scandens and Tradescantia. At the other end of the scale is the 'delicate' group (Acalypha, Calathea, Gardenia etc). These are a challenge and are best left to the experienced house plant enthusiast.

QUESTION 3: HOW MUCH DO I WANT TO SPEND?
The usual way of obtaining a plant is to buy one in a 3-5 in. pot, but one type may be much, much dearer than another. The expensive ones have a major drawback for the professional grower, such as slowness of growth or difficulty in propagation. If you want lots of foliage and money is limited then buy small plants for growing on or you can sow seeds and strike cuttings.

QUESTION 4: WHAT SIZE AND SHAPE DO I WANT?
Think about size and shape as well as the beauty of the flowers or the foliage. Read pages 6-7.

QUESTION 5: WHAT WILL THE GROWING CONDITIONS BE LIKE?
The all-important questions — how much light will be available and will the spot be heated in winter? Read page 8.

THE NAMING OF HOUSE PLANTS

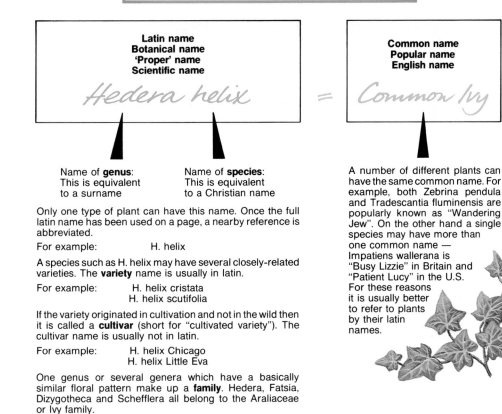

Latin name
Botanical name
'Proper' name
Scientific name

Hedera helix

=

Common name
Popular name
English name

Common Ivy

Name of **genus**:
This is equivalent
to a surname

Name of **species**:
This is equivalent
to a Christian name

Only one type of plant can have this name. Once the full latin name has been used on a page, a nearby reference is abbreviated.

For example: H. helix

A species such as H. helix may have several closely-related varieties. The **variety** name is usually in latin.

For example: H. helix cristata
H. helix scutifolia

If the variety originated in cultivation and not in the wild then it is called a **cultivar** (short for "cultivated variety"). The cultivar name is usually not in latin.

For example: H. helix Chicago
H. helix Little Eva

One genus or several genera which have a basically similar floral pattern make up a **family**. Hedera, Fatsia, Dizygotheca and Schefflera all belong to the Araliaceae or Ivy family.

A number of different plants can have the same common name. For example, both Zebrina pendula and Tradescantia fluminensis are popularly known as "Wandering Jew". On the other hand a single species may have more than one common name — Impatiens wallerana is "Busy Lizzie" in Britain and "Patient Lucy" in the U.S. For these reasons it is usually better to refer to plants by their latin names.

The Ancient Greek philosopher Theophrastus began it all with a list of about 450 plants. That was over 2000 years ago, but it was not until 1753 when Linnaeus published his masterpiece *Species Plantarum* that plant naming was put on to a scientific and orderly footing.

It was Linnaeus who founded the binomial (two-name) system outlined above, and each genus has a different name. There are two main types of generic name, and the most popular one is the *Descriptive* name. This is usually a Greek word which has been latinised. The description may be of an unusual part of the plant, the plant's appearance, its resemblance to another plant, its practical use and so on. Cryptanthus (hidden flower) is an example.

The second major type is the *Commemorative* name — a latinised version of a person's name which was considered worthy of posterity. Linnaeus coined many of the names and he was Swedish, so it is perhaps not surprising that many Swedish scientists have been immortalised in house plant names, such as Billbergia, Bromeliad, Browallia, Sparmannia, Tillandsia etc. Botanists from many other countries have given their names to house plants, and so have patrons, soldiers, garden curators, noblemen and so on. One of the surprises is that very few discoverers and collectors have been remembered in this way — Allamanda and Saintpaulia are exceptions.

Descriptions and proper names are the major sources of plant names, but the list does not end there. The *Native* name has sometimes been retained (Kalanchoe, Ananas, Yucca etc) and the old *Classical* name may have been kept, as in the case of Amaryllis and Euphorbia.

Every plant name tells a story, but we are not always sure of the story. The origin of a few generic names, such as Rhoeo and Setcreasea, remains a mystery and others are a matter of dispute. Polyscias is a good example. We know it is Greek in origin, but some authorities believe it means 'shade-loving' and others claim the proper meaning is 'much-divided'.

Another complication is that an old and well-established genus name may be replaced by a new one, and the scientists expect us to follow them. An example is Scindapsus which is now referred to as Epipremnum. In this book, however, the better-known genus name is used rather than the 'technically correct' one.

THE SHAPE OF HOUSE PLANTS

Both size and shape are extremely important considerations when choosing a plant. A small, low-growing variety can look completely out-of-place against a large, bare wall .. a tall, tree-like plant can look distinctly unsafe on a narrow windowsill. Remember that you may be buying a young specimen — in your home a small neat Dracaena or Ficus can become a man-sized tree in a few seasons. There are six basic plant shapes and nearly all indoor plants fit into one or other of these groups. But there are borderline cases, and a few plants will change with age from one shape type to another.

GRASSY PLANTS

GRASSY PLANTS have long, narrow leaves and a grass-like growth habit. Very few true grasses are offered as house plants because their leaf form has never been generally accepted for indoor decoration. Several grass-like plants with long and extremely narrow leaves are listed as indoor plants, but they are not often seen.

Examples: Acorus
Arundinaria
Carex
Ophiopogon

Broad-leaved Grassy Plants are much more popular — Chlorophytum comosum is one of the most widely grown of all foliage house plants. Several flowering plants have grassy leaves of this type — good examples are Billbergia nutans, Vallota, Tillandsia lindenii and Narcissus.

BUSHY PLANTS

BUSHY PLANTS are a vast collection of varieties which do not fit into the other groups. The standard pattern is an arrangement of several stems arising out of the compost, with a growth habit which is neither markedly vertical nor horizontal. They may be small and compact like Peperomia or tall and shrubby like Aucuba. Some plants are naturally bushy, regularly producing side shoots; others must be pinched out regularly to induce bushiness. The Secrets of Success listed for each bushy plant will tell you if pinching out is necessary.

Examples: Achimenes
Begonia rex
Coleus
Hypocyrta
Maranta
Pilea

UPRIGHT PLANTS

UPRIGHT PLANTS bear stems with a distinctly vertical growth habit. They vary in height from an inch to the tallest house plants available. Medium-sized upright plants are an essential component of the mixed group, providing a feeling of height to offset the horizontal effect created by rosette plants, trailing plants and low bushes. Tall, upright plants are often displayed as solitary specimens, serving as effective focal points.

Column Plants have thick vertical stems which are either leafless or bear leaves which do not detract from the column effect. Many Cacti and some Succulents have this growth habit.

Examples: Cereus peruvianus
Cleistocactus straussii
Haworthia reinwardtii
Kleinia articulata
Notocactus leninghausii
Trichocereus candicans

Trees are an extremely important group, providing spectacular Specimen Plants for large displays and the centrepiece in many collections. All trees have the same basic form — a central branched or unbranched stem bearing leaves with relatively small leaf bases. Some are quite small, such as miniature Succulent 'trees' or a young Croton — others are capable of growing until they reach the ceiling.

Examples: Aphelandra
Citrus
Codiaeum
Ficus benjamina
Ficus elastica decora
Laurus
Schefflera

False Palms have stems which are completely clothed by the elongated stem bases when the plant is young. In a mature plant usually only the upper part of the stem is covered by leaves and the characteristically Palm-like effect is created. Large False Palms are often used as specimen plants in public buildings.

Examples: Beaucarnea
Dieffenbachia
Dracaena
Pandanus
Yucca

CLIMBING & TRAILING PLANTS

CLIMBING & TRAILING PLANTS bear stems which, when mature, are either provided with support to grow upwards or are left to hang downwards on the outside of the container. Many (but not all) varieties can be used in both ways. As climbers they are trained on canes, strings, trelliswork, wire hoops or vertical poles; they can be grown in wall-mounted pots to frame windows or they can be trained up stout supports to serve as room dividers. As trailers they can be used to spread horizontally as ground cover in indoor gardens or left to trail over the sides of pots or hanging baskets.

Climbers are always grown as upright plants. Twining varieties are allowed to twist around the supports provided. Clinging varieties bearing tendrils must be attached to the supports at frequent intervals; if left to grow unattended the stems will soon become tangled together. Varieties bearing aerial roots are best grown on a moss stick (see page 223).

Examples: Dipladenia
Passiflora
Philodendron hastatum
Stephanotis

Climber/Trailers are extremely useful house plants and many popular varieties belong to this group. When growing them as climbers it is usually advisable not to tie all the stems to a single cane — it is more attractive to spread out the stems on a trellis or on several canes inserted in the pot. When growing them as trailers it is sometimes necessary to pinch out the growing tips occasionally to prevent straggly growth.

Examples: Ficus pumila
Hedera
Philodendron scandens
Scindapsus

Trailers are always grown as pendant plants, with stems hanging downwards, or as creeping plants, with stems growing along the soil surface. Many trailers have striking foliage or attractive flowers and are best grown in hanging baskets or stood on high pedestals.

Examples: Begonia pendula
Campanula isophylla
Columnea
Fittonia
Helxine
Nertera
Sedum morganianum
Senecio rowleyanus
Zygocactus

ROSETTE PLANTS

ROSETTE PLANTS bear leaves which form a circular cluster around the central growing point. Most rosette plants are low-growing and combine well with bushy and upright plants in Pot Groups and in Indoor Gardens.

Flat Rosette Plants have large leaves which lie almost horizontally, forming a loose rosette. A number of attractive flowering plants have this growth habit.

Examples: Gloxinia
Primula
Saintpaulia

Succulent Rosette Plants have fleshy leaves borne in several layers and often tightly packed together. The leaves may be horizontal or nearly upright. This arrangement helps to conserve moisture in the natural desert habitat.

Examples: Aloe humilis
Aeonium tabulaeforme
Echeveria setosa
Haworthia fasciata
Sempervivum tectorum

Funnel Rosette Plants are common among the Bromeliads. The basal area of the strap-like leaves forms a 'vase' which holds rainwater in the natural tropical habitat. Plants are usually large and spreading.

Examples: Aechmea
Guzmania
Nidularium
Vriesea

BALL PLANTS

BALL PLANTS are leafless and have a distinctly globular shape. They are all Cacti, and the stem surface may be smooth or covered with hair and spines.

Examples: Astrophytum
Echinocactus grusonii
Ferocactus
Mammillaria
Parodia
Rebutia miniscula

THE GROWING CONDITIONS FOR HOUSE PLANTS

Most people choose a house plant which has the right shape, appearance and price. It is essential, however, that it should also be right for the light and warmth it will receive in its new home. There are three important points to remember.

- **Each plant has its own likes and dislikes.** Some plants need an unheated room in winter, and a few will grow quite happily in full sun, but many would die under such conditions. Don't guess — look up your plant's special needs in the A–Z guide.

- **A new plant gets homesick even in good conditions.** Many varieties suffer a distinct shock when they are moved from their well-lit and humid glasshouse home to your walled-in and dry living room. Don't assume that the conditions must be wrong if the plant looks jaded for the first few weeks — read page 9.

- **An established plant may adapt to poor conditions.** The Secrets of Success given for each plant in the A–Z guide describe the *ideal* growing conditions; here the plant will flourish. But many plants are capable of slowly adapting to a poorer environment.

SITUATION	N ←	SUITABLE PLANTS
SHADE Well away from a window, but enough light to allow you to read a newspaper		Aglaonema, Aspidistra, Asplenium, Fittonia, Helxine, Philodendron scandens, Sansevieria, Scindapsus (variegation will fade). Any of the Semi-Shade group can be grown here for a month or two; some will survive permanently
SEMI-SHADE Near a sunless window or some distance away from a bright window		Aglaonema, Aspidistra, Dracaena fragrans, Dracaena marginata, Fatshedera, Fatsia, Ferns, Ficus pumila, Fittonia, Hedera helix, Helxine, Howea, Maranta, Neanthe, Philodendron scandens, Sansevieria, Scindapsus, Tolmiea
BRIGHT BUT SUNLESS On a sunless windowsill or near a bright window		Anthurium, Asparagus, Azalea, Begonia rex, Bromeliads, Chlorophytum, Columnea, Cyclamen, Dieffenbachia, Dizygotheca, Fuchsia, Garden Bulbs, Hedera, Monstera, Peperomia, Philodendron, Pilea, Schefflera, Scindapsus, Spathiphyllum, Vines, Zygocactus
SOME DIRECT SUNLIGHT On or very close to an east- or west-facing windowsill. May need protection from hot summer sun		Beloperone, Capsicum, Chlorophytum, Chrysanthemum, Codiaeum, Cordyline terminalis, Cuphea, Ficus elastica decora, Gynura, Hoya, Impatiens, Nertera, Plumbago, Poinsettia, Saintpaulia, Sansevieria, Solanum, Sparmannia, Tradescantia, Zebrina
SUNNY WINDOW On or very close to a south-facing windowsill. Light shading may be necessary in midsummer		Acacia, Agapanthus, Bedding Plants, Bougainvillea, Bouvardia, Cacti & Succulents, Callistemon, Celosia, Citrus, Coleus, Heliotropium, Hibiscus, Hippeastrum, Iresine, Jasminum, Lantana, Nerine, Nerium, Oxalis, Passiflora, Pelargonium, Rosa, Zebrina
NO HEAT IN WINTER		Araucaria, Aspidistra, Beloperone, Cacti & Succulents, Chlorophytum, Cineraria, Clivia, Cyclamen, Fatshedera, Fatsia, Grevillea, Hedera helix, Helxine, Hydrangea, Nertera, Rosa, Saxifraga sarmentosa, Setcreasea, Streptocarpus, Tolmiea
CENTRAL HEATING IN WINTER		Increase humidity to counteract desert-dry air (see page 232). Otherwise choose Aechmea, Billbergia, Cacti & Succulents, Chlorophytum, Dracaena godseffiana, Ficus elastica decora, Grevillea, Impatiens, Nerium, Palms, Pelargonium, Peperomia, Zebrina

BUYING A HOUSE PLANT . . .

Indoor plants are raised in glasshouses in which the air is warm and humid. The world outside is far less accommodating, so always buy from a reputable supplier who will have made sure that the plants have been properly hardened off. In this way the shock of moving into a new home will be reduced to a minimum.

House plants can, of course, be bought at any time of the year, but it is preferable to purchase delicate varieties between late spring and mid autumn. But some plants can only be bought in winter, and you should be extra careful at this time of the year. Plants stood outside the shop or on a market stall will have been damaged by the cold unless they are hardy varieties — avoid buying delicate plants which are stood in the open as 'bargain' offers.

Now you are ready to buy. If you are shopping for flower seeds, choose F_1 hybrids if available. If you are picking bulbs, make sure that they are firm, rot-free and without holes or shoots. When buying house plants, ensure that the specimen is not too big for the space you have in mind and then look for the danger signs. None present? Then you have a good buy.

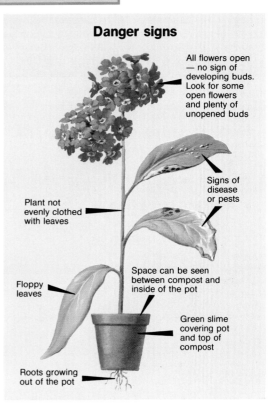

Danger signs

All flowers open — no sign of developing buds. Look for some open flowers and plenty of unopened buds

Signs of disease or pests

Plant not evenly clothed with leaves

Space can be seen between compost and inside of the pot

Floppy leaves

Green slime covering pot and top of compost

Roots growing out of the pot

. . . AND TAKING IT HOME

Make sure the plant is properly wrapped before leaving the shop or nursery. The purpose of this wrapping is twofold — to protect stray leaves from damage and to keep out draughts. In winter the protecting cover should be closed at the top.

Much has been written about the danger of walking home with a delicate house plant in the depths of winter, but just as much damage is done by putting plants in the boot of a car in the height of summer. When taking a plant home by car the best plan is to secure it in a box and place it on a seat. Be careful not to crush the leaves or the stems.

Once your new plant is home it will need a period of acclimatisation. For a few weeks keep it out of direct sunlight and draughts, and be careful not to give it too much heat or water. It is quite normal for a delicate variety to lose a leaf or two during this settling-in period, and the worst thing you can do is to keep on moving it from one spot to another in order to find the 'proper' home. Just leave it alone in a moderately warm spot out of the sun.

Flowering pot plants (such as Azalea, Chrysanthemum and Cyclamen) which are purchased in flower during the winter months require different treatment — put them in their permanent quarters immediately and give them as much light as possible.

HOUSING YOUR PLANT

Most of this book is devoted to descriptions of hundreds of different varieties of indoor plants, but hardly any of them can be grown if they are not planted in a suitable growing medium within a suitable receptacle. Unfortunately the words 'receptacle', 'pot' and 'container' are used interchangeably and this leads to confusion. The best plan is to use the word **Receptacle** to describe any of the three basic types of housing used for one or more plants. They come in all shapes and sizes, from egg cups for tiny Saintpaulias to massive room-sized indoor gardens. Note that the oddities (bark for Staghorn Fern, driftwood for Air Plants etc) are excluded.

THE 3 TYPES OF RECEPTACLE

POTS	POT HOLDERS	CONTAINERS
A receptacle with a drainage hole or holes at the base. It is used for potting one or more plants. A pot holder or drip tray is necessary	(Other names: Pot Hider, Cachepot) A receptacle with no drainage holes and a waterproof base. It is used for holding and hiding a single pot	A waterproof receptacle with no holes at the base. It is used for potting one or more plants or for holding several pots

POTS

The basic pot is made of clay or plastic. Each type has its own group of devotees, but both sorts will support perfectly good plants. Their watering requirements are rather different, so try to keep a plant in one type or the other — repotting from a plastic pot into a clay one will mean that you will have to change your watering routine.

All clay pots have the same earthy terracotta appearance, but plastic pots come in a wide variety of shapes and surfaces. If your room is unheated in winter the insulating properties of foam plastic pots can be a distinct advantage.

PLANTING A SPECIMEN PLANT IN A POT

Choose a pot with a central drainage hole or several small drainage holes

Pick a colour which is in keeping with the plant and its surroundings

Use a drip tray

Clay Pots v Plastic Pots

Advantages:
- Heavy — much less liable to topple over.
- Waterlogging is less likely because of porous nature.
- Traditional 'natural' appearance — no chance of colour clashes.
- Damaging salts are leached away from the compost.

Advantages:
- Lightweight — much less liable to break if dropped.
- Watering is needed less often.
- Decorative and colourful forms available.
- No crocking needed — easy to clean.

Pot Size

A wide range is available with diameters between 1½ and 15 inches. Ideally you should move up only 1 in. every time you repot, but this would call for a large store of pots. You can manage by taking the following steps when repotting, provided you use a good peat-based compost and follow the instructions on page 13. If you wish to stop before the large pot stage, root prune before repotting (see page 12).

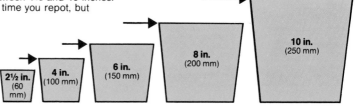

2½ in. (60 mm) 4 in. (100 mm) 6 in. (150 mm) 8 in. (200 mm) 10 in. (250 mm)

POT HOLDERS

Some people enjoy the natural look of a clay pot, especially when the appearance of the plant rather than its furnishing value in the room is all-important. The overall effect of most Specimen Plants is, however, improved by being placed in a pot holder. These pot holders come in many materials, shapes and prices — you can buy ones made of wire, plastic, pottery, wood, glass fibre, cane or metal. Apart from these shop-bought types there are also many ordinary household objects which can be used — popular examples include copper bowls and kettles. The one rule for any pot holder is that either the lower part or all of it must be waterproof.

A wide choice, but do make sure that the style of the pot holder is in keeping with the style of the room. Stainless steel cylinders are splendid in ultra-modern surroundings. Wicker baskets and plant-filled china tea pots are charming in period rooms. But change them round and the display will seem out of place.

The style of the pot holder is therefore important and so is its size. It should be at least 1 in. wider than the pot — a rather larger space is preferable. The pot holder should also be taller than the pot, and the treatment of the space between the pot holder and pot depends on the plant. For dry-air plants (Cacti, Succulents, Aspidistra etc) leave the space empty — for other plants fill the void with, and stand the pot on, damp peat. This damp peat increases the moisture around the plant — see page 232.

BALANCE

The pot holder must be large enough to provide stability. It must also be wide enough — as a general rule a spreading plant should be no more than 2–5 times wider than the pot holder.

COLOUR

The purpose of the pot holder is to provide a suitable base for the beauty of the plant. It should not compete with it and on no account should it overwhelm the display.

CONTAINERS

PLANTING A SPECIMEN PLANT IN A CONTAINER

Potting or Multipurpose compost

Narrow layer of small lumps of charcoal

Layer of small pebbles filling the bottom ¼ of the container

Pot holders have their limitations with regard to both size and shape because they have to house standard-shaped pots. Containers have no such limitations because the usual practice is to take the plants out of their pots and then plant them directly into the compost-filled receptacle.

The only basic rule for containers is that they *must* be waterproof. Basket-type containers must have an inner liner and wooden ones must be treated with a sealant. Apart from this restriction there are hardly any hard-and-fast rules. The catalogues are dominated by rectangular, circular and square containers made out of rigid plastic, but all sorts of things are used. You will find brass coal scuttles, tables with built-in planters, teak jardinières and so on. Glazed earthenware containers are popular, but do make sure that the colour and decoration are muted.

Perhaps the most popular container of all is the humble bulb bowl. Planting here is an exception to the usual container rules — bulb fibre made of peat, charcoal and oyster shell is employed instead of ordinary potting compost, and dormant bulbs rather than growing plants are used.

Container growing poses one great problem. Excess water cannot escape and this means that waterlogging will occur unless you take care when watering. This problem is most serious with small containers — here you should bore holes in the base if you can and place the receptacle on a drip tray. With a large tub it may be impractical to bore holes, so follow the instructions on the left.

REPOTTING YOUR PLANT

When you buy a plant the nurseryman will have already chosen a suitable pot, but in a year or two it will probably become pot-bound. The time has come for repotting — you will have to pick a satisfactory pot and the correct compost to house the roots, and you will have to ensure that the plant will settle down successfully in its new home. This chapter will show you how.

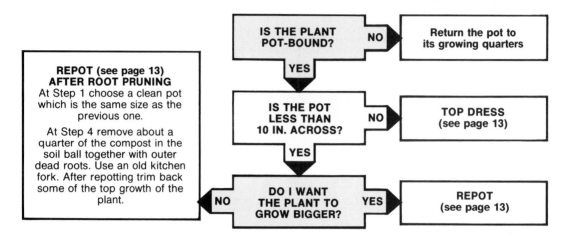

REPOT (see page 13) AFTER ROOT PRUNING
At Step 1 choose a clean pot which is the same size as the previous one.

At Step 4 remove about a quarter of the compost in the soil ball together with outer dead roots. Use an old kitchen fork. After repotting trim back some of the top growth of the plant.

IS THE PLANT POT-BOUND? — NO → **Return the pot to its growing quarters**

YES

IS THE POT LESS THAN 10 IN. ACROSS? — NO → **TOP DRESS (see page 13)**

YES

NO ← **DO I WANT THE PLANT TO GROW BIGGER?** — YES → **REPOT (see page 13)**

CHOOSING THE GROWING MEDIUM

Soil taken straight from the garden is totally unsuitable for filling pots. It may well contain pests and disease organisms which would flourish under the warmer conditions indoors, and its restriction within a pot which is then regularly watered is almost bound to lead to a complete loss of structure. For these reasons indoor plants are grown in special mixtures known as *composts*. In nearly every case multipurpose composts are used, but you can buy special mixes.

Soil Composts

The basis is loam, made from turves stacked grass-downwards until well-rotted. Shortage of supply has meant that good-quality topsoil has been substituted in most cases — poor-quality soil will always produce an unsatisfactory compost. Other organic ingredients are added, and all are sterilised before blending with fertilizer, lime and sand. The introduction of the John Innes Composts has removed the need for a wide array of mixtures.

Soilless Composts

Because loam is difficult to obtain and its quality is variable, modern composts are based on peat, or peat and sand. These soilless composts have many advantages over soil-based composts. Their quality does not vary and they are lighter and cleaner to handle. Perhaps the most important advantage is that the plant to be repotted was almost certainly raised in a peat-based compost, and plants do not like a change in growing medium. Most manufacturers of soilless composts produce a single grade which provides an average plant with enough food for a few months. This fertilizer content makes potting compost too rich for sowing seeds or taking cuttings.

Soilless composts can have one or two drawbacks. All-peat composts tend to be difficult to water once they have been allowed to dry out and lightness can be a disadvantage when a large plant is to be potted. Use a multi-compost which contains soil and sand as well as peat if extra weight is required.

Aggregates

In hydroculture, porous clay aggregates replace compost as anchorage for the roots, and both roots and aggregates are bathed in a dilute fertilizer solution. The system is usually housed in a special container — the hydropot. These hydropots first appeared in 1976 but have not become popular and are difficult to obtain. They are expensive, but have the advantage of requiring water only once every few weeks.

The plants grown in hydroculture develop thick, fleshy roots in place of the thin fibrous ones which grow in soil. Some plants succeed better than others. Cacti do surprisingly well — so do Aglaonema, Philodendron, Scindapsus and Spathiphyllum.

RECOGNISING A POT-BOUND PLANT

Most house plants thrive best in pots which appear to the beginner to be too small for the amount of leaf and stem present. It is a mistake to repot into a larger receptacle unless the plant is definitely pot-bound. Check in the A–Z guide — some plants will only flower when in this condition and there are others, such as Bromeliads, which should never need repotting.

Stem and leaf growth very slow even when the plant is fed regularly in spring and summer

Soil dries out quickly, so frequent watering is required

Roots growing through drainage hole

Final check:
Remove the pot in the way described below. If the plant is pot-bound there will be a matted mass of roots on the outside, and not much soil will be visible.

If it is not pot-bound, simply replace the soil ball back into the original pot; no harm will have been done.

TECHNIQUE 1: REPOTTING

The best time is in spring, so that the roots will have plenty of time to become established before the onset of the resting season. Choose a pot which is only slightly larger than the previous one — too large a difference will result in a severe check to growth (see page 10). Have everything ready before you start — pots, compost, watering can etc. Check in the A–Z guide to see if the plant can be divided up at repotting time.

(1) If the pot has been used before, it must be thoroughly scrubbed out. A new clay pot should be soaked in water overnight before use.

(2) If a clay pot is used, cover the drainage hole with 'crocks' (broken pieces of pot or brick). Place a shallow layer of potting compost over the crock layer.

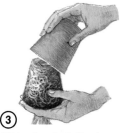

(3) Water the plant. One hour later remove it from the pot by spreading the fingers of one hand over the soil surface. Invert, and gently knock the rim on a table. Run a knife around the edge if it is necessary. Remove the pot with the other hand.

(4) Take away the old crocks. Carefully tease out some of the matted outside roots. Remove any rotten roots but avoid at all costs causing extensive root damage.

(5) Place the plant on top of the compost layer in the new pot and gradually fill around the soil ball with potting compost, which should be slightly damp.

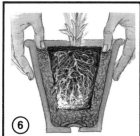

(6) Firm the compost down with the thumbs, adding more until level with the base of the stem. Finally, tap the pot on the table several times to settle the compost.

(7) Water carefully and place in the shade for about a week, misting the leaves daily to avoid wilting. Then place the plant in its growing quarters and treat normally.

TECHNIQUE 2: TOP DRESSING

For a variety of reasons, especially with large pots and trained specimens, you may not wish or be able to disturb by repotting. In this case the pot should be top dressed every spring by carefully removing the top inch of compost (2 inches for large pots). The removed material is then replaced by fresh potting compost.

FACTS & FIGURES

HOW MUCH WE SPEND

In 1984 the average household spent £5.50 on house plants. In the mid 1980s the market was increasing by more than 20 per cent each year, but it began to slow down. In 1990 the annual increase in sales was 7 per cent. Present annual purchases are £14 per household.

Source: Mintel

WHAT WE BUY

There is no universally agreed Top 20 list for the U.K. The alphabetical list of best-sellers set out below is based on the latest sales recorded through auctions in Holland and the findings of a series of market surveys.

AZALEA
BEGONIA
BULBS IN BOWLS
CACTI & SUCCULENTS
CHLOROPHYTUM
CHRYSANTHEMUM
CYCLAMEN
DIEFFENBACHIA
DRACAENA
FERNS

FICUS
GERANIUM
HEDERA
IMPATIENS
KALANCHOE
MONSTERA
PALMS
POINSETTIA
SAINTPAULIA
SCINDAPSUS

The Second Division is headed by Sansevieria, Primula, Cissus and Solanum.

FOLIAGE OR FLOWERS

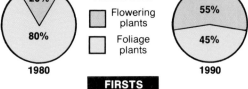

Annual sales:
▨ Flowering plants
☐ Foliage plants

1980 — 20% / 80%
1990 — 55% / 45%

FIRSTS

● The first recorded plant collectors were the soldiers in the army of Thothmes III, Pharaoh of Egypt, 3500 years ago. In the Temple of Karnak these soldiers are shown bringing back 300 plants as booty from the campaign in Syria.

● The first Maidenhair Fern, Philodendron scandens and Peperomia magnoliaefolia were brought to Britain by Captain Bligh of HMS Bounty fame.

● The first heated greenhouses were built in Ancient Rome before the birth of Christ.

● The first cultivated Orchids were grown in China 2500 years ago.

● The first 'Chelsea' Flower Show was not held at Chelsea. It started with the Horticultural Society's Fête held at Chiswick in 1827. The first RHS Flower Show to be held at Chelsea was in 1913.

HOW WE COMPARE WITH OTHER COUNTRIES

Amount spent per person each year

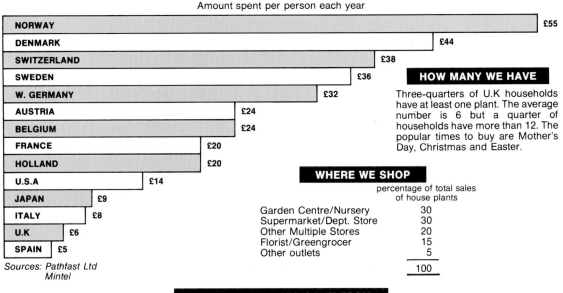

Country	Amount
NORWAY	£55
DENMARK	£44
SWITZERLAND	£38
SWEDEN	£36
W. GERMANY	£32
AUSTRIA	£24
BELGIUM	£24
FRANCE	£20
HOLLAND	£20
U.S.A	£14
JAPAN	£9
ITALY	£8
U.K	£6
SPAIN	£5

Sources: Pathfast Ltd
Mintel

HOW MANY WE HAVE

Three-quarters of U.K households have at least one plant. The average number is 6 but a quarter of households have more than 12. The popular times to buy are Mother's Day, Christmas and Easter.

WHERE WE SHOP

percentage of total sales of house plants

Garden Centre/Nursery	30
Supermarket/Dept. Store	30
Other Multiple Stores	20
Florist/Greengrocer	15
Other outlets	5
	100

WHERE THE NAMES CAME FROM

AECHMEA Greek — 'a point'. The bracts in the flower-head are spear-like.

AGLAONEMA Greek — 'bright thread'. The stamens are eye-catching.

ASPARAGUS Greek — 'to rip'. Some species have stems with sharp spines.

AZALEA Greek — 'dry'. An odd origin for this moisture-loving plant. The name was first given to a N. European plant which thrives in dry conditions.

BEGONIA Named after Michael Begon, 18th century Governor of French Canada.

CALATHEA Greek — 'basket'. The plant was used by American Indians for basket-making.

CHLOROPHYTUM Greek — 'green plant'. No one knows why this plant was chosen to bear the basic name for foliage plants.

FUCHSIA Named after Leonhart Fuchs, 16th century German physician and botanist.

IMPATIENS Latin — 'impatient'. Ripe seed pods burst and eject seeds when touched.

MONSTERA Latin — 'monstrous'. An obscure name, which probably refers to the large and deeply-divided leaves.

ORCHID Greek — 'a testicle'. Swollen pseudobulbs appear at the base of some species.

PHILODENDRON Greek — 'tree lover'. An apt name for this climber which attaches itself to trees in its natural habitat.

SAINTPAULIA Named after Baron Walter von Saint Paul-Illaire, 19th century District Officer in German East Africa who discovered the plant.

TRADESCANTIA Named after John Tradescant, 17th century gardener to Charles I.

CHAPTER 2
DISPLAYING INDOOR PLANTS

There are two basic approaches to the use of house plants around the home. The first one is to regard them as green pets to be set out as individual specimens in an environment which is the best one you can provide for their needs. These pets are then carefully tended when alive and mourned when dead.

The second approach is to regard house plants as living decor which serves to improve the appearance of one or more rooms. Here we look for the right plants to suit the environment and the plants may be stood singly or massed together for maximum effect. The temporary ones, such as the flowering pot plants, are no more mourned than an attractive cut flower arrangement when the final hour arrives.

To understand the principles of indoor plant display, look out of the window. The garden is brought alive by its contrasting shapes and colours — bold specimens may stand on their own but bedding plants need to be massed in order to produce a bold display.

There are very few rules to tell you how to arrange plants correctly. They should be in keeping with their surroundings — large architectural plants in spacious rooms, small pots on tiny windowsills. Let dramatic ones stand on their own as specimens, but always gather insignificant and below-par ones into a group. Pick up ideas from magazines, TV and other people's homes, but above all create displays which please *you*.

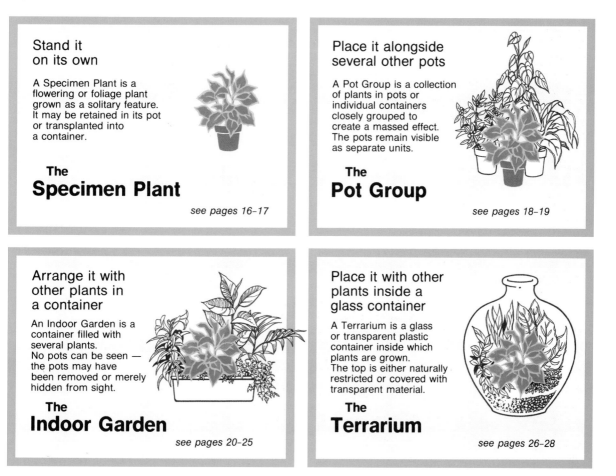

Stand it on its own

A Specimen Plant is a flowering or foliage plant grown as a solitary feature. It may be retained in its pot or transplanted into a container.

The
Specimen Plant

see pages 16–17

Place it alongside several other pots

A Pot Group is a collection of plants in pots or individual containers closely grouped to create a massed effect. The pots remain visible as separate units.

The
Pot Group

see pages 18–19

Arrange it with other plants in a container

An Indoor Garden is a container filled with several plants. No pots can be seen — the pots may have been removed or merely hidden from sight.

The
Indoor Garden

see pages 20–25

Place it with other plants inside a glass container

A Terrarium is a glass or transparent plastic container inside which plants are grown. The top is either naturally restricted or covered with transparent material.

The
Terrarium

see pages 26–28

A Specimen Plant is a flowering or foliage plant grown as a solitary feature. It may be retained in its pot or transplanted into a container.

The Specimen Plant

Most ordinary plants need to be grouped together to achieve an eye-catching effect, but some are best seen on their own in a prominent place. These are the Specimen Plants. Of course, correct plant choice is all-important, but you must also pay attention to the position, receptacle, lighting and background — see page 30.

You may want a large specimen which will cover an area of several square feet. Unfortunately the cost of a mature floor-standing house plant which can dominate a corner or wall could well be prohibitive. A good plan is to buy a young plant, repot regularly and then place it in its permanent position once it has reached the required height. Alternatively stand a hanging plant on a pedestal or grow a vigorous climber to clothe the required area.

ARCHITECTURAL PLANTS

An Architectural plant (also called a Decorator, Accent or Statement plant) has a shape which is large, distinctive and attractive. Its basic use is to act as a focal point, although it may be used to either clothe a bare space or divide off a section of the room. Palms, False Palms and tree-like plants are the types most frequently used, and interior decorators usually choose tall specimens from the following list:

    Araucaria heterophylla
    Cyperus
    Dieffenbachia
    Dracaena
    Fatsia japonica
    Ficus benjamina
    Ficus elastica decora
    Ficus lyrata
    Grevillea robusta
    Palms
    Philodendron bipinnatifidum
    Schefflera actinophylla
    Yucca

CLIMBING PLANTS

Many climbers make excellent Specimen Plants, and the more vigorous ones can be used to provide a large, leafy specimen at the lowest possible cost. You can choose a foliage type (Philodendrons, Vines, etc) or a flowering climber (Hoya, Thunbergia, etc). Good examples are

    Cissus
    Monstera
    Passiflora
    Philodendron hastatum
    Philodendron panduriforme
    Rhoicissus
    Scindapsus
    Stephanotis

HANGING PLANTS

Some hanging plants are showy enough to be displayed on their own in hanging baskets or on pedestals rather than as part of a Plant Group. Good examples are

    Chlorophytum
    Columnea
    Nephrolepis
    Zygocactus

MULTICOLOURED FOLIAGE PLANTS

Many popular house plants have multicoloured foliage, and the most dramatic varieties are frequently used as Specimen Plants. Good examples are

    Begonia rex
    Caladium
    Codiaeum
    Cordyline terminalis
    Nidularium
    Rhoeo

FLOWERING POT PLANTS

Some flowering pot plants are so colourful that they are best displayed on their own. Good examples are

    Begonia tuberhybrida
    Bulbs
    Cyclamen
    Gloxinia
    Hydrangea
    Pelargonium
    Poinsettia
    Rhododendron simsii

THE FOCAL POINT SPECIMEN PLANT

A Specimen Plant is often used to produce an extra point of interest in the room — a part of the decor which has to compete with other furnishing items for attention. In the larger room a bold Specimen Plant can be used as a focal point — a prominent feature which is designed to be the centre of attention. Shown here is a floor-to-ceiling Dracaena marginata.

A Pot Group is a collection of plants in pots or individual containers closely grouped to create a massed effect. The pots remain visible as separate units.

The Pot Group

The simple step of bringing together several isolated plants to make a Pot Group can add a new dimension to your indoor display. There are three basic reasons for this transformation:

- The overall effect is much bolder than can be achieved with individual pots. Plants at the rear of the group can be raised to give added height.
- Small-leaved plants such as Ficus pumila, Adiantum, Helxine and Tradescantia can seem insignificant and uninteresting when grown in isolated pots, but suddenly come to life when grouped with large-leaved varieties and so add an important ingredient to the overall effect.
- Individual perfection, so important with the Specimen Plant, is not vital. Bare stems, lop-sided growth and damaged leaves can all be easily hidden by surrounding them with other plants.

The advantage of grouping is not just a matter of appearance — there are also cultural benefits. Watering is an easier task when plants are collected together rather than scattered around the room. The close proximity of other plants and a large expanse of moist compost means that the air humidity around the foliage is increased, and this can be vitally important for a delicate variety.

The house plant owner has the satisfaction of creating an individual arrangement. Various groupings are shown on these two pages, but there are no hard and fast rules except that plants should, wherever possible, have the same basic light and warmth requirements.

THE STANDARD GROUP

Between four and a dozen clay or plastic pots are closely grouped together to produce a pleasing arrangement in which both shapes and tints are varied. In the most usual grouping foliage plants are used to provide the permanent framework and flowering pot plants are used to provide splashes of colour. The taller plants, the darker greens and the larger leaves are placed at the back of the group.

It is a basic error to assume that you *must* create a riot of different colours and a wide variety of shapes in order to give your Pot Group a professional touch. The skilled interior decorator will sometimes use only foliage plants, relying on different leaf forms and variegation to produce an attractive display.

THE PROFESSIONAL GROUP

This type of display, much loved by interior designers, is the big brother of the Standard Group described on page 18. Although it is usually found in public buildings, a simple version is worth considering for a bare corner in your home. Pot holders are an important feature of the Professional Group — they are decorative and of different heights. The one at the back is either much taller than the others or is raised on a block of wood to display to the maximum the pinnacle plant it contains — a Kentia Palm in the illustration above. The pot holder at the front holds a large flowering pot plant which is replaced when its display is finished. A trailing plant is grown in one of the middle receptacles and its stems are allowed to drape over the base unit.

THE PEBBLE TRAY

Grouping plants within a shallow tray is a useful technique for maintaining plants which need high humidity in a centrally-heated room. If you have difficulty in growing African Violets then try them in a Pebble Tray. The tray should be about 2 in. high, and can be made of any waterproof material. The dimensions are up to you, but avoid a dangerously wide overhang if the tray is to be stood on a windowsill.

Place 1 in. of gravel in the bottom of the tray and keep the bottom of this layer wet at all times. The water level, however, must not be allowed to cover the top of the gravel. Group the plants on the surface.

A favourite place for a Pebble Tray is on a radiator shelf below a windowsill. In this situation the humidity around the plants in winter will be trebled. Watering plants is a simple matter — allow excess water to run out of the pots and into the gravel.

THE COLLECTION

A group of pots containing closely related plants can be found in the homes of people at both ends of the house plant knowledge scale. The young beginner often starts with a collection of Succulents and Cacti — grouped neatly on a windowsill . . . in the home of the keen indoor gardener you will often find a prized collection of his or her speciality — Ferns, African Violets, Orchids, etc. In the U.K collections are usually housed in a spot exposed to natural light; in the U.S the fluorescent-lit plant table is popular — see page 229.

Collections, big and small, have one feature in common. Unlike the Standard Group (page 18) where the overall decorative effect is all-important, the basic purpose of the Collection is to highlight the individuality, rarity or beauty of each plant.

THE DISPLAY WINDOW

The Display Window turns an ordinary window into a tiered arrangement of flowers and greenery. Shelves of glass or transparent plastic are fixed across the window opening at convenient heights, and the pots are arranged along each shelf. You will either love or hate the Display Window — to some it is an excellent way to show off their Cacti and Succulents, or their range of flowering plants and other sun lovers. To others this type of Pot Group is far too regimented, with several rows of pots one above the other standing at attention. If you do go ahead, go all the way and make sure that the whole of the glass area is used for display purposes. A thing of beauty for you, perhaps, but a nightmare for the window cleaner!

THE VERTICAL DISPLAY

The Pot Group is nearly always horizontal, although the pots are sometimes set at different heights. The Vertical Display, however, is both easily arranged and can be extremely effective. The traditonal version is a corner shelf unit with a pot on each shelf — use the same variety of colourful trailing plant to produce a column of foliage or flowers. A series of hanging baskets attached to each other can be used to give the same effect — the metal or cane plant stand which carries pots at different heights has the advantage of portability.

An Indoor Garden is a container filled with several plants. No pots can be seen — the pots may have been removed or merely hidden from sight.

The Indoor Garden

Indoor gardening remains an unusual concept because there is still a strange reluctance to growing house plants in groups rather than as individual specimens. Colourful plants such as Begonia semperflorens and Coleus can be bedded out in the home as they are in the garden, but they are nearly always grown indoors as single plants in solitary pots.

Find a container which is large enough to hold several indoor plants — it should be attractive in shape, colour and design. Now plant out the specimens into potting compost you have placed inside the container; alternatively stand the pots on a layer of peat, sand, gravel or pebbles and surround each pot with damp peat so that the clay or plastic is no longer visible. You now have an Indoor Garden.

Your Indoor Garden may be five small plants in a bowl or it may be a forest of greenery and flowers in a multi-tiered Planter, but the basic advantages and principles of construction remain the same. Some of the advantages of the Indoor Garden are similar to those of the Pot Group — the creation of a bold effect, the proper utilisation of insignificant foliage and flowers, the hiding of ugly bare stems and damaged leaves, the ease of watering and the creation of moist conditions around the foliage. But the 'natural' effect is much more dramatic than with the Pot Group — here you are truly gardening.

There are several reasons why most plants grow much better in an Indoor Garden than in a solitary pot. Higher humidity, insulation of the roots from sudden changes in temperature and the water reservoir below each pot are amongst the most important benefits. But there are dangers. Close planting means reduced ventilation, and so the chance of pest and disease attack is increased. Prune or remove plants to avoid overcrowding and cut off mouldy leaves or flowers immediately they are seen.

The Ingredients of the Indoor Garden

PLANT
All the plants will receive approximately the same conditions of moisture and warmth. Light conditions will also be similar across a small Indoor Garden, but the plants in the centre of a large square unit may receive appreciably less light than the unshaded plants at the edges. The standard pattern is to have a permanent foliage background with splashes of colour provided by flowering plants.

POT
It is much better to leave the plants in their pots rather than planting them directly into the compost. In this way plants can be occasionally turned to prevent one-sided growth. Plants can also be easily removed when flowering is over or when repotting is necessary. The individual pots must have drainage holes.

PEAT
Make sure that the peat reaches to the rim of each pot and keep it moist but not saturated. This damp peat will provide a moisture reserve beneath each pot, which means that a plant will survive much better in an Indoor Garden than in an isolated pot if regular watering is interrupted at holiday time.

CONTAINER
There is an almost limitless range of watertight containers from which you can take your choice — plastic tubs, ornate jardinières, old copper steamers, home-made boxes and so on. If the container is made of wood, the inner surface and corners must be waterproofed with a sealant. Do not use creosote.

SOAKAWAY
A soakaway is not essential but it is a good idea to place a layer of gravel, small pebbles or coarse sand at the bottom of the container before adding peat.

THE PLANTER

The single Planter is the most popular of all Indoor Gardens. Until recently long troughs of metal, wood or plastic were the only popular containers, but there is now a wide range of cylindrical and cubic containers in every shade of tough plastic. A black or white Planter is recommended for modern decor.

Water carefully so that the surrounding peat does not become waterlogged. If the pots are stood on a thick layer of peat, the roots can be allowed to grow through the drainage holes and into the moist peat so that the Planter becomes a self-watering one. The usual recommendation where the pots stand on a shallow layer of gravel or peat is to lift or turn the pots occasionally to prevent rooting.

The size of Planters varies enormously. Egg cups have been used for tiny Succulents — at the other end of the scale Indoor Gardens draining into the hardcore of the house have been built into the floors of the homes of the rich and design-conscious.

Whatever the size, the effect will be enhanced if you choose the right background for your Planter. Plain wood and a mirror or mirror tiles are ideal.

THE HANGING BASKET

A group of attractive indoor plants in a Hanging Basket will indeed provide a beautiful display, but do not rush into hanging a container from a hook in the ceiling or a bracket on the wall until you have carefully studied the difficulties.

The air will be warmer and drier than at floor or windowsill level. The height of the display usually makes watering difficult, and when water is applied too liberally the basket may drip on to the floor.

You must choose a container which is suitable for indoors. The standard wire basket lined with sphagnum moss is ideal for outdoors, but in the home you will have the problem of water dripping on to the floor. You can line the basket with polythene sheeting, but waterlogging may then be a problem. The best answer is to put the pots of plants in a large waterproof container which bears the holding wires, chains or cords. The space between the pots and the hanging container should be filled with moist peat. A variation is a plastic hanging pot with a built-in drip tray. Always use a peat-based potting compost rather than a soil one — excess weight can be a problem.

To make watering and misting an easier task place the display at eye level or if you must suspend it over head-high then have a pulley arrangement instead of an ordinary hook. You can buy a pump action watering can if the display cannot be lowered. Ensure that the hook is securely fixed to a ceiling joist or the bracket is firmly attached to the wall, and finally make sure that your choice of plants is suited to the light available — flowering plants and variegated foliage house plants will need a spot near a window.

Good hanging basket plants:

Aporocactus	Chlorophytum	Hoya	Setcreasea
Asparagus	Episcia	Lobelia	Tradescantia
Begonia	Fuchsia	Pelargonium	Zebrina
Campanula	Hedera	Scindapsus	Zygocactus

THE MULTIPLE PLANTER

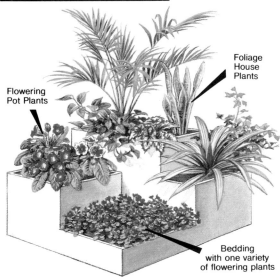

Flowering
Pot Plants

Foliage
House
Plants

Bedding
with one variety
of flowering plants

The simplest type consists of two or more ordinary containers pushed together to form a Multiple Planter. The best type is a tailor-made garden designed to fit the allotted space. The average handyman can quite easily construct a Multiple Planter from plastic-coated board — for maximum effect the planting units should be on different levels. The cracks between the boards must be sealed.

Each planting unit can be treated individually from both the planting and cultural standpoint. In the illustration flowering pot plants are grown in the unit closest to the window, the lowest unit is used for indoor bedding (Wax Begonia, Coleus, Crocus, Poinsettia, etc) which changes with the season and finally the tallest units provide a permanent backcloth of foliage house plants. An added advantage is that each unit can be individually watered so that moisture-lovers can be grown alongside Cacti and Succulents.

Several proprietary types of vertical Multiple Planter are available. Each unit is clipped on to the one below to form a tower — plants are potted into the open side of each unit.

THE MIXED BOWL

One of the simplest of all Indoor Gardens, in which a small selection of foliage plants and one or two flowering plants are removed from their pots and planted in a peat-based compost. The traditional pattern is to have a large pinnacle plant towards the back of the bowl, several compact bushy plants in the middle and a trailing plant at the front. The container is usually a bulb bowl, but any waterproof bowl will do.

A Mixed Bowl is always a welcome present to receive, but it is not a *permanent* Indoor Garden. When the flowers fade the best plan is to break up the arrangement and repot the individual plants before the roots become hopelessly intertwined. Explain to the donor, if necessary, that you are not destroying his or her present — you are preserving it.

Planting Suggestions for an Indoor Garden

You will be able to make your selection from scores of different varieties. Aim for closely-matched requirements for heat, light and water whenever you can.

The next step is to make sure that the height and shape of the plants are in keeping with the size of the container. Aim for a variation in height, a contrast in leaf shape and texture, and a controlled use of colour.

First of all, the tall pinnacle plants which give height to the display. Be careful in small Indoor Gardens that you don't choose a wide-spreading giant. Sansevieria provides height without spread, and feathery-leaved plants such as Grevillea and Dizygotheca avoid the shading effect of large leaves. The choice of pinnacle plants for a large Planter is of course much easier — Palms, Dracaena, Ficus, Monstera and Philodendron are all widely used.

For most displays it is the medium-sized range of plants which form the basic framework. If you don't want to rely on flowering pot plants for colour you can use some non-green foliage varieties — red-leaved Cordyline terminalis, yellow Scindapsus, variegated Chlorophytum and Ivies, and the multicoloured Croton, Coleus and Begonia rex.

Finally, don't forget the trailers which are needed to soften the hard line of the edge of the container. The popular four are Ivy, Tradescantia, Ficus pumila and Zebrina.

THE MINIATURE GARDEN

This special type of Indoor Garden is an attempt to reproduce an outdoor garden on a small scale. Paths, pools, figurines, etc, are used for decoration and mossy turfs plus tiny-leaved plants are used for landscaping. Japanese styles are popular, and the Miniature Garden is usually kept on a trolley so that it can be wheeled outside in fine weather and into the kitchen for watering. This style of Indoor Garden is really for the keen hobbyist, as upkeep is difficult and without a high degree of artistry the result can appear distinctly amateurish.

THE DISH GARDEN

A small Indoor Garden made in a shallow dish using carefully-chosen Succulents. Unlike other Indoor Garden containers the dish usually has drainage holes. For further details see page 212.

THE LIVING SCREEN

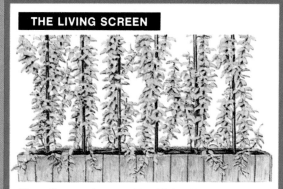

The eating area in a combined living/dining room can be separated in many ways. A wooden divider unit is sometimes used — a few pots in the open spaces will help to enliven such a unit. A living screen is preferred by many plant-lovers. A deep and reasonably wide trough is placed on the floor and a trellis or series of decorative poles secured in the compost so the support runs from floor to ceiling. Pots are then inserted in the compost — suitable plants are Cissus, Syngonium, Hedera, Ficus benjamina, Scindapsus, Philodendron scandens and Ficus pumila.

THE POT-ET-FLEUR

The Pot-et-Fleur is essentially a small Planter in which a group of foliage house plants is grown. During its construction a glass tube or metal florist tube is sunk into the peat between the pots. Subsequently this tube is filled with water and used for arranging cut flowers. In this way flowers from the garden or florist can be used to produce ever-changing and colourful displays.

At the beginning of the year 3 or 4 Daffodils against a living green backcloth look most attractive. During summer a few blooms from the flower garden or shrub border — Roses are excellent. Do not aim for a skilled arrangement — just a few points of colour to add interest to a group of house plants. The obvious favourite for Christmas time is a sprig or two of berried Holly.

Surprisingly the idea has never become popular — flower arrangers find the Pot-et-Fleur too limiting for their skills. The mistake is regarding it as a hybrid of pot plant culture and flower arranging — it is in fact a house plant display with a few seasonal flowers to brighten it up.

A Terrarium is a glass or transparent plastic container inside which plants are grown. The top is either naturally restricted or covered with transparent material.

The Terrarium

A Terrarium has two basic features. It surrounds the plants completely or almost completely with glass or some other transparent material, and access to the outside air is either strictly limited or non-existent. As a result plant-killing draughts are excluded and the air within is always moister than the room atmosphere. Because of this a wide range of delicate plants can be grown which would fail miserably if grown outside the Terrarium under ordinary room conditions.

Planting suggestions for a Bottle Garden

The range of plants you can grow in a Bottle Garden with a restricted or closed top is strictly limited. Do not use flowering plants, quick-growing foliage plants, Cacti or Succulents.

Choose from the following list and buy small specimens:

Acorus	Hedera helix (small-leaved var.)
Begonia rex (small-leaved var.)	Maranta
Calathea	Neanthe bella
Cryptanthus	Pellionia
Dracaena sanderiana	Peperomia
Ferns	Pilea
Ficus pumila	Saxifraga sarmentosa
Fittonia	Selaginella

The varieties to choose depend, of course, on where you place the Terrarium. If placed well away from the light it can be used to house Ferns and other green-leaved plants. When part of a window, the Terrarium is an excellent home for Orchids, Bromeliads, exotic foliage plants and all the dazzling flowering plants listed in the A–Z guide as needing some direct sun and moist air.

The reason why the Terrarium has remained the Cinderella of indoor plants is hard to understand. It cannot be a matter of cost, because suitable containers are to be found in most homes. All you need is a goldfish bowl, fish tank, large bottle or even a large glass mixing bowl. The only requirements are transparent sides and either a restricted neck or an opening which can be covered with glass or transparent plastic. Nor can this lack of general acceptance be due to the newness of the idea. Fern-cases were all the rage in the 1850s — these were used to house delicate Ferns and a variety of other moisture-loving foliage plants in Victorian parlours. Also in Victorian times the noted horticultural author Shirley Hibberd actively promoted the idea of a glass extension for plants built out from an ordinary window — his *hortus fenestralis*.

So it has been a story of ups and downs for Terraria. After the Victorian boom the idea was neglected in Britain, but the Plant Window became popular in some countries during the 20th century. For the U.K it was the Bottle (Carboy) Garden which first reached some degree of popularity, but it is the shop-bought version of the Fishtank Garden, made from soldered metal strips and glass panes, which is now beginning to overtake the glass carboy.

THE PLANT WINDOW

The most successful of all Terraria is the Plant Window. It is essentially a window with an external pane or panes of glass (doubled-glazed to provide winter insulation) and an internal fully-glazed door which can be opened to get to the space within. At the base of this space is a tray filled with gravel in which the pots are housed and then hidden with damp peat.

Plant Windows are a feature of many homes in Germany, Scandinavia, Holland and parts of the U.S — but are a rarity in British houses. This type of display is generally built at the time of house construction — it is a difficult task to construct one on to an existing building. The Plant Window floor is generally 1½–2½ ft wide and there are a number of basic features which must be provided. Some form of shading will be needed if the window faces south, and a ventilator is usually essential. There are all sorts of optional extras — fluorescent lighting, piped water supply, under-floor heating, automatically controlled humidifiers and ventilators, etc.

A Plant Window can truly be a thing of beauty. The atmosphere is even better than that in a conservatory for jungle plants. Here you can grow Orchids, Anthuriums, Bougainvilleas, Columneas, Caladiums and Acalyphas to perfection, but a lot of work is involved. Careful watering is essential and ventilation must be regularly adjusted to prevent misting. Plants must be groomed and the glass must be cleaned at regular intervals.

THE BOTTLE GARDEN

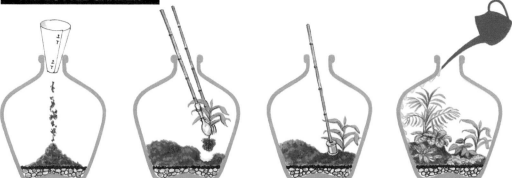

It is curious that until recently the only popular type of Terrarium in Britain was the Carboy or Bottle Garden. It is difficult to make, requiring special tools and some dexterity. First of all, make sure that the bottle is clean and dry. Insert a stiff paper cone in the mouth and pour in a 2 in. layer of gravel. Add a thin layer of charcoal and finally a thick layer of Seed and Cutting Compost. Firm the compost with a tamper (a cotton reel at the end of a bamboo cane) and then build up the compost to form the back of the garden.

Now introduce the plants — for planting suggestions, see page 26. You will need about six, including one tree-like specimen and at least one trailer. The planting tools are a dessert spoon at the end of one cane and a fork at the end of another. Firm the compost around each plant with the tamper.

Your Bottle Garden is now finished and is ready for watering. Use a long-necked watering can and train a gentle stream of water against the glass. Use very little water — just enough to clean the glass and moisten the surface. Insert the stopper; if the glass clouds over later, then remove the stopper until the condensation disappears. Re-insert the stopper — you will probably never have to water again.

THE FISHTANK GARDEN

A glass-cased garden which opens at the top is known as a Fishtank Garden — the many attractive glass cases which open at the side are sold simply as Terraria.

The treatment of both is the same. Begin by placing a layer of gravel and charcoal at the bottom of the container and then add a 2 in. layer of Seed and Cutting Compost. You can landscape the 'ground' into hills and valleys — use stones and pebbles if you wish but do not incorporate wood.

There is an extensive range of plants which are suitable for the Fishtank Garden or shop-bought Terrarium. It is a pity to waste such a good home on commonplace plants. Delicate Ferns, Crotons, Fittonia, Maranta, Cryptanthus, Calathea, Selaginella and Rhoeo will all flourish. Between the foliage add flowering varieties to provide splashes of colour — African Violets and small Orchids are ideal. Two warnings — never use Cacti or Succulents and always leave room between the plants so that they will be able to spread without becoming cramped.

After planting cover the top with a sheet of glass with bevelled edges. Close the door if present of a standard Terrarium. Stand it in a well-lit spot out of direct sunlight. If excessive condensation appears, slide open the lid or door for a few hours, but keep it shut at other times. There is little else to do — remove dead or diseased leaves and water every few months. This portable mini-jungle is the easiest way to grow exotic plants.

POSITIONING YOUR PLANTS FOR MAXIMUM EFFECT

The standard advice for getting the best visual effect from your plants is to study their future home *before* making your purchase. They may be required for general decoration — a bright splash of colour or a medley of green foliage to liven up a dull room. The first step here is to go through the questions on page 4 and take your list of suitable plants to your supplier. Once you have brought them home you should move the pots around the room so as to get the most pleasing effect.

In other cases the choice is more limited — the plants are required to do a specific job, such as covering an empty fireplace or serving as a divider between parts of a room. Here the final position is already fixed, so you should look carefully at the background before making your decision.

Much of this is a counsel of perfection. At least 50 per cent of all house plants are impulse purchases — the plant is bought solely on the basis of catching your eye in the shop and the instructions are then read when the pot arrives home. In this case you must find a spot in the house which will give the plant the light and heat it needs, and you should consider the background and lighting to enhance its beauty.

BACKGROUND

For most plants the best background is a non-patterned, pale pastel colour. This is especially true for all-green foliage plants and for brightly coloured flowers.

Heavily variegated leaves and plants bearing masses of pale blooms may look insipid when set against a pale background. A dark surface is visually more effective.

Small leaves are often lost against an intricately-patterned background. Move such plants in front of a plain wall — use large-leaved types against patterned surfaces.

For a bold effect aim for contrasts in colour and shapes. A background with a strongly perpendicular look can be improved by placing a spreading plant in front of it.

LIGHTING

For life-giving illumination the plants must rely on daylight or fluorescent lighting. For display purposes the light of an ordinary bulb directed on to the foliage or flowers will greatly enhance the appearance of a Specimen Plant in the evening. The best type of bulb to use is a spotlight or floodlight, but overheating can be a problem. Switch on the light and place your hand just above the leaves nearest the bulb. If you can feel the warmth then the plant is too close.

- **SPOTLIGHTING** A light or lights (usually spotlights recessed in the ceiling or set on a track) which are above the plant or plants. There are 2 benefits — plants in groups are brought into a unified whole and the details of individual plants are heightened.

- **UPLIGHTING** A light or lights which are set at ground level in front of the plant or plants. Leaves are illuminated, but the main purpose is to cast interesting shadows against the wall. Move the light to seek the most dramatic effect.

- **BACKLIGHTING** A light or lights which are set at ground level behind the plant or plants. The basic purpose is to turn the plant into a silhouette as clearly shown on page 30. This is not a technique for ordinary displays — you need space and large plants.

ONE PLANT – NINE DIFFERENT APPEARANCES

Dusty leaves

Washed leaves

Polished leaves

Plain background

Mirrored background

Patterned background

Uplighting

Spotlighting

Backlighting

PLACING PLANTS AROUND THE ROOM

HANGING FROM THE CEILING There is no finer way of displaying a trailing plant than suspending it in a container attached to the ceiling or a wall bracket. Nothing impedes the cascading stems, and the sight of living plants in mid-air has a special attraction. We notice the plants in a hanging basket on the wall of a house and we wouldn't give them a second glance if they were growing in the bed below. A hanging Specimen Plant can be used to add height to a floor-standing display or to add interest and colour to a dull side or alcove window. There is, unfortunately, a rather long list of warnings. Don't have a hanging display in the line of traffic if the ceiling is low — plants must never be part of an obstacle course. Choose the container with care and make sure that the attachment is strong enough to withstand the weight of the container and the compost just after watering. The plant must be a fine specimen and in peak condition — a bedraggled Ivy or a trailing stem or two of Philodendron scandens may actually diminish the beauty of the environment. Plant care is not easy — it is obviously more difficult to water a hanging display than its floor-standing or windowsill-sitting counterpart.

STANDING ON A WINDOWSILL People who regard their house plants as green pets rather than display material generally choose the windowsill as the favourite place to house them. This does not mean that plants in the window do not fit into the interior decorator's scheme of things, but the line of several separated pots neatly placed along the sill is neither one thing nor the other. From the display point of view it is much better to use an eye-catching Specimen Plant — low and bushy if sited in the middle of the window or tall and narrow if placed on one side. Choose a type with leaves which are enhanced by light shining through or on them — examples are Hypoestes and Iresine. Of course you must choose a plant which will be in keeping with its surroundings, a small and insignificant plant in a large window has little display value. Choose the plant with care — if the window faces east, south or west you will need one which can withstand some direct sun. A south-facing window will need some form of screen against the hot summer sun. Check the compost frequently — with the sun in summer and the radiator below in winter, watering can be a never-ending chore! If the view from the window is not important and you don't need the light, consider having a hanging plant above and a sill-borne one below.

STANDING ON THE FLOOR The place for the large Specimen Plant is on the floor — placing a heavy pot on a table can make it look unsafe. Bold Architectural plants are the usual choice, but there are other possibilities. Flowering standards are best displayed in this way and tall climbers with large leaves (Philodendron, Monstera etc) also make excellent floor-standing specimens. Interior designers love these tall Specimen Plants. A matched pair on either side of a door adds symmetry to a large room — a pot stood near a patio door brings the garden indoors. A floor-standing plant must be chosen with care. Narrow, upright plants can make the ceiling look higher — low, spreading ones have the opposite effect. Remember the receptacle can damage the carpet so place a piece of wood or cork below it.

STANDING ON FURNITURE Small Specimen Plants need to be raised off the ground so that they can be enjoyed at close range. The usual way to do this is to place the pot on a windowsill, shelf or piece of furniture. You must use a drip tray which is deep enough to protect the surface of the furniture — mop up any spillage immediately.

STANDING ON A PEDESTAL A number of indoor plants produce long pendulous stems or arching leaves and the display is often spoilt if the pot is stood on a sideboard or windowsill. The place for such plants is in a hanging container or on a pedestal. You can buy a reproduction antique pedestal if your home is decorated in this style, but for modern surroundings it is extremely simple to make a wooden pillar with straight sides. To house several pots in a pedestal-like arrangement you can buy a metal or cane plant stand — see page 19 for details.

GROWING AGAINST A WALL The plants most usually grown against a wall are flowering types (to provide a splash of colour against a pastel wall) and trailers (to frame windows, pictures, etc). There are a number of difficulties — it is not easy to create moist conditions, the pot is often small which means that constant watering is essential, and it is difficult to tell when the plant requires watering in a high-mounted display. Choose a receptacle which is soundly made, not too ornate and with a saucer which is both large and deep.

A ROOM-BY-ROOM GUIDE TO HOUSE PLANTS

The six basic sites for indoor plants around the house are shown below, and these together with the conservatory are the places where you may find plants growing for decorative purposes. Note the phrase 'where you *may* find plants growing'. There is no room where you can be certain to find foliage or flowering specimens. Most living rooms have at least one pot and the kitchen is also a popular place, but less than one bathroom in ten has an indoor plant and they are just as rare in the bedroom. This is, perhaps, a shame — there is no doubt that there is something especially eye-catching about finding a fine-looking specimen in an unusual place.

Much has been written about the elements of good design, but the only fundamental rule is that the arrangement should be pleasing to you and your family and also acceptable to the plants concerned. Apart from this there are just a few assorted rules. A Specimen Plant should be a point of real interest because of its shape, foliage or flowers — run-of-the-mill plants are better in a group. Scale is important — big rooms need big plants. Style is also important — strongly architectural plants with bare stems or stiff leaves (e.g Dracaena marginata) look better in modern rather than in old-world settings. Groups of plants are generally improved if there is a focal point — one or more plants which really catch the eye surrounded by other plants which serve to add extra colour and interest. The final rule is to avoid overdoing it, except in the conservatory. Your living room is not a garden centre and should not be made to look like one.

Most of us are prepared to accept that the showy flowering pot plants (page 57) have a strictly limited life, but we often expect the foliage and flowering house plants (pages 51 and 55) to be permanent features in the room we have chosen for them. One of the tricks of the skilled house plant enthusiast, however, is to move some plants from one room to another. A number of flowering house plants (e.g Bougainvillea, Heliotropium, Hoya, Pittosporum, Passiflora etc) need cool winter conditions so during these months the pots are moved from the centrally-heated living room to an unheated bedroom. Plants suffering from low air humidity are moved to the bathroom or kitchen to recuperate — specimens affected by the low light intensity in the hall are moved to a bright room in order to recover before being returned.

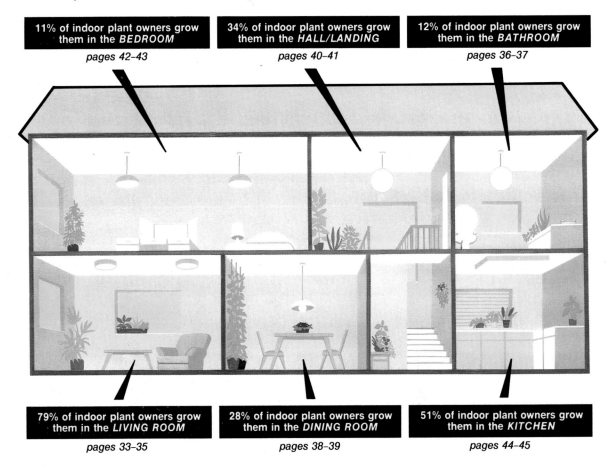

11% of indoor plant owners grow them in the BEDROOM
pages 42–43

34% of indoor plant owners grow them in the HALL/LANDING
pages 40–41

12% of indoor plant owners grow them in the BATHROOM
pages 36–37

79% of indoor plant owners grow them in the LIVING ROOM
pages 33–35

28% of indoor plant owners grow them in the DINING ROOM
pages 38–39

51% of indoor plant owners grow them in the KITCHEN
pages 44–45

The Living Room

The living room is the area where the family gathers. It is here that the adults relax, the children play and everyone seeks comfort. It is also the spot in the average home where most of the indoor plants can be found.

It is here where one usually finds the showiest and most expensive plants, and yet nearly every living room can be improved by introducing new types and altering the arrangement of the ones which are already there. The thing to avoid is scattering a few pots of nondescript greenery and run-of-the-mill flowering plants around the room — a couple on the windowsill, one on the mantlepiece, another on the TV set and so on. The interior designer sets out to create a number of *plant stations*, each of which is bold enough and attractive enough to be admired. The four types of plant station are summarised on page 15 and described on pages 16–28, and each of these types has its own advantages and its own special role to play. By choosing Specimen Plants with care you can change the basic appearance of the room — high ceilings will appear lower if you use hanging baskets and cascading plants whereas low rooms will appear higher if you use a bold and upright plant. Plants with arching branches and small leaves will give the illusion of added width to a narrow room.

The rules of good design appear on page 32. Scale is important — a small Pilea may look pathetic in a large area and a stately Dracaena would overpower a tiny room. Contrast is also important. A richly ornamental room is improved by using plants with large and simple leaves, but a drab area benefits from intricately-shaped and multicoloured foliage.

Make use of plants to enliven dull features. A fireplace filled with glowing coals may be a welcome sight in winter, but the empty hearth is unattractive for the rest of the year. The unused fireplace is therefore a popular spot for house plants — but remember that the light level is often low and so consider using shade-loving foliage plants or temporary displays of flowering ones. Radiators are rarely things of beauty and they can be improved by installing a shelf above in order to house a Pebble Tray (see page 19).

The living room is a moderately good home for many plants — the light level is usually good and there is always space for a plant station or two. But there are problems — the humidity of centrally-heated rooms is low in winter and the environment may be too warm in the dormant season for plants which need cool winter conditions. However, there are still hundreds of varieties from which to make your choice.

THE FIREPLACE ARRANGEMENT

Asplenium, Nephrolepis, Cissus . . . a group of shade-loving foliage plants add interest to a fireplace in summer time.

THE PLANT LOVER'S ARRANGEMENT

*A room in which practically all of the colour is provided by a wide array
of foliage and flowering plants. Many shapes and sizes are present here and
the effect can be quite stunning. But do be careful — this number and variety
of plants in a colourful over-furnished room would be overpowering.*

THE FUNCTIONAL ARRANGEMENT

Here the plants have a specific furnishing job to do. The walls are oddly shaped and the view uninteresting. The tall Ficus benjamina and Cissus antarctica are used to add interest to the walls and the small pots between them break up the straight lines of the window.

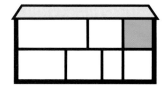

The Bathroom

A plant display in the bathroom is much more likely to be seen in a magazine than in the home, but with a little thought plants can always be used here to add a touch of interest or even luxury.

It is strange that so few bathrooms contain house plants. A warm bathroom with a large frosted-glass window is perhaps the best room in the house for the beautiful varieties which have come to us from humid habitats. In addition few other locations in the house need the softness and greenness of plants to reduce the hardness of their surfaces.

The problem bathroom is the small one — unheated in winter and with a tiny window of frosted glass. The answer is to choose a tough, glossy-leaved foliage variety such as Philodendron scandens (often called the Bathroom Plant in the U.S), Cissus antarctica or Scindapsus aureus. There is no floor space available, so put the pot on the windowsill or in a wall-mounted pot holder. A hanging basket over the bath is sometimes recommended, as the basket is provided with a ready-made if oversized drip-tray below!

In a larger bathroom with a decent-sized window you have a much greater choice of plants and display types. A Specimen Plant such as a Palm, Boston Fern or Weeping Fig can transform the appearance of the room. Alternatively you can create a Plant Window or Indoor Garden filled with Asparagus, Ivies, Heptapleurum, Syngonium, Ferns etc. Bath surrounds are usually too narrow to support plant pots — this precarious placing is best avoided, especially if there are children around.

The large, well-lit bathroom really comes into its own when it is centrally heated. It then becomes the best room in the house for the cultivation of colourful exotics — Anthurium, Calathea, Caladium, Maranta, Cymbidium and so on. Bromeliads will flourish here and so will all moisture-loving plants. You might be tempted to create a tropical jungle, but do make sure that such a scheme meets with the approval of the rest of the family.

Finally, a few points on bathroom plant care. Misting should not be necessary if the room is in regular use but the leaves will need sponging at fairly frequent intervals — talcum powder and hair lacquer aerosols are pore-blocking agents. Choose pot holders with care — wicker-work is ideal for a Victorian bathroom but for ultra-modern settings a metal or plastic one may be better.

THE SIMPLE ARRANGEMENT

Many people try to avoid a cluttered look in a bathroom, especially where space is strictly limited. However, a single Specimen Plant, such as this Ficus benjamina variegata, can add a welcome touch of living colour.

THE JUNGLE ARRANGEMENT

This bathroom is strictly for the plant enthusiast who must be surrounded
by living green all year round. The tropical nature of the large-leaved Fig, the Philodendron
and Palm add to the jungle feel of the room. The overhead Boston Ferns
add to the effect, but the blue duck seems quite out of place.

The Dining Room

It may seem strange that only one in four dining rooms contains indoor plants. This area is widely used for entertaining (and impressing) friends, there are ample horizontal surfaces for housing pots and the location is close to the kitchen which makes for easy watering. In addition, the decor is often sparse and would benefit from attractive leaves and colourful flowers.

The problem is one of space — most dining rooms are quite small and are filled with the chairs, table and serving surfaces they have to contain. Floor-standing pots would hamper free movement or could be knocked over when chairs are pulled back — plants must never, never turn a room into an obstacle course.

Even in the most compact dining room, however, a centrepiece of house plants instead of cut flowers on the dining table is an excellent idea . . . with three provisos.

Firstly, the plants must be low growing so as not to interfere with conversation between people on opposite sides of the table. Good examples here include Saintpaulia, Crocus, dwarf Cyclamen, Peperomia, Begonia semperflorens, Pilea and the small-leaved Ivy. Secondly, the plants must be in good condition —

dusty, diseased leaves and live greenfly are distinctly distasteful for the guest and embarrassing for the host. Finally, avoid strong-smelling plants — this means highly fragrant ones such as Hyacinth which can mask the taste of the food, and unpleasantly pungent ones like Exacum in full flower. Other places for plants in the small dining room are on the windowsill (choose carefully if it faces south) or in a pot holder on the wall.

If you have a large dining room then house plants can make a splendid contribution. The bold Specimen Plant in the corner, the pendant variety on a pedestal, the bold Pot Group on the sideboard — all are possible.

It is sometimes desirable to separate the eating area in a combined living/dining room, and indoor plants offer one of the cheapest and most satisfactory ways of doing this. A living screen can be created by growing vigorous climbers up an attractive framework. The plants are stood at ground level in pots either in individual drip trays or in a waterproof trough. Pots of colourful hanging plants can be used to soften the lines of a wooden island unit which divides the dining area from the rest of the room.

THE SIMPLE ARRANGEMENT

Nothing could be simpler. Just a few pots of low-growing African Violets in a casserole which matches the dinner service. Simple, but effective.

THE BOLD ARRANGEMENT

A pool of dramatic shapes in a sparsely-furnished room.
This Pot Group of Begonia, Scindapsus, Rubber Plant and Kentia Palm
is greatly enhanced by backlighting — see page 29.

The Hall/Landing

Indoor plants are a vital feature of the well-furnished hall. It is here that visitors gain their first impression of the inside of your home. Beautiful leaves and flowers are an immediate indication of a well-tended house. If your hall is large, well-lit and heated in winter then you are indeed fortunate and should make the most of the opportunity. Don't scatter a few pots about — go for the bold and the unusual. A Moth Orchid in flower may not attract much attention in a large living room where it is surrounded by ornaments, pictures, books etc, but it certainly would if stood in solitary splendour on a hall table. Here is the place for the large and illuminated Indoor Garden, the stately tree, the group of Azaleas in full flower, and so on.

Unfortunately most halls present a very different scene. They are poorly lit, subject to draughts, cold at night and tend to be narrow passageways rather than square or rectangular rooms. Flourishing but unexciting plants will look better than struggling exotics, so choose from the 'easy' group listed on page 4 if you want a permanent resident in a problem hall. But your display does not have to be unexciting if you are prepared to treat it as temporary, and there are two ways of doing this. You can place brightly-flowered but inexpensive plants there and treat them as disposable displays in the same way as cut flowers. Alternatively you can practice rotation with foliage plants. This calls for removing the pots when the plants start to look sickly and placing them in your well-lit 'hospital' room (spare bedroom, kitchen etc) until they recover.

The favourite site is a table near the front door. Make sure the plants are kept out of the line of traffic at this congested spot. Never obstruct the staircase. Do not choose spiky or thorny types such as Cacti. Ferns are usually an excellent choice.

A well-lit spot near the hall window or at the top of the stairs is often the best hallway environment. Garden Bulbs, Azalea, Cyclamen, Erica, Cineraria and Primula will usually last longer on a hall or landing windowsill than in a centrally-heated living room. Keep the size of the plant in keeping with the space available. A large plant in a small hall will make the area look even smaller. Consider using the same varieties in both hall and landing to link the two areas together.

THE SIMPLE ARRANGEMENT

This long and narrow hall does not have space for a large group of plants, nor does it need such an arrangement. Just one or two pots will do, but the plants must be in good condition and should be bold enough to be eye-catching.

THE SPECIAL ARRANGEMENT

*Palms and Peace Lilies — a muted yet spectacular display
in the Indoor Garden of a large, well-lit hallway.*

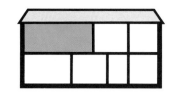

The Bedroom

The bedroom is the least popular room for displaying indoor plants. While it is generally agreed that all living rooms, kitchens and halls can be improved with living plants, there is a difference of opinion over bedrooms. Some interior designers feel that bedrooms are in use for too short a time during the waking hours to make a house plant display worthwhile. Having to look after pots and troughs in rooms so far away from the watering can, plant food, pruners etc kept in the kitchen just prolongs the time spent on housework. The final point made by the anti-school is that there are too few visitors to bedrooms to justify the expenditure on impressive plants.

Fortunately most interior decorators take the opposite view. They know that the bedroom is regarded as a very special room by many people. Despite the limited time spent there and the absence of visitors it is the one area which can truly reflect the design sense of the occupant. You don't have to worry about the views of the whole family or what friends will think. Here you can create your *own* arrangement.

The conditions in a centrally-heated bedroom really are too good to waste. It is an excellent spot for plants which hate too much heat in winter and tend to suffer in living rooms which are heated during the day. Examples are Cyclamen, Heliotrope, Beloperone, Hydrangea, Campanula, Buxus, Bougainvillea, Yucca and Abutilon.

Perhaps the best plan is to have one or two really eye-catching Specimen Plants rather than aiming for the group displays which belong in the living room and the kitchen. A floor-standing architectural plant is the designer's choice for a large bedroom — in a smaller one you can have a hanging display or else set attractive pot holders on the windowsill or dressing table. An unused fireplace can be masked by a foliage plant display. Whatever arrangement you choose there is the pleasure of waking to the sight of green foliage and you can go to sleep amid natural fragrance if you choose sweet-smelling types such as Jasmine, Hyacinth and Stephanotis. And forget the old wives' tale that plants are unhealthy in a bedroom — they are not.

Bedrooms which are heated for all or part of the night in winter make good house plant hospitals. This is a place to overwinter plants which need a rest from high temperatures during the non-flowering season. The bedroom can be a place of relaxation and recuperation for you and the Fuchsias and the Pelargoniums.

THE SIMPLE ARRANGEMENT

Plants in the bedroom are not everybody's choice, but there can be no doubt that the two matched displays of Scindapsus aureus give a touch of symmetry to the odd collection of furniture.

THE GROUP ARRANGEMENT

A Pot Group can add interest to a drab corner of a bedroom.
Here Maidenhair Fern, Kentia Palm, Red Dracaena, Creeping Fig
and Chinese Evergreen add colour to the pale cream decor.

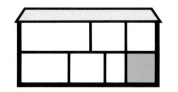

The Kitchen

The kitchen is second only to the living room as the most popular place for indoor plants — more than half have at least one pot or plant trough. This popularity is not really surprising as there are several factors which make the kitchen a good place for many foliage plants and flowers. Some members of the family may spend much of the day here and the moist environment is beneficial for most plants. In addition the somewhat clinical appearance of white or pastel units, steel sinks etc can be softened and enlivened by the presence of colourful plants.

By far the most popular spot for kitchen plants is the windowsill. There is usually a hotch-potch of types — African Violets next to recently-rooted cuttings, pots of Cacti next to Bulbs in bowls, sickly plants taken from other rooms next to Primulas and Ivies. It is also the place for herbs — Parsley, Chives, Basil etc and even for miniature fruits such as miniature Tomatoes.

The windowsill in front of the sink is a good environment in many ways — you cannot help but keep an eye on the plants when working at the sink, water is readily to hand and so is the equipment for feeding, polishing and removing dead foliage and flowers. In addition this part of the kitchen generally has the moistest air and the light is usually good. Still, there are points to watch. Splashing foliage with hot soapy water can be troublesome and an untidy jungle can spoil the view and make the kitchen rather dark.

Natural gas is not a danger to plants but kitchens can be an undesirable residence for some plants with a delicate constitution. Draughts occur as a result of the opening and closing of outside doors and there are hot spots around cookers, toasters, refrigerators etc. The best plan is to choose colourful workaday plants rather than expensive temperamental ones. Good examples include Begonia, Impatiens, Scindapsus, Zebrina, Hypoestes, Pelargonium and Garden Bulbs. Although the plants may not be unusual the pot holders can be — teapots, terracotta jars, brass kettles etc.

The kitchen is a busy place and plants must be kept out of the way — they must never block free passage between one work area and another. The bold Specimen Plant such as a Weeping Fig is fine, but only if you really do have the floor space. Space on work surfaces is usually (but not always) too limited to devote to plants. It is generally better to put pots on shelves or in wall containers. Hanging baskets are attractive, but they must be out of the line of traffic. Big or small, there is always room for at least one house plant in any kitchen.

THE BOLD ARRANGEMENT

A neat arrangement of house plants brightens a corner of this modern kitchen — Tulips on the counter plus Weeping Fig and Aglaonema on the floor.

THE SIMPLE ARRANGEMENT

A kitchen should not be cluttered with plants if space is limited.
In this small room three pots of Ivy are used to soften the
collection of squares and rectangles. The spot above the oven is
far from ideal, but the plants are cheap and easily replaceable.

The Garden Room

The dividing lines between *greenhouse*, *conservatory* and *garden room* are vague, and experts disagree over the definitions. It is best to regard a greenhouse (or glasshouse) as a structure made entirely or mainly of glass or transparent plastic and which is entered from the garden. It is arranged almost exclusively for the comfort of the plants rather than for the people who tend or look at them.

A conservatory is similar in physical appearance with glazed walls and roof but is generally more ornate than the standard greenhouse. The basic difference, however, is that entry is generally through the house and there is provision for people to sit and enjoy the plants. Still, the beauty and welfare of the plants and their arrangement are the key factors.

The garden room (other names: sun room, plant room) is also entered through the house, but is often an integral part of the house rather than an extension. The walls consist entirely or mainly of glass or transparent plastic, but the ceiling may be made of standard building material which is not transparent. Here human comfort is the key consideration with extensive plant displays serving as an attractive background.

It is a great mistake to fill a garden room or conservatory with common-or-garden varieties. Using the popular house plants is all right as long as you separate them with eye-catching tropical beauties. Look through the A–Z guide — typical ones include Agapanthus, Hibiscus, Datura, Citrus, Clianthus, Strelitzia, Orchids, Abutilon, Columnea, Passiflora, Caladium and Gloriosa. The plants you are able to grow will depend on the amount of heat you can provide in winter. A minimum of 55°F means that nearly all of the exotic types will be suitable. You will find some at your garden centre but it will be necessary to order the rarer types from specialist nurseries.

You will have to provide a number of things apart from heat in winter. Shading will be needed to protect delicate foliage from the hot summer sun, and there must be some way of ventilating the room. Avoid polished wood furniture — cane, plastic or rust-proof metal is a much better choice for the damp atmosphere. Floors should be covered with a rot-proof surface such as tiles or polypropylene carpeting. It is essential to have a tap somewhere near the room as there will be a great deal of watering to do.

THE VICTORIAN ARRANGEMENT

Marble statuary and muted colours give this arrangement
a distinctly 19th Century appearance.

THE JUNGLE ARRANGEMENT

*A wide variety of large foliage plants is used to produce
a jungle-like effect in this garden room.*

THE WELL-BALANCED ARRANGEMENT

*In this garden room there is a good balance between plants
and living space. Neither aspect dominates the other.*

CHAPTER 3

THE CLASSIFICATION OF HOUSE PLANTS

There are four basic groups, each one with its own special characteristics. The main features of each group are outlined below. The single most important dividing line is between the Flowering Pot Plants which have only a limited display life in the room and the other three groups which under good conditions can be expected to be permanent residents.

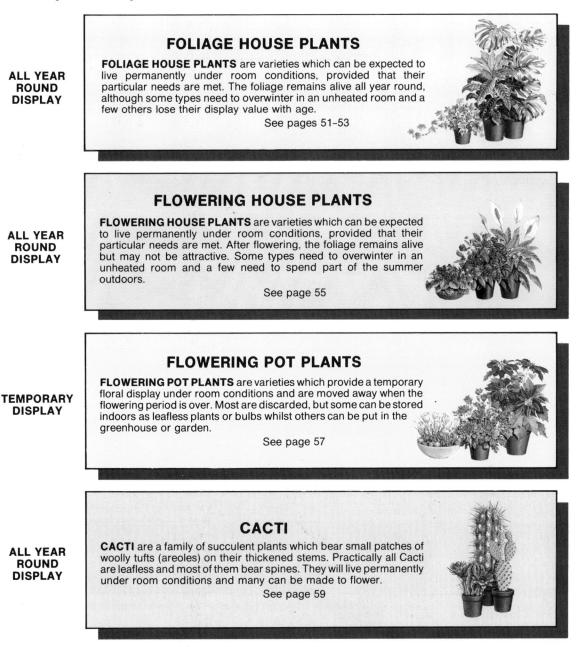

ALL YEAR ROUND DISPLAY

FOLIAGE HOUSE PLANTS

FOLIAGE HOUSE PLANTS are varieties which can be expected to live permanently under room conditions, provided that their particular needs are met. The foliage remains alive all year round, although some types need to overwinter in an unheated room and a few others lose their display value with age.

See pages 51–53

ALL YEAR ROUND DISPLAY

FLOWERING HOUSE PLANTS

FLOWERING HOUSE PLANTS are varieties which can be expected to live permanently under room conditions, provided that their particular needs are met. After flowering, the foliage remains alive but may not be attractive. Some types need to overwinter in an unheated room and a few need to spend part of the summer outdoors.

See page 55

TEMPORARY DISPLAY

FLOWERING POT PLANTS

FLOWERING POT PLANTS are varieties which provide a temporary floral display under room conditions and are moved away when the flowering period is over. Most are discarded, but some can be stored indoors as leafless plants or bulbs whilst others can be put in the greenhouse or garden.

See page 57

ALL YEAR ROUND DISPLAY

CACTI

CACTI are a family of succulent plants which bear small patches of woolly tufts (areoles) on their thickened stems. Practically all Cacti are leafless and most of them bear spines. They will live permanently under room conditions and many can be made to flower.

See page 59

FOLIAGE HOUSE PLANTS

At the start of the house plant boom in the 1950s it was the Foliage House Plants which dominated the scene. The Ivies and Rubber Plants led the way and were soon followed by a host of others.

Today the foliage plants have to share the stage with the flowering ones, but the leafy types still provide the permanent framework of most indoor plant collections. These are the plants grown for their foliage or stems rather than for their flowers, the attraction arising from the beauty of each leaf (e.g Monstera deliciosa and Begonia rex) or from their overall effect (e.g Asparagus and Boston Fern).

A few of these plants, such as Zebrina, Sansevieria and Peperomia, occasionally produce small flowers, but it is for their foliage and general growth habit that specimens of this group are grown. This, of course, does not mean that the purpose of Foliage House Plants is to provide an all-green background for brightly-coloured flowering types. A year-round multicoloured display can be obtained with plants such as Croton, Coleus, Iresine, Begonia rex, Cordyline terminalis, Dracaena marginata and so on. Even more types have foliage which is lined, splashed, edged or spotted with white or cream — the popular varieties of Tradescantia, Dieffenbachia, Aglaonema, Chlorophytum, Scindapsus and Ivy are just a few examples. There is an increasing trend towards growing variegated versions of old favourites. The variegated types of Ficus benjamina, Fatsia japonica, Monstera deliciosa and Heptapleurum arboricola have begun to take over from their all-green parents.

It is not only new varieties of established plants which have appeared in recent years — during the 1980s and into the 1990s new genera have appeared in the shops. Radermachera is now seen in many outlets alongside other recent introductions such as Breynia, Leea and the Air Plants.

The Foliage House Plants *belong* indoors. Some of them appreciate a winter holiday in a frost-free unheated room away from the family,

but not for them the fate of Flowering Pot Plants — the end-of-season dustbin, the enforced summer outdoors or a stemless winter indoors. The concept of permanence has been stressed several times on this page, and it is true that with proper care many types are capable of outliving their owners. But it is equally true that a few types deteriorate quite quickly with age. Coleus is a well-known example but there are others — both Gynura and Hypoestes become leggy and unattractive after two or three years. In addition there are temperamental Foliage House Plants which become gaunt and partly leafless if the conditions are not right. The answer is to raise cuttings or buy another specimen to replace the worn-out plant. The only truly 'temporary' Foliage House Plant is Caladium, which spends each winter as a dormant tuber.

It is impossible to generalise about the proper care of Foliage House Plants — a few are extremely delicate and some have cast-iron constitutions. The popular types which have all-green, large and shiny leaves are usually tolerant of indifferent conditions. Variegated types need more care — fleshy-leaved varieties need less frequent watering. But each plant has its own needs — always check in the A–Z guide.

KEY TO THE FOLIAGE HOUSE PLANT GROUPS

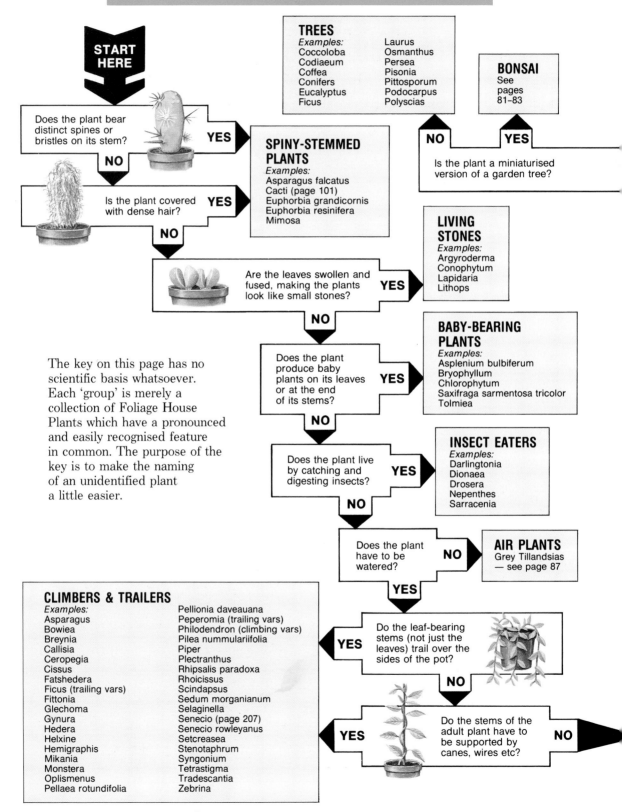

START HERE

Does the plant bear distinct spines or bristles on its stem?

YES

NO

Is the plant covered with dense hair?

YES

NO

SPINY-STEMMED PLANTS
Examples:
Asparagus falcatus
Cacti (page 101)
Euphorbia grandicornis
Euphorbia resinifera
Mimosa

TREES
Examples:
Coccoloba   Laurus
Codiaeum   Osmanthus
Coffea   Persea
Conifers   Pisonia
Eucalyptus   Pittosporum
Ficus   Podocarpus
                Polyscias

NO   **YES**

Is the plant a miniaturised version of a garden tree?

BONSAI
See pages 81–83

Are the leaves swollen and fused, making the plants look like small stones?

YES

NO

LIVING STONES
Examples:
Argyroderma
Conophytum
Lapidaria
Lithops

Does the plant produce baby plants on its leaves or at the end of its stems?

YES

NO

BABY-BEARING PLANTS
Examples:
Asplenium bulbiferum
Bryophyllum
Chlorophytum
Saxifraga sarmentosa tricolor
Tolmiea

The key on this page has no scientific basis whatsoever. Each 'group' is merely a collection of Foliage House Plants which have a pronounced and easily recognised feature in common. The purpose of the key is to make the naming of an unidentified plant a little easier.

Does the plant live by catching and digesting insects?

YES

NO

INSECT EATERS
Examples:
Darlingtonia
Dionaea
Drosera
Nepenthes
Sarracenia

Does the plant have to be watered?

NO

YES

AIR PLANTS
Grey Tillandsias — see page 87

CLIMBERS & TRAILERS
Examples:
Asparagus
Bowiea
Breynia
Callisia
Ceropegia
Cissus
Fatshedera
Ficus (trailing vars)
Fittonia
Glechoma
Gynura
Hedera
Helxine
Hemigraphis
Mikania
Monstera
Oplismenus
Pellaea rotundifolia

Pellionia daveauana
Peperomia (trailing vars)
Philodendron (climbing vars)
Pilea nummulariifolia
Piper
Plectranthus
Rhipsalis paradoxa
Rhoicissus
Scindapsus
Sedum morganianum
Selaginella
Senecio (page 207)
Senecio rowleyanus
Setcreasea
Stenotaphrum
Syngonium
Tetrastigma
Tradescantia
Zebrina

YES

Do the leaf-bearing stems (not just the leaves) trail over the sides of the pot?

NO

YES

Do the stems of the adult plant have to be supported by canes, wires etc?

NO

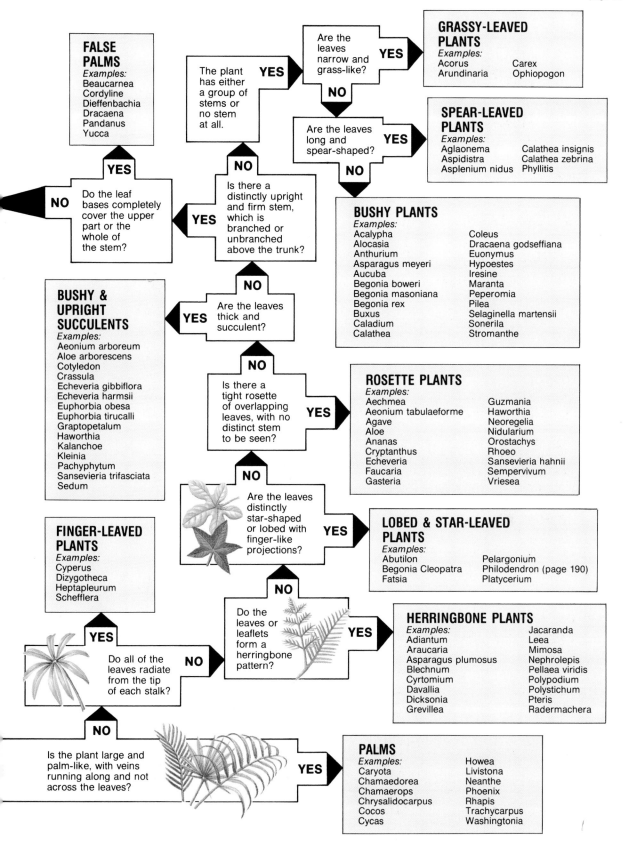

FALSE PALMS
Examples:
Beaucarnea
Cordyline
Dieffenbachia
Dracaena
Pandanus
Yucca

The plant has either a group of stems or no stem at all.

YES Are the leaves narrow and grass-like?

YES **GRASSY-LEAVED PLANTS**
Examples:
Acorus
Arundinaria
Carex
Ophiopogon

NO Are the leaves long and spear-shaped?

YES **SPEAR-LEAVED PLANTS**
Examples:
Aglaonema
Aspidistra
Asplenium nidus
Calathea insignis
Calathea zebrina
Phyllitis

YES Do the leaf bases completely cover the upper part or the whole of the stem?

NO

NO Is there a distinctly upright and firm stem, which is branched or unbranched above the trunk?

YES

NO **BUSHY PLANTS**
Examples:
Acalypha
Alocasia
Anthurium
Asparagus meyeri
Aucuba
Begonia boweri
Begonia masoniana
Begonia rex
Buxus
Caladium
Calathea
Coleus
Dracaena godseffiana
Euonymus
Hypoestes
Iresine
Maranta
Peperomia
Pilea
Selaginella martensii
Sonerila
Stromanthe

BUSHY & UPRIGHT SUCCULENTS
Examples:
Aeonium arboreum
Aloe arborescens
Cotyledon
Crassula
Echeveria gibbiflora
Echeveria harmsii
Euphorbia obesa
Euphorbia tirucalli
Graptopetalum
Haworthia
Kalanchoe
Kleinia
Pachyphytum
Sansevieria trifasciata
Sedum

YES Are the leaves thick and succulent?

NO Is there a tight rosette of overlapping leaves, with no distinct stem to be seen?

YES **ROSETTE PLANTS**
Examples:
Aechmea
Aeonium tabulaeforme
Agave
Aloe
Ananas
Cryptanthus
Echeveria
Faucaria
Gasteria
Guzmania
Haworthia
Neoregelia
Nidularium
Orostachys
Rhoeo
Sansevieria hahnii
Sempervivum
Vriesea

NO Are the leaves distinctly star-shaped or lobed with finger-like projections?

YES **LOBED & STAR-LEAVED PLANTS**
Examples:
Abutilon
Begonia Cleopatra
Fatsia
Pelargonium
Philodendron (page 190)
Platycerium

FINGER-LEAVED PLANTS
Examples:
Cyperus
Dizygotheca
Heptapleurum
Schefflera

NO Do the leaves or leaflets form a herringbone pattern?

YES **HERRINGBONE PLANTS**
Examples:
Adiantum
Araucaria
Asparagus plumosus
Blechnum
Cyrtomium
Davallia
Dicksonia
Grevillea
Jacaranda
Leea
Mimosa
Nephrolepis
Pellaea viridis
Polypodium
Polystichum
Pteris
Radermachera

YES Do all of the leaves radiate from the tip of each stalk?

NO

NO Is the plant large and palm-like, with veins running along and not across the leaves?

YES **PALMS**
Examples:
Caryota
Chamaedorea
Chamaerops
Chrysalidocarpus
Cocos
Cycas
Howea
Livistona
Neanthe
Phoenix
Rhapis
Trachycarpus
Washingtonia

FLOWERING HOUSE PLANTS

Flowering plants are playing an increasingly important role in house plant displays. Both colour and interest are added to a Pot Group or Indoor Garden when one or more varieties in flower are added. Cut flowers have, of course, been popular for centuries as a way of bringing living blooms indoors, but the flowering plant in a pot has an added ingredient. There is the fascination of watching the buds open into full bloom, and in many cases waiting for new buds to appear.

These flowering plants are of two types — there are the many varieties which provide a temporary display indoors (see page 57) and there are the remaining varieties which can take up permanent residence in your room. This latter group is made up of the Flowering House Plants.

These plants come in many sizes, shapes and smells and the range is vast. You can grow a spectacular Bird of Paradise with 6 in. blooms or a Stapelia gigantea with blooms as large as a dinner plate — or you can buy a Kalanchoe or Heliotrope where each individual bloom is tiny. The plant may fit into an egg cup if you grow Saintpaulia Pip Squeek but you will need a large tub for a fully-grown Datura or Acacia. Odours range from the strong, heady perfumes of Gardenia, Oleander and Jasmine to the unpleasant stench of the Carrion Flower.

You can take your choice of flowering season — there are Kalanchoe and Pink Jasmine to brighten up the living room in winter, plants such as Spathiphyllum and Anthurium for blooming in spring and Hibiscus and Campanula for summer blooms. Aphelandra and Oleander bloom in autumn, and there are numerous types which can with care be made to flower nearly all year round — Saintpaulia, Impatiens, Brunfelsia and Beloperone are examples. Not all Flowering House Plants are grown for their blooms — at least three (Citrus, Ardisia and Duchesnea) are bought for their fruit rather than their floral display.

Each Hibiscus bloom lasts for only a day or two — at the other end of the scale the flower-head of an Aechmea can be expected to last for several months. The floral season may be fleeting or may occur intermittently for most of the year, but with all these plants there comes a time when it is no longer in flower. In most cases the plant is not particularly attractive at this stage. Such types are best grown in a Pot Group or Indoor Garden so that their plainness when not in bloom can be hidden by showier types. Some varieties, however, have leaves which are so striking that they are worth growing for their foliage alone — good examples include Aphelandra, Bromeliads, Fancy-leaved Geraniums, Sanchezia, Pittosporum and Sparmannia. Because of this advantage these types can be used as year-round Specimen Plants.

There are few general rules for cultivation. You will find that nearly all Flowering House Plants need more light than foliage ones but you should always look up specific needs in the A–Z guide. During the 1980s the range of flowering house plants increased (e.g merrily-coloured and gaily-patterned Impatiens and Saintpaulias) and people have become more adventurous (Orchids and a number of Bromeliads are now offered in supermarkets). No doubt the 1990s will see further developments.

FLOWERING POT PLANTS

Unlike the Flowering House Plants, the members of this group can only be temporary residents in your living room, kitchen or hall. Once the flowers fade their display days are over and the next stage depends on the plant in question. Most are thrown away, some can be kept for another year by moving them into the garden or a cool room and others are stored as bulbs for replanting at the proper time of the year.

It is a cardinal rule to check before buying whether that plant in bloom and which looks so attractive on the shelves in the shop or bench in the garden centre is a Flowering House or Pot Plant. Obviously you should never choose a Flowering Pot Plant if you want something which will adorn your living room as a permanent feature.

This lack of permanence is, of course, a disadvantage and it may seem strange at first that such plants should be so popular. But it is not really strange for some of our most spectacular flowering plants are to be found here — the Poinsettia, Azalea, Gloxinia, Cineraria, Chrysanthemum and Hyacinth.

An important group of Flowering Pot Plants, sometimes referred to as 'florist' or 'gift' plants, have an essential part to play in the indoor plants scene. During the dark winter months they provide a welcome splash of colour when garden flowers are absent and cut flowers are expensive. The Azalea, Poinsettia, Cyclamen and Chrysanthemum are bright in bud or full flower — the Solanum and Capsicum are bought in fruit. These plants are to be found in countless homes as the first flowers or bright fruits to welcome in the New Year.

The second important group are the Garden Bulbs, providing the basic spring display of flowers indoors — Hyacinth, Crocus, Tulip and Narcissus. The remaining Flowering Pot Plants are a mixed bag — there are the showy ones such as Cineraria, Gloxinia and Begonia, the quick-growing climbers such as Thunbergia and Gloriosa, and scores of pretty annuals such as Exacum and Browallia which are raised from seed. Shrubs feature here — there are types such as Pomegranate and Miniature Roses which lose their leaves in winter. Also included are a number of Indoor (non-hardy) Bulbs.

After a few weeks or perhaps months the flowers will fade and in nearly all types the leaves fall and the plant may die. This is not your fault, because it is a basic feature of the group. Poinsettias can keep their showy heads for a few months and most of the popular types should stay in bloom for 4–7 weeks — this means that you should regard these plants as a long-lasting substitute for cut flowers rather than as house plants with a very short life.

Of course, flower fading and leaf fall should not take place in a matter of days — this would indicate that you were doing something wrong. As a general rule Flowering Pot Plants need bright, cool conditions and moist compost — warm air is generally the biggest enemy of all.

When flowering comes to an end the A–Z guide will tell you what to do. Some plants can be made to provide a repeat display next season — millions are needlessly thrown away every year.

CACTI

Cacti have perhaps lost a little of the popularity they enjoyed 50 years ago. No longer do they top the best-seller lists, but they still are to be found in millions of homes and they still remain the least understood of all indoor plants.

They are often regarded as plants which actually thrive on neglect. Hardly any other indoor living thing can put up with such poor conditions and yet outlive its owner. And so there are millions of Cacti in homes throughout the country which are kept as semi-alive, green ornaments which, apart from some increase in size, hardly change their appearance over the years. After all, as everybody knows, they are desert plants which thrive on a staple diet of sandy soil, drought and year-round heat, and if you are lucky they will bloom every seven years.

All of which is nonsense. Too much fine sand may actually kill them. Summer drought will put them to sleep. For proper development and regular flowering they need winter temperatures which will make you shiver and in summer many prefer fresh air outdoors to overheated stuffy rooms. Given proper treatment as outlined in the Secrets of Success on page 101, your dusty Desert Cactus will come alive and, depending on the variety, may flower as regularly as the Daffodils in spring.

The Cacti are a vast and varied family of plants which in nature range from tiny ground-hugging types to towering pillars seen in the deserts of the American South West. Although there is such a wide variety of sizes, shapes and flower types there are still a few features they have in common. All of them (except Pereskia and young Opuntia) are leafless. On the stems you will find a number of areoles (woolly or bristly cushions). In most cases you will find outgrowths from these areoles — there may be spines, needles, long hairs or short hooks.

The Cactus family is divided into two groups — the Desert Cacti and the Forest Cacti. The original home and cultural needs of these two groups are different — see pages 101–109.

DESERT CACTI

Natural home is the warm semi-desert regions of America. Despite the name of the group very few can exist in sand alone.

Nearly all Cacti belong to this group and there are hundreds to choose from. Most types are easily propagated from cuttings.

Need very little or no water between mid autumn and early spring.

Require as much sunshine as possible, especially for flowering. Suitable for south-facing windowsills.

FOREST CACTI

Natural home is the forest regions of tropical America, where they grow as epiphytes on trees.

Only a few varieties are commercially available, and most of them can be recognised by their trailing habit and their flattened leaf-like stems.

May need some water and feeding during winter months.

Require some shade during hottest months of the year. Suitable for north- and east-facing windowsills.

In this chapter you will find illustrations and descriptions of hundreds of house plants. Some are too well known to need much description, and a few are rare enough to be regarded as collectors' items. Many are perfectly happy in the living room, and one or two really belong in the conservatory. Most appear under their latin name, but a number have been grouped together because they share many features in common — examples are 'Ferns', 'Succulents', 'Bromeliads' and 'Orchids'. If you want to find out more about a particular plant, then look up either its latin or common name in the Index and then turn to the appropriate page.

CHAPTER 4
HOUSE PLANTS A~Z

ABUTILON

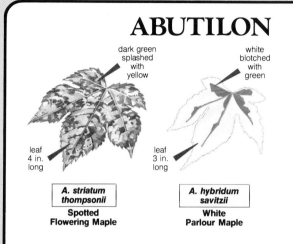

dark green splashed with yellow

white blotched with green

leaf 4 in. long

leaf 3 in. long

A. striatum thompsonii
Spotted Flowering Maple

A. hybridum savitzii
White Parlour Maple

FOLIAGE HOUSE PLANT
page 51

FLOWERING HOUSE PLANT
page 55

The typical Abutilon or Flowering Maple is a vigorous shrub with large Sycamore-like leaves and pendant blooms which are borne on slender stalks between early summer and autumn. It is a plant which needs room to spread — a large window which receives some filtered sunlight during the day is ideal.

The leaves are often variegated with white or yellow patches and a couple of varieties (A. striatum thompsonii and A. hybridum savitzii) are regarded as foliage house plants which bear summer flowers as a bonus.

Abutilon is not a difficult plant to grow despite its exotic appearance. It needs neither unduly warm conditions nor moist air and it benefits from being stood outdoors in summer. Mealy bugs and aphids are the only pests which are likely to be a problem and cuttings root quite readily. Prune the shoots back a little in spring and then feed regularly until the autumn. With the onset of winter the plant should be cut back to about half its size to ensure a bushy growth habit in the following season.

TYPES

Abutilon striatum thompsonii is the best-known foliage type. Unlike other Abutilons the variegated leaves are free from hairs — this quick-growing shrub will reach 5 ft or more and the orange-red flowers appear in summer. **A. megapotamicum** is a trailer suitable for hanging baskets or for tying to supports as a 4 ft climber. Its arrow-shaped leaves are about 3 in. long and the lantern-like blooms hang down from the wiry stems — hence its common name Weeping Chinese Lantern. There is a colourful variety (**variegata**) with yellow-splashed leaves. **A. hybridum** is quite different — it forms a spreading tree about 5 ft high. The Maple-like leaves are about 3 in. across and the bell-like flowers are 2 in. long. A wide range of varieties is available — look for **Canary Bird** (yellow), **Boule de Neige** (white), **Fireball** (red) and **Souvenir de Bonn** (pink).

SECRETS OF SUCCESS

Temperature: Average warmth. Keep cool (50°-60°F) in winter.

Light: Choose a well-lit spot — a few hours sunlight each day is beneficial.

Water: Water liberally from spring to late autumn. Water sparingly in winter.

Air Humidity: Mist leaves occasionally.

Repotting: Repot in spring every year. Make sure that the new pot is not too large — abundant flowering calls for the compost ball to be full of roots.

Propagation: Take stem cuttings or sow seeds in spring for green-leaved varieties — for variegated types take cuttings rather than sowing seeds.

Abutilon striatum thompsonii

Abutilon megapotamicum

Abutilon hybridum Canary Bird

ACACIA

FLOWERING HOUSE PLANT
page 55

Acacia dealbata

ball-like
flower-head
½ in. across

spiny
'leaf'
1 in.
long

A. armata
Kangaroo Thorn

Acacias are useful shrubs where space is not a problem, but they have never been popular house plants. The spreading branches bear feathery leaves or spiny false leaves known as phylloclades, and in winter or spring the characteristic yellow flower-heads appear. These are clusters of small powder-puffs which are much more popular in flower arrangements than in house plant collections. Keep the plant under control by cutting back straggly and unwanted growth once flowering has finished, and keep it robust by feeding and watering regularly during the growing season. If you can, place the pot outside in a sheltered spot once summer arrives. Bring it back indoors in autumn.

SECRETS OF SUCCESS

Temperature: Average warmth. Keep fairly cool in winter — minimum temperature 50°F.

Light: Provide as much light as possible.

Water: Water freely from spring to autumn — sparingly in winter.

Air Humidity: Misting is not necessary. Fresh air is beneficial in summer.

Repotting: Repot in spring every 2 years after flowering.

Propagation: Take semi-ripe (not woody) cuttings in summer. Seeds sown in spring at 70°F germinate quickly.

TYPES

Acacia armata (Kangaroo Thorn or Wattle) is the best-known type, growing about 3–4 ft high. The 'leaves' are dark green and the scented flower-heads appear in late spring. **A. dealbata** (the Mimosa sold by florists) is a larger plant bearing 9 in. long feathery fronds. The delicately scented fluffy flowers are present between mid winter and early spring. **A. podalyriifolia** (Queensland Wattle) is a vigorous silvery-leaved species which bears its golden-yellow blooms in winter. All of these Acacia types are generally trouble-free and easy to grow.

ACALYPHA

FOLIAGE HOUSE PLANT
page 51

FLOWERING HOUSE PLANT
page 55

Acalypha wilkesiana

pendant
spike
1½ ft
long

hairy
leaf
6 in.
long

A. hispida
Red-hot Catstail
(Chenille Plant)

There are two distinct groups of Acalypha. The more popular type bears long tassels of tiny flowers amongst its plain foliage and the other type has colourful foliage with insignificant blooms. All Acalyphas are woody shrubs which are quick growing but are unfortunately difficult to overwinter in the average room. The problem is the high humidity requirement which can be readily satisfied in the greenhouse or conservatory but not in the home. When the air is dry leaf drop occurs and red spider mites flourish, so the usual practice is to take cuttings each year to provide a regular supply of young and vigorous plants. Remove dead tassels from old plants and prune back to half size in late summer or early spring.

SECRETS OF SUCCESS

Temperature: Warmth is essential — 65°–80°F during the day and a minimum of 60°F at night.

Light: Bright light with little or no direct sun.

Water: Keep compost moist at all times.

Air Humidity: Moist air is vital. Surround the pot with damp peat or stand on a pebble tray. Mist leaves frequently.

Repotting: Repot in spring every year. Large plants should be top-dressed rather than repotted.

Propagation: Take stem cuttings in spring. Use a rooting hormone and provide bottom heat.

TYPES

Acalypha hispida (Chenille Plant or Red-hot Catstail) is a tall shrub which can reach a height of 6 ft or more. The long drooping spikes appear in late summer and autumn — the usual flower colour is red but an unusual white variety (**alba**) is available. Remove the spikes once the flowers start to fade. The bright foliage Acalypha is **A. wilkesiana** — popularly known as Copperleaf because of the coppery-red 5 in. long leaves which cover the 4 ft shrub. There are several fine varieties — for example **godseffiana** (green edged with white) and **musaica** (red, orange and copper).

ACHIMENES

FLOWERING POT PLANT
page 57

stems
6–12 in.
high

leaf
1–1½ in.
across —
heart-shaped,
serrated and
velvety

trumpet-like
flared flower

A. hybrida
Cupid's Bower
(Hot Water Plant)

Achimenes hybrida English Waltz

The modern varieties of Achimenes bear masses of large flowers amid glistening hairy leaves. White, blue, purple, pink and yellow varieties are available. Each bloom is short-lived, but the flowering season extends from June to October. The stems are weak and wiry, making this plant an excellent subject for a hanging basket in a well-lit spot. If you want to grow it as a bushy plant then pinch out the tips of young shoots and tie tall stems to canes. Care is quite easy — just keep the plant reasonably warm and make sure that the compost does not dry out for even a single day.

SECRETS OF SUCCESS

Temperature: Average warmth — minimum 55°F during the growing season.

Light: Brightly lit spot away from summer sun.

Water: Keep compost moist at all times during the growing season.

Air Humidity: Mist occasionally around the plants — do not wet the leaves.

Care After Flowering: Stop watering once flowering has finished. Start into growth in spring by watering with tepid water. Alternatively remove rhizomes in winter and store in dry peat for planting in spring.

Propagation: Separate the rhizomes in early spring and plant 5 or 6 in a compost-filled pot — set them ½–1 in. below the surface. Achimenes can be raised from spring-sown seed.

TYPES

Achimenes erecta (**A. coccinea**) is a trailer despite its name — the 18 in. long reddish stems bear bright red blooms. **A. longiflora** with 3 in. long leaves is another trailer growing 1–1½ ft high when staked. The flowers are usually purple, but the variety **alba** bears purple-spotted white blooms. The tallest species is **A. grandiflora** which grows about 2 ft high, its drooping stems carrying flowers measuring 2 in. across. These species are not easy to find — at your local shop you will be offered one of the many types of **A. hybrida**. Named varieties include **Rose**, **Little Beauty** and **Pink Beauty** (pink), **Purple King** and **Paul Arnold** (purple), **Yellow Beauty** (yellow), **Schneewitschen** (white), **Master Ingram** (red) and **Ambroise Verschaffelt** (white, veined purple).

AESCHYNANTHUS

FOLIAGE HOUSE PLANT
page 51

FLOWERING HOUSE PLANT
page 55

tubular 2 in. long
red flower — brown calyx
below, borne at stem tip

leaf
1½ in.
long —
waxy and
edged with
purple

stems
1½ ft
long

A. lobbianus
Lipstick Vine

Aeschynanthus speciosus

The general popular name for Aeschynanthus is Basket Vine or Basket Plant. The trailing stems with their leathery leaves and red flowers are best displayed in a hanging basket or suspended pot. Unfortunately they are not easy to grow under ordinary room conditions. They may flower profusely and then fail to produce any blooms at all in the following year. The major requirements for regular flowering between June and September seem to be humid air in summer and a period of rest in winter with temperatures in the 55°–65°F range. Once the flowering season is over, cut back the stems immediately if growth is becoming straggly and make sure that the plant is kept well lit in winter.

SECRETS OF SUCCESS

Temperature: Average or above average warmth in summer. Keep fairly cool in winter — minimum temperature 55°F.

Light: Bright light — avoid direct sunshine.

Water: Water freely from spring to autumn — sparingly in winter. Use tepid water.

Air Humidity: Mist leaves frequently, especially in hot weather.

Repotting: Repot in spring every 2–3 years.

Propagation: Take stem cuttings in spring. Use a rooting hormone and provide bottom heat.

TYPES

The most popular variety (**Aeschynanthus lobbianus**) has a characteristic flower form and a descriptive common name — the Lipstick Vine. The cream-throated red flowers arise from brown 'lipstick' cases. **A. pulcher**, **A. javanicus** and **A. radicans** are all similar to the Lipstick Vine, but **A. speciosus** is quite different. The 2 ft stems bear leaves in whorls and the 3 in. long flowers stand erect, darkening from yellow bases to red mouths. The Zebra Basket Vine (**A. marmoratus**) is uncommon but well worth looking for. It is grown for its foliage rather than its dull green flowers — the leaves are intricately mottled above and dark red below. Aeschynanthus is sometimes confused with Columnea. Look at the flower — the upper lobes of the Columnea bloom fuse to form a prominent hood — the Aeschynanthus hood is much less pronounced.

ACORUS

FOLIAGE HOUSE PLANT
page 51

Acorus gramineus variegatus

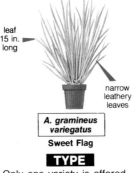

leaf 15 in. long

narrow leathery leaves

A. gramineus variegatus

Sweet Flag

TYPE

Only one variety is offered — **Acorus gramineus variegatus**. This is the white-striped form — not particularly showy, but useful in a terrarium. It is an uncommon house plant and is not widely available.

The white-striped leaves of this grassy plant form fan-shaped tufts. Its great advantage as a background plant among more spectacular specimens is that it will withstand poor conditions — it is not affected by waterlogging, draughts or cold winter nights. It suffers from few problems, but leaf tips will turn brown if the compost is short of water. In a warm room red spider mite can be a problem.

SECRETS OF SUCCESS

Temperature: Prefers cool conditions — keep in an unheated room in winter.

Light: Bright light or semi-shade — not direct sun.

Water: Keep compost wet at all times.

Air Humidity: Misting is not necessary.

Repotting: Repot, if necessary, in spring.

Propagation: Divide plants at any time of the year.

AGAPANTHUS

FLOWERING HOUSE PLANT
page 55

Agapanthus orientalis alba

ball-like flower-head 3–8 in. across

strap-like leaf 1 ft long

A. africanus

Blue African Lily

TYPES

Agapanthus africanus bears its blooms on 2 ft flower-stalks. Plant in a tub or large pot. **A. orientalis** is larger and will need even more space.

Large round heads of tubular flowers on tall stalks appear in succession throughout the summer. There is no difficulty in growing this plant as long as you can move it to a frost-free room in winter. There it will need very little water until spring, when it should be brought back to a well-lit spot and started into growth by watering and feeding. Do not repot frequently as this plant blooms best when it is pot-bound.

SECRETS OF SUCCESS

Temperature: Average warmth. Keep cool (40°–60°F) in winter.

Light: Choose sunniest spot available.

Water: Keep compost moist at all times during the growing season. Water sparingly in winter.

Air Humidity: Misting is not necessary.

Repotting: Not required until division takes place.

Propagation: Divide plants in spring every 4–5 years.

ALLAMANDA

FLOWERING HOUSE PLANT
page 55

Allamanda cathartica grandiflora

leaf 4 in. long

tubular flower 3 in. across

A. cathartica

Golden Trumpet

TYPES

Allamanda cathartica is truly a beauty with flaring yellow trumpets. Two varieties are available — **grandiflora** (compact, pale yellow flowers) and **hendersonii** (red buds, golden flowers).

A spectacular climbing plant which would undoubtedly be much more popular if it had a more robust constitution. The leaves are glossy and the large blooms appear all summer long. Its demand for warmth and a humid atmosphere plus plenty of sunlight means that it is a plant for the conservatory rather than the living room.

SECRETS OF SUCCESS

Temperature: Keep the plant warm — minimum 60°F in winter.

Light: Some direct sun is essential.

Water: Water moderately from spring to autumn. Water sparingly in winter.

Air Humidity: Surround pot with damp peat and mist frequently.

Repotting: Repot in spring every year.

Propagation: Take stem cuttings in spring. Use a rooting hormone and provide bottom heat.

AGLAONEMA

FOLIAGE HOUSE PLANT page 51

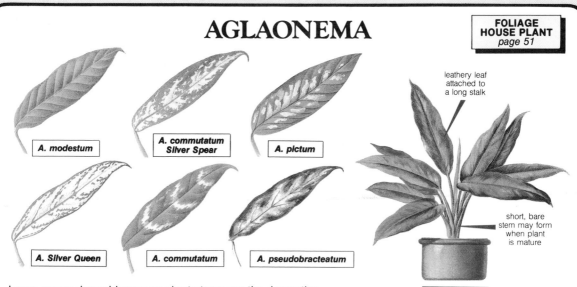

A. modestum

A. commutatum Silver Spear

A. pictum

A. Silver Queen

A. commutatum

A. pseudobracteatum

leathery leaf attached to a long stalk

short, bare stem may form when plant is mature

A. modestum
Chinese Evergreen

Large, spear-shaped leaves on short stems are the decorative feature of Aglaonema, the Chinese Evergreen. Its virtue, according to the textbooks, is an ability to thrive in poorly-lit conditions, but this is only true of the all-green varieties. The ones with white or yellow variegated foliage need brighter conditions.

According to some European authorities the shade tolerance of this slow-growing plant is its *only* virtue — it has even been described as being far too difficult for growing in the home. In the United States, however, it is regarded as one of the most tolerant and reliable of house plants.

The best advice is to treat it as a moderately easy plant with a few special needs. Grow it in a shallow pot and keep it well away from draughts and smoky air. In winter it requires warm and moist air.

Aglaonema is a slow-growing plant which requires frequent feeding and infrequent repotting. Young specimens are virtually stemless, but older ones have a short trunk which is scarred with old leaf bases.

SECRETS OF SUCCESS

Temperature: Warm in summer — minimum 60°F in winter.

Light: Semi-shade or bright light. Keep well away from direct sunlight.

Water: Water sparingly in winter. For the rest of the year water thoroughly.

Air Humidity: Moist air is necessary. Mist leaves regularly, but never use a coarse spray. Surround pot with damp peat.

Repotting: Repot in spring every 3 years.

Propagation: In spring or summer pot up basal shoots with a few leaves and roots attached. Air layering is an alternative.

SPECIAL PROBLEMS

LEAVES SHRIVELLED. BROWN TIPS
Cause: Air too dry.

LEAVES CURLED. BROWN EDGES
Cause: Air too cool, or cold draughts.

INSECTS: Mealy bugs at the base of the leaf stalks can be a serious problem — so can red spider mite if the light is too bright.

TYPES

Aglaonema Silver Queen

The Aglaonemas are popular house plants — the Arum-like flowers which appear in summer are not particularly showy, so they are grown primarily for their large and colourful foliage. Aglaonemas tolerate some shade, but near-white varieties need a well-lit situation. The baby of the group is **Aglaonema pictum** (6 in. speckled and velvety leaves) — the giant is **A. nitidum** (18 in. plain green leaves). The usual plain green species is **A. modestum**, but it is the variegated types which are generally chosen. **A. commutatum** has silver bands — **A. pseudobracteatum** (Golden Evergreen) is blotched with yellow, cream and pale green. **A. commutatum Silver Spear** is an attractive variety, but perhaps the best of all the Aglaonemas are the hybrids **A. Silver Queen** and **A. Silver King** with foliage which is almost entirely silvery-grey.

Aglaonema pseudobracteatum

Alocasia amazonica

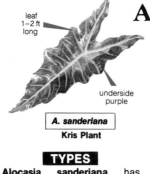

leaf 1–2 ft long

underside purple

A. sanderiana
Kris Plant

ALOCASIA

FOLIAGE
HOUSE PLANT
page 51

The Alocasias are distinctly uncommon — you will find them in few textbooks and even fewer shops. They certainly arouse attention — the erect stems bear enormous arrow-shaped leaves with pale-coloured veins. Unfortunately these spectacular plants are not really happy in the living room and need to return to greenhouse conditions after a few months.

SECRETS OF SUCCESS

Temperature: Warm — above 70°F in summer and at least 65°F in winter.

Light: Bright in winter, semi-shade in summer.

Water: Keep compost moist at all times. Water very sparingly in winter.

Air Humidity: Mist leaves very frequently.

Repotting: Repot in early spring every year.

Propagation: Divide plants at repotting time.

TYPES

Alocasia sanderiana has metallic green leaves with scalloped edges — **A. amazonica** is easier to find and the leaves are darker, contrasting sharply with the bold white veins.

ANTHURIUM

FOLIAGE
HOUSE PLANT
page 51

FLOWERING
HOUSE PLANT
page 55

Anthuriums are not cheap, but they do have a distinct air of luxury. The flowering ones are the only types you are likely to find — large waxy 'palettes' each with a coloured 'tail' at the centre. These exotic blooms last for many weeks and the flowering season stretches from spring to late summer. Unfortunately Anthuriums are not easy to grow and only the most popular one (Anthurium scherzerianum) is reasonably tolerant of ordinary room conditions.

The Crystal Anthurium is one of the most eye-catching of all foliage house plants, but it is not easy to care for nor easy to obtain. It needs moist air and careful watering, and the aerial roots should be pushed into the damp compost.

lance-shaped leaf 8 in. long

waxy 'flower' 2 in. long with curly orange tail

glossy, puckered 'flower' 4 in. long with straight or arched yellow tail

A. scherzerianum
Flamingo Flower

leaf 1–2 ft long

velvety surface

A. crystallinum
Crystal Anthurium

heart-shaped leaf 9 in. long

A. andreanum
Oilcloth Flower

SECRETS OF SUCCESS

Temperature: Average warmth — minimum 60°F in winter.

Light: Bright in winter — protect from summer sun.

Water: Give a little water every few days to keep compost moist at all times.

Air Humidity: Mist leaves very frequently.

Repotting: Repot in spring every 2 years.

Propagation: Divide plant at repotting time.

TYPES

Anthurium scherzerianum (Flamingo Flower or Pigtail Plant) is the one to choose for the home. It grows about 1 ft high and has a curly tail. Brilliant red is the usual colour but a white variety (**album**) is available. **A. andreanum** (Oilcloth Flower or Painter's Palette) is a much larger plant (2–3 ft high) and is more suited to the conservatory than the living room. White, pink, orange and red varieties are available. There is a single foliage species — **A. crystallinum** (Crystal Anthurium). The leaf colour changes from bronzy-purple to deep green with age — the foliage hangs vertically, displaying the prominent silvery veins.

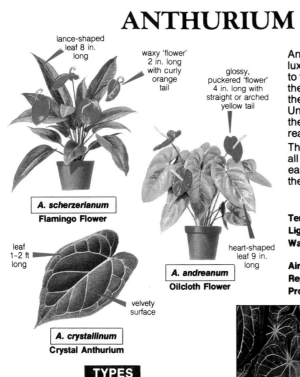

Anthurium crystallinum

Anthurium scherzerianum

AMARANTHUS

FLOWERING HOUSE PLANT
page 55

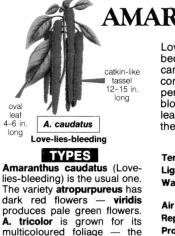

catkin-like
tassel
12–15 in.
long

oval
leaf
4–6 in.
long

A. caudatus
Love-lies-bleeding

Amaranthus viridis

Love-lies-bleeding is better known as a bold bedding plant rather than as an indoor plant, but it can be grown successfully on a windowsill or in the conservatory. In summer and autumn the long and pendant tassels appear, each one made up of tiny blooms. The shrub bears reddish stems and the leaves turn bronzy as they age. Look for this one in the outdoor plant section of the garden centre.

TYPES

Amaranthus caudatus (Love-lies-bleeding) is the usual one. The variety **atropurpureus** has dark red flowers — **viridis** produces pale green flowers. **A. tricolor** is grown for its multicoloured foliage — the flowers are insignificant.

SECRETS OF SUCCESS

Temperature: Average warmth — minimum 50°F in winter.

Light: Full sun or light shade.

Water: Water freely from spring to autumn — sparingly in winter.

Air Humidity: Mist leaves occasionally.

Repotting: Repot in spring every 2 years.

Propagation: Take stem cuttings in spring. Use a rooting hormone and provide bottom heat.

APHELANDRA

FOLIAGE HOUSE PLANT
page 51

FLOWERING HOUSE PLANT
page 55

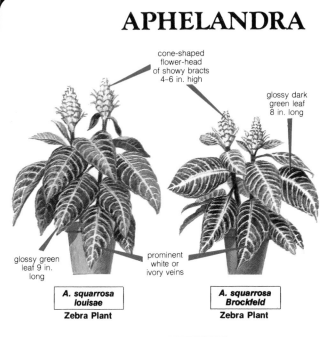

cone-shaped
flower-head
of showy bracts
4–6 in. high

glossy dark
green leaf
8 in. long

glossy green
leaf 9 in.
long

prominent
white or
ivory veins

A. squarrosa louisae
Zebra Plant

A. squarrosa Brockfeld
Zebra Plant

Aphelandra is a double-purpose plant — all year round its large leaves with silvery veins provide an attractive feature, and then for about 6 weeks in autumn it is crowned by a golden cone. Not surprisingly it has been a favourite for generations, but it is not easy to keep an Aphelandra under ordinary room conditions for more than a few months. The fate of nearly all of them is to become leggy and leafless. The way to avoid this is to feed regularly, never allow the compost to dry out, mist frequently and keep warm in winter. Remove dead blooms after flowering.

SECRETS OF SUCCESS

Temperature: Average warmth — minimum 55°F in winter.

Light: Brightly lit spot away from direct sun in summer.

Water: Keep compost moist at all times but never waterlogged. Reduce watering in winter. Use soft, tepid water.

Air Humidity: Mist leaves frequently.

Repotting: Repot in spring every year.

Propagation: Take stem cuttings in spring. Use a rooting hormone and provide bottom heat.

TYPES

The flower is made up of bracts which are nearly always yellow or golden, but there is a species with orange-scarlet blooms and grey-veined leaves — **Aphelandra aurantica**. The most popular species is **A. squarrosa**, but the basic species is not often grown as it can reach 3–4 ft. The usual choice is a variety which is less vigorous. **Louisae** is a 1½–2 ft sturdy bush with red-tipped bracts — more compact types include **Brockfeld** and the golden **Dania**. **Fritz Prinsler** has the most eye-catching veining.

SPECIAL PROBLEMS

LOSS OF LEAVES
Cause: Most likely reason is dryness at the roots — even a short period of drying out can cause serious leaf loss. Cold air is another common cause of defoliation. Other possibilities are too much sun or draughts.

BROWN LEAF TIPS
Cause: Air humidity too low. Surround the pot with moist peat — mist leaves regularly.

Aphelandra squarrosa Dania

ARAUCARIA

FOLIAGE HOUSE PLANT page 51

Araucaria heterophylla

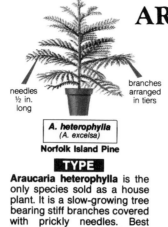

needles ½ in. long

branches arranged in tiers

A. heterophylla
(A. excelsa)
Norfolk Island Pine

TYPE

Araucaria heterophylla is the only species sold as a house plant. It is a slow-growing tree bearing stiff branches covered with prickly needles. Best grown as a specimen plant to ensure symmetrical growth.

A handsome and easy-to-grow conifer with many uses — seedlings for the terrarium, small plants for table display and tall trees as bold specimens in halls or large rooms. It flourishes in cool and light conditions, and will grow to about 5 ft. Keep it pot-bound to restrict growth. The major problem is leaf drop and loss of lower branches — the main cause is either hot, dry air or drying out of the compost.

SECRETS OF SUCCESS

Temperature: Average warmth. Keep cool in winter.

Light: Bright light or semi-shade — avoid summer sun.

Water: Water regularly from spring to autumn. Water sparingly in winter.

Air Humidity: Mist leaves occasionally, especially if room is heated in winter. Ventilate in summer.

Repotting: Repot in spring every 3–4 years.

Propagation: Difficult — best to buy plants.

ARDISIA

FLOWERING HOUSE PLANT page 55

Ardisia crenata

stem 3 ft high

fragrant flowers followed by red berries

A. crenata
Coral Berry

TYPE

Ardisia crenata is a handsome tree, sometimes sold as **A. crispa**. The leaves are oval and leathery and the flowers are white or pale pink. Stand outdoors in summer — cut back when the display of berries is over.

The glossy leathery leaves make this slow-growing shrub an attractive foliage plant, but its main feature is the presence of red berries at Christmas. These berries follow the tiny flowers which appear in summer and they stay on the plant for many months. The Coral Berry should be kept cool in winter and away from draughts at all times. Never let the compost dry out and prune back in early spring.

SECRETS OF SUCCESS

Temperature: Average warmth — minimum 45°F in winter.

Light: Brightly lit spot away from direct sun.

Water: Keep compost moist at all times. Reduce watering in winter.

Air Humidity: Mist leaves frequently with tepid water.

Repotting: Repot, if necessary, in spring.

Propagation: Take stem cuttings in spring or summer. Sow seeds in early spring.

ARUNDINARIA

FOLIAGE HOUSE PLANT page 51

Arundinaria variegata

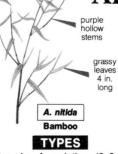

purple hollow stems

grassy leaves 4 in. long

A. nitida
Bamboo

TYPES

The dwarf varieties (2–3 ft) have colourful foliage — **Arundinaria variegata** bears cream-striped leaves. The tall ones (8–10 ft) have coloured stems — **A. nitida** (purple) and **A. murielae** (yellow).

Bamboo is a rarity in indoor plant displays but it does have a part to play in the conservatory or larger room. The house plant Bamboos have Reed-like stems and short branches bearing grassy leaves. There are several varieties available and they all do well in cool airy conditions. The taller varieties make exotic tub plants — water and feed regularly during the growing season.

SECRETS OF SUCCESS

Temperature: Prefers cool conditions — keep in an unheated room in winter.

Light: Bright light or semi-shade — not direct sun.

Water: Keep compost moist at all times during the growing season. Water sparingly in winter.

Air Humidity: Misting is not necessary.

Repotting: Repot, if necessary, in spring.

Propagation: Divide plants at repotting time.

ASPARAGUS

FOLIAGE HOUSE PLANT page 51

horizontal branchlets on wiry stems

1½ in. long heart-shaped 'leaves'

climbing or trailing stems

feathery 'leaves'

A. plumosus
(A. setaceus)
Asparagus Fern

arching wiry stems

A. asparagoides
Smilax

dense needle-like foliage

1 in. long needle-like 'leaves'

A. densiflorus sprengeri
Asparagus Fern
(Emerald Fern)

climbing stems

'leaf' 1 in. long

2 in. long 'leaves'

A. meyeri
Plume Asparagus
(Foxtail Fern)

A. falcatus
Sicklethorn

The two popular Asparagus Ferns (A. plumosus and A. densiflorus sprengeri) are grown for their graceful feathery foliage, which is often used in flower arrangements. But all is not what it seems — they are not Ferns, and the 'leaves' are really needle-like branches.

Asparagus Fern is an easy plant to grow, much easier than most true Ferns, because it will adapt to wide variations in light, heat and frequency of watering. It does not demand a humid atmosphere and can be easily propagated. For maximum effect make sure that the arching or trailing branches are not impeded by other plants — a hanging basket is the ideal home.

The flat-leaved variety called Smilax by florists is A. asparagoides. It is more difficult to grow indoors than the ferny varieties, but it is sometimes recommended for hanging displays.

SECRETS OF SUCCESS

Temperature: Average warmth — minimum 50°F at night. Constant high temperatures can be harmful.

Light: Can adapt to bright or semi-shady conditions. Keep away from direct sunlight.

Water: Water regularly from spring to autumn. Occasionally water from below. Water sparingly in winter.

Air Humidity: Mist occasionally, especially in winter if room is heated.

Repotting: Repot in spring every year.

Propagation: Divide plants at any time of the year. Sow seeds in spring.

SPECIAL PROBLEMS

YELLOWING FOLIAGE, BROWN-EDGED OR SCORCHED. LEAF DROP
Cause: Too much sun, or compost has been allowed to dry out.

YELLOWING FOLIAGE, NO SCORCH. LEAF DROP
Cause: Temperature too high or not enough light.

PLANT DEATH
Cause: Root rot disease is the likely culprit, caused by faulty watering. For more details see page 245.

TYPES

The Asparagus species which have become popular as house plants have needle-like 'leaves'. They have a ferny look — **Asparagus plumosus** is a compact plant with graceful, spreading branches when young but the thin stems become straggly with age. Berries sometimes appear and the smallest type is **A. plumosus nanus**. **A. densiflorus sprengeri** has trailing stems with bright green 'leaves' (hence the common name Emerald Fern) and red berries. Less well known but more attractive is the Plume Asparagus — **A. meyeri**. The erect and stiff stems are 15–18 in. long and densely covered with needles — a green bottle-brush plant which serves as a useful contrast to large-leaved plants in pot groups. There is nothing fern-like about **A. falcatus** — the sickle-shaped 'leaves' are large and the 3 ft high stems are distinctly prickly. Finally there is the old fashioned Smilax — **A. asparagoides**. A vigorous plant with trailing stems which can reach 5 ft or more — the shiny foliage remains fresh for a long time after cutting.

Asparagus plumosus

Asparagus densiflorus sprengeri

Aspidistra elatior variegata

leaf 1½ ft long

rolled base

prominent ribs

A. elatior
Cast Iron Plant

TYPES

The dark green leaves of **Aspidistra elatior** withstand both air pollution and neglect but are scorched by sunlight. A cream-striped variety (**A. elatior variegata**) is available — it is more attractive but less hardy.

ASPIDISTRA

FOLIAGE HOUSE PLANT
page 51

An old favourite, once maligned but now regaining some of its former popularity. The common name of Cast Iron Plant indicates its tolerance of neglect. It can withstand periods of dryness at the roots if the temperature is not too high, but it does have two strong dislikes — it will die if the soil is constantly saturated and it will be harmed by frequent repotting.

SECRETS OF SUCCESS

Temperature: Average warmth. Keep cool but frost-free in winter.

Light: Extremely tolerant, but not of direct sun.

Water: Water regularly from spring to autumn. Water sparingly in winter.

Air Humidity: Can stand dry air but wash leaves occasionally.

Repotting: Repot in spring every 4–5 years.

Propagation: Divide plants at repotting time.

Astilbe arendsii Ostrich Plume

tiny flowers in feathery plumes

fern-like foliage

A. arendsii
Perennial Spiraea

TYPES

Several varieties of **Astilbe arendsii** (1–1½ ft) are available — **Fanal** (red), **Irrlicht** (white), **Bressingham Pink** (pink) etc. **Ostrich Plume** (pink) bears pendant flower-heads.

ASTILBE

FLOWERING POT PLANT
page 57

This popular garden plant is sometimes offered for sale in spring as a flowering pot plant. Its most important requirement is for abundant moisture — thorough and frequent watering is essential and the leaves should be misted in warm weather. Despite the attractiveness of Astilbe indoors its real home is the garden, and it should be planted outside once the flowers have faded.

SECRETS OF SUCCESS

Temperature: Cool or average warmth — minimum 50°F.

Light: Brightly lit spot, but shade from hot summer sun.

Water: Keep compost moist at all times.

Air Humidity: Mist leaves occasionally.

Care After Flowering: Place the pot in a cool, well-ventilated room for a few days, then plant outdoors in a shady site.

Propagation: Divide plants in spring.

Aucuba japonica variegata

serrated leaves

leaf 5 in. long

A. japonica variegata
Spotted Laurel

TYPES

Aucuba japonica is an outdoor shrub with leathery, glossy foliage. Only the variegated types are used indoors. **Variegata** is the most popular — **goldiana** (almost all-yellow) is the most colourful.

AUCUBA

FOLIAGE HOUSE PLANT
page 51

A useful plant for a shady spot which is not heated in winter. It is not suitable for hot and dry locations as serious leaf fall will occur. Brown edges in summer mean that you are not watering frequently enough. When small, the Spotted Laurel can be stood on a windowsill or table. It will reach 5 ft or more, but it can be kept in check by pruning in the spring.

SECRETS OF SUCCESS

Temperature: Average warmth. Keep cool in winter — minimum temperature 40°F.

Light: Bright light or shade — avoid direct sun in summer.

Water: Water regularly from spring to autumn. Water sparingly in winter.

Air Humidity: Mist plant frequently, especially in winter.

Repotting: Repot in spring every year.

Propagation: Take stem cuttings in late summer.

AZALEA

FLOWERING POT PLANT page 57

open, bell-shaped flower 1½–2 in. across

leathery leaf 1½ in. long

underside hairy

Rhododendron simsii
(Azalea indica)
Azalea
(Indian Azalea)

funnel-shaped flower 1 in. across

glossy leaf 1–1½ in. long

Rhododendron obtusum
Japanese Azalea

Two sorts of Azalea are widely available as flowering pot plants. The Indian Azalea (Rhododendron simsii) is by far the most popular one — the less usual type is the Japanese Azalea (Rhododendron obtusum). Both are dwarf shrubs which grow about 1–1½ ft high.

Countless Indian Azaleas are bought every year at Christmas time to provide decoration during the holiday season and into the New Year. When buying a plant pick one with a few open flowers and a mass of buds. Without correct care the flowers wilt and the leaves drop in a week or two. The secret of keeping a plant in bloom for many weeks and capable of coming back into flower the following year is to keep it wet (not just moist), distinctly cool and brightly lit. Remove faded flowers promptly.

SECRETS OF SUCCESS

Temperature: Keep the plant cool — 50°–60°F is ideal.

Light: Brightly lit spot away from direct sunlight.

Water: Keep compost wet at all times, using soft water.

Air Humidity: Mist leaves daily during flowering season.

Care After Flowering: Move to a cool but frost-free room — continue watering. Place pot in a shady spot in the garden once the danger of frost is past — keep fed, watered and sprayed until early autumn. Bring into a cool room — when flowers open move into display area.

SPECIAL PROBLEMS

SHRIVELLED LEAVES
Cause: The most likely reason for leaf shrivelling and leaf loss is underwatering. A thorough soaking may be needed several times each week. Other common causes are too little moisture in the air (surround pot with damp peat), too much heat or too much sun.

SHORT FLOWERING PERIOD
Cause: Hot dry air is the usual culprit. Keep the pot well away from radiators and mist the foliage daily. Too much sun and too little water can also bring flowering to a premature end.

YELLOWING LEAVES
Cause: Lime in the compost or lime in the water. Treat with MultiTonic, water with soft water.

TYPES

The variety range of **Rhododendron simsii** (Indian Azalea or just plain 'Azalea') is enormous. Pink is the popular colour, but there are whites, reds and purples. There are attractive bicolours, such as the white-edged pink **Inga** and the pink-hearted white **Osta**. Both single and double varieties are available and so are ones with ruffled petals. Recent novelties include trailing Azaleas and pyramid-shaped types. The blooms of the Japanese Azalea are smaller than the Indian Azalea ones, but this plant has the distinct advantage of thriving as a garden shrub if planted out when flowering is over.

Rhododendron simsii Stella Maris

Rhododendron simsii Ambrosus

Rhododendron obtusum Rex

BEDDING PLANTS

FLOWERING POT PLANT page 57

TYPES

Many flowering pot plants can be raised at home from seed. Examples include Exacum, Browallia, Celosia, Salpiglossis, Schizanthus and Thunbergia. Outside this limited list there is a large number of popular garden annuals and biennials which can be grown indoors as flowering pot plants, although they will not be found in the house plant section of the garden centre. Some of the most successful examples are illustrated here. The technique of propagating from seed is described on page 240, and a vital requirement is to ensure that the seedlings receive maximum light by keeping them in a greenhouse or on a sunny windowsill. Failure to provide ample light will result in spindly growth with few flowers. If you don't wish to raise plants at home then obtain them as seedlings offered as bedding plants at your local garden shop. The best plan is to buy them in small pots and repot them at home. If you wish to create an indoor bedding scheme then buy the young plants in strips or trays or as plugs (see The Bedding Plant Expert for details). Feed regularly when the plants are established. When in flower, pots of annuals should be given as much light as possible, but temperatures should be below average.

Ageratum houstonianum
Ageratum

Height 8 in. In flower all summer. Pick a compact blue (**Blue Mink** or **Blue Blazer**). Or choose **Summer Snow** (white) and **Fairy Pink** (rose).

Antirrhinum majus
Snapdragon

Height 9 in. In flower all summer. Choose a dwarf variety — **Magic Carpet**, **Floral Carpet** or **Tom Thumb**. Pinch out tip when 3 in. high.

Calendula officinalis
Pot Marigold

Height 1–2 ft. In flower all summer. Colours range from pale cream to deep orange. The best compact variety is the 1 ft **Fiesta Gitana**.

Centaurea cyanus
Cornflower

Height 1 ft. In flower all summer. Choose a dwarf variety such as **Polka Dot** or **Jubilee Gem**. The leaves are grey-green.

Clarkia elegans
Clarkia

Height 1½ ft. In flower all summer (spring if sown in autumn). Available in white, pink, red and purple. **C. pulchella** (1 ft) is a daintier species.

Convolvulus tricolor
Dwarf Morning Glory

Height 9 in. In flower all summer. Bright-coloured trumpets on bushy plants — sow the compact type **Blue Flash** or **Rainbow Flash**. Remove dead flowers.

Godetia grandiflora
Godetia

Height 9 in. –1½ ft. In flower all summer (spring if sown in autumn). Choose a short, bushy variety — e.g **Kelvedon Glory** or **Sybil Sherwood**.

Iberis umbellata
Candytuft

Height 9 in. In flower late winter if sown in summer. **Fairy Mixture** will give a variety of white, pink and red fragrant flowers.

Ipomoea tricolor
Morning Glory

Height 6 ft. In flower all summer. Each large trumpet-shaped flower lasts only a day — choose **Heavenly Blue** or the striped **Flying Saucers**.

Lathyrus odoratus
Sweet Pea

Height 1 ft. In flower all summer. Grow a dwarf variety — no support will be needed. **Bijou**, **Little Sweethearts** and **Patio** are examples.

Linum grandiflorum
Flax

Height 1 ft. In flower midsummer. The best one to choose is Scarlet Flax (**L. grandiflorum rubrum**). For white flowers grow **album**.

Lobelia erinus
Lobelia

Height 4–8 in. In flower all summer. The deep blue variety is **Mrs Clibran Improved** — for hanging baskets grow **Sapphire** or **Cascade Mixed**.

Matthiola incana
Stock

Height 1–2 ft. In flower winter (spring if sown in summer). For a long flowering season sow both **Brompton** and **Ten Week** strains. Excellent for fragrance.

Mesembryanthemum criniflorum
Livingstone Daisy

Height 4–6 in. In flower all summer. Usually sold as a multicoloured mixture — **M. Lunette** is all-yellow. A windowsill plant — direct sunlight is necessary.

Myosotis alpestris
Forget-me-not

Height 6 in. –1 ft. In flower spring if sown in summer and kept outdoors until frosts arrive. Compact varieties are best — try **Ultramarine** (deep blue).

Nemesia strumosa
Nemesia

Height 9 in. In flower midsummer (winter if sown in midsummer). Sow **Carnival** or **Sparklers** mixture. Grow numerous plants for a bold display.

Nicotiana hybrida
Tobacco Plant

Height 9 in. –1½ ft. In flower all summer. Buy a day-flowering compact hybrid, such as **Tinkerbelle**, **Nicki Mixed**, **Red Devil** or **Domino Mixed**.

Petunia hybrida
Petunia

Height 6 in. -1½ ft. In flower all summer. Catalogues offer a wide range of single and double varieties in a large and varied assortment of colours.

Phlox drummondii
Annual Phlox

Height 6–9 in. In flower all summer. Pick from the **nana compacta** group — examples include **Twinkle**, **Beauty Mixed** and **Dwarf Petticoat**.

Salvia splendens
Salvia

Height 9 in. -1 ft. In flower all summer. Choose a compact variety such as **Blaze of Fire** (red). **Dress Parade Mixed** provides various colours.

Tagetes erecta
African Marigold

Height 1–2 ft. In flower all summer. Grow one of the dwarf varieties which rarely exceed 1½ ft — **Gay Ladies**, **Inca Yellow**, **Space Age Mixed**, etc.

Tagetes patula
French Marigold

Height 6–9 in. In flower all summer. All sorts of blends of yellow, orange, red and mahogany in single and double blooms are listed in catalogues.

Tropaeolum majus
Nasturtium

Height 6 in. -1 ft. In flower all summer. The **Gleam** hybrids are the most popular choice — good for hanging baskets. Dwarfs (6 in.) are also available.

Verbena hybrida
Verbena

Height 6 in. -1 ft. In flower midsummer. Pick one of the compact varieties — **Sparkle**, **Springtime** and **Dwarf Compact Mixed** are all good choices.

Viola tricolor
Pansy

Height 6–9 in. In flower at any time of the year, depending on variety and date of sowing. For the largest flowers, choose one of the **Swiss Giants**.

Viola hybrida
Viola

Height 6–9 in. In flower spring, summer or autumn, depending on date of sowing. Various colours, such as **Blue Heaven** and **Yellow Bedder**.

Zinnia elegans
Zinnia

Height 6 in. -1½ ft. Select a low-growing strain, not one of the 2½ ft giants. Good ones include **Thumbelina**, **Pulchino**, **Peter Pan** and **Lilliput**.

Calendula officinalis

Lobelia erinus

Petunia hybrida

Phlox drummondii

Tagetes erecta

Tropaeolum majus

BEGONIA

| FOLIAGE HOUSE PLANT *page 51* | FLOWERING HOUSE PLANT *page 55* | FLOWERING POT PLANT *page 57* |

The estimated number of Begonia hybrids is between 1000 and 2000. Within this enormous assembly there are plants which are small enough to grow in an egg cup and others which can cover a conservatory wall. Many Begonias have been selected or bred to be cultivated as house plants, and some form of classification is necessary to make some sense of this vast genus.

Firstly, all Begonias have a few basic features in common. A key fact is that the flowers are either male or female and they are generally borne in clusters. Stems are often fleshy and the leaves are usually lop-sided. Botanically there are three basic groups, depending on the nature of the underground portion. The Rhizomatous Group bear thickened underground stems which are used for propagation — the members of this group are generally grown for their attractive foliage and Begonia rex belongs here. The Tuberous Group have thickened roots which are used for propagation — here you will find the large-flowered types. Finally there is the Fibrous-rooted Group with ordinary roots which are not used for propagation — the well-known Wax Begonia (B. semperflorens) belongs here.

This method of classification may be of value to the botanist but for the ordinary indoor gardener it is more useful to divide Begonias into groups depending on their use in the home or conservatory. Accordingly in this chapter they are divided into Flowering Pot Plant Begonias, Foliage Begonias and Flowering House Plant Begonias.

FLOWERING POT PLANT BEGONIAS

● TUBEROUS TYPES

single or double flower 3-5 in. across

pointed, serrated leaf 6-9 in. long

brittle leaf 4 in. across

stems and flower-stalks thin and pendant

B. tuberhybrida pendula
Basket Begonia

flower 2-3 in. across

B. tuberhybrida

single or double flower 2 in. across

pointed, serrated leaf 4 in. long

B. multiflora

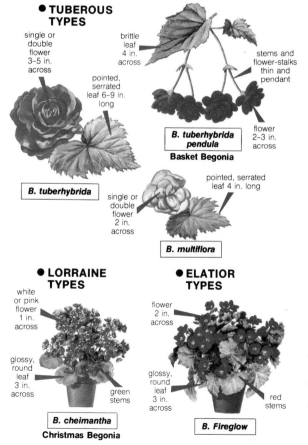

● LORRAINE TYPES

white or pink flower 1 in. across

glossy, round leaf 3 in. across

green stems

B. cheimantha
Christmas Begonia

● ELATIOR TYPES

flower 2 in. across

glossy, round leaf 3 in. across

red stems

B. Fireglow

These are the Begonias which are used as temporary residents to provide a bright splash of floral colour. There are three main types of this pot plant group.

The most spectacular ones are the Tuberous Begonias, which bloom in summer and autumn. Included here are the pendulous Basket Begonias. All of them can be raised by planting tubers in spring in boxes of moist peat. Keep at 60°–70°F and when shoots are a couple of inches high transplant into 5 in. pots. Repot later into 8 in. pots. At the end of the flowering season withhold water, cut off shoots, lift tubers and store in peat.

The second type are the Lorraine or Cheimantha Hybrids. These winter-flowering Begonias grow about 1½ ft tall and bear rather weak stems which require some form of support. Pinching out the tips when the plants are young will keep them bushy. The parentage is somewhat complex with B. socotrana and B. dregei involved, and they have been around since the last century.

The third type, the Elatior Hybrids, have become the stars of the Pot Begonia world. These are rather similar to Lorraine Begonias but bear larger flowers. They have become very popular in recent years and can be bought in flower all year round.

SECRETS OF SUCCESS

Temperature: Average warmth — minimum 55°F in winter. Avoid temperatures above 70°F.

Light: A bright spot away from direct sunlight. A few hours of winter sun are beneficial.

Water: Water freely when plant is in flower, but do not keep compost constantly soggy.

Air Humidity: Moist air is needed — surround pots with damp peat and mist air around plant.

Care After Flowering: Tuberous Begonias — see above. Other types are usually discarded — otherwise cut back and keep cool with little water. Increase water in spring. New shoots can be used as cuttings.

SPECIAL PROBLEMS

BROWN BLOTCHES, TURNING GREY & MOULDY
Cause: Botrytis. Move away from other Begonias, cut off diseased parts and spray with a systemic fungicide. Avoid low light and over-damp conditions. Improve ventilation.

INSECTS
Keep watch for aphid and red spider mite.

YELLOWING LEAVES
Cause: Too little light; too little or too much water. Look for other symptoms.

LOSS OF LEAVES
Cause: There are a number of possible causes and you must look for other symptoms. There is not enough light if the stems are thin and leggy; too much heat if leaves are dry and curled; and too much water if leaves are wilted and rotten.

LEAVES WITH BROWN TIPS
Cause: Air humidity too low. Follow rules in Secrets of Success.

PALE, ROTTING LEAVES
Cause: Overwatering. Follow rules in Secrets of Success.

WHITE POWDERY SPOTS
Cause: Powdery mildew. Move away from other Begonias, cut off diseased leaves and spray with a systemic fungicide. Avoid over-damp conditions and low temperatures. Improve ventilation.

FLOWER BUDS DROP
Cause: Dry air or underwatering.

PLANT COLLAPSE
Cause: Several possible reasons — stem rot disease due to overwatering, root knot eelworm (look for swollen bumps on roots) or vine weevil (look for tunnels in tubers).

TYPES

The most popular Tuberous Begonias are the **Begonia tuberhybrida** hybrids — single, semi-double and double in a wide range of colours and colour combinations. The 1 ft high fleshy-stemmed plants bear large and showy male flowers and smaller female ones. Single colours include **Sugar Candy** (pale pink), **Gold Plate** (yellow), **Guardsman** (red) and **Diana Wynward** (white). Picotees are available — look for **Seville** (yellow, edged pink) and **Double Picotee** (cream, edged red). **B. multiflora** flowers are similar in shape but they are more numerous and smaller. The Basket Begonias are varieties of **B. tuberhybrida pendula** — the flowers are single and semi-double in white, yellow, pink, orange and red. One Tuberous Begonia can be raised from seed — **B. sutherlandii** is a trailing species with 1–1½ ft stems and small coppery flowers from spring until autumn. The remaining Pot Begonias are usually bought in flower although a few can be raised from seed. The Lorraine Hybrids bear a mass of small flowers in winter. By far the best-known variety is the pink **Gloire de Lorraine** — the F$_1$ hybrid **Love Me** (pink) can be raised from seed. The third group, the **B. elatior** hybrids, are seen everywhere — compact plants bearing a mass of single or double flowers in bright colours. The Reiger strain has a good reputation for reliability and some of the popular B. elatior varieties include **Heidi** (red), **Fireglow** (red), **Schwabenland** (red), **Elfe** (pink), **Barbara** (pink), **Mandela** (yellow) and **Marco** (white). You can raise **Charisma** (double, orange) from seed.

Begonia tuberhybrida Sugar Candy   *Begonia tuberhybrida pendula Bridal Cascade*   *Begonia Fireglow*

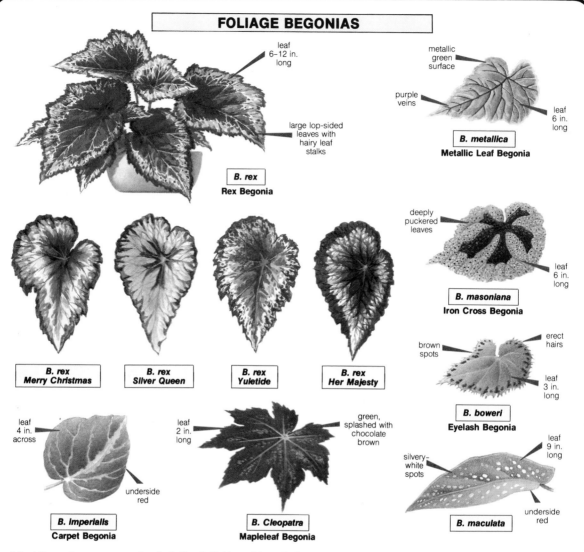

FOLIAGE BEGONIAS

B. rex — Rex Begonia
leaf 6–12 in. long
large lop-sided leaves with hairy leaf stalks

B. metallica — Metallic Leaf Begonia
metallic green surface
purple veins
leaf 6 in. long

B. rex Merry Christmas

B. rex Silver Queen

B. rex Yuletide

B. rex Her Majesty

B. masoniana — Iron Cross Begonia
deeply puckered leaves
leaf 6 in. long

B. boweri — Eyelash Begonia
brown spots
erect hairs
leaf 3 in. long

B. imperialis — Carpet Begonia
leaf 4 in. across
underside red

B. Cleopatra — Mapleleaf Begonia
leaf 2 in. long
green, splashed with chocolate brown

B. maculata
silvery-white spots
leaf 9 in. long
underside red

Most Begonias are grown for their floral display, although these varieties may also have attractive foliage. The situation with the types described here is reversed — they are grown for their foliage display although some have flowers as a bonus. The original Begonia rex came from India, but the species no longer exists and all the colourful ones you see on display are hybrids. The flowers are insignificant and should be removed. The off-centre heart-shaped leaves are easy to recognise, but the Foliage Begonias include many other shapes — stars, ovals, spears etc. Leaf size varies enormously, ranging from the 1 ft long foliage of B. Ricky Minter and some varieties of B. rex to the ½ in. leaves of B. foliosa. Surfaces range from waxy and smooth to dull and deeply puckered. Most Foliage Begonias bear thick rhizomes which creep over or just under the soil surface. Growth habit is generally bushy or trailing, but a few tall Foliage Begonias are available. If you cannot generalise about appearance you can about cultivation. All detest overwatering and direct summer sun, and they are not difficult as long as there is some room heat in winter. Do not expect Foliage Begonias to become part of the family like Monstera, Palms and Chlorophytum — even with care these foliage varieties usually last for only a year or two under ordinary room conditions. But take heart — new plants can be easily raised from leaf cuttings.

SECRETS OF SUCCESS

Temperature: Average warmth — minimum 60°F in winter.

Light: A bright spot away from direct sunlight. A few hours of morning or evening sun in winter are beneficial. Turn pots occasionally.

Water: The compost should be kept moist from spring to autumn — allow surface to dry between waterings. Water sparingly in winter.

Air Humidity: Moist air is needed — surround pots with damp peat. Mist surrounding air, but never wet the leaves.

Repotting: Repot in spring every year. Leaves of pot-bound plants lose colour.

Propagation: Leaf cuttings root easily. Plants can be divided at repotting time.

SPECIAL PROBLEMS

See leaf and stem problems on page 75. Diseases are a menace — see page 245.

TYPES

The types described and illustrated on these 2 pages are grown primarily or solely for their foliage. This group is dominated by the many hybrids of **Begonia rex**, so widely used in plant groups where a contrast to plain green varieties is required. Scores of varieties are available — old favourites include **President Carnot** (green and silver), **Helen Teupel** (red, green and pink) and **King Edward IV** (purple and red). Miniature Rex Begonias are available. Similar to the familiar Rex but with puckered leaves and a dark cross-shaped heart is **B. masoniana**. **B. maculata** is quite different — cane-like stems several feet high bear 9 in. long leaves, white-spotted above and red below. **B. metallica** is another tall-growing species, metallic green above and red-veined below. Although listed here because of its attractive foliage, some people group this species with the Flowering House Plant Begonias as it bears clusters of 1 in. wide flowers in summer or autumn (see page 79). The Beefsteak Begonia (**B. feastii** or **B. erythrophylla**) has fleshy round leaves which are shiny green above and red below — the variety **bunchii** has leaves with crested and frilly margins. Where space is limited grow the compact **B. boweri** (6–9 in. high) or its hybrid **B. Tiger**. **B. Cleopatra** (also known as **B. Maphil**) is a small bushy plant (6–9 in. high) grown for its glistening bronzy leaves. The underside of the foliage bears white hairs, and the shape of the leaf is much more like a Maple or Sycamore than a Begonia — hence the common name (Mapleleaf Begonia). Most of the Begonias described above produce small flowers in either winter or summer, depending on the species.

Trailing Begonias are generally grown for their floral display but a few trailing Foliage types are occasionally seen. Examples include **B. solanthera** (waxy foliage) and **B. imperialis** (velvety foliage). You would never guess that **B. foliosa** was a Begonia — its pendant stems clothed with tiny oval leaves have a distinctly Fern-like appearance.

Begonia rex Bettina Rothschild

Begonia feastii bunchii

Begonia Tiger

Begonia solanthera

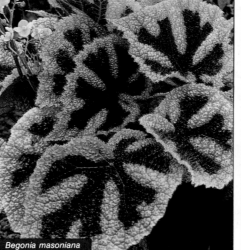

Begonia masoniana

Begonia Cleopatra

FLOWERING HOUSE PLANT BEGONIAS

Flowering Begonias are many and varied and identification is often difficult. There are a few basic points which can help you through the maze. The showiest blooms are generally borne by the Tuberous Begonias and some fibrous-rooted ones which become dormant after flowering (see pages 74–75). These are all Flowering Pot Plants, grown for temporary display and then discarded or kept for replanting to provide fresh blooms next season.

The Flowering Begonias which are shown here are the evergreen ones — less spectacular in bloom, perhaps, but with the advantage of keeping their leaves all year round. The height range is enormous, from 6 in. high bushes to 10 ft tall climbers. To succeed with these Begonias you have to avoid hot dry days, really cold nights, too much water and too much sun.

SECRETS OF SUCCESS

Temperature: Average warmth — minimum 55°F in winter.

Light: Bright light — avoid direct sunshine. A few hours of morning or evening sun in winter are beneficial.

Water: The compost should be kept moist from spring to autumn — allow surface to dry out slightly between waterings. Water sparingly in winter.

Air Humidity: Moist air is necessary. Surround the pot with damp peat. Mist around the plants — do not wet the leaves.

Repotting: Repot, if necessary, in spring.

Propagation: Stem cuttings root easily — take cuttings from low down on the plant. Germinate seeds at 70°F.

SPECIAL PROBLEMS

See the leaf and stem problems diagram on page 75.
Diseases are a menace — see page 245.

TYPES

● CANE-STEMMED TYPES

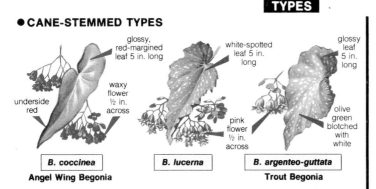

glossy, red-margined leaf 5 in. long

waxy flower ½ in. across

underside red

B. coccinea

Angel Wing Begonia

white-spotted leaf 5 in. long

pink flower ½ in. across

B. lucerna

glossy leaf 5 in. long

olive green blotched with white

B. argenteo-guttata

Trout Begonia

● TRAILING TYPES

glossy leaf 5 in. long

stems and flower-stalks thin and pendant

flower 1 in. across

B. glaucophylla
(B. limmingheiana)

Shrimp Begonia

These Begonias are the giants of the group, reaching 6 ft or more if left unpruned. However, it is usually a good idea to pinch them back in spring to induce bushiness. Use a heavy clay pot to prevent the plant from toppling over and stake the tall, Bamboo-like stems. The flower trusses are pendulous and the most popular species is **Begonia lucerna** — tall-growing and often sold under its full name **B. Corallina de Lucerna**. Flowers appear all year round and the truss bears 30–60 flowers. **B. coccinea** is more compact and summer-flowering — **B. argenteo-guttata** is bushy and not often seen.

Begonia glaucophylla (often sold as **B. limmingheiana**) is grown in hanging baskets when winter flowers are required and the much more popular Basket Begonias (page 75) are at rest. The leaves are less lop-sided than other large-leaved Begonias and the blooms are rose-red.

Begonia coccinea

Begonia lucerna

Begonia glaucophylla

● BUSHY TYPES

single or double flower 1 in. across

serrated, glossy leaf 1½ in. long

plant 3 ft high

round, waxy leaf 2 in. across

pink or red flower 1 in. across

pale pink flower ½ in. across

plant 2 ft high

hairy leaf 8 in. long

underside red

deep pink flower ½ in. across

lobed, serrated leaf 3 in. long

green blotched with red

B. semperflorens	**B. fuchsioides**	**B. haageana**	**B. serratipetala**
Wax Begonia	Fuchsia Begonia	Elephant Ear Begonia	Pink Spot Begonia

Begonia fuchsioides

By far the most popular of the bushy types is the Wax Begonia — **Begonia semperflorens**. The plant is a leafy bush 6–12 in. high and is the easiest Flowering Begonia to grow. There are hybrids with leaves ranging from greenish-yellow to deepest red, and there is a wide range of flower types in white, pink, orange and red. The Wax Begonia blooms at any time of the year — bedding plants in the garden can be dug up and potted in autumn for winter display indoors. The other types are much less common. **B. haageana** is the only reasonably easy one — the flowers appear in summer amid the very large leaves. **B. fuchsioides** is attractive but difficult — the drooping clusters of flowers which appear during the winter months give it a Fuchsia-like appearance. **B. serratipetala** is easy to identify — the arching stems bear leaves which are deeply notched — the flowers open in summer. **B. metallica** is another Begonia which is easy to recognise — the dark green leaves have deeply sunken purplish veins. Although often regarded as a Foliage Begonia (see pages 76–77), this species bears clusters of white blooms flanked with pink in late summer or early autumn.

Begonia semperflorens

BEAUCARNEA

FOLIAGE HOUSE PLANT page 51

leaf 3-5 ft long

swollen base

B. recurvata (Nolina tuberculata)

Pony Tail (Elephant Foot)

TYPE

One species is sold — **Beaucarnea recurvata**. It grows slowly, but with time the trunk will reach 6 ft or more and the base will be swollen like a huge bulb.

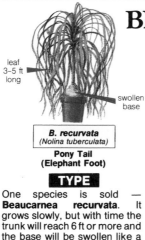

Beaucarnea recurvata

A curiosity rather than a thing of beauty, the Pony Tail is still very useful if you want a tall specimen plant which will not require a lot of attention. The swollen bulb-like base stores water, so occasional dryness at the roots will do no harm. The plume of long strap-like leaves gives the plant its common name. It is a rarity in Britain but is popular in the U.S, where it flourishes and may reach ceiling height.

SECRETS OF SUCCESS

Temperature: Average warmth — minimum 50°F in winter.

Light: Brightly lit spot — some sun is beneficial.

Water: Water thoroughly, then leave until compost is moderately dry. Avoid overwatering.

Air Humidity: Misting is not necessary.

Repotting: Repot, if necessary, in spring.

Propagation: Plant up offsets at repotting time. Not easy — best to buy plants.

BELOPERONE

FLOWERING HOUSE PLANT
page 55

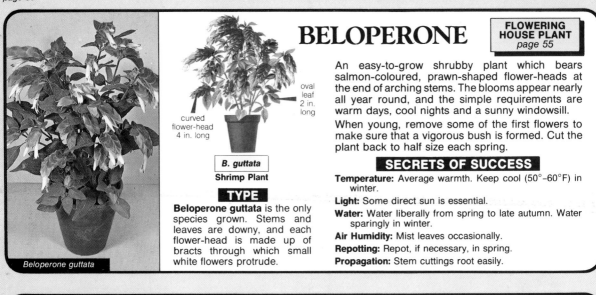

oval leaf 2 in. long

curved flower-head 4 in. long

B. guttata
Shrimp Plant

An easy-to-grow shrubby plant which bears salmon-coloured, prawn-shaped flower-heads at the end of arching stems. The blooms appear nearly all year round, and the simple requirements are warm days, cool nights and a sunny windowsill.

When young, remove some of the first flowers to make sure that a vigorous bush is formed. Cut the plant back to half size each spring.

TYPE

Beloperone guttata is the only species grown. Stems and leaves are downy, and each flower-head is made up of bracts through which small white flowers protrude.

SECRETS OF SUCCESS

Temperature: Average warmth. Keep cool (50°–60°F) in winter.

Light: Some direct sun is essential.

Water: Water liberally from spring to late autumn. Water sparingly in winter.

Air Humidity: Mist leaves occasionally.

Repotting: Repot, if necessary, in spring.

Propagation: Stem cuttings root easily.

Beloperone guttata

BERTOLONIA

FOLIAGE HOUSE PLANT
page 51

quilted leaves, 6 in. long with broad white stripes

purple below

B. marmorata
Jewel Plant

A rarity, but well worth looking for if you have a terrarium or plant window to fill. Not a good choice, however, for the living room — it needs the high humidity of its jungle home. Small purple flowers may appear but are of little decorative value. Bertolonia has a creeping growth habit — the plants grow only a few inches high.

SECRETS OF SUCCESS

Temperature: Warm — minimum 60°F in winter.

Light: Bright in winter, semi-shade in summer. No direct sun.

Water: Keep compost moist at all times during the growing season. Water sparingly in winter.

Air Humidity: Moist air is vital. Stand on a pebble tray. Mist leaves frequently.

Repotting: Repot, if necessary, in spring.

Propagation: Take stem cuttings in spring. Use a rooting hormone and provide bottom heat.

TYPES

Bertolonia marmorata has heart-shaped leaves which are mossy green and furry. There are prominent white stripes — the variety **sanderiana** has leaves heavily splashed with silver. **B. maculata** has oval leaves with pale green veins.

Bertolonia maculata

BOUGAINVILLEA

FLOWERING HOUSE PLANT
page 55

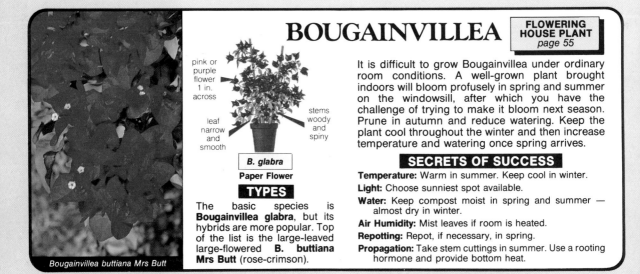

pink or purple flower 1 in. across

leaf narrow and smooth

stems woody and spiny

B. glabra
Paper Flower

It is difficult to grow Bougainvillea under ordinary room conditions. A well-grown plant brought indoors will bloom profusely in spring and summer on the windowsill, after which you have the challenge of trying to make it bloom next season. Prune in autumn and reduce watering. Keep the plant cool throughout the winter and then increase temperature and watering once spring arrives.

SECRETS OF SUCCESS

Temperature: Warm in summer. Keep cool in winter.

Light: Choose sunniest spot available.

Water: Keep compost moist in spring and summer — almost dry in winter.

Air Humidity: Mist leaves if room is heated.

Repotting: Repot, if necessary, in spring.

Propagation: Take stem cuttings in summer. Use a rooting hormone and provide bottom heat.

TYPES

The basic species is **Bougainvillea glabra**, but its hybrids are more popular. Top of the list is the large-leaved large-flowered **B. buttiana Mrs Butt** (rose-crimson).

Bougainvillea buttiana Mrs Butt

BONSAI

FOLIAGE HOUSE PLANT
page 51

FLOWERING HOUSE PLANT
page 55

Bonsai were introduced into Japan about 1000 years ago and the first examples in Britain arrived at the beginning of the 20th century. It was not, however, until the 1980s that they really caught the public eye. Now you will find examples in all sorts of gardening shops, and there are numerous books on the subject.

The sight of a mature but miniature-sized tree growing in a small pot has a special fascination. It seems to be an ideal house plant, but be warned. The popular types such as Pines, Maples, Junipers etc belong to the **Outdoor Bonsai** group, and these can only be brought inside for four or five days at a time. In recent years **Indoor Bonsai** have been introduced — the basic difference from the outdoor ones is that frost-sensitive trees and shrubs are used instead of hardy ones and these types can be kept indoors for most of the year.

Bonsai trees are not naturally dwarf varieties — they are ordinary sorts which have been cultivated and trained in such a way so as to produce the traditional growth forms shown below. This takes time and skill, which explains the high price of the specimens you will see at the garden centre.

BONSAI STYLES

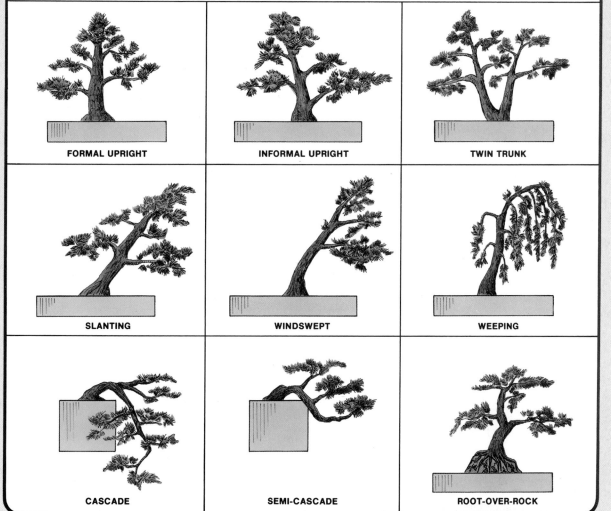

| FORMAL UPRIGHT | INFORMAL UPRIGHT | TWIN TRUNK |

| SLANTING | WINDSWEPT | WEEPING |

| CASCADE | SEMI-CASCADE | ROOT-OVER-ROCK |

Acer palmatum

Chamaecyparis pisifera

Juniperus chinensis

Pyracantha angustifolia

OUTDOOR BONSAI

The word *bonsai* simply means 'a plant in a tray'. The miniaturisation, however, is not achieved by keeping the plant in a pot and leaving it there to cramp the roots. According to the official definition a bonsai is "a tree encouraged to conform in all aspects with ordinary trees, except for its miniature size. The technique consists of keeping the tree confined to its pot by pinching out the top growth and pruning the roots to strike a balance between the foliage above and the roots below, and at the same time to develop a satisfactory shape."

The Outdoor Bonsai on offer at the nursery will usually be about 4 years old. During the basic training period the plant will have been kept in a pot and each year both root and stem pruning will have taken place. In addition the branches will have been trained into attractive shapes by using stiff wire known as 'bonsai wire'. When the bonsai was about 3–4 years old it will have been moved to a shallow frost-proof tray or pot which has drainage holes.

Growing Outdoor Bonsai is a fascinating hobby, but you must know what you are doing. First of all, it is essential to know that they are *not* house plants. The hardy specimens which are used begin to suffer when kept indoors for more than a few days — the air in the average room is too hot and too dry. Outdoors some form of protection is needed against wind and rain. Next, you must realise that growing bonsai requires time and money. Even a modest collection can cost £100 or more, and daily watering will be necessary in the summer months when the weather is dry.

There is no such thing as 'bargain bonsai'. A specimen which appears surprisingly inexpensive will be either an attractively shaped but untrained seedling of an ordinary variety or a mature plant of a naturally dwarf variety. The only way to grow bonsai inexpensively is to start with an ordinary seedling or rooted cutting and train it yourself. A few notes on the procedure are set out on page 83, but you really will have to buy a book on the subject.

SECRETS OF SUCCESS

Temperature: Not usually a problem outdoors, but you must provide some protection to prevent the compost being baked by hot summer sun or frozen solid by a cold snap in winter. Keep as close to outdoor temperature as possible during the brief stay indoors.

Light: Some shading is needed outdoors, but flowering and fruiting types need several hours sunshine on cloudless days. Put in a brightly lit spot during stay indoors.

Water: Keep compost moist at all times — daily watering may be necessary.

Air Humidity: Mist leaves daily during stay indoors.

Repotting: Repot in spring every 2 years. With a trained plant some of the old compost is removed from around the roots and about ⅓ of the root growth is cut away. Replace in the same container, using fresh compost.

TYPES

The favourite subjects for classical bonsai are conifers — the leaves are generally small and evergreen and the plants are remarkably long-lived. Popular types include **Juniperus chinensis**, **Chamaecyparis pisifera**, **Larix kaempferi**, **Cryptomeria japonica** and **Pinus sylvestris**. Not all the favourite ones are evergreens — **Acer palmatum** (Japanese Maple) and **Zelkova serrata** (Grey-bark Elm) are widely grown. Flowering and fruiting trees are especially interesting, and there is a long list of subjects which are known to produce attractive bonsai — Cherry, Apricot, Peach, Japanese Azalea, Quince, Magnolia, compact Roses, Wisteria, Apple (especially the Crab varieties), Laburnum and Pyracantha are examples. In fact nearly any hardy tree can be treated in this way, so you can use an Oak, Beech, Birch or Sycamore seedling from the garden.

INDOOR BONSAI

Indoor Bonsai is a relatively new idea which has not come from Japan. The centre of interest appears to be Germany but the concept has now spread to other countries. You can buy Indoor Bonsai trees from garden centres and nurseries throughout Britain.

The basic difference from the traditional Outdoor Bonsai is that non-hardy trees and shrubs are used here. Indoor Bonsai are generally much better suited than hardy types to the conditions found in the average home, and of course they *must* be kept indoors during the winter. Thus they can be regarded as true house plants, although during the summer months they should be given the standard bonsai treatment. This calls for keeping them outdoors and then bringing them inside for a few days at a time.

Ficus benjamina

Obviously the easiest plan is to buy a mature and trained specimen but they are expensive. If you have the time and patience you can begin from scratch. Pot up the chosen seedling or rooted cutting in the ordinary way in a 3 or 3½ in. pot and care for it as advised in the appropriate section of this A–Z guide. When the main stem has reached the desired height the growing point should be pinched out. Remove some of the lower branches and pinch out the tips of upper side branches to encourage bushiness at the head of the tree. After 2 years repotting is necessary and so is root pruning. In spring remove the plant from the pot and cut away about ⅓ of the roots — replant in a pot or bonsai tray. During the growing season continue to pinch out growing tips, remove unwanted growth, train branches with bonsai wire and cut off sun-scorched leaves. You will need to carry out this repotting and root pruning process every 2 years.

Like their hardy outdoor counterparts, Indoor Bonsai are fascinating to grow but they are a lot of trouble. Moist air is essential and you must keep them well away from draughts and radiators. Watering is the big problem — a daily soaking is often necessary. Feed every 4–6 weeks.

Sageretia theezans

SECRETS OF SUCCESS

Temperature: Average warmth, or temperature recommended in the appropriate section of this A–Z guide.

Light: Most types require a brightly lit spot away from direct sunlight — all should be protected from hot summer sun.

Water: The compost must be kept moist (but not wet) at all times. This may call for daily watering — use rainwater or tepid tap water. The recommended method of watering is by immersion but overhead watering using a fine rose is generally satisfactory.

Air Humidity: Moist air is vital. Stand the pot on a pebble tray and mist leaves occasionally.

Repotting: Repot in spring every 2 years. With a trained plant some of the old compost is removed from around the roots and ⅓ of the root growth is cut away. Replace in the same container, using fresh compost.

Punica granatum

TYPES

Several of the house plants described in this A–Z section can be cultivated and trained as Indoor Bonsai. **Ficus benjamina** (Weeping Fig) is the favourite one — others include **Heptapleurum** (Parasol Plant), **Bougainvillea**, **Acacia**, **Hibiscus**, **Allamanda**, **Gardenia**, **Ixora**, **Jasminum primulinum** (Primrose Jasmine), **Schefflera** (Umbrella Tree), **Punica granatum** (Pomegranate) and **Crassula argentea** (Jade Plant). Some of the Indoor Bonsai are sub-tropical or tropical trees which are grown only in this dwarfened form — examples here are **Sageretia theezans**, **Carmona microphylla** (Fukien Tea), **Pistacia** (Pistachio), **Sterculia**, **Tamarix**, **Swietenia** (Mahogany) and **Olea** (Olive). Seedlings of these trees can be bought for training from specialist nurseries. Cheapest of all are Oranges, Lemons and Coffee raised from pips or unroasted beans at home — see pages 117 and 122.

Carmona microphylla

BOUVARDIA

FLOWERING HOUSE PLANT *page 55*

Bouvardia domestica Mary

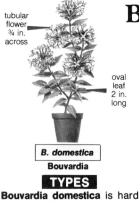

tubular flower ¾ in. across

oval leaf 2 in. long

B. domestica
Bouvardia

TYPES

Bouvardia domestica is hard to find. There are several named varieties — **Mary** (white and pink) and **Bridesmaid** (double, pink) are examples.

Fragrant flowers appear from midsummer to early winter — the tubular blooms are borne in large clusters above the leaves. The main requirement is for a brightly lit spot which is cool in winter. Pinch out the tips of young plants to promote bushy growth and cut back the stems once flowering is over. With proper care the shrub will grow about 2 ft high, but even in expert hands it will deteriorate after a few years.

SECRETS OF SUCCESS

Temperature: Average warmth — minimum 50°F in winter.

Light: Brightly lit spot but shade from hot summer sun.

Water: Water liberally from spring until flowering stops, then keep compost fairly dry.

Air Humidity: Mist leaves regularly.

Repotting: Repot, if necessary, in spring.

Propagation: Take stem cuttings in spring.

BOWIEA

FOLIAGE HOUSE PLANT *page 51*

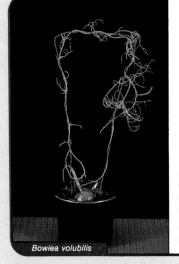

Bowiea volubilis

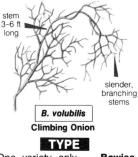

stem 3-6 ft long

slender, branching stems

B. volubilis
Climbing Onion

TYPE

One variety only — **Bowiea volubilis**. The large above-ground bulb produces straggly stems in winter. A few short-lived leaves and small greenish flowers appear before the stems die down in late spring.

So many of the plants in this book can be classed as both popular and attractive. The Sea Onion or Climbing Onion is neither — it is both rare and repulsive. It is grown only as a novelty, so that visitors can express their surprise. Easier to find in the U.S than in Britain — look for it in the catalogues of specialist nurseries.

SECRETS OF SUCCESS

Temperature: Cool or average warmth — tolerates 50°F quite happily.

Light: Moderately well lit but away from direct sunlight.

Water: Water sparingly for most of the year. Keep the compost moist when stems start to grow in winter. Do not water in summer.

Air Humidity: Misting is not necessary.

Repotting: Repot when offsets fill the pot.

Propagation: Plant up offsets at repotting time.

BREYNIA

FOLIAGE HOUSE PLANT *page 51*

Breynia nivosa roseopicta

oval leaf 1 in. across

B. nivosa roseopicta
Leaf Flower

TYPES

Breynia nivosa has green leaves marbled with white. The variety **roseopicta** is the usual choice. The pink, white and green variegated leaves have a flower-like appearance — hence the common name.

You will find this plant in a number of garden centres and department stores but in very few textbooks. It is basically a greenhouse plant which was introduced as a house plant in the 1980s. Under glass it will grow into a shrub — in the living room it is grown as a small bush, with slender branches densely clothed with colourful leaves. Humidity is the problem — it needs a moist atmosphere.

SECRETS OF SUCCESS

Temperature: Average warmth — minimum 55°F in winter.

Light: Bright light — avoid direct sunshine.

Water: Keep compost moist at all times during the growing season. Water sparingly in winter.

Air Humidity: Mist leaves frequently.

Repotting: Repot in spring every 2 years.

Propagation: Take stem cuttings in summer. Make sure each cutting has a heel at the base.

BROMELIADS

| FOLIAGE HOUSE PLANT page 51 | FLOWERING HOUSE PLANT page 55 |

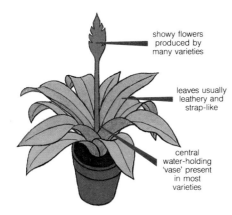

showy flowers produced by many varieties

leaves usually leathery and strap-like

central water-holding 'vase' present in most varieties

Some Bromeliads are grown for the beauty of their foliage and there are others which are admired for the beauty of their flowers. A few, such as the popular Aechmea fasciata and Vriesea splendens, belong in both camps. These dual-purpose plants are cultivated for both their attractive foliage and bold flower-heads.

The usual pattern is a rosette of leathery, strap-like foliage and a flower-head which arises on a stalk from the cup-like centre of this rosette. It may take several years to reach the flowering stage, but the display may last for several months. Once the flower-head fades the rosette of leaves starts to die and is replaced by the offsets at the base. In most cases the colourful display of the flower-head is due to the presence of showy bracts — the true flowers are small and short-lived.

Interior decorators look upon Bromeliads as almost essential for their modern decor schemes, but beginners often feel that these spectacular plants must be too difficult for them to grow. It is true that it takes patience, skill and warmth to induce a large-leaved specimen to flower, but foliage types and plants in flower are surprisingly easy to care for.

One of the oddities is the method of watering — water is poured into the central cup or 'vase' rather than over the surface of the compost. There is a group of Bromeliads which do not need watering at all — see page 87 for details of the Air Plants.

The native home of the Bromeliads is the American jungle, where they dwell among the Orchids in the trees or on the forest floor. A novel way of growing them and showing your plants is to create a Bromeliad tree. Otherwise you can keep them in peat-based compost in small pots bearing drainage holes. Remember that they all have tiny root systems which means that over-potting and overwatering can be fatal.

HOW TO MAKE A BROMELIAD TREE

Leafy Bromeliad — Choose plants with a well pronounced 'cup' in the heart of the rosette. Remove from pot, wrap roots with sphagnum moss and then tightly attach with plastic-covered wire to branch

Tillandsia usneoides (Spanish Moss) — a unique Bromeliad which grows as grey-green strands in moist air. No watering required

Keep cup filled with water and spray sphagnum moss with water at weekly intervals

Pebbles

Branch set in Plaster of Paris and stones

Leafy Bromeliad

Sphagnum moss

Container

SECRETS OF SUCCESS

Temperature: High temperatures (above 75°F) may be required to bring plants into flower, but average warmth (minimum 50°F) is satisfactory for foliage types or plants in flower.

Light: Most Bromeliads require a brightly lit spot away from direct sunlight. Pineapple and the Earth Stars will thrive in full sun.

Water: Never overwater, and ensure that there is good drainage. Keep the central 'vase' filled with water — use rainwater in hard water areas. Empty and refill the 'vase' every 1–2 months. Water the compost only when it dries out. With non-vase varieties keep the compost moist, but never wet.

Air Humidity: Mist leaves in summer. Feeding through the leaves is the natural method of nutrition, so occasionally use dilute liquid fertilizer instead of water in the sprayer.

Repotting: Rarely, if ever, necessary.

Propagation: Offsets appear at the base of the plant. When the offset is several months old remove it with some roots attached and plant shallowly in Seed & Cutting Compost. Keep warm until established.

SPECIAL PROBLEMS

LEAVES WITH PALE BROWN PATCHES
Cause: Sun scorch. Move plant away from direct sunlight.

LEAVES WITH BROWN TIPS
Cause: Dry air is a likely reason — mist during the summer months. Other possibility is failure to fill 'vase' with water or use of hard water.

PLANT DEATH
Cause: Overwatering if plant has not yet flowered. If it has flowered then rotting and death of the rosette which bore the flower-stalk is natural.

INSECTS
Scale and mealy bug can be troublesome.

AECHMEA

TYPES

The Aechmeas are typical Bromeliads with leathery, arching leaves and a distinct central 'vase' from which a stout stalk bearing a bold flower-head emerges. **Aechmea fasciata** (**A. rhodocyanea**) is by far the most popular one. It is good enough to be the showpiece of any living room or florist window — the arching 2 ft grey-green leaves are banded with silvery powder and the floral spike which appears when the plant is a few years old is striking. The pink floral ball appears in midsummer and lasts until early winter. This showy Urn Plant is one of the easiest Bromeliads to grow, but there are other Aechmeas worth considering. **A. chantinii** is rather larger and the flower-head is brighter and more open. **A. caudata** has branching heads of yellow flowers and the attractive **A. fulgens discolor** has purple-backed foliage and purple flowers which are followed by long-lasting berries. Where space is limited there are dwarfs such as **A. Foster's Favorite**.

A. fasciata

A. fulgens discolor

A. Foster's Favorite

A. chantinii

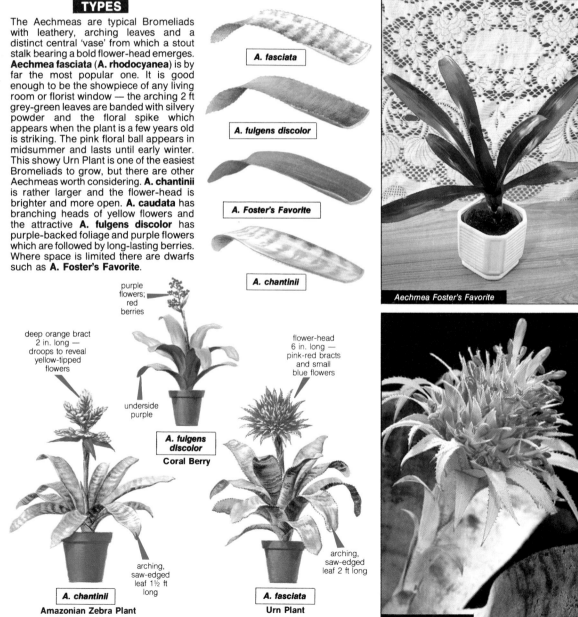

Aechmea Foster's Favorite

purple flowers; red berries

deep orange bract 2 in. long — droops to reveal yellow-tipped flowers

underside purple

flower-head 6 in. long — pink-red bracts and small blue flowers

A. fulgens discolor
Coral Berry

arching, saw-edged leaf 1½ ft long

A. chantinii
Amazonian Zebra Plant

arching, saw-edged leaf 2 ft long

A. fasciata
Urn Plant

Aechmea fasciata

ANANAS

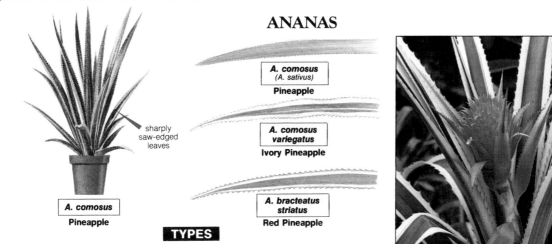

A. comosus
sharply saw-edged leaves

A. comosus
(A. sativus)
Pineapple

A. comosus variegatus
Ivory Pineapple

A. bracteatus striatus
Red Pineapple

A. comosus
Pineapple

TYPES

Most types of Pineapple produce pink flower-heads on mature plants and these are followed by small aromatic but inedible fruits if the plants have been kept under warm and humid conditions. But Pineapples are generally grown for their foliage — the ordinary one (**Ananas comosus**) is too large and dull for the living room — the smaller and colourful form **variegatus** is a better choice. Best of all is **A. bracteatus striatus** with brightly-striped 1–2 ft arching leaves in green, cream and pink.

Ananas bracteatus striatus

AIR PLANTS

TYPES

These are the Grey Tillandsias, which differ from their normal green relatives (see page 88) by bearing absorbent furry scales on their foliage. These scales take up water from humid air, and obtain nutrients from air-borne dust — they literally live on air! The most widespread species is **Tillandsia usneoides**, the familiar Spanish Moss which hangs from trees throughout the warmer regions of America. Until recently the Air Plants were virtually unknown as house plants in Britain, but you can now find several species on sale in garden centres everywhere. These plants are stuck on coral, shells, driftwood etc — they are not planted in compost. The leaves around the flowers may change colour and provide a long-lasting bright display, but the blooms themselves last for only a few days. **T. caput-medusae** is perhaps the most popular species. Thick and twisted leaves arise from a bulbous base — the red bracts and blue flowers are very showy. **T. ionantha** forms a compact rosette of arching silvery leaves. It grows only a couple of inches high, and the inner foliage turns red when the stalkless violet flowers appear. **T. juncea** is a long-leaved species — Rush-like foliage spreads outwards and a single flower-stalk bears the terminal blooms well above the heart of the plant. **T. argentea** is a silvery species — the short leaves spread untidily outwards as the plant develops.

Tillandsia caput-medusae

Tillandsia ionantha

Tillandsia argentea

BILLBERGIA

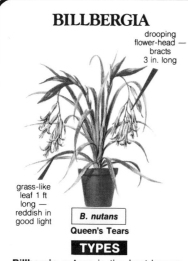

drooping flower-head — bracts 3 in. long

grass-like leaf 1 ft long — reddish in good light

B. nutans

Queen's Tears

TYPES

Billbergia nutans is the best-known Billbergia and is by far the easiest Bromeliad to grow — young plants flower quite readily. **B. windii** is larger — the flower-stalks are 18 in. long and the foliage is grey-green. Billbergia can withstand winter temperatures as low as 35°–40°F.

Billbergia windii

GUZMANIA

bright red or orange bract 1½ in. long — central cluster of small white flowers

arching, smooth-edged leaf 4 in. long

G. lingulata minor

Scarlet Star

TYPES

The Guzmanias are generally grown for their showy flower-heads. **Guzmania lingulata** (leaves 1½ ft long) bears orange and red bracts — so does its variety **minor** which is much more compact. **G. zahnii** is the giant with 2 ft long leaves — some types (e.g **G. Omer Morobe** and **G. musaica**) are grown for their striped or banded foliage.

Guzmania lingulata Broadway

TILLANDSIA

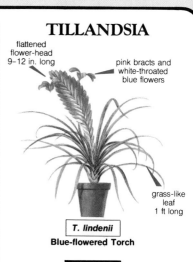

flattened flower-head 9–12 in. long

pink bracts and white-throated blue flowers

grass-like leaf 1 ft long

T. lindenii

Blue-flowered Torch

TYPES

The two most popular Tillandsias have grassy leaves like Billbergia, but their flowers are quite different. **Tillandsia lindenii** is shown above — **T. cyanea** has a more compact flower-head with flowers which are all-blue. The Air Plants are shown on page 87.

Tillandsia cyanea

CRYPTANTHUS

small wavy-edged leaves

TYPES

The Earth Stars are best kept in a glass container. There is a wide range to choose from — plain, striped and banded in green, red, brown and yellow. Leaf sizes range from **Cryptanthus bivittatus** (4 in.) to **C. fosterianus** (15 in.). The brightest (and most difficult to grow) is **C. bromelioides tricolor.**

C. acaulis

Green Earth Star

C. bivittatus

C. acaulis roseo-pictus

C. bromelioides tricolor

Rainbow Star

C. fosterianus

C. zonatus

Cryptanthus zonatus

NEOREGELIA

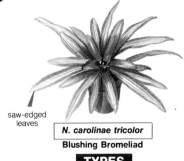

saw-edged leaves

N. carolinae tricolor

Blushing Bromeliad

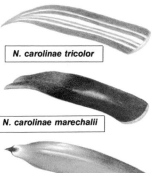

N. carolinae tricolor

N. carolinae marechalii

N. spectabilis

Fingernail Plant

Neoregelia spectabilis

TYPES

The favourite variety, **Neoregelia carolinae tricolor**, blushes at the centre when about to flower, whereas the Fingernail Plant reddens at the leaf tips. The glossy leaves are about a foot long, and with age the foliage of the tricolor variety becomes suffused with pink.

NIDULARIUM

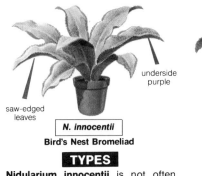

underside purple

saw-edged leaves

N. innocentii

Bird's Nest Bromeliad

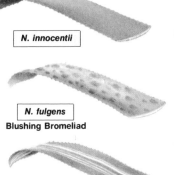

N. innocentii

N. fulgens

Blushing Bromeliad

N. innocentii striatum

Nidularium fulgens

TYPES

Nidularium innocentii is not often seen. It differs from the more popular and rather similar Neoregelia by having a central rosette of very short leaves. This 'bird's nest' turns bright red at flowering time. Leaves below the bird's nest are about 1 ft long and 2 in. wide.

VRIESEA

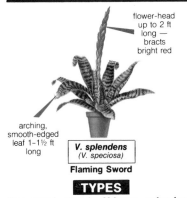

flower-head up to 2 ft long — bracts bright red

arching, smooth-edged leaf 1–1½ ft long

V. splendens
(V. speciosa)

Flaming Sword

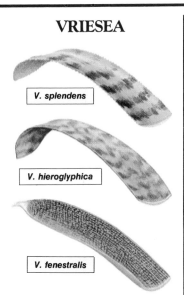

V. splendens

V. hieroglyphica

V. fenestralis

Vriesea carinata

TYPES

The usual one is **Vriesea splendens** with its all-red, sword-like flower-head. Other types generally have more spreading flower-heads — there is the all-red **V. vulcana**, maroon and yellow **V. Favorite**, red and yellow **V. carinata** and the yellow **V. rodigasiana**. Some species are grown for their foliage — e.g **V. hieroglyphica** and **V. fenestralis**.

BROWALLIA

FLOWERING POT PLANT
page 57

drooping leaf 2 in. long

star-shaped tubular flower 2 in. across

B. speciosa
Bush Violet

TYPES

Browallia speciosa bears violet flowers with white throats. The stems are weak — stake to maintain bushy shape. Varieties **major** (large, blue-violet) and **alba** (white) are available.

Browallia major

The Bush Violet is usually bought in flower, but it can be easily raised from seed. Sow in early spring for summer flowers or delay sowing until summer for winter flowering. Pinch out the growing tips occasionally to promote bushiness. With proper care the flowering period will last for many weeks — keep the pot in a cool room. Feed regularly and pick off the flowers as they fade.

SECRETS OF SUCCESS

Temperature: Cool — 50°–60°F is ideal during the flowering season.

Light: Bright light with some direct sun.

Water: Keep compost moist at all times.

Air Humidity: Mist leaves occasionally.

Care After Flowering: Plant should be discarded.

Propagation: Sow seeds in spring or summer.

BRUNFELSIA

FLOWERING HOUSE PLANT
page 55

fragrant white-eyed flower 2 in. across

leathery leaf 3 in. long

B. calycina
Yesterday, Today and Tomorrow

TYPE

Brunfelsia calycina is an evergreen which bears clusters of flowers. These blooms are borne nearly all year round. Place outdoors occasionally during the day in summer.

Brunfelsia calycina

A slow-growing evergreen shrub with an unusual common name — Yesterday, Today and Tomorrow. It describes the changing flower colours — yesterday's purple, today's pale violet and tomorrow's white. Success depends on putting the plant in a room where there will be no sudden changes in temperature. With care the shrub will grow 2 ft tall, and can be kept compact by light pruning.

SECRETS OF SUCCESS

Temperature: Average warmth — minimum 50°F in winter.

Light: Semi-shade in summer — a well-lit spot in winter with a little direct sunlight.

Water: Water freely from spring to autumn. Water sparingly in winter.

Air Humidity: Mist leaves in summer.

Repotting: Repot, if necessary, in spring.

Propagation: Take stem cuttings in summer.

BUXUS

FOLIAGE HOUSE PLANT
page 51

leaf 1 in. long

glossy, leathery leaves

B. sempervirens
Common Box

TYPES

The popular **Buxus sempervirens** (Common Box) can be grown, but the Small-leaved Box (**B. microphylla**) is a better choice. Slow growing — prune to keep in shape. Can be trimmed to decorative shapes.

Buxus microphylla

Box is a popular shrub outdoors, but has only recently been accepted as a house plant. It is tolerant of cool conditions and draughts, producing a dense screen of shiny small leaves. There is an essential requirement — good light, especially in winter. Stand the pot outdoors in summer. These shrubs can be clipped and trained at any time of the year. The only danger is overwatering.

SECRETS OF SUCCESS

Temperature: Average or below average warmth. Keep cool in winter.

Light: A well-lit spot — some direct sunlight is beneficial.

Water: Water thoroughly but let the compost become dryish between waterings.

Air Humidity: Mist leaves occasionally.

Repotting: Repot, if necessary, in spring.

Propagation: Take stem cuttings in late summer.

BULBS - GARDEN TYPES

FLOWERING
POT PLANT
page 57

Many of the popular bulbs which flower in the garden during the spring months can be grown indoors. For many people, helping to plant up a bowl of Tulips or Hyacinths was their first introduction to the world of indoor gardening. There are two basic growing techniques. Large bulbs are nearly always 'forced' so that they will bloom well ahead of their garden counterparts —this **forcing technique** involves keeping them cold and dark to make the roots grow and then providing more light and warmth for leaf and flower development. Hyacinths are the most reliable —Tulips the least satisfactory. The second growing method (the **non-forcing technique**) is used for small bulbs and is simpler than forcing. The pots are placed outdoors after planting and then simply brought indoors when the flower buds have formed and are ready to open. In this case flowering will only be a few days ahead of similar bulbs grown in the garden.

SECRETS OF SUCCESS

FORCING TECHNIQUE
for Hyacinths, Tulips & Narcissi

Planting: Choose varieties which are recommended for indoor cultivation and make sure that the bulbs are good-sized, disease-free and firm. Bulb fibre is sometimes used as the growing medium, but if you intend to save the bulbs for garden use after blooming then choose Seed & Cutting Compost. Place a layer of moist compost in the bottom of the bowl and set the bulbs on it. They should be close together but must not touch each other nor the sides of the bowl. Never force bulbs downwards into compost. Fill up with more compost, pressing it firmly but not too tightly around the bulbs. When finished the tips should be above the surface and there should be about ½ in. between the top of the compost and the rim of the bowl.

Care After Planting: The bulbs need a 'plunging' period of complete darkness and a temperature of about 40°F. The best spot is in the garden covering the bowl with about 4 in. of peat. Failing this, place the container in a black polythene bag and stand it in a shed, cellar or garage. Any warmth at this stage will lead to failure. The plunging period lasts for about 6–10 weeks. Check occasionally to make sure that the compost is still moist.

Care During Growth: When the shoots are about 1–2 in. high move the bowl into a cool room indoors — 50°F is the ideal temperature. Place in a shady spot at first, then move near to the window after a few days. The leaves will now develop and in a few weeks the flower buds will appear. Now is the time to move the bowl to the chosen site for flowering. This spot should be bright but not sunny, free from draughts, away from a radiator or heater and not too warm — 60°–70°F is the ideal. Keep the compost moist at all times. Turn the bowl occasionally so that growth will be even and provide some support for tall-flowering types. Feed with a liquid fertilizer.

Care After Flowering: Cut off flowers, not flower-stalks. Continue watering and feeding until leaves have withered. Remove bulbs and allow to dry, then remove dead foliage and store in a cool dry place. These bulbs will not provide a second display indoors — plant in the garden in autumn.

NON-FORCING TECHNIQUE
for other bulbs

Planting: It is essential to choose a container with adequate drainage holes. Place a layer of crocks at the bottom and add a layer of Bulb Fibre or Seed & Cutting Compost. Plant the bulbs closely together and add more compost. The tips of the bulbs should be completely covered.

Care After Planting: Place the pot in the garden.

Care During Growth: When the plants are fully grown and flower buds are present bring the pot indoors to the site chosen for flowering. Treat in the same way as forced bulbs.

Care After Flowering: Treat in the same way as forced bulbs.

HOW TO MAKE BULBS BLOOM AT CHRISTMAS

It is quite simple to raise Hyacinths, Narcissi and Tulips which will be in bloom on Christmas Day, but it is not a matter of planting the bulbs earlier than the recommended time. The essential step is to buy bulbs which have been specially prepared for early flowering. These bulbs are more expensive than ordinary garden types and they must be planted as soon as possible after purchase. September is the usual time for planting, and the forcing technique should be followed. Bring the pots indoors when the shoots are 1 in. high — this should not be later than the first day of December. After flowering the bulbs can be stored for planting outdoors in autumn.

SPECIAL PROBLEMS

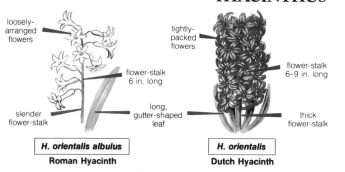

YELLOW LEAVES
Cause: Draughts are the usual reason. Other possible causes are incorrect watering and keeping the bowl in a spot with insufficient light.

STUNTED GROWTH
Cause: The usual reason is that the bowl has not been kept in the dark for the required period — the shoots should be an inch or two high before being exposed to light. Another cause is dry compost.

BUDS FAIL TO OPEN
Cause: Water is the problem here. Erratic watering can cause buds to die without opening; so can wetting the buds by watering carelessly.

NO FLOWERS AT ALL
Cause: There are several possible reasons. The trouble may start at planting time by using undersized bulbs. Keeping the bowl too warm or bringing it too quickly into bright sunlight will have this effect. Dry compost will also inhibit flowering.

ERRATIC FLOWERING
Cause: The most likely reason is that the bulbs were either different in size or vigour. If the bulbs were evenly matched then the probable cause was failure to turn the bowl occasionally.

DEFORMED FLOWERS
Cause: A clear symptom of keeping the bowl too warm during the plunging period. At this first stage the temperature should be about 40°F — do not keep the pot in a stuffy cupboard or sunny room even if unheated.

LONG, LIMP LEAVES
Cause: A clear sign of keeping the bowl in the dark for too long. Another possibility is too little light at flowering time.

ROTTING FLOWERS
Cause: Overwatering is the problem. A bowl without drainage holes kept under cool conditions can easily become waterlogged — take care. Remove excess water by carefully tipping the bowl.

HYACINTHUS

loosely-arranged flowers

slender flower-stalk

flower-stalk 6 in. long

long, gutter-shaped leaf

H. orientalis albulus
Roman Hyacinth

tightly-packed flowers

flower-stalk 6–9 in. long

thick flower-stalk

H. orientalis
Dutch Hyacinth

TYPES

The Dutch or Common Hyacinth (**Hyacinthus orientalis**) is the most popular of all indoor bulbs. The leafless flower-stalks bear 30 or more crowded bell-like flowers with a fragrance that can fill a room. Each bulb bears a single stalk and the waxy 1–2 in. long blooms last for 2–3 weeks. Bulbs specially prepared for Christmas blooming should be planted in September — bulbs for January–March flowering are planted in October. There are scores of varieties. The range of colours is demonstrated by **L'Innocence** (white), **Yellow Hammer** (yellow), **Lady Derby** (pink), **Jan Bos** (red), **Ostara** (blue) and **Amethyst** (violet). Roman Hyacinths (**H. orientalis albulus**) differ in a number of ways — 2 or 3 stalks are produced by each bulb and the flowers are smaller and less tightly packed. The flower-stalks are thinner and the colour range is restricted to white, pink and blue. Plant in August–September for December–January flowering. A third group, the Multiflora Hyacinths, bear several flower-stalks per bulb.

Hyacinthus orientalis Pink Pearl

NARCISSUS

TYPES

Pots of Narcissi and Daffodils continue to be the heralds of spring in countless households. Nearly all types can be grown indoors, but the 5 groups described below are generally considered to be the most reliable. The name 'Daffodil' is used when the large central tube ('trumpet') is at least as long as one of the petals — all the rest of the plants are called Narcissi. Some of the large-flowered types are quite suitable for indoor cultivation, but perhaps the best group of all are the Tazettas which produce bunches of flowers on each stem at Christmas or early in the New Year.

Plant: August–October
In flower: January–April (Tazettas: December–January)

N. hybrida	N. hybrida	N. hybrida	N. cyclamineus	N. tazetta
Daffodil	**Single Narcissus**	**Double Narcissus**	**Cyclamineus Narcissus**	**Tazetta Narcissus**
12–20 in. tall One flower per stem — central trumpet surrounded by shorter petals.	12–24 in. tall One flower per stem — central cup surrounded by longer petals.	12–18 in. tall More than one ring of petals — cup and petals indistinguishable.	6–12 in. tall Drooping flowers with long trumpets and strongly reflexed petals.	12–18 in. tall Several flowers per stem — central cup surrounded by longer petals.
Examples: **King Alfred** (yellow) **Spellbinder** (white and yellow) **Dutch Master** (yellow)	Examples: **Carlton** (yellow) **Verona** (white) **La Riante** (white and orange)	Examples: **White Lion** (white and yellow) **Golden Ducat** (yellow) **Texas** (yellow and orange)	Examples: **Peeping Tom** (yellow) **Tête-a-Tête** (yellow) **February Gold** (yellow)	Examples: **Soleil d'Or** (yellow) **Paperwhite** (white) **Geranium** (white and orange)

Narcissus Dutch Master

Narcissus Carlton

Narcissus Golden Ducat

Narcissus Tête-a-Tête

Narcissus Paperwhite

Narcissus Geranium

TULIPA

TYPES

The most satisfactory Tulips to grow indoors are the compact hybrids classed as Single Earlies (one ring of petals) and Double Earlies (several rings of petals). Some Species Tulips are also excellent for indoor use — both **Tulipa kaufmanniana** and **T. greigii** include suitable varieties. The tall-growing Tulips which are so colourful outdoors in May are much less useful for growing in bowls or pots. The best ones to choose are the strong-stemmed Darwin and Lily-flowered hybrids.

Plant: September–October (early September for bulbs prepared for Christmas flowering)

In flower: Late December–April

T. hybrida	T. hybrida	T. hybrida	T. hybrida	T. kaufmanniana	T. greigii
Single Early Tulip	**Double Early Tulip**	**Darwin Tulip**	**Lily-flowered Tulip**	**Species Tulip**	**Species Tulip**
9–16 in. tall Blooms rather small — open flat when mature.	9–16 in. tall Long-lasting — petals sometimes frilled.	24–30 in. tall Very large flowers opening in April.	20–24 in. tall Long flowers with pointed reflexed petals.	6–10 in. tall The Water Lily Tulip — the pointed petals opening flat in sunlight.	8–12 in. tall Later than T. kaufmanniana — leaves are streaked or mottled with brown.
Examples: **Brilliant Star** (red) **Princess Margaret** (pink) **Keizerskroon** (yellow and red)	Examples: **Peach Blossom** (rosy-pink) **Orange Nassau** (orange) **Scarlet Cardinal** (red)	Examples: **Apeldoorn** (red) **Striped Apeldoorn** (yellow and red) **Sunkist** (gold)	Examples: **West Point** (yellow) **China Pink** (pink) **Aladdin** (red and yellow)	Examples: **The First** (white and red) **Stresa** (red and yellow)	Examples: **Red Riding Hood** (red) **Plaisir** (cream and red)

Tulipa hybrida Keizerskroon

Tulipa hybrida Peach Blossom

Tulipa hybrida Apeldoorn

Tulipa hybrida Aladdin

Tulipa kaufmanniana Stresa

Tulipa greigii Plaisir

CROCUS

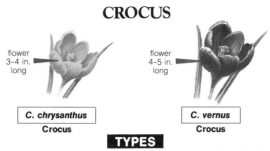

flower 3–4 in. long

C. chrysanthus
Crocus

flower 4–5 in. long

C. vernus
Crocus

TYPES

Crocus corms are planted in the autumn for flowering in early spring. The varieties of **Crocus chrysanthus** are often yellow (**Cream Beauty**, **E. A. Bowles**, **Goldilocks**, etc), but pale blues and mauves also occur, often with a golden base — **Blue Pearl**, **Princess Beatrix**, and so on. Flowering time is January–February — the varieties of **C. vernus** bloom a few weeks later, the flowers are larger, and blues and whites predominate. Popular types include **Vanguard** (silvery–pink) and **Pickwick** (mauve, striped purple).

Crocus chrysanthus Cream Beauty

Crocus vernus Vanguard

CONVALLARIA

bell-like flower ¼ in. long

oval leaf 8 in. long

C. majalis
Lily of the Valley

TYPES

The dainty white bells and heavy fragrance are well known. For Christmas flowers you will have to buy specially-prepared crowns ('pips') and plant in mid November. Alternatively, lift crowns from outdoor plants and pot up in October for blooming in February.

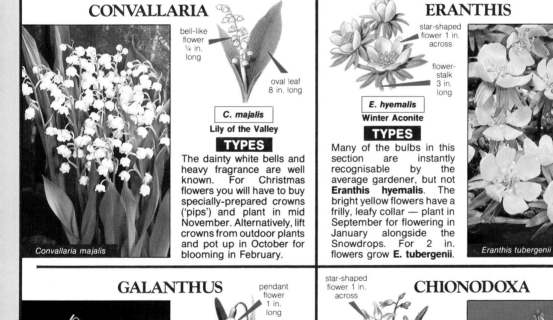
Convallaria majalis

ERANTHIS

star-shaped flower 1 in. across

flower-stalk 3 in. long

E. hyemalis
Winter Aconite

TYPES

Many of the bulbs in this section are instantly recognisable by the average gardener, but not **Eranthis hyemalis**. The bright yellow flowers have a frilly, leafy collar — plant in September for flowering in January alongside the Snowdrops. For 2 in. flowers grow **E. tubergenii**.

Eranthis tubergenii

GALANTHUS

pendant flower 1 in. long

green-tipped inner petals

flower-stalk 6 in. long

G. nivalis
Snowdrop

TYPES

Planting time is September — flowering time is January. The one you are most likely to see is the Common Snowdrop (**Galanthus nivalis**). The best variety is **S. Arnott** (9 in.) — for double flowers choose **flore pleno**. The tallest Snowdrop is **G. elwesii** (10 in.).

Galanthus Neil Frazer

CHIONODOXA

star-shaped flower 1 in. across

flower-stalk 6 in. long

C. luciliae
Glory of the Snow

TYPES

The popular Chionodoxa is **Chionodoxa luciliae** — 10 white-centred, blue starry flowers appear on each slender stalk in late winter. **C. sardensis** has all-blue flowers, and the largest blooms (1½ in. across) are borne by **C. gigantea**. Plant the bulbs in September for February flowers.

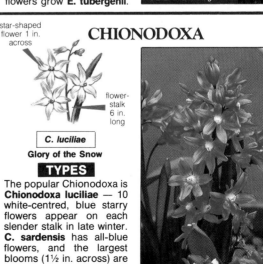
Chionodoxa sardensis

IRIS

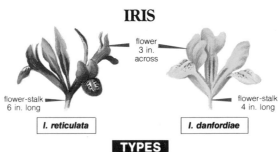

flower 3 in. across

flower-stalk 6 in. long

I. reticulata

flower-stalk 4 in. long

I. danfordiae

Iris reticulata

Iris danfordiae

TYPES

Dwarf Irises are excellent for growing indoors, producing large blooms in January and February. They have never gained the popularity of Crocuses, Hyacinths, etc, but there are at least 3 species which are well worth cultivating in the house. Plant the bulbs in September and provide plenty of light once the leaves have appeared above the compost. Choose from **Iris histrioides major** (deep blue, white centres), **I. reticulata** (purple, yellow centres — fragrant) and **I. danfordiae** (yellow — fragrant).

SCILLA

strap-like leaf

pendant flower ½ in. long

S. siberica
Bluebell

Scilla tubergeniana

TYPES

Some garden species can be grown indoors — plant in September–October for blooming in January–March. **Scilla tubergeniana** (3 in.) is the earliest species — **S. siberica** (6 in.) is the popular one. There are tender types (**S. adlamii**, **S. violacea**) which can be kept indoors for years.

MUSCARI

urn-shaped flower ¼ in. long

strap-like leaf

M. armeniacum
Grape Hyacinth

TYPES

Often seen outdoors but rarely recommended in house plant books. It is still a good choice — plant in September for January–March flowers. The usual species is **Muscari armeniacum** (8 in., blue flowers with white rims) — for sky blue flowers pick **M. botryoides** (6 in.).

Muscari armeniacum

GLADIOLUS

trumpet-shaped flower 3 in. across

flower-stalk 2 ft long

G. Columbine

TYPES

Gladioli are not usually thought of as indoor bulbs, and the large-flowering types are not suitable. Choose one of the Primulinus or the Miniature Hybrids such as **Columbine**, **Robin** or **Bo Peep**, or pick a low-growing species such as **G. colvillii** (1–2 ft).

Gladiolus primulinus Robin

GALTONIA

pendant flower 1½ in. long

flower-stalk 3–4 ft long

G. candicans
Summer Hyacinth

TYPE

This imposing plant is in marked contrast to the many dainty dwarfs in this section. Bulbs are planted in large pots in September and each flower-stalk bears 20 or more white bells in May-June. The strap-like leaves are 2 ft long.

Galtonia candicans

BULBS~INDOOR TYPES

FLOWERING POT PLANT page 57

A large number of the plants that are grown indoors produce 'bulbs' which can be used for propagation. Some produce true bulbs (see page 247 for definitions) and others form rhizomes, tubers and corms.

Some of these bulb-forming plants (Clivia, Eucharis, Vallota etc) keep their leaves all year round and are therefore regarded as Flowering House Plants rather than 'Bulbs'. Most of the flowering bulbs, however, lose their leaves during the dormant period, which means that they are Flowering Pot Plants. They are left on display until flowering is over and then moved out of sight.

These temporary-display bulbs are divided into two basic groups. First of all there are the frost-hardy ones which are happy outdoors but need special treatment for blooming indoors. They must be subjected to cold conditions during the rooting stage and are only placed in the living room, hall etc when the flower buds have formed. These are the *Garden* or *Outdoor Bulbs* (see pages 91-96).

The other group are the *Indoor Bulbs* described in this section. These plants cannot tolerate frost and are never placed outdoors in winter. They are left in the pot when the foliage dies down — the compost is kept almost dry until growth starts again. This is the way to treat the true bulbs and most corms, tubers and rhizomes. A few (Achimenes, Tuberous Begonia and Canna) are stored in slightly moist peat during the dormant period and then potted up prior to the start of the growing season.

The list of Indoor bulbs is an impressive one, and can provide colour all year round. Some of the important ones are described individually in this A–Z chapter — see table on the left. The remainder are illustrated and described here. For the really keen there are also Lycoris aurea (Golden Spider Lily), Sprekelia formosissima (Jacobean Lily) and Habranthus robustus.

OTHER INDOOR BULBS

	page
ACHIMENES	63
TUBEROUS BEGONIA	74
GLORIOSA	152
GLOXINIA	152
LACHENALIA	166
LILIUM	168
RECHSTEINERIA	198
SMITHIANTHA	208

TYPES

Hippeastrum Safari

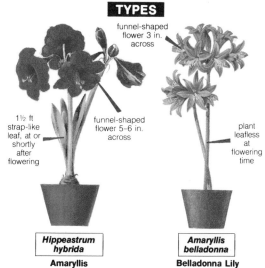

funnel-shaped flower 3 in. across

1½ ft strap-like leaf, at or shortly after flowering

funnel-shaped flower 5-6 in. across

plant leafless at flowering time

Hippeastrum hybrida
Amaryllis

Amaryllis belladonna
Belladonna Lily

Amaryllis belladonna alba

Hippeastrum Apple Blossom

These 2 plants are often confused — both are large bulbs which produce clusters of trumpet-like flowers on thick stalks. The Belladonna Lily, however, is not often seen — the popular 'Amaryllis' offered for sale in autumn is really a Hippeastrum hybrid. These hybrids are orange, purple, white, pink or red — sometimes edged or striped in other shades. **Hippeastrum hybrida** has hollow stalks and there are 3-6 flowers per cluster. **Amaryllis belladonna** has solid stalks and 6-12 flowers per cluster. Hippeastrum blooms in winter or spring (Amaryllis — autumn).

Hippeastrum Ludwig's Dazzler

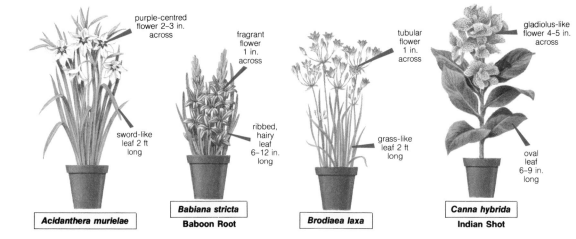

purple-centred flower 2–3 in. across

sword-like leaf 2 ft long

Acidanthera murielae

fragrant flower 1 in. across

ribbed, hairy leaf 6–12 in. long

Babiana stricta
Baboon Root

tubular flower 1 in. across

grass-like leaf 2 ft long

Brodiaea laxa

gladiolus-like flower 4–5 in. across

oval leaf 6–9 in. long

Canna hybrida
Indian Shot

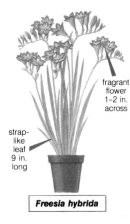

fragrant flower 1–2 in. across

strap-like leaf 9 in. long

Freesia hybrida

Acidanthera murielae is a Gladiolus-like plant, bearing sweetly-scented blooms in late summer or autumn. Plant the corms in late winter. **Babiana stricta** is also related to the Gladiolus but it is a much smaller plant — the flower-stalks grow 6–12 in. high. Plant in autumn for spring flowers — hybrids with white, yellow, red, blue or purple blooms are available. Brodiaea is an uncommon bulb for people who prefer delicate blooms to big showy ones. **Brodiaea laxa** bears white or blue blooms in large clusters — it flowers in spring, unlike **B. coronaria** which blooms in summer. **B. ida-maia** is quite different — the flowers are pendant, red and edged with green. **Canna hybrida** plants are big, bold and colourful. The large flowers are borne on a 2–4 ft stalk, and specialist growers can offer a bewildering array of varieties — white, yellow, pink and red; plain, striped and spotted. There is also a choice of leaf colour — standard green, dark green and bronzy-purple. The funnel-shaped flowers of **Freesia hybrida** grow on one side of the 1–1½ ft long wiry stems — all varieties are sweet-smelling and you can choose from white, yellow, blue, lilac, orange, pink and red. Plants can be raised from seeds or corms. **Eucomis comosa** needs lots of space. The long leaves form a large rosette and the cylindrical spike of small flowers bears a leafy crown. **E. bicolor** (purplish-green flowers, purple-spotted stalk) is smaller.

flower-head 1 ft long

lance-shaped leaf 1½ ft long

Eucomis comosa
Pineapple Lily

Acidanthera murielae

Canna hybrida J.B. van der Schoot

Freesia hybrida Marie Louise

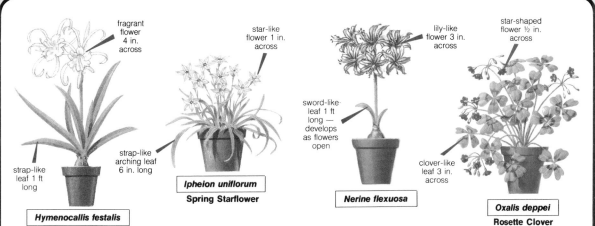

fragrant
flower
4 in.
across

strap-like
arching leaf
6 in. long

strap-like
leaf 1 ft
long

Hymenocallis festalis

Spider Lily

star-like
flower 1 in.
across

Ipheion uniflorum

Spring Starflower

lily-like
flower 3 in.
across

sword-like
leaf 1 ft
long —
develops
as flowers
open

Nerine flexuosa

star-shaped
flower ½ in.
across

clover-like
leaf 3 in.
across

Oxalis deppei

Rosette Clover

star-shaped
flower 2 in.
across

sword-
like
leaf
1 ft
long

Ixia hybrida

African Corn Lily

Hymenocallis festalis is cultivated for its attractive sweet-smelling blooms which appear in late spring or summer. These flowers look like Daffodils with long and narrow petals, borne on 2 ft stalks above the arching leaves. The foliage of H. festalis dies down in winter. **Ipheion uniflorum** is a low-growing plant, its starry blooms appearing on top of the 6 in. stems in spring. Use your nose for identification — the blue or white flowers have a pleasant smell, but the crushed leaves have the pungent odour of garlic. **Nerine flexuosa** is an uncommon plant — a cluster of wavy-petalled pink or white bells are borne on 2 ft flower-stalks in autumn. **N. sarniensis** is the Guernsey Lily — narrow-petalled white, orange or red flowers tightly clustered crowning the stalks. The leaves appear after flowering. Oxalis has never become a popular plant, despite its Shamrock-like appearance. **Oxalis deppei** has red flowers in spring, **O. cernua** (Bermuda Buttercup) bears yellow blooms and **O. bowiei** is pale purple. The leaves close at night, and so do the flowers of some species. Buy Oxalis plants in bloom or raise your own from bulbs. The strap-like leaves of **Ornithogalum thyrsoides** arise from the bulb, followed by a 1½ ft stalk crowned with about 20 starry flowers in late spring. A close relative (**O. caudatum**) has a 3 ft stalk which bears up to 100 green-striped blooms. **Ixia hybrida** is known for its gaily-coloured flowers, but is much less popular than Freesia. You can identify Ixia from its 6-petalled dark-centred flowers borne on upright wiry stalks. Many varieties are available — flowers appear in early summer.

fragrant
flower
1 in.
across

strap-like
leaf 1 ft
long

Ornithogalum thyrsoides

Chincherinchee

Ipheion uniflorum Wisley Blue

Nerine sarniensis

Hymenocallis festalis

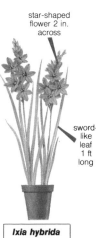

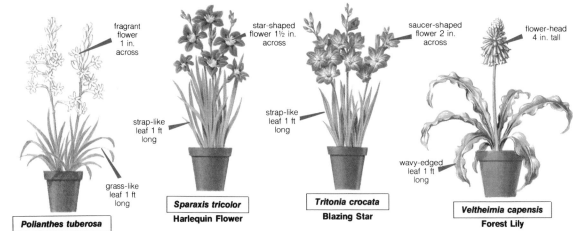

fragrant flower 1 in. across

grass-like leaf 1 ft long

Polianthes tuberosa
Tuberose

star-shaped flower 1½ in. across

strap-like leaf 1 ft long

Sparaxis tricolor
Harlequin Flower

saucer-shaped flower 2 in. across

strap-like leaf 1 ft long

Tritonia crocata
Blazing Star

flower-head 4 in. tall

wavy-edged leaf 1 ft long

Veltheimia capensis
Forest Lily

trumpet-shaped flower 6–9 in. long

arrow-shaped leaf 1½ ft long

Zantedeschia aethiopica
Calla Lily

Polianthes tuberosa is widely planted outdoors in the Tropics but is not often seen as a pot plant in Europe. The bulb-like rhizomes are planted in spring to bloom in winter. The leaves are narrow and the flowering spike can reach 2–3 ft. The flowers are white and waxy. A mixture of **Sparaxis tricolor** hybrids will produce a riot of colour in late spring when the flowers open above the dense foliage. Many (but not all) types have a black-edged yellow throat. Plant the corms in autumn. Like its relatives Ixia and Sparaxis, **Tritonia crocata** produces a fan of narrow leaves. In summer the floral display appears on wiry stalks — varieties in white, glowing orange, deep pink and several other bright colours are available. Somewhat like the Red Hot Poker of the garden, **Veltheimia capensis** is a good choice for indoors. Plant the large bulb in early autumn and about 3 or 4 months later the 1 ft flower-stalk arises from the centre of the leaf rosette. This stalk bears about 60 small but long-lasting bell-like flowers. Calla Lily is one of the real beauties of the indoor plant world. **Zantedeschia aethiopica** bears its upturned white trumpets on 3 ft stalks in early spring — other species include **Z. rehmannii** (pink) and **Z. elliottiana** (yellow), plus many hybrids in various colours. The Zephyr Lily is a much smaller and more dainty plant — **Zephyranthes grandiflora** produces 6 in. flower-stalks in early summer, each bearing a Crocus-like bloom which soon opens out into a pink star. **Z. candida** (white) is even smaller, but there are several large-flowering hybrids.

crocus-like flower 3 in. across

strap-like leaf 5 in. long

Zephyranthes grandiflora
Zephyr Lily

Veltheimia capensis

Zantedeschia aethiopica

Zephyranthes grandiflora

CACTI ~ DESERT TYPES

CACTI
page 59

HOW TO MAKE A DESERT CACTUS BLOOM

Although some cacti, especially the ones illustrated, will bloom when the plant is still quite young, there are others, such as Opuntia and Cereus, which are more difficult to bring into bloom.

About half the cactus varieties can be expected to flower indoors by the time they are three or four years old. They will continue to bloom each year, and although spring is the usual flowering season even a modest collection can be selected to provide a few blooms all year round.

The secret lies in the fact that most cacti will only flower on new growth. This calls for summer care and winter 'neglect' as described in Secrets of Success. Another point to remember is that flowering is stimulated when the plant is slightly pot-bound.

Chamaecereus **Echinopsis** **Gymnocalycium** **Lobivia**

Mammillaria **Notocactus** **Parodia** **Rebutia**

SECRETS OF SUCCESS

Temperature: Average warmth from spring to autumn. Keep cool in winter — 50°-55°F is ideal but no harm will occur at 40°F. Windowsill plants should be brought into the room at night if the weather is very cold and there is no artificial heat. The hairy cacti (Cephalocereus senilis and Espostoa lanata) need a minimum of 60°F in winter.

Light: Choose the sunniest spot available, especially in winter. In the greenhouse some shading may be necessary in the hottest months.

Water: Increase watering in spring, and in the late spring-late summer period treat as an ordinary house plant by watering thoroughly when the compost begins to dry out. Use tepid water. In late summer give less water and after mid autumn keep almost dry — just enough water to prevent shrivelling.

Air Humidity: Do not mist in summer (exception — Cleistocactus). The main requirement is for fresh air — open windows on hot summer days.

Repotting: Repot annually when young; after that only repot when essential. Transfer in spring into a pot which is only slightly larger than the previous one.

Propagation: Cuttings of most varieties root easily. Take stem cuttings or offsets in spring or summer. It is vital to let the cuttings dry for a few days (large cuttings for 1-2 weeks) before inserting in peat-based compost. Another propagation method is seed sowing — germination temperature 70°-80°F.

SPECIAL PROBLEMS

STEM TIP SHRIVELLED, SOFT ROT BELOW
Cause: Overwatering, especially in winter. Carry out standard remedial treatment (see page 246).

NO GROWTH
Cause: Underwatering in summer or overwatering in winter. Follow rules in Secrets of Success.

BRONZY MOTTLING ON SURFACE
Cause: Red spider mite (see page 244).

CORKY PATCHES ON SURFACE
Cause: Localised damage due to insects, physical injury or sudden chilling. Another possible reason is underwatering in summer.

BROWN SOFT PATCHES
Cause: Stem rot disease — well-grown plants are rarely attacked. Cut out infected tissue and water compost with carbendazim. Improve growing conditions.

STEM ELONGATED & MISSHAPEN
Cause: Too much warmth in winter or too little light in summer. Follow rules in Secrets of Success; turn pots occasionally to ensure even growth.

PATCHES OF WHITE WOOL ON SURFACE
Cause: Mealy bug (see page 244).

BROWN HARD SHELLS ON SURFACE
Cause: Scale insect (see page 244).

ROT AT BASE FOLLOWED BY STEM COLLAPSE
Cause: Basal rot disease, due to overwet conditions in winter. Use upper stem for propagation. Next time avoid overwatering in winter, and cover compost surface with a layer of stone chippings.

TYPES

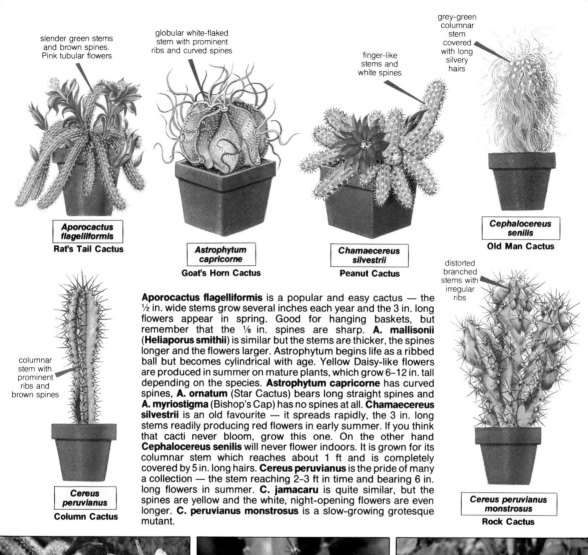

slender green stems and brown spines. Pink tubular flowers

Aporocactus flagelliformis

Rat's Tail Cactus

globular white-flaked stem with prominent ribs and curved spines

Astrophytum capricorne

Goat's Horn Cactus

finger-like stems and white spines

Chamaecereus silvestrii

Peanut Cactus

grey-green columnar stem covered with long silvery hairs

Cephalocereus senilis

Old Man Cactus

columnar stem with prominent ribs and brown spines

Cereus peruvianus

Column Cactus

distorted branched stems with irregular ribs

Cereus peruvianus monstrosus

Rock Cactus

Aporocactus flagelliformis is a popular and easy cactus — the ½ in. wide stems grow several inches each year and the 3 in. long flowers appear in spring. Good for hanging baskets, but remember that the ⅛ in. spines are sharp. **A. mallisonii** (**Heliaporus smithii**) is similar but the stems are thicker, the spines longer and the flowers larger. Astrophytum begins life as a ribbed ball but becomes cylindrical with age. Yellow Daisy-like flowers are produced in summer on mature plants, which grow 6–12 in. tall depending on the species. **Astrophytum capricorne** has curved spines, **A. ornatum** (Star Cactus) bears long straight spines and **A. myriostigma** (Bishop's Cap) has no spines at all. **Chamaecereus silvestrii** is an old favourite — it spreads rapidly, the 3 in. long stems readily producing red flowers in early summer. If you think that cacti never bloom, grow this one. On the other hand **Cephalocereus senilis** will never flower indoors. It is grown for its columnar stem which reaches about 1 ft and is completely covered by 5 in. long hairs. **Cereus peruvianus** is the pride of many a collection — the stem reaching 2–3 ft in time and bearing 6 in. long flowers in summer. **C. jamacaru** is quite similar, but the spines are yellow and the white, night-opening flowers are even longer. **C. peruvianus monstrosus** is a slow-growing grotesque mutant.

Aporocactus flagelliformis

Cereus jamacaru

Astrophytum ornatum

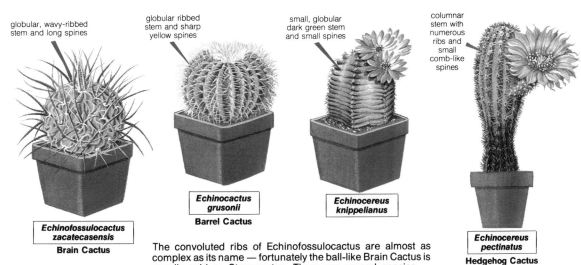

globular, wavy-ribbed stem and long spines

Echinofossulocactus zacatecasensis
Brain Cactus

globular ribbed stem and sharp yellow spines

Echinocactus grusonii
Barrel Cactus

small, globular dark green stem and small spines

Echinocereus knippelianus

columnar stem with numerous ribs and small comb-like spines

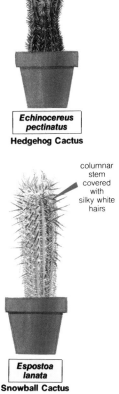

Echinocereus pectinatus
Hedgehog Cactus

slender many-ribbed columnar stem covered with fine white bristles

Cleistocactus straussii
Silver Torch Cactus

The convoluted ribs of Echinofossulocactus are almost as complex as its name — fortunately the ball-like Brain Cactus is usually sold as Stenocactus. There are several species — **Echinofossulocactus multicostatus**, **E. hastatus**, **E. zacatecasensis** etc, and the usual form is a 6 in. globe with 1 in. spines. Echinocactus is a slow-growing ball — it will take 10 years or more to reach a diameter of 9 in. **Echinocactus grusonii** is the common one — there is a golden crown of woolly hairs at the top and prominent spines along the ribs. It will not flower indoors — for deep pink flowers grow **E. horizonthalonius**. There are many species of Echinocereus and some confusion over their names. The column-like one covered with spines is either **Echinocereus pectinatus** or the very similar **E. rigidissimus**. Height is about 10 in. and the pink flowers are scented. The much smaller **E. knippelianus** is more ball-like and less spiny. **E. salm-dyckianus** produces bright orange flowers. The Cleistocacti are slow-growing, tall and densely covered with spines. Flowering does not begin until the plants are many years old. **Cleistocactus straussii** is the favourite species, reaching 4 ft or more after several decades. The wool and spines are white, giving the plant a silvery appearance. Espostoa, like Cephalocereus, is a densely hairy species — the main difference is the presence of sharp spines on Espostoa. **Espostoa lanata** is a 1–2 ft column which does not bloom indoors. **E. melanostele** is white at first, but later the hairs turn black.

columnar stem covered with silky white hairs

Espostoa lanata
Snowball Cactus

Echinocactus horizonthalonius

Echinocereus salm-dyckianus

Espostoa melanostele

globular or short columnar stem and short spines

globular or columnar stem and long spines

grey-green globular stem with prominent ribs and large red hooked spines

brightly-coloured stem grafted on to another cactus stock

Echinopsis eyriesii
Sea Urchin Cactus

Echinopsis rhodotricha
Sea Urchin Cactus

Ferocactus latispinus
Fish Hook Cactus

Gymnocalycium mihanovichii friedrichii
Hibotan Cactus

columnar stem and dense cover of yellow spines

globular or short columnar stem. Flowers followed by red fruits

There is nothing special about the ball-like or oval stems of Echinopsis — the notable feature is the outstanding floral display which appears each summer. **Echinopsis eyriesii** is the popular one, bearing ¼ in. brown spines on prominent ribs — the 6 in. long flowers are scented. The large Sea Urchin Cactus is **E. rhodotricha** which bears 1 in. spines and scentless flowers. Ferocactus is a fearsome plant — barrel-shaped and armed with stout spines. The red bristles of **Ferocactus latispinus** are hooked — hence the common name. This cactus rarely blooms indoors — for orange flowers in summer grow **F. acanthodes**. Gymnocalycium is the Chin Cactus, and most species and varieties are rather ordinary. The small globular bodies are green, ribbed and spined, but there is one group which is entirely red or yellow. These strains of **Gymnocalycium mihanovichii friedrichii** are the Hibotan or Red Cap Cacti — their brightly-coloured stems lack chlorophyll and so are grafted on to a green cactus. Most of the cacti in this chapter are reasonably common, but Haageocereus appears in few shops and even fewer textbooks. The basic species is **Haageocereus chosicensis** — a broadly columnar cactus with the green surface hidden by bristle-like spines. **Hamatocactus setispinus** is a close relative of Ferocactus — there are prominent ribs and large hooked spines. The ribs, however, are curved and notched, and the yellow blooms are readily produced each summer.

Haageocereus chosicensis

Hamatocactus setispinus
Strawberry Cactus

Echinopsis rhodotricha

Ferocactus acanthodes

Gymnocalycium mihanovichii friedrichii

globular stem with many ribs and pale brown spines

Lobivia aurea

Golden Lily Cactus

columnar stem with many ribs and yellow spreading spines

Lobivia famatimensis

Sunset Cactus

globular stem with hooked spines and dense white hairs

Mammillaria bocasana

Powder Puff Cactus

short columnar stem with prominent tubercles and hooked spines

Mammillaria wildii

columnar stem with prominent ribs. Closely-packed areoles form white line

Lemaireocereus marginatus

Organ Pipe Cactus

Lobivia is a good cactus for the beginner — it remains compact (3–6 in. high) and readily produces red or yellow blooms. Several species are available — the oval **Lobivia famatimensis** is covered with flat yellow bristles and bears large golden flowers. Both **L. aurea** and **L. hertrichiana** are ball-shaped with prominent ribs and the summer blooms measure several inches in diameter. Any large collection of cacti will contain several Mammillaria species and varieties. Their popularity is based on the compact growth habit and their free-flowering nature even when quite young — many bear attractive fruits once the small flowers have faded. One of the recognition features is the presence of tubercles in place of ribs, each tubercle bearing spines at the apex. The favourite species is **Mammillaria bocasana** — a cluster-forming silvery plant which bears a ring of small white blooms around the stem in spring. The oval-shaped **M. wildii** is quite similar — **M. rhodantha** and **M. hahniana** bear pink flowers. In contrast to Lobivia and Mammillaria, Lemaireocereus is not easy to grow and often succumbs to disease. It is one of the much-branched cacti seen in Western films, growing 20 ft or more, but in the home **Lemaireocereus marginatus** is usually a single column with dense white wool along the ribs to tell you that it is not a Cereus (page 102). **Myrtillocactus geometrizans** is an unusual type, with stems which branch and turn blue with age. **Heliocereus speciosus** (Sun Cactus) is another odd one — its green stems branch at the base and trail downwards. Bright red flowers appear in early summer.

branched columnar stem with prominent ribs and long spines

Myrtillocactus geometrizans

Blue Myrtle Cactus

Lobivia hertrichiana

Mammillaria hahniana

Heliocereus speciosus

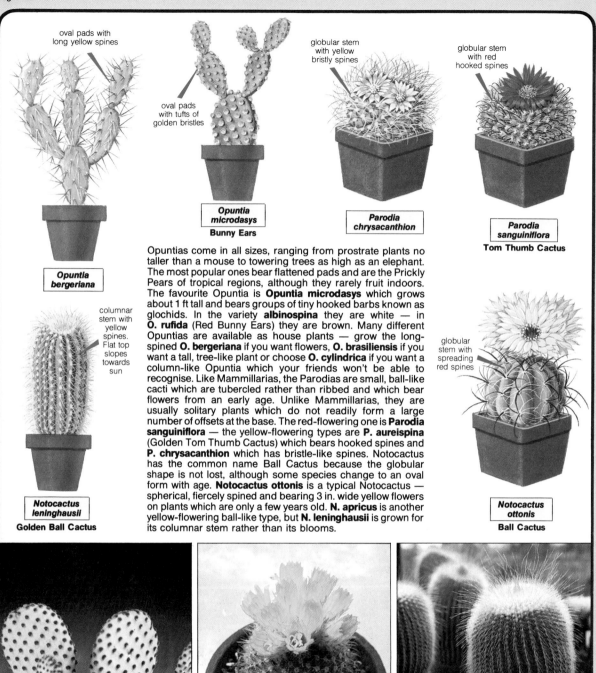

oval pads with long yellow spines

oval pads with tufts of golden bristles

globular stem with yellow bristly spines

globular stem with red hooked spines

Opuntia microdasys
Bunny Ears

Parodia chrysacanthion

Parodia sanguiniflora
Tom Thumb Cactus

Opuntia bergeriana

columnar stem with yellow spines. Flat top slopes towards sun

globular stem with spreading red spines

Notocactus leninghausii
Golden Ball Cactus

Opuntias come in all sizes, ranging from prostrate plants no taller than a mouse to towering trees as high as an elephant. The most popular ones bear flattened pads and are the Prickly Pears of tropical regions, although they rarely fruit indoors. The favourite Opuntia is **Opuntia microdasys** which grows about 1 ft tall and bears groups of tiny hooked barbs known as glochids. In the variety **albinospina** they are white — in **O. rufida** (Red Bunny Ears) they are brown. Many different Opuntias are available as house plants — grow the long-spined **O. bergeriana** if you want flowers, **O. brasiliensis** if you want a tall, tree-like plant or choose **O. cylindrica** if you want a column-like Opuntia which your friends won't be able to recognise. Like Mammillarias, the Parodias are small, ball-like cacti which are tubercled rather than ribbed and which bear flowers from an early age. Unlike Mammillarias, they are usually solitary plants which do not readily form a large number of offsets at the base. The red-flowering one is **Parodia sanguiniflora** — the yellow-flowering types are **P. aureispina** (Golden Tom Thumb Cactus) which bears hooked spines and **P. chrysacanthion** which has bristle-like spines. Notocactus has the common name Ball Cactus because the globular shape is not lost, although some species change to an oval form with age. **Notocactus ottonis** is a typical Notocactus — spherical, fiercely spined and bearing 3 in. wide yellow flowers on plants which are only a few years old. **N. apricus** is another yellow-flowering ball-like type, but **N. leninghausii** is grown for its columnar stem rather than its blooms.

Notocactus ottonis
Ball Cactus

Opuntia rufida

Parodia aureispina

Notocactus leninghausii

columnar stem with yellow spines and long white hairs

globular stems and short white spines

finger-like stems and tiny spines

columnar stem with large areoles and long yellow spines

Rebutia miniscula

Mexican Sunball

Rebutia pygmaea

Trichocereus candicans

Torch Cactus

Oreocereus celsianus

Old Man of the Andes

semi-evergreen shrub with spiny stems and green leaves

Pereskia aculeata

Rose Cactus

semi-evergreen shrub with spiny stems and leaves red on underside

Pereskia godseffiana

Rose Cactus

Oreocereus celsianus is an oval cactus bearing white hairs and a woolly top — the common name of this plant from the S. American mountains seems quite appropriate. With age the yellow spines turn red, branches arise from the base and red flowers appear. **O. trollii** is a less common species which is smaller and bears fewer ribs. Rebutia is a popular cactus because it is small and starts to flower while still quite young. It is similar to Mammillaria in many ways — the globular stems are covered with tubercles rather than ribs and offsets are readily produced at the base. The bright funnel-shaped flowers, however, are borne close to the base rather than as a ring around the top as occurs with so many Mammillarias. **Rebutia miniscula** is the favourite one — 2 in. balls bearing orange or pink flowers in early summer. The variety **grandiflora** bears large red blooms — **violaciflora** produces mauve ones. The baby is **R. pygmaea** (less than 1 in. high) and the giants are **R. kupperiana** and **R. senilis** (3–4 in. high). Trichocereus is the Torch Cactus, grown for its columnar stems and huge white flowers which are borne on mature plants. **Trichocereus candicans** branches freely and grows about 3 ft tall — the more popular **T. spachianus** forms an impressive bristly column reaching 5 ft or more. The odd man out — Pereskia bears thin spiny stems and true leaves. The flowers look like wild roses — hence the common name. **Pereskia aculeata** is the usual one, growing to 6 ft — the golden-leaved **P. godseffiana** is attractive but hard to find.

Oreocereus celsianus

Rebutia senilis

Pereskia aculeata

CACTI ~ FOREST TYPES

CACTI
page 59

In their natural home the Forest Cacti are attached to trees in woodlands and jungles, and so it is not surprising that they are so different in form and requirements from the spine-covered Desert Cacti. There is an exception — the Rat's Tail Cactus (Aporocactus flagelliformis) grows on trees in its ancestral home in Mexico, but it looks like and should be treated as a Desert Cactus (see page 101).

The typical Forest Cactus has leaf-like stems and a trailing growth habit, making it suitable for hanging baskets. A few, such as Rhipsalis, are grown for their stem form but their main attraction is their flowers. The most spectacular group are the Epiphyllums, with their fragrant saucer-size blooms.

Unfortunately the Forest Cacti can be shy bloomers, and there are rules to follow if you want a good display every year. Provide a cool and dry resting period, never move a plant once buds appear and allow stems to harden outdoors during summer. There are also specific needs for each type, as illustrated on page 109.

SECRETS OF SUCCESS

Temperature: Ideal temperature range is 55°–70°F. During resting period (see page 109) keep at 50°–55°F.

Light: Choose a well-lit spot, shaded from direct sunlight for most varieties. Epiphyllum thrives on an east-facing windowsill.

Water: Increase watering when resting period is over and buds begin to form. Treat as an ordinary house plant when flowers appear and during active growth — water liberally when compost begins to dry out. Use rainwater if tap water is very hard.

Air Humidity: Mist leaves frequently.

Repotting: Repot annually shortly after flowering has finished. Epiphyllum is an exception — flowering is encouraged by pot-bound conditions so do not repot annually.

Propagation: Cuttings of most varieties root easily. Take stem cuttings in summer, using a terminal 'leaf' pad or stem tip. Allow cutting to dry for a few days before inserting in peat-based compost.

TYPES

Rhipsalis burchellii

pale green stems

creamy flowers followed by round white fruits

Rhipsalis cassutha
Mistletoe Cactus

In its natural habitat **Rhipsalis cassutha** hangs from trees — indoors its long, branching stems trail over the rim of the pot. The fruits have a Mistletoe-like appearance. **R. burchellii** is another Mistletoe Cactus — the fruits are pink.

triangular winged stems

stem section 3 in. long

Rhipsalis paradoxa
Chain Cactus

The long stems of **Rhipsalis paradoxa** are narrowed at intervals, giving a branched chain effect. A suitable plant for a hanging basket — white flowers appear in summer. Another hanging basket Rhipsalis is **R. houlletiana** (leaf-like branches, white flowers).

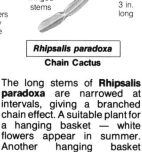

Rhipsalis paradoxa

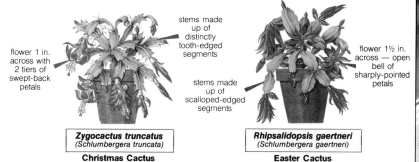

flower 1 in. across with 2 tiers of swept-back petals

stems made up of distinctly tooth-edged segments

stems made up of scalloped-edged segments

flower 1½ in. across — open bell of sharply-pointed petals

Zygocactus truncatus
(Schlumbergera truncata)
Christmas Cactus

Rhipsalidopsis gaertneri
(Schlumbergera gaertneri)
Easter Cactus

Rhipsalidopsis gaertneri

Both the popular Christmas and the Easter Cactus have branching and arching stems composed of leaf-like flattened segments which are 1½–2 in. long. The margins are the key to identification — the segments of **Zygocactus truncatus** bear pointed projections whereas those of **Rhipsalidopsis gaertneri** and the smaller **R. rosea** are shallowly scalloped. Plants are usually bought in bud and many varieties are available. Z. truncatus varieties bloom between mid November and late January — white, pink, red or purple. R. gaertneri varieties range from pink to dark red and bloom in April or May. These shop-bought specimens usually produce a large number of blooms, but in unskilled hands never flower again. The reason is that these forest cacti need both a resting period (when water and warmth are decreased) and a spell outdoors in order to produce next year's flower buds.

	Christmas Cactus	Easter Cactus	Epiphyllum
JAN	FLOWERING PERIOD	RESTING PERIOD	RESTING PERIOD Keep cool (maximum temperature 50°F). Water infrequently
FEB	RESTING PERIOD Keep cool (55°F). Water infrequently	PRE-FLOWERING PERIOD Keep dryish and cool until flower buds form. Then increase water and temperature	
MAR			PRE-FLOWERING PERIOD Keep dryish and cool until flower buds form. Then increase water and temperature
APR	Treat normally; water thoroughly when compost begins to dry out	FLOWERING PERIOD Water normally. Maintain a minimum temperature of 60°F	
MAY			FLOWERING PERIOD Water normally. Maintain a minimum temperature of 60°F
JUN			
JUL	OUTDOORS Place in a shady spot; protect from slugs	OUTDOORS Place in a shady spot; protect from slugs	OUTDOORS Place in a shady spot; protect from slugs
AUG			
SEP			
OCT	PRE-FLOWERING PERIOD Keep dryish and cool until flower buds form. Then increase water and temperature	RESTING PERIOD Keep cool (55°F). The soil ball should be moist, but do not overwater	Treat normally; water thoroughly when compost begins to dry out
NOV	FLOWERING PERIOD Water normally. Maintain a minimum temperature of 55°F		
DEC			RESTING PERIOD

notched stem 2 ft long

funnel-shaped flower 4–6 in. across

Epiphyllum ackermanii
Orchid Cactus

The Epiphyllums are untidy plants, the strap-shaped stems sprawling outwards unless staked when in flower. This lack of an attractive growth habit is more than made up for by the flowers — flaring, multi-petalled trumpets which can be as large as a saucer. Nearly all the commercial varieties are hybrids of **Epiphyllum ackermanii** — day-flowering plants which are available in a wide range of shades. The white, night-flowering Epiphyllums are hybrids of **E. cooperi** — the 5 in. flowers are very fragrant. This cactus is closely related to the Easter and Christmas Cacti and like them will bloom every year with proper treatment. The range of colours is illustrated by **London Glory** (red), **Gloria** (orange), **Little Sister** (white), **Midnight** (purple), **Reward** (yellow), **Padre** (pink) . . . but no blue.

Epiphyllum Sabra

CALADIUM

FOLIAGE HOUSE PLANT
page 51

The striking arrow-shaped leaves are spectacular — paper thin and beautifully marked and coloured. This dazzling foliage, however, is not permanent and lasts only from late spring to early autumn.

Plant Caladium tubers in Potting Compost in spring and keep moist at 75°F or more. When shoots appear mist daily and slowly adjust to living room temperature. Warmth at all times is vital — at no stage should the temperature fall below 60°F. If you buy a Caladium plant, protect it from cold on the way home.

SECRETS OF SUCCESS

Temperature: Warm. Above 70°F whenever possible, never below 60°F.

Light: Moderately well-lit but away from direct sunlight.

Water: Water freely during the growing season.

Air Humidity: Mist leaves frequently, especially in spring.

After Care: Foliage dies down in autumn. Stop watering — keep tubers at about 60°F in pots or in peat. Replant tubers in spring — small 'daughter' tubers can be potted up separately.

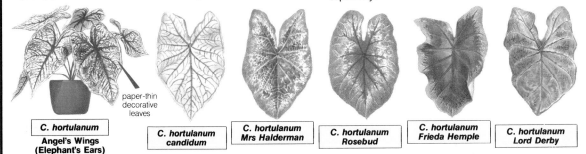

paper-thin decorative leaves

C. hortulanum
Angel's Wings (Elephant's Ears)

C. hortulanum candidum

C. hortulanum Mrs Halderman

C. hortulanum Rosebud

C. hortulanum Frieda Hemple

C. hortulanum Lord Derby

TYPES

There are scores of varieties available but they are usually sold unnamed. The textbooks can't agree whether these hybrids should be listed under **Caladium bicolor** or **C. hortulanum** — obviously naming a Caladium is not easy! Several are illustrated here — **C. hortulanum candidum** is easily recognised (white with green veins) and so is its reverse image **Seagull** (green with white veins). **Pink Blush** is pink/dark red/dark green — **John Peel** bears orange/red/green foliage. Easier to grow than the showy hybrids is the smaller **C. humboldtii**. The green arrow-shaped foliage is blotched with white. **C. picturatum** has long and narrow green leaves with prominent white veins.

Caladium hortulanum candidum

Caladium hortulanum Triomphe de Compte

CALCEOLARIA

FLOWERING POT PLANT
page 57

The Slipper Flower is a springtime favourite. The soft leaves are large and hairy and the flowers are curious and colourful. The plant is bought in flower (propagation is a skilled job best left to the nurseryman) and should last about a month. Provide moist conditions, keep away from draughts and keep careful watch for aphids.

SECRETS OF SUCCESS

Temperature: Cool — 50°-60°F is ideal.

Light: Bright light away from direct sunlight.

Water: Keep compost moist at all times.

Air Humidity: Stand the pot on a pebble tray or surround with moist peat. Mist occasionally but do not wet the leaves.

Care After Flowering: Plant should be discarded.

Propagation: Difficult — sow seeds in summer in a cool greenhouse for flowering next year.

hairy leaf 4–6 in. across

pouch-like flower 1–2 in. across

C. herbeohybrida
Slipper Flower

TYPES

Calceolaria herbeohybrida is the only popular species. The plants grow about 1½ ft high and the pouch-shaped flowers are available in several colours — yellow, orange, red or white with dark-coloured blotches.

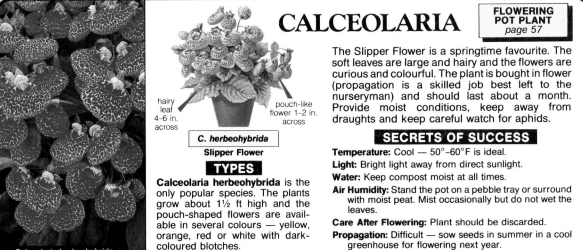

Calceolaria herbeohybrida

CALLIANDRA

FLOWERING HOUSE PLANT
page 55

Calliandra tweedyi

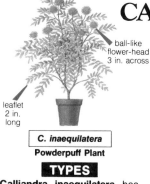

ball-like flower-head 3 in. across

leaflet 2 in. long

C. inaequilatera
Powderpuff Plant

TYPES

Calliandra inaequilatera has bright red flowers and dark green foliage. A better choice is the hardier **C. tweedyi** — the flowers are smaller and the leaves are feathery.

A popular plant in the U.S but rarely grown in Britain. The leaves are made up of a large number of segments and the flowers are made up entirely of stamens. It blooms in winter and the 'powder-puffs' last for 6–8 weeks. It needs light, warmth and moist air which means that it is more suited to the conservatory than the living room. Keep it pruned to 2–3 ft by trimming in spring.

SECRETS OF SUCCESS

Temperature: Warm — minimum 60°F in winter.

Light: As much light as possible. Shade from hot sun.

Water: Keep compost moist at all times — reduce watering in winter.

Air Humidity: Mist leaves frequently.

Repotting: Repot, if necessary, in early spring.

Propagation: Take stem cuttings in spring. Use a rooting hormone and provide bottom heat.

CALLISTEMON

FLOWERING HOUSE PLANT
page 55

Callistemon citrinus splendens

erect spike 3 in. long

narrow leaf 3 in. long

C. citrinus
Bottlebrush Plant

TYPE

Callistemon citrinus will reach about 3 ft high and in summer the cylindrical flower-spikes appear — no petals, just yellow-tipped red stamens. Leaves bronzy when young.

An excellent choice if you want a 'novelty' plant, and it is also a good one to pick if you want an easy-to-grow specimen which blooms in summer. It does not mind dry air — all it needs is a sunny spot, cool conditions in winter and a good soaking in spring and summer. Prune in early spring and stand the pot outdoors in summer.

SECRETS OF SUCCESS

Temperature: Average warmth — minimum 45°F in winter.

Light: As much light as possible. Shade from hot sun.

Water: Water liberally from spring to late autumn. Water sparingly in winter.

Air Humidity: Misting is not necessary.

Repotting: Repot, if necessary, in spring.

Propagation: Take stem cuttings in spring. Use a rooting hormone and provide bottom heat. Sow seeds in spring.

CAMELLIA

FLOWERING HOUSE PLANT
page 55

Camellia japonica Florentine

glossy leaf 4 in. long

single or double flower 3-5 in. across

C. japonica
Camellia

TYPES

Camellia japonica is the basic species. Well-known varieties include **Adolphe Audusson** (red, semi-double), **Alba Simplex** (white, single) and **Pink Perfection** (pink, double).

It is a waste of time and money to try to grow this temperamental shrub if the conditions are not right. The room must be cool and airy. Buds appear in profusion in early spring, but they will rapidly drop if the plant is moved or if there is a sudden change in temperature or soil moisture. Stand the pot outdoors during summer.

SECRETS OF SUCCESS

Temperature: Cool — keep in the 45°-60°F range.

Light: Brightly lit spot away from direct sun in summer.

Water: Keep compost moist at all times but never waterlogged. Use soft water.

Air Humidity: Mist leaves frequently.

Repotting: Repot in spring — do not repot unless root bound.

Propagation: Take stem cuttings in summer. Use a rooting hormone and provide bottom heat.

Campanula isophylla alba

CAMPANULA

FLOWERING HOUSE PLANT
page 55

grey-green hairy stems 1½ ft long

star-shaped flower 1½ in. wide

C. isophylla
Italian Bellflower

The Italian Bellflower is one of the best of all summer-flowering trailing plants. For generations it has been grown on windowsills and sideboards, its long grey-green stems tumbling down the side of the pot. During the summer these stems bear a profusion of small star-shaped flowers. The blooms are clustered at the tips of the stems, and one of the secrets of success for prolonging the display is to remove the flowers once they have faded. Campanulas are no problem — all you have to provide are bright and fairly cool conditions and a compost which is kept moist throughout the growing season. Once flowering is over, cut back the stems and keep cool and fairly dry during the winter rest period.

SECRETS OF SUCCESS

Temperature: Cool or average warmth — minimum 45°F in winter.

Light: Brightly lit spot away from direct sun in summer.

Water: Keep compost moist at all times — reduce watering in winter.

Air Humidity: Mist leaves occasionally.

Repotting: Repot, if necessary, in spring.

Propagation: Take stem cuttings or sow seeds in spring.

TYPES

Several species of Campanula are grown as house plants. By far the most popular one is **Campanula isophylla** which has many popular names — Italian Bellflower, Star of Bethlehem, Falling Stars, Trailing Campanula etc. The small leaves are pale green and the height of the plant is rarely more than 9 in. The usual flower colour used to be blue, but these days the popular ones are a white variety (**alba**) and a mauve one (**mayi**). **C. fragilis** is quite similar to C. isophylla, bearing blue flowers on 1 ft pendant stems. The main difference is that C. fragilis bears somewhat fleshy leaves. Raise this one from seed.

Capsicum annuum Red Missile

CAPSICUM

FLOWERING POT PLANT
page 57

white, star-shaped flowers followed by fruit

oval leaf 4 in. long

upright fruits darkening with age

C. annuum
Christmas Pepper

These plants are grown for their decorative fruits rather than their leaves or flowers. The leaves are plain and the white blooms which appear in summer or autumn are small. The flowers are followed by the fruits — green at first and then generally turning to shades of yellow, orange or red. They are oval or pointed, depending on the variety, and with care should remain attractive for 2 or 3 months. One of the popular names of this plant is Christmas Pepper as large quantities are sold in December to provide traditional colour during the festive season. A few tips — some direct sunlight is essential, the compost must not be allowed to dry out and hot dry air will cause the fruit to fall.

SECRETS OF SUCCESS

Temperature: Cool or average warmth — minimum 55°F.

Light: Brightly lit spot with morning or afternoon sun.

Water: Keep compost moist at all times. Water occasionally by the immersion method.

Air Humidity: Mist leaves frequently.

Care After Flowering: Plant should be discarded.

Propagation: Difficult — sow seeds in early spring.

TYPES

There are many varieties of **Capsicum annuum** but these are rarely named in the shops. A few bear ball-like fruits, but the popular types bear erect cone-like peppers. These may be 1 in. (**Christmas Greeting**) or 2 in. long (**Fiesta**) and the usual pattern is for them to change from green to yellow and finally red. There are variations — some varieties bear purple fruits (**Variegated Flash** is an example) and some are in full colour in summer — making the common name rather meaningless. These Christmas Peppers have been bred from Chilli and Cayenne Peppers, so the ornamental fruits are definitely not for eating as they are fiery.

Carex morrowii variegata

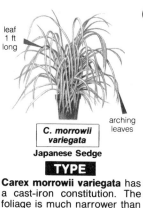

leaf 1 ft long

arching leaves

C. morrowii variegata
Japanese Sedge

TYPE

Carex morrowii variegata has a cast-iron constitution. The foliage is much narrower than the leaves of Chlorophytum and is an excellent choice — but hardly anyone sells it.

CAREX

FOLIAGE HOUSE PLANT page 51

From the vast family of Sedges only one or two are suitable as house plants. The Japanese Sedge is not often seen but is extremely easy to look after indoors. Its white-striped leaves make it a useful specimen for a terrarium or for growing among other plants in an indoor garden. It is one of the most durable of foliage plants, growing happily in sun or shade, low temperatures and in wet or dryish compost.

SECRETS OF SUCCESS

Temperature: Average warmth. Keep cool in winter.
Light: Not fussy — semi-shade, well-lit or sunny.
Water: Keep compost moist but it should not be kept waterlogged.
Air Humidity: Ventilate on warm days.
Repotting: Repot in spring every 2 years.
Propagation: Divide plants at any time of the year.

Catharanthus roseus

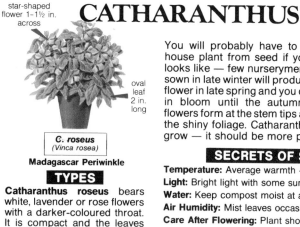

star-shaped flower 1–1½ in. across

oval leaf 2 in. long

C. roseus
(Vinca rosea)
Madagascar Periwinkle

TYPES

Catharanthus roseus bears white, lavender or rose flowers with a darker-coloured throat. It is compact and the leaves have a pale midrib.

CATHARANTHUS

FLOWERING POT PLANT page 57

You will probably have to raise this uncommon house plant from seed if you want to see what it looks like — few nurserymen offer it for sale. Seed sown in late winter will produce plants which start to flower in late spring and you can expect them to stay in bloom until the autumn. The Periwinkle-like flowers form at the stem tips and may cover much of the shiny foliage. Catharanthus is an easy plant to grow — it should be more popular.

SECRETS OF SUCCESS

Temperature: Average warmth — minimum 50°F.
Light: Bright light with some sun.
Water: Keep compost moist at all times.
Air Humidity: Mist leaves occasionally.
Care After Flowering: Plant should be discarded.
Propagation: Sow seeds in late winter or early spring.

Celosia cristata

conical flower-head 6–9 in. long

lance-shaped leaf 4 in. long

C. plumosa
Plume Flower

TYPES

Celosia plumosa bears its red or yellow plumes in summer — dwarfs (8–12 in.) such as **Golden Plume** and **Kewpie** are available. **C. cristata** has a convoluted flower-head.

CELOSIA

FLOWERING POT PLANT page 57

There are two distinct types. Celosia plumosa has feathery plumes — C. cristata has a curious velvety 'cockscomb'. Celosia is sometimes sold for bedding outdoors, but it can be kept in full flower for many weeks indoors. Some direct sunlight is essential, and regular feeding is necessary. It needs cool, airy conditions to prolong the flowering season. The usual height is 1½–2 ft. Celosia can be raised from seed, but it is usually more satisfactory to buy nursery-grown plants.

SECRETS OF SUCCESS

Temperature: Cool — 50°–60°F is ideal.
Light: As much light as possible. Shade from hot sun.
Water: Keep compost moist at all times.
Air Humidity: Mist leaves occasionally.
Care After Flowering: Plant should be discarded.
Propagation: Sow seeds in spring at 60°–65°F.

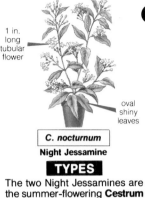

1 in. long tubular flower

oval shiny leaves

C. nocturnum
Night Jessamine

Cestrum elegans

CESTRUM

FLOWERING HOUSE PLANT
page 55

These Jasmine-like plants are all tall, weak-stemmed shrubs which reach 6–10 ft. They are obviously more suited to the conservatory than to the living room, but despite their size the Night Jessamine group are increasing in popularity as house plants in the U.S. These plants can fill a room with the intense fragrance of their white tubular flowers which open at night.

TYPES

The two Night Jessamines are the summer-flowering **Cestrum nocturnum** and **C. parqui**. The Day Jessamines include **C. elegans** (red flowers) and **C. auranticum** (orange flowers).

SECRETS OF SUCCESS

Temperature: Average warmth — minimum 45°F in winter.

Light: Brightly lit spot — protect from summer sun.

Water: Keep compost moist at all times — reduce watering in winter.

Air Humidity: Mist leaves occasionally.

Repotting: Repot, if necessary, in spring.

Propagation: Take stem cuttings in spring. Use a rooting hormone and provide bottom heat.

CHLOROPHYTUM

FOLIAGE HOUSE PLANT
page 51

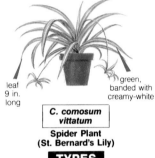

leaf 9 in. long

green, banded with creamy-white

C. comosum vittatum
Spider Plant (St. Bernard's Lily)

TYPES

Chlorophytum comosum has been grown as an indoor plant for over 200 years and is available everywhere. Arching leaves form an attractive rosette, and the long stalks bear plantlets. Several varieties are available. **Vittatum** is the usual one — **variegatum** has green leaves edged with white. **Mandaianum** is compact with yellow-striped leaves.

Chlorophytum is one of the most popular of all house plants. This popularity is not surprising — it is quick growing with attractive arching leaves, and in spring and summer the cascading wiry stems produce small white flowers followed by tiny plantlets. Left on the mother plant, these plantlets grow to give an attractive display, especially in a hanging basket. Removed from the mother plant they can be used to produce new plants. Above all the Spider Plant has the prime requirement for popularity — it is extremely adaptable. It will grow in hot or cool rooms, in sun or shade and doesn't mind dry air.

SECRETS OF SUCCESS

Temperature: Average warmth — minimum 45°F in winter.

Light: A well-lit spot away from direct sunlight.

Water: Water liberally from spring to autumn. Water sparingly in winter.

Air Humidity: Mist leaves occasionally in summer.

Repotting: Repot, if necessary, in spring.

Propagation: Peg down plantlets in compost — cut stem when rooted. Alternatively divide plants at repotting time.

Chlorophytum comosum vittatum

SPECIAL PROBLEMS

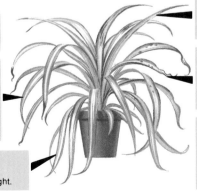

INSECTS
Chlorophytum is virtually pest-free. Aphid may attack if plants are weak.

LEAVES WITH BROWN TIPS
Cause: Most likely reason is underfeeding — don't forget to feed with every watering. Other possible causes are bruising and excessively hot air. Cut off damaged tips and correct the fault.

LEAVES PALE & LIMP IN WINTER. SOME YELLOWING & LEAF FALL
Cause: Too much heat and too little light.

LEAVES WITH BROWN STREAKS IN WINTER
Cause: Too much water under cool conditions when the plant is not growing. Water sparingly in winter.

LEAVES CURLED WITH BROWN SPOTS & EDGES. SOME YELLOWING & LEAF FALL
Cause: The soil around the roots has dried out. Chlorophytum needs a plentiful supply of water when it is actively growing.

NO STEMS
Cause: The plant is too young; stems bearing plantlets will not form until the plant is mature. If it is mature, then lack of space is the most likely cause; avoid overcrowding.

CHRYSANTHEMUM

FLOWERING POT PLANT *page 57*

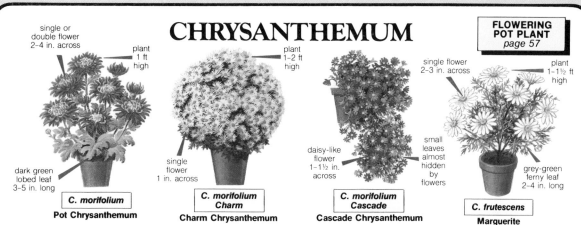

single or double flower 2-4 in. across — plant 1 ft high

dark green lobed leaf 3-5 in. long

C. morifolium
Pot Chrysanthemum

plant 1-2 ft high — single flower 1 in. across

C. morifolium Charm
Charm Chrysanthemum

daisy-like flower 1-1½ in. across

C. morifolium Cascade
Cascade Chrysanthemum

single flower 2-3 in. across — plant 1-1½ ft high

small leaves almost hidden by flowers

grey-green ferny leaf 2-4 in. long

C. frutescens
Marguerite

In recent years the Pot Chrysanthemum has become a favourite pot plant. The nurseryman uses chemicals to dwarf its growth and keeps it in the dark for part of the day to make it bloom on a set date. By this means Pot Chrysanthemums, less than 1 ft high but large-flowered in every colour but blue, are offered for sale in bloom throughout the year. If you choose your plant carefully and look after it properly then it should stay in bloom for 6-8 weeks. In the shop there should be a few open blooms and a mass of buds which are showing colour. At home place the pot in a cool room on a windowsill where it will get some early morning or evening sunlight. By comparison the other types (Marguerites, Charm Chrysanthemums and Cascade Chrysanthemums) are almost rarities.

SECRETS OF SUCCESS

Temperature: Cool — 50°-60°F is ideal.

Light: Bright light is essential, but Pot Chrysanthemums must be shaded from midday sun.

Water: Keep compost moist at all times. It may be necessary to water several times each week.

Air Humidity: Mist leaves occasionally.

Care After Flowering: Most plants are discarded, but Pot Chrysanthemums can be planted out in the garden where they will revert to their natural growth habit.

Propagation: Raising Pot Chrysanthemums is for the professional. Marguerites — take stem cuttings in early summer. Cascade and Charm Chrysanthemums — sow seeds in spring.

SPECIAL PROBLEMS

WILTED LEAVES
Cause: Underwatering is the most likely reason. Even a short period of dryness will lead to wilting and this generally causes the lower leaves to fall.

FLOWER BUDS FAIL TO OPEN
Cause: Two major reasons cause buds not to open. The buds may have been all-green when the plant was purchased or the plant was not placed in a bright enough spot.

SHORT FLOWERING PERIOD
Cause: The plant is too warm. Temperatures of 70°-75°F result in the flowers rapidly opening and then wilting.

INSECTS
Aphid and red spider mite can be problems — see Chapter 7.

TYPES

Unlike the ordinary types of **Chrysanthemum morifolium** which are grown in the greenhouse, the Pot Chrysanthemum is usually bought by colour and not by variety name. The Charm Chrysanthemum is a variety of C. morifolium which produces its single flowers so abundantly in summer and autumn that the foliage may be almost entirely covered. White, orange, yellow, pink and red strains are available. You will have to raise your own plants from seed — the same course of action is necessary for obtaining specimens of Cascade Chrysanthemums. The trailing stems can be trained into decorative shapes on wire frames — a mass of flowers cover the stems in late summer and autumn. The baby of the house plant Chrysanthemums is the Mini-Mum (single flowers, 6-8 in. high).

Marguerites (**C. frutescens**) are generally summer flowering. The central disc of each flower is yellow — the surrounding petals may be white, yellow or pink.

Chrysanthemum morifolium Princess Anne

Chrysanthemum frutescens

CINERARIA

FLOWERING POT PLANT
page 57

daisy-like flower 1-3 in. across

plant 9 in.-2½ ft tall

underside usually purple

heart-shaped leaf up to 8 in. across

Senecio cruentus
(Senecio hybridus)

Cineraria

A well-grown Cineraria (proper name Senecio cruentus) is always a welcome gift. Masses of Daisy-like flowers cover the soft, heart-shaped leaves and the colour range is impressive — white, blue, purple, pink and red varieties are available. The showiest strain is the Grandiflora group — large-flowered plants about 18 in. high. The tallest Cinerarias are varieties belonging to the Stellata group, reaching a height of 2 ft or more with small, star-shaped flowers. At the other end of the scale is the Nana group, small and compact, with masses of brightly-coloured flowers. Buy plants with some open flowers and masses of unopened buds. They should last for 4-6 weeks. Unfortunately Cineraria can be a disappointing plant and will collapse in a week or two in a hot room or if it is not watered properly.

SPECIAL PROBLEMS

YELLOWING, WILTED FOLIAGE
Cause: Cold draughts are the usual culprit, although wilting is the first sign of underwatering. A wilted plant may recover if watered and moved to a draught-free spot, but the flowering period is bound to be shortened.

SHORT FLOWERING PERIOD
Cause: Too much warmth — temperature above 60°F speeds up flower death. Too much sun and too little water can also bring flowering to a premature end.

SUDDEN PLANT COLLAPSE
Cause: Waterlogging due to overwatering or poor drainage.

SECRETS OF SUCCESS

Temperature: Cool — 45°-55°F is ideal.

Light: Bright light away from direct sunlight.

Water: Keep compost moist at all times with tepid water. Take care not to overwater.

Air Humidity: Stand pot on a pebble tray (see page 19) or surround with damp peat. Occasionally mist air around the plant.

Care After Flowering: Plant should be discarded.

Propagation: Not easy — sow seeds in midsummer in a cool greenhouse.

TYPES

There are scores of **Senecio cruentus** hybrids, varying in height, colour and flower form. The usual flower form is the typical Daisy pattern — a central boss of stamens and a ring of wide or narrow petals. In the Grandiflora group the petals generally have an inner white ring and with a typical Cineraria the flower-head measures about 9 in. across. Double-flowered types in which the central disc is hidden by petals are available, but they are not popular. The growth form is a leafy bush — large and rounded in the Grandifloras (which occasionally need staking) or small and compact with the Multiflora Nana group. The exception is the Stellata group — the stems are branched and spreading. Cinerarias are bought between late winter and mid spring — after brightening the home for several weeks they are thrown away.

GRANDIFLORA
bloom 2-3 in. across
plant 1½-2 ft high

DOUBLE
bloom 2 in. across
plant 1-2 ft high

Exhibition Mixed (Grandiflora strain. Height 1½ ft)

Spring Glory (Multiflora Nana strain. Height 9 in.)

Gaytime (Multiflora Nana strain. Height 10 in.)

Triumph (Multiflora Nana strain. Height 1 ft)

Gubler's Mixed (Double strain. Height 1½ ft)

Mixed Star (Double strain. Height 2 ft)

MULTIFLORA NANA
bloom 1-2 in. across
plant 9 in.-1¼ ft high

STELLATA
bloom 1-1½ in. across
plant 2-2½ ft high

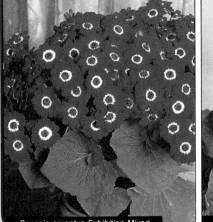

Senecio cruentus Exhibition Mixed

Senecio cruentus Spring Glory

Senecio cruentus Gubler's Mixed

CITRUS

FOLIAGE HOUSE PLANT page 51

FLOWERING HOUSE PLANT page 55

leathery leaf 3 in. long

white fragrant flowers followed by small fruit — flowers and fruit appear all year round

C. mitis

Calamondin Orange

There is an obvious fascination in having an orange or lemon tree at home, but if you want it to bear fruit then you will have to buy a Citrus tree selected for its ability to grow indoors. The problem is that plants raised at home from pips will not fruit until they are too large for an ordinary room. The dwarfs sold as house plants are shrubby trees which have glossy leaves and produce fruit while the plant is still quite young. Summer is the usual flowering period, but the Calamondin Orange may produce white fragrant flowers and small bitter oranges nearly all year round. Cultivation is straightforward — the basic requirements are good drainage, freedom from draughts, careful watering, ample feeding and cool but not cold conditions in winter. Summer should be spent outdoors. Two tips — pollinate the flowers by dabbing with cotton wool and apply MultiTonic if yellowing leaves reveal magnesium deficiency.

SECRETS OF SUCCESS

Temperature: Average warmth — minimum 50°F in winter.

Light: Choose the sunniest spot available.

Water: Water moderately all year round.

Air Humidity: Mist leaves occasionally.

Repotting: Repot, if necessary, in spring.

Propagation: Take stem cuttings in spring. Use a rooting hormone and provide bottom heat.

TYPES

A number of Citrus species and varieties can be relied upon to form oranges or lemons indoors, but you will have to provide good conditions and even then you cannot expect to match the quality of shop-bought fruits. **Citrus mitis (Citrofortunella mitis)** is the most popular species — a 4 ft bush which bears small (1–1½ in. diameter) bitter oranges whilst the plant is still quite small. Other indoor types include the Sweet Orange (**C. sinensis** — 4 ft, spiny, 2½ in. fruits under greenhouse conditions), Lemon (**C. limon** — the dwarf varieties are **meyeri** and the large-fruited **Ponderosa**) and Seville Orange (**C. aurantium** or **C. sinensis** — 3 ft spiny tree). An interesting house plant variety, if you can find it, is the Otaheite Orange (**C. taitensis**). The pink-tinged white flowers are very fragrant and are followed by orange-coloured fruit.

Citrus mitis

Citrus limon

CLERODENDRUM

FLOWERING HOUSE PLANT page 55

inflated flower 1 in. long — white with red tip

leaf 5 in. long

C. thomsoniae

Glory Bower

TYPE

Clerodendrum thomsoniae has long, weak stems — pinch out tips for room display. Allow stems to trail or to twine around an upright support. The leaves have a quilted look.

The Glory Bower is usually regarded as a greenhouse plant, its climbing stems reaching 8 ft or more. By pruning in winter, however, it can be trained as a bush or hanging basket plant. The flowers appear in summer among the heart-shaped leaves. In summer it requires high air humidity, good light and warmth — in winter it must be given a rest with infrequent watering and cool conditions.

SECRETS OF SUCCESS

Temperature: Warm or average warmth. Keep cool (55°–60°F) in winter.

Light: Brightly lit spot away from direct sunlight.

Water: Keep compost moist at all times throughout spring and summer — water very sparingly in winter.

Air Humidity: Mist leaves frequently.

Repotting: Repot in spring every year.

Propagation: Take stem cuttings in spring.

Clerodendrum thomsoniae

CLEYERA

FOLIAGE HOUSE PLANT page 51

Cleyera japonica variegata

leaves reddish when young

leaf 3 in. long

C. japonica variegata

TYPES

Cleyera japonica grows about 2 ft tall. The glossy-leaved variegated form — **C. (or Eurya) japonica variegata** is the one to look for, but you will certainly not find it at your local garden centre.

Cleyera japonica is a rarity in Britain. It deserves to be more popular as it is easy to grow and does not drop its leaves at the first change in conditions — an annoying habit of some other variegated-leaved shrubby plants. It is slow growing and it can be kept compact by occasionally removing the shoot tips. Small white flowers may appear as a bonus.

SECRETS OF SUCCESS

Temperature: Average warmth. Keep cool in winter — minimum temperature 50°F.

Light: Well-lit but away from direct sunlight.

Water: Keep compost moist at all times. Use rainwater if tap water is hard.

Air Humidity: Mist leaves occasionally.

Repotting: Repot, if necessary, in spring.

Propagation: Take stem cuttings in summer.

CLIANTHUS

FLOWERING HOUSE PLANT page 55

Clianthus formosus

beak-like flower 2 in. long

feathery leaf 6 in. long

C. formosus

Glory Pea

TYPES

Two types are grown — both are rarities. They are **Clianthus formosus** (2 ft, late spring-summer flowers) and **C. puniceus** (10 ft climber, late spring flowers).

Lobster Claw is an apt description of the large claw-like red flowers which are borne in clusters in late spring or summer. Prune and train the stems once flowering is over and in summer provide adequate ventilation. The low-growing C. formosus is short-lived and is best treated as an annual — the tall-growing C. puniceus (Parrot Bill) can be kept as a room plant but is best grown in the conservatory.

SECRETS OF SUCCESS

Temperature: Average warmth. Keep cool in winter.

Light: Keep in full sun.

Water: Water liberally from spring to autumn. Water sparingly in winter.

Air Humidity: Mist leaves occasionally on hot days.

Repotting: Repot, if necessary, in spring.

Propagation: Sow seeds in warm conditions in spring. Take Parrot Bill stem cuttings in summer.

CLIVIA

FLOWERING HOUSE PLANT page 55

Clivia miniata

bell-shaped flower 3 in. across

strap-like leaf 1½ ft long

C. miniata

Kaffir Lily

TYPES

Clivia miniata bears clusters of 10–20 flowers in early spring on top of a tall stalk. Orange, red, yellow and cream varieties are available.

An old favourite which will fail to bloom year after year if it is left in a heated room in winter or if the watering rules are not followed. It needs space. It needs winter rest — an unheated room, no fertilizer and just enough water to prevent wilting. And it needs to be undisturbed — don't move the pot when in bud or flower and don't repot unless the plant is pushing out of the container.

SECRETS OF SUCCESS

Temperature: Cool or average warmth. Keep cool (40°–50°F) in winter.

Light: Bright light — avoid direct sun in summer.

Water: Water moderately from spring to autumn. Water sparingly from late autumn until stalk is 4–6 in. high.

Air Humidity: Sponge leaves occasionally.

Repotting: Repot, if necessary, after flowering.

Propagation: Divide plants at repotting time.

CODIAEUM (CROTON)

FOLIAGE HOUSE PLANT page 51

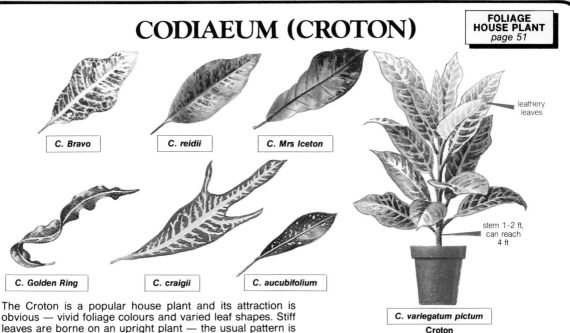

C. Bravo

C. reidii

C. Mrs Iceton

C. Golden Ring

C. craigii

C. aucubifolium

leathery leaves

stem 1–2 ft, can reach 4 ft

C. variegatum pictum
Croton
(Joseph's Coat)

The Croton is a popular house plant and its attraction is obvious — vivid foliage colours and varied leaf shapes. Stiff leaves are borne on an upright plant — the usual pattern is large and lobed foliage on which there are distinctly coloured veins. A tough-looking plant in the shop or garden centre, but before you buy one of the hybrids of Codiaeum variegatum pictum you must make sure that you can satisfy its fussy requirements. It will need a fairly constant temperature which will not drop below 60°F and it will need high air humidity. The compost will have to be kept moist at all times during the growing season with tepid water, and you will have to keep the pot away from draughts. Regular feeding is necessary during the growing season but it should be stopped in winter when proper care calls for moderately warm air and rather dry compost. Your reward for creating the right conditions will be a colourful bush with the clear sign of the expert . . . the lower stem of a Croton fully clothed with leaves.

SECRETS OF SUCCESS

Temperature: Warm — minimum 60°F in winter.

Light: Good light is necessary — an east- or west-facing windowsill is ideal.

Water: Water liberally from spring to autumn. Water sparingly in winter.

Air Humidity: Air must be moist. Mist leaves regularly — daily if possible. Wash leaves frequently.

Repotting: Repot, if necessary, in spring.

Propagation: Take stem cuttings in spring. Use a rooting hormone and provide bottom heat.

SPECIAL PROBLEMS

LOSS OF LOWER LEAVES
Cause: If brown tips are present — air or compost is too dry. If brown edges are present — temperature is too low.

LOSS OF LEAF COLOUR
Cause: Not enough light.

INSECTS
Red spider mite and scale can be problems — see Chapter 7 for details.

TYPES

The basic variety is **Codiaeum variegatum pictum**, and over the years hundreds of different named types have appeared. Most have Laurel-like foliage, but there are also forked leaves, long ribbons, lobed leaves, twisted and curled types. Identification is not easy — the colour often changes with age, a pink or red hue taking over from the yellows and greens. Examples of well-known varieties include **Appleleaf** and **Vulcan** (yellow with red edges and green veins), **Norma** (green with red veins and splashes of yellow), **aucubifolium** (green with yellow spots), **Bravo** (green splashed with yellow). **Reidii** is popular — so are the lobed varieties such as **craigii** and **holuffiana**. There are many, many others, such as **Mrs Iceton**, **Excellent**, **Gold Finger**, **Gold Sun**, **Julietta**, **Petra**, **Europa**, **Gold Star** and **Gold Moon**.

Codiaeum Norma

Codiaeum Gold Finger

COLEUS

**FOLIAGE
HOUSE PLANT**
page 51

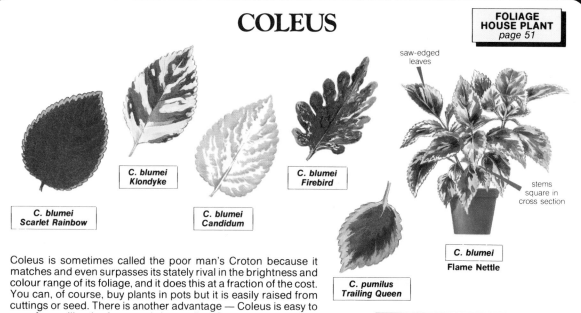

C. blumei
Klondyke

C. blumei
Scarlet Rainbow

C. blumei
Candidum

C. blumei
Firebird

saw-edged leaves

stems square in cross section

C. blumei
Flame Nettle

C. pumilus
Trailing Queen

Coleus is sometimes called the poor man's Croton because it matches and even surpasses its stately rival in the brightness and colour range of its foliage, and it does this at a fraction of the cost. You can, of course, buy plants in pots but it is easily raised from cuttings or seed. There is another advantage — Coleus is easy to care for, unlike the fussy and demanding Croton.

But there are features where Coleus is clearly inferior to the imposing and long-lived Croton. The bushy 1 ft high plants are soft-stemmed and need pinching out regularly to stop the plant becoming leggy and defoliated. In addition the specimens remain attractive for only a short time — they can be overwintered but the best plan is to treat this foliage plant as an annual by sowing seeds or taking cuttings each spring.

Coleus offers a multicoloured display at minimum cost if you follow a few simple rules. Good light is essential — winter colours are more muted than summer ones. Use soft water if you can and the compost should be only just moist during the winter months. Mist the leaves in summer and keep watch for aphids.

SECRETS OF SUCCESS

Temperature: Average warmth — minimum 50°F.

Light: Give as much light as possible, but shade from summer noonday sun.

Water: Keep compost moist at all times — reduce watering in winter. Use rainwater if tap water is hard.

Air Humidity: Moist air is necessary. Mist leaves frequently.

Repotting: Cut back and repot in spring.

Propagation: Take stem cuttings in spring or summer. Alternatively sow seeds in early spring.

SPECIAL PROBLEMS

LEGGY STEMS
Cause: Young plants — not enough light or failure to pinch out tips. Old plants — normal effect, nothing can be done.

LEAF DROP
Cause: Not enough water; in summer it may be necessary to water every day.

TYPES

There is a bewildering choice of **Coleus blumei** hybrids. The usual height is 1–2 ft, but dwarf varieties such as **Sabre** are available. Most (but not all) have nettle-like leaves — there are also ruffled ones (e.g **The Chief**), frilly ones (e.g **Firebird**) and wavy-edged ones (e.g **Butterfly**). There is no basic colour — almost every conceivable mixture can be found. There are some attractive single-coloured varieties, such as **Golden Bedder** (yellow) and **Volcano** (deep red), but the usual choice is for a multicoloured Coleus. Several varieties (e.g **Scarlet Poncho**, **Milky Way** and **Fashion Parade**) can be grown from seed. There is a trailing species — **C. pumilus** (**C. rehneltianus**). The largest and most colourful leaves are borne by **C. verschaffeltii** — numerous varieties are available from specialist suppliers.

Coleus Salmon Lace

Coleus Glory of Luxembourg

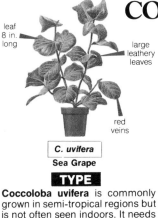

leaf
8 in.
long

large
leathery
leaves

red
veins

C. uvifera
Sea Grape

Coccoloba uvifera

COCCOLOBA

FOLIAGE
HOUSE PLANT
page 51

Coccoloba is a plant for the lover of rarities — it will grow in the house but it is more suited to the conservatory. As an indoor plant it is grown for its stiff, olive-green leaves — the red veins turn pale cream with age. Under natural conditions fragrant white flowers appear and these are followed by red grape-like fruits — unfortunately the plant won't flower indoors.

SECRETS OF SUCCESS

Temperature: Average warmth — minimum 55°F in winter.

Light: Well-lit but away from direct sunlight.

Water: Keep compost moist at all times.

Air Humidity: Mist leaves regularly.

Repotting: Repot, if necessary, in spring.

Propagation: Take stem cuttings in summer. Use a rooting hormone and provide bottom heat.

TYPE

Coccoloba uvifera is commonly grown in semi-tropical regions but is not often seen indoors. It needs space — grow it in a large tub so that it can show off its leaves.

COLUMNEA

FLOWERING
HOUSE PLANT
page 55

leaf covered with reddish hairs

tubular 3 in. long scarlet flower — yellow throated

stems 3 ft long, much less branching than C. banksii

C. gloriosa
Goldfish Plant

leaf smooth and waxy, underside red

branching stems 3 ft long

tubular 2½ in. long scarlet flower — yellow-lined at mouth

C. banksii
Goldfish Plant

There are numerous varieties of Columnea which with proper care will bear abundant yellow, orange or red tubular flowers year after year in winter or early spring. It belongs in a hanging basket or in a pot where its trailing stems can be allowed to hang freely.

It is not an easy plant to care for. Columnea may survive under poor conditions, but leaves will fall and flowers will refuse to appear unless it is pampered. This calls for meeting a number of special requirements — top of the list is frequent misting to maintain a moist atmosphere around the foliage. The compost must be kept on the dry side in winter and during this period you should aim to maintain the night-time temperature at 55°–65°F. Very few pests attack this attractive plant but botrytis will be a problem if you overwater. Feed at regular intervals in spring and summer, and trim back the stems once flowering is over.

SECRETS OF SUCCESS

Temperature: Average warmth — minimum 55°F in winter.

Light: Bright light — avoid direct sunshine.

Water: Keep compost moist at all times during the growing season. Water sparingly in winter.

Air Humidity: Mist leaves frequently.

Repotting: Repot in late spring every 2 years.

Propagation: Take stem cuttings after flowering. Use a rooting hormone and provide bottom heat.

TYPES

Unless you are skilled it is wise to choose one of the easier types. Perhaps the most popular one is **Columnea banksii** with its small, dark green foliage and yellow-marked red flowers. **C. Stavanger** is quite similar — smooth leaves, yellow and red flowers and branching stems, but the leaves and blooms are larger. The hairy-leaved Columneas are more difficult to grow. **C. gloriosa** is an old favourite and so is **C. microphylla** which has 4 ft long stems, tiny leaves and C. gloriosa-like flowers. **C. hirta** is a smaller plant with creeping stems which produces flowers very freely in spring. A few types (e.g **C. crassifolia**) have an erect or semi-erect growth habit.

Columnea banksii

Columnea gloriosa

COFFEA

FOLIAGE HOUSE PLANT
page 51

Coffea won't disappoint if you expect an attractive bush with dark, shiny and wavy-edged leaves. It will disappoint if you expect coffee beans for breakfast. It is an undemanding plant, but the compost must never be allowed to dry out, and draughts are positively harmful. It can reach 4 ft or more, but you can keep it in check by pruning in spring.

leaf 6 in. long

wavy-edged leaves

C. arabica
Coffee Tree

TYPES

The true Coffee Tree (**Coffea arabica**) can be grown indoors and may flower after a few years. The variety **nana** is smaller but flowers more readily.

Coffea arabica

SECRETS OF SUCCESS

Temperature: Average warmth — minimum 50°F in winter.

Light: Bright light — avoid direct sunshine.

Water: Keep compost moist at all times.

Air Humidity: Mist leaves occasionally.

Repotting: Repot in spring every 2 years.

Propagation: Take stem cuttings in summer. Plants can be raised from unroasted coffee beans.

CONIFERS

FOLIAGE HOUSE PLANT
page 51

Until recently Conifers were not regarded as house plants. Nowadays there are several varieties of Cupressus and Chamaecyparis which have proved their worth in the home — all are slow growing but it may be necessary to prune the stems in early spring to keep the plants in bounds. They are easy to look after and are best used in group plantings as a background to more colourful specimens.

scale-like leaves

yellow feathery sprays

Cupressus macrocarpa
Goldcrest

TYPES

Cupressus macrocarpa Goldcrest (upright) and **C. cashmeriana** (weeping) are attractive trees. Recent introductions are the **Chamaecyparis pisifera** varieties **squarrosa intermedia** and **squarrosa sulphurea**.

Chamaecyparis pisifera squarrosa sulphurea

SECRETS OF SUCCESS

Temperature: Average warmth — minimum 45°F in winter.

Light: Bright light — avoid direct sunshine.

Water: Water liberally from spring to autumn. Water sparingly in winter.

Air Humidity: Mist leaves occasionally.

Repotting: Repot in spring every 2 years.

Propagation: Take stem cuttings in spring.

COSTUS

FLOWERING POT PLANT
page 57

The place for Costus is a greenhouse or conservatory — it will deteriorate in the living room. The leaves are large and in some species attractively marked — they spiral around the stem. The flowers appear in late spring — colourful but short-lived. Costus has a resting period in winter when the leaves die.

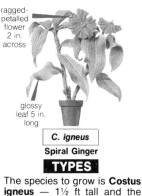

ragged-petalled flower 2 in. across

glossy leaf 5 in. long

C. igneus
Spiral Ginger

TYPES

The species to grow is **Costus igneus** — 1½ ft tall and the most popular Spiral Ginger. The other species are large and spreading. Examples are **C. speciosus** (6 ft) and **C. lucanusianus** (5 ft).

Costus igneus

SECRETS OF SUCCESS

Temperature: Warm — minimum 55°F in winter.

Light: Provide as much light as possible, but shade from midday summer sun.

Water: Keep compost very moist during the growing season.

Air Humidity: Surround the pot with damp peat or stand pot on a pebble tray.

Repotting: Repot, if necessary, in spring.

Propagation: Divide plants at repotting time.

CRINUM

FLOWERING HOUSE PLANT *page 55*

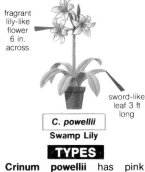

fragrant lily-like flower 6 in. across

sword-like leaf 3 ft long

C. powellii
Swamp Lily

Everything about Crinum is extraordinarily large — the 6 in. bulb, the 3 ft tall flower-stalk and the magnificent 7 in. long trumpets in late summer. You will need patience if you begin by planting a bulb — it will take several years before flowering starts. The floral display lasts for 4–5 weeks, after which it needs to rest in a cool room or greenhouse.

SECRETS OF SUCCESS

Temperature: Average warmth. Keep cool in winter.

Light: Bright light with some direct sun.

Water: Water liberally from spring until flowering stops. Water sparingly in winter.

Air Humidity: Sponge leaves occasionally.

Repotting: Repot in spring every 3–4 years.

Propagation: Detach offsets from mature plants and pot up in summer.

TYPES

Crinum powellii has pink drooping flowers. There are several hybrids with white, pink or red blooms. **C. bulbispermum** flowers are white inside, deep pink outside.

Crinum powellii

CROSSANDRA

FLOWERING HOUSE PLANT *page 55*

tubular flower 1½ in. across

glossy leaf 3 in. long

C. undulifolia
Firecracker Flower

Crossandra starts to flower when only a few months old and the flowering season lasts from spring to autumn. The blooms are borne on top of green flowering spikes. The disadvantage of the Firecracker Flower is its need for moist air — it will probably not survive unless frequently misted and surrounded by other plants. Remove dead blooms to prolong the flowering season.

SECRETS OF SUCCESS

Temperature: Average warmth — minimum 55°F in winter.

Light: Bright light — avoid direct sun in summer.

Water: Keep compost moist at all times. Reduce watering in winter.

Air Humidity: Mist leaves frequently.

Repotting: Repot, if necessary, in spring.

Propagation: Take stem cuttings in summer. Use a rooting hormone and provide bottom heat.

TYPES

Crossandra undulifolia (sometimes sold as **C. infundibuliformis**) grows about 1–2 ft high. The variety **Mona Wallhed** is reputed to be the best type.

Crossandra undulifolia

CUPHEA

FLOWERING HOUSE PLANT *page 55*

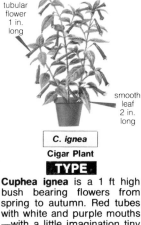

tubular flower 1 in. long

smooth leaf 2 in. long

C. ignea
Cigar Plant

A pretty plant, rather than a spectacular one. It can be used in a mixed display, but is not bold enough to serve as a specimen plant. It grows quickly, reaching its full height in a single season. Cigar-shaped flowers are borne in profusion among the narrow leaves. Overwinter the plant in a cool room and water sparingly. Cut back the stems in early spring.

SECRETS OF SUCCESS

Temperature: Average warmth — minimum 45°F in winter.

Light: Choose a well-lit spot — some direct sunlight is beneficial.

Water: Keep compost moist at all times. Reduce watering in winter.

Air Humidity: Misting is not necessary.

Repotting: Repot, if necessary, in spring.

Propagation: Take stem cuttings in spring or summer. Sow seeds in spring.

TYPE

Cuphea ignea is a 1 ft high bush bearing flowers from spring to autumn. Red tubes with white and purple mouths —with a little imagination tiny ash-tipped cigars.

Cuphea ignea

CYCLAMEN

FLOWERING POT PLANT
page 57

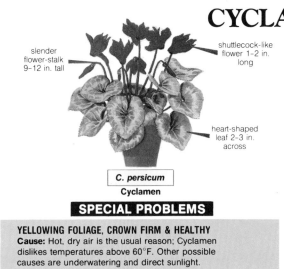

slender
flower-stalk
9–12 in. tall

shuttlecock-like
flower 1–2 in.
long

heart-shaped
leaf 2–3 in.
across

C. persicum
Cyclamen

Cyclamen is one of the most popular of all winter-flowering pot plants and its charm is obvious. Compact growth, beautiful swept-back flowers on long stalks and decorative foliage which is patterned in silver and green. The blooms are in bright colours or pastel shades, large and eye-catching or small and perfumed.

Most Cyclamens are unfortunately consigned to the dustbin after a few weeks. With care they will bloom indoors for several months and then can be kept to provide another display next winter. First of all, try to buy a plant in autumn and not in mid winter, and choose one with plenty of unopened buds. Then put it in a suitable home — a north-facing windowsill is ideal. The spot must be cool and away from direct sunlight — a warm room means a short life for a Cyclamen.

SPECIAL PROBLEMS

YELLOWING FOLIAGE, CROWN FIRM & HEALTHY
Cause: Hot, dry air is the usual reason; Cyclamen dislikes temperatures above 60°F. Other possible causes are underwatering and direct sunlight.

PLANT COLLAPSE, CROWN SOFT & ROTTEN
Cause: Overwatering, especially from above. Never let water stand on the fleshy crown.

SHORT FLOWERING PERIOD
Cause: There are many possible reasons — too much warmth, incorrect watering and dry air are common causes. Feed regularly during the growing and flowering season.

TWISTED, STUNTED LEAVES
Cause: Cyclamen mite — see page 244 for details.

SECRETS OF SUCCESS

Temperature: Cool — 50°–60°F is ideal.

Light: Bright light away from direct sunlight.

Water: Keep compost moist at all times. Employ the immersion method (see page 231) using soft water.

Air Humidity: Stand pot on a pebble tray (see page 19) or surround with damp peat. Occasionally mist air around the plant.

Care After Flowering: Reduce watering and stop feeding. Place pot on its side in a cool spot and keep it dry until midsummer. Then repot using fresh compost, burying the tuber to half its depth. Stand the pot in a cool, well-lit spot — water to keep the compost moist.

Propagation: Sow seeds in late summer at 60°–70°F. Most varieties take 15–18 months to flower — miniatures take only 6–8 months.

TYPES

The wild **Cyclamen persicum** of the Middle East has narrow, pink petals — the hybrids which first began to appear about 100 years ago are sometimes listed as **C. persicum giganteum**. These plants have wide petals which may be frilled and are available in many colours — white, pink, red, purple and salmon. Fragrant varieties are available and the foliage is usually edged, marbled or lined in white. This leaf patterning is sometimes bold enough to rival the flowers in display value. Cyclamens are bought in vast numbers between autumn and early spring. You can save the tubers for planting in summer but it is usually better to buy fresh ones. You can also raise Cyclamen from seed, but you may have to wait about 1½ years for the plants to bloom. Move established standard seedlings into 5 in. pots — 3½ in. pots for miniatures. Once there were only standard-sized hybrids but now there are also dwarfs with pretty scented flowers on stalks which are only a few inches high.

Cyclamen persicum Decora

Standard varieties: Height 12 in.

Triumph series: Large and abundant flowers. Attractive leaves.

Rex series: Compact plants. Leaves boldly marbled in silver.

Decora series: Noted for pastel shades (salmon, lavender etc). Leaves marbled in silver.

Sweetheart series: Fragrant flowers in a wide range of colours. Leaves marked in silver.

Firmament series: Large flowers. Noted for early flowering.

Ruffled series: Fringed petals.

Other standard varieties include **Candlestick** (pink), **Vogt's Double** (double pink), **Cardinal** (red) and **Cattleya** (lavender).

Intermediate variety: Height 9 in.

Turbo/Laser series: Compact and fast growing. Up to 35 flowers at one time.

Miniature varieties: Height 6 in. or less

Mirabelle series: Small leaves, wide colour range.

Tiny Mites series: Smallest of all — dainty flowers in a wide range of colours.

Puppet series: Scented flowers.

Kaori series: Scented flowers with a distinct eye.

Cyclamen persicum Suttons Puppet

CYPERUS

FOLIAGE HOUSE PLANT *page 51*

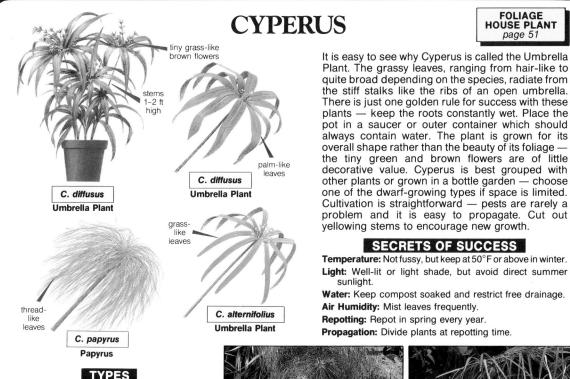

tiny grass-like brown flowers

stems 1–2 ft high

C. diffusus
Umbrella Plant

palm-like leaves

C. diffusus
Umbrella Plant

grass-like leaves

thread-like leaves

C. papyrus
Papyrus

C. alternifolius
Umbrella Plant

It is easy to see why Cyperus is called the Umbrella Plant. The grassy leaves, ranging from hair-like to quite broad depending on the species, radiate from the stiff stalks like the ribs of an open umbrella. There is just one golden rule for success with these plants — keep the roots constantly wet. Place the pot in a saucer or outer container which should always contain water. The plant is grown for its overall shape rather than the beauty of its foliage — the tiny green and brown flowers are of little decorative value. Cyperus is best grouped with other plants or grown in a bottle garden — choose one of the dwarf-growing types if space is limited. Cultivation is straightforward — pests are rarely a problem and it is easy to propagate. Cut out yellowing stems to encourage new growth.

SECRETS OF SUCCESS

Temperature: Not fussy, but keep at 50°F or above in winter.

Light: Well-lit or light shade, but avoid direct summer sunlight.

Water: Keep compost soaked and restrict free drainage.

Air Humidity: Mist leaves frequently.

Repotting: Repot in spring every year.

Propagation: Divide plants at repotting time.

TYPES

Cyperus papyrus (5–8 ft) is an interesting plant as it was the source of both paper and Moses' cradle in biblical times, but it is too tall and difficult for most homes. The popular one is **C. alternifolius** which bears long and narrow leaves and grows about 3 ft tall when mature. There are several attractive varieties, including the white-striped **variegatus** and the dwarf (1–1½ ft) **gracilis**. Another compact type is **C. diffusus** which is easy to find — the 1 ft **C. esculentus** which produces Tiger nuts underground is much more difficult to obtain. The showiest flower-heads are borne by **C. haspan**.

Cyperus papyrus

Cyperus alternifolius variegatus

CYTISUS

FLOWERING POT PLANT *page 57*

Cytisus racemosus

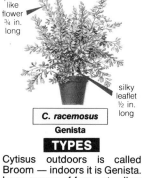

pea-like flower ¾ in. long

silky leaflet ½ in. long

C. racemosus
Genista

TYPES

Cytisus outdoors is called Broom — indoors it is Genista. Long sprays of fragrant yellow flowers appear in spring at the end of arching branches. Choose **Cytisus racemosus** rather than **C. canariensis**.

Two types of Cytisus are sold for indoor cultivation — C. canariensis and the more attractive C. racemosus. These shrubs must spend their summers outdoors. They are stood out after the shoots which have borne flowers are cut back. In early autumn the plants are brought back indoors and kept in a cool room. In mid winter move to a bright, warmer spot and water more freely.

SECRETS OF SUCCESS

Temperature: Cool — minimum 40°F in winter.

Light: Well-lit during the flowering season — light shade in winter.

Water: Water liberally during the flowering season.

Air Humidity: Mist leaves frequently during the flowering season.

Repotting: Repot, if necessary, after flowering.

Propagation: Take stem cuttings in summer.

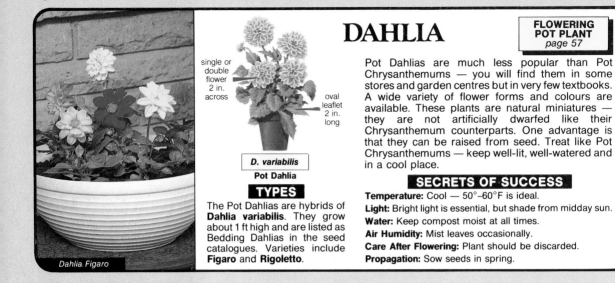

DAHLIA

FLOWERING POT PLANT page 57

single or double flower 2 in. across

oval leaflet 2 in. long

D. variabilis

Pot Dahlia

TYPES

The Pot Dahlias are hybrids of **Dahlia variabilis**. They grow about 1 ft high and are listed as Bedding Dahlias in the seed catalogues. Varieties include **Figaro** and **Rigoletto**.

Dahlia Figaro

Pot Dahlias are much less popular than Pot Chrysanthemums — you will find them in some stores and garden centres but in very few textbooks. A wide variety of flower forms and colours are available. These plants are natural miniatures — they are not artificially dwarfed like their Chrysanthemum counterparts. One advantage is that they can be raised from seed. Treat like Pot Chrysanthemums — keep well-lit, well-watered and in a cool place.

SECRETS OF SUCCESS

Temperature: Cool — 50°–60°F is ideal.

Light: Bright light is essential, but shade from midday sun.

Water: Keep compost moist at all times.

Air Humidity: Mist leaves occasionally.

Care After Flowering: Plant should be discarded.

Propagation: Sow seeds in spring.

DATURA

FLOWERING HOUSE PLANT page 55

oval leaf 9 in. long

tubular flower 8–10 in. long

D. candida

Angel's Trumpet

TYPES

Two species are sold as house plants — **Datura candida** and **D. suaveolens**. Both bear sweet-smelling white flowers in summer — D. candida is the better choice.

Datura suaveolens

The magnificent 10 in. long flaring trumpets in the photograph may tempt you to rush off and buy a Datura. Before you do, remember that these exotic plants need space and care, and all parts are poisonous. They are tub plants, spending part of the summer outdoors and the whole of the winter in a cool, well-lit place.

SECRETS OF SUCCESS

Temperature: Average warmth. Keep cool in winter.

Light: A well-lit spot — some direct sunlight is beneficial.

Water: Water regularly from spring to autumn. Water sparingly in winter.

Air Humidity: Mist leaves occasionally.

Repotting: Repot, if necessary, in spring.

Propagation: Take stem cuttings in spring. Use a rooting hormone and provide bottom heat.

DIANTHUS

FLOWERING POT PLANT page 57

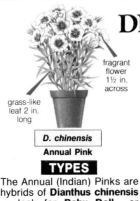

fragrant flower 1½ in. across

grass-like leaf 2 in. long

D. chinensis

Annual Pink

TYPES

The Annual (Indian) Pinks are hybrids of **Dianthus chinensis** — look for **Baby Doll** or **Telstar**. The Annual Carnations (hybrids of **D. caryophyllus**) have blooms which are larger and double.

Dianthus caryophyllus

You may occasionally find pots of Dianthus for sale in the house plant section of a garden centre. You will not, however, find them in most textbooks — Pinks and Annual Carnations are not accepted as house plants. They do need cool conditions and are not always long-lasting, but they are easily raised from seed and the white, pink or red frilly-edged blooms are attractive. Give them a well-lit spot and do not let the compost dry out. Provide fresh air on hot days.

SECRETS OF SUCCESS

Temperature: Cool — 50°–60°F is ideal.

Light: Bright light is essential, but shade from midday sun.

Water: Keep compost moist at all times.

Air Humidity: Mist leaves occasionally.

Care After Flowering: Plant should be discarded.

Propagation: Sow seeds in spring.

DIEFFENBACHIA

FOLIAGE HOUSE PLANT page 51

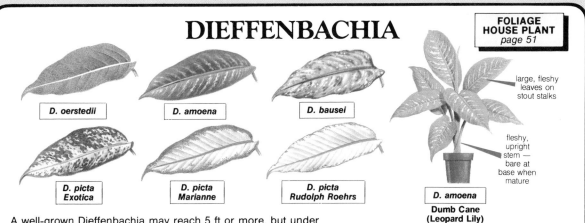

D. oerstedii

D. amoena

D. bausei

D. picta Exotica

D. picta Marianne

D. picta Rudolph Roehrs

large, fleshy leaves on stout stalks

fleshy, upright stem — bare at base when mature

D. amoena
Dumb Cane (Leopard Lily)

A well-grown Dieffenbachia may reach 5 ft or more, but under ordinary room conditions some of the lower leaves will fall to give a False Palm effect. It is not an easy plant to grow — it will not tolerate low winter temperatures or cold draughts. Dry air and fluctuating temperatures can be fatal to some delicate varieties, but the most popular types (varieties of D. picta and D. amoena) are fairly tolerant and not at all difficult to grow in the centrally heated home. With age or bad management the plant may become leggy and unattractive. Cut off the cane, leaving a 4 in. stump. The crown of leaves can be used as a cutting — the stump will resprout to produce a new plant.

The large and highly decorative leaves of this plant make it a great favourite with interior designers, who use large ones as solitary specimen plants and smaller examples as a key part of plant groups. Its common name, Dumb Cane, is derived from the unpleasant effect of its poisonous sap on the mouth and throat. Remember to wash your hands after taking cuttings.

SECRETS OF SUCCESS

Temperature: Average or above average warmth — minimum 60°F in winter.

Light: Partial shade in summer — bright light in winter.

Water: Water regularly from spring to autumn. Water sparingly in winter.

Air Humidity: Mist frequently. Surround pot with damp peat. Wash leaves occasionally.

Repotting: Repot in spring every year.

Propagation: There are several methods. Remove and pot up top crown of leaves — use a rooting hormone and provide bottom heat. Pieces of stem, 2 or 3 in. long, can be used as cane cuttings. Some varieties produce daughter plants at the base — remove and use as cuttings.

SPECIAL PROBLEMS

INSECTS
Keep watch for scale and red spider mite.

STEM BASE SOFT & DISCOLOURED
Cause: Stem rot disease. This condition is encouraged by overwatering and low temperatures. If damage is slight — cut out diseased area, spray with carbendazim and repot. If damage is severe — discard plant; use top as a cutting.

LOWER LEAVES YELLOW & WILTED
Cause: Low winter temperatures or cold draughts are the most likely reason. Plants will survive at 50°-55°F but lower leaves will suffer.

LOSS OF COLOUR
Cause: Direct sunlight or excessive brightness will give leaves a washed-out appearance. Move to a shadier spot.

LOSS OF LEAVES
Cause: Most likely reasons are temperature too cool, dry air or cold draughts if leaves are young. Old leaves tend to drop naturally with age.

LEAVES WITH BROWN EDGES
Cause: Compost has been allowed to dry out; it should be kept moist but not soggy at all times. Cold air can have a similar effect.

TYPES

There is much confusion over the naming of Dieffenbachias — no two experts seem to agree! The only all-green one you are likely to see is **Dieffenbachia oerstedii** — look for the prominent white mid-rib. **D. picta (D. maculata)** is the most popular species, bearing oval leaves with ivory white blotches or markings. These markings are variable on the variety **Exotica** — on **Camilla**, **Marianne** and **Rudolph Roehrs** almost the whole of the leaf is ivory or cream. If you want a larger plant choose **D. amoena** — the stems reach 5 ft when fully grown and the leaves are 1½ ft long. The foliage is dark green with white bars — this striped effect is most marked in the variety **Tropic Snow**. Unusual species include the yellow-green **D. bausei** and the giant-leaved (2 ft or more) **D. bowmannii**.

Dieffenbachia amoena Tropic Snow

Dieffenbachia picta Camilla

DIPLADENIA

FLOWERING HOUSE PLANT page 55

leaf 2 in. long

trumpet-shaped flower 3 in. across

twining woody stems

D. sanderi rosea

Large flowers appear in summer on the twining stems. Dipladenia can be grown as a climber, reaching 10 ft or more, or it can be pruned back once flowering is finished in order to maintain it as a bush. The pink blossoms appear on the plant while it is still small, and the glossy leaves make it attractive all year round, but it has never become popular.

SECRETS OF SUCCESS

Temperature: Warm — minimum 55°F in winter.

Light: Bright light or semi-shade — not direct sun.

Water: Water regularly from spring to autumn. Water sparingly in winter.

Air Humidity: Mist regularly, especially when in bud or flower.

Repotting: Repot in spring every year.

Propagation: Take stem cuttings in spring. Use a rooting hormone and provide bottom heat.

TYPES

Dipladenia sanderi rosea is grown for its yellow-throated, pink flowers. **D. (Mandevilla) splendens** is larger-leaved with pink-throated flowers.

Dipladenia sanderi rosea

DIZYGOTHECA

FOLIAGE HOUSE PLANT page 51

saw-toothed edge

leaflets coppery when young

D. elegantissima
(Aralia elegantissima)

False Aralia (Finger Aralia)

A graceful plant with leaves divided into finger-like serrated leaflets which are dark green or almost black. The bush has a splendid lacy effect when young. It has the usual problems of so many delicate plants — it detests soggy compost but it drops its leaves if the soil ball is allowed to dry out. It does not like sudden changes in temperature and the air must be moist.

SECRETS OF SUCCESS

Temperature: Average warmth — minimum 60°F in winter.

Light: Bright light — not direct sun.

Water: Water moderately from spring to autumn. Water sparingly in winter.

Air Humidity: Mist leaves frequently.

Repotting: Repot in spring every 2 years.

Propagation: Difficult. Try stem cuttings in spring — use a rooting hormone and provide bottom heat.

TYPES

Dizygotheca elegantissima is the popular species — delicate in both appearance and constitution. This plant can grow up to 6 ft high. **D. veitchii** has wider leaves with wavy (not serrated) edges.

Dizygotheca elegantissima

DUCHESNEA

FLOWERING HOUSE PLANT page 55

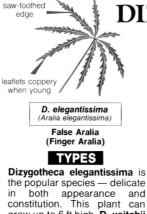

branching runners

strawberry-like fruits ¾ in. across

D. indica
(Fragaria indica)

Indian Strawberry

There has been a rapid increase in the popularity of hanging plants in recent years. Some excellent trailers, however, still remain rarities and the Indian Strawberry is a good example. It is vigorous and easy to care for. In summer the flowers appear and these are followed by small strawberry-like fruits. These are edible, but unfortunately they are completely tasteless.

SECRETS OF SUCCESS

Temperature: Cool or average warmth — keep cool but frost-free in winter.

Light: Bright light — not direct sun.

Water: Keep compost moist. Water sparingly in winter.

Air Humidity: Mist leaves occasionally.

Repotting: Repot in spring every year.

Propagation: Divide plants at repotting time. Layer runners in spring.

TYPE

Duchesnea indica bears trailing runners and bright yellow flowers in summer. It will not flower if it is kept in a semi-shady spot. Place outdoors occasionally in summer.

Duchesnea indica

The DRACAENA Group

FOLIAGE HOUSE PLANT page 51

HOW TO GROW A TI TREE

Ti Trees are grown by planting pieces of mature cane cut from Dracaena, Cordyline or Yucca. The crown of leaves which appears at the top of the cane gives an 'instant palm' effect. Nursery-raised Ti Trees can be obtained but you can also grow your own — Ti Canes (cut from outdoor tropical plants and dried before shipment) are becoming increasingly available.

Crown of leaves appears at the side of the cane once rooting has taken place

Dry cane planted firmly in Seed & Cutting Compost. Keep compost moist but not wet

An old Dracaena, after its top has been removed and used as a cutting, will grow as a Ti Tree.

SPECIAL PROBLEMS

LEAVES WITH BROWN TIPS & YELLOW EDGES
Cause: The most likely reason is dry air. Most Dracaenas need high air humidity — surround pot with moist peat and mist regularly. Cold draughts can have a similar effect, and so can underwatering. If dryness at the roots is the cause there will also be brown spotting on the foliage — see below.

LEAVES SOFT & CURLED WITH BROWN EDGES
Cause: Temperature too low. Delicate Dracaenas will quickly show these symptoms if kept close to a window on cold winter nights.

YELLOWING LOWER LEAVES
Cause: If this effect occurs slowly it is the natural and unavoidable process of old age. Dracaenas are False Palms with a characteristic crown of leaves on top of a bare stem. This growth habit is due to the limited life span of the foliage, each leaf turning yellow and dying after about 2 years.

LEAVES WITH BROWN SPOTS
Cause: Underwatering. The soil ball must be kept moist.

PLANT DEATH
Cause: One of 2 fatal faults — either too much water has been given in winter or the plant has been kept too cold.

LEAVES WITH BLEACHED DRY PATCHES
Cause: Too much sun. Move to a shadier spot.

Dracaena is becoming increasingly popular as a specimen plant, providing a bold and attractive focal point for a living room or hallway. Tall specimens are much in demand for public buildings, and the choice is far larger than it was a few years ago. The popular Cordylines are generally more compact but their foliage is equally or even more colourful.

Most Dracaenas and Cordylines are False Palms — the leafless woody trunk and crown of leaves giving a distinct Palm-like appearance, but in fact they are unrelated to the True Palms. These stately plants are ideal for the contemporary or hi-tech living room, but they are not new to the house plant scene. The Dracaena was much admired in Victorian times, but only recently has it reached the bestseller lists. It now outsells nearly every other large foliage plant.

There is some confusion over the naming of plants in this group. There is also some confusion over the ease (or difficulty) of growing these False Palms, with their cane-like stems and crown of leaves. The simple answer is that they can be easy or difficult; it all depends on which variety you choose.

There are three easy ones — Dracaena marginata, D. draco and Cordyline australis. These will stand some shade, some neglect and quite low winter temperatures. The remainder of the group need more care — higher winter temperatures, careful watering to ensure moist but not soggy compost, and frequent misting.

Not all the Dracaenas are Palm-like — D. godseffiana is a shrub which bears no similarity to its relatives. It is a robust plant, withstanding lower winter temperatures and drier air than the delicate varieties.

DRACAENA OR CORDYLINE?

The species and varieties of Cordylines are often confused with and sold as Dracaenas. You may find the popular Cordyline terminalis labelled as Dracaena terminalis and its favourite English name is Red Dracaena.

Despite the confusion there are clear-cut differences. Cordyline has a creeping rootstock and its roots are white and knobbly. Dracaena has a non-creeping rootstock and the smooth-surfaced roots are deep yellow or orange.

SECRETS OF SUCCESS

Temperature: Average warmth — minimum 55°F in winter. The easy types (see above) can withstand lower temperatures.

Light: Light shade is the best general position — close to an east or west window is an ideal spot. Some varieties, such as C. terminalis, must have good light, but two — D. marginata and D. fragrans — will grow in shade.

Water: Keep compost moist at all times. Reduce watering in winter but do not let it dry out.

Air Humidity: Mist leaves regularly. Only D. draco and D. godseffiana can grow happily in dry air.

Repotting: Repot in spring every 2 years.

Propagation: There are several methods to choose from. Remove crown from old leggy canes and plant in Potting Compost; use a rooting hormone and provide bottom heat. Alternatively, air layer the crown before potting up. Pieces of stem, 2 or 3 in. long, can be used as cane cuttings.

DRACAENA DEREMENSIS

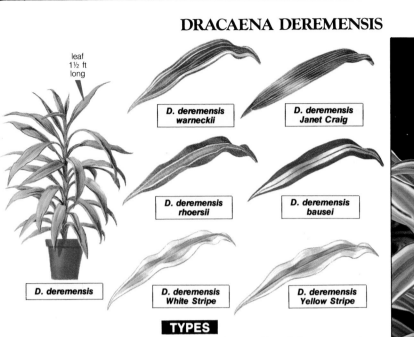

leaf
1½ ft
long

D. deremensis warneckii	**D. deremensis Janet Craig**
D. deremensis rhoersii	**D. deremensis bausei**

D. deremensis

D. deremensis White Stripe

D. deremensis Yellow Stripe

TYPES

Dracaena deremensis is a slow-growing species reaching 4 ft or more when mature. One variety (**Janet Craig**) is all-green — the usual foliage colour is dark green with one or more longitudinal stripes in a different colour. **Bausei** has two broad white bands at the centre — **warneckii** bears its white bands close to the edge. The 'Stripe' series produces foliage with distinctly coloured margins — **White Stripe**, **Yellow Stripe** and **Green Stripe**. Grow the variety **compacta** if the space you have available is limited.

Dracaena deremensis warneckii

DRACAENA MARGINATA

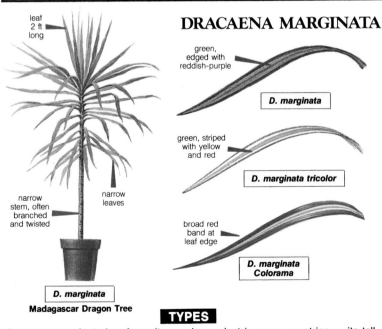

leaf
2 ft
long

green,
edged with
reddish-purple

D. marginata

green, striped
with yellow
and red

D. marginata tricolor

broad red
band at
leaf edge

D. marginata Colorama

narrow
stem, often
branched
and twisted

narrow
leaves

D. marginata
Madagascar Dragon Tree

TYPES

Dracaena marginata is a favourite specimen plant in many countries — its tall snake-like trunk branches with age and can grow up to 10 ft high. The basic species has narrow, arching leaves which are edged with red. The green colour predominates — in the variety **tricolor** a band of yellow separates the green and red stripes and the overall effect is greenish-gold. In the modern variety **Colorama** the red banding is more prominent and here the leaves appear distinctly reddish.

Dracaena marginata tricolor

DRACAENA DRACO

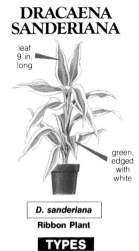

leaf 1½ ft long

tough, sword-shaped leaves — resin ('dragon's blood') exudes from trunk

D. draco
Dragon Tree

TYPE

Dracaena draco is a giant in its natural habitat but grows to only 4 ft indoors. Leaves are red-edged if kept in good light — old foliage arches downwards.

Dracaena draco

DRACAENA SANDERIANA

leaf 9 in. long

green, edged with white

D. sanderiana
Ribbon Plant

TYPES

Where space is limited, the usual choice is **Dracaena sanderiana**. The grey-green twisted leaves are not wide-spreading and the maximum height is 2–3 ft. The variety **borinquensis** has dark green-edged leaves.

Dracaena sanderiana

DRACAENA REFLEXA

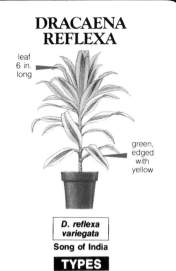

leaf 6 in. long

green, edged with yellow

D. reflexa variegata
Song of India

TYPES

Dracaena reflexa (formerly called **Pleomele reflexa**) is a weak-stemmed plant which is not easy to grow. Moist air is essential. The yellow-edged **variegata** is the only type you are likely to find at the garden centre.

Dracaena reflexa variegata

DRACAENA GODSEFFIANA

leaf 3 in. long

glossy leaves

wiry stems

D. godseffiana
Gold Dust Dracaena

D. godseffiana kelleri

D. godseffiana Florida Beauty

TYPES

The odd man out in the Dracaena world — **Dracaena godseffiana** is distinctly shrubby rather than Palm-like and the leaves are broadly oval rather than long and grassy. This branching plant grows about 2 ft high and the amount of spotting on the leaves depends on the variety. The foliage of the popular **Florida Beauty** is usually more cream than green.

Dracaena godseffiana Florida Beauty

DRACAENA FRAGRANS

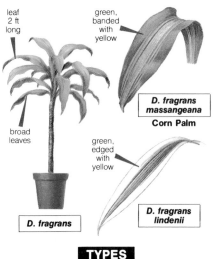

leaf 2 ft long

broad leaves

green, banded with yellow

D. fragrans massangeana

Corn Palm

D. fragrans

green, edged with yellow

D. fragrans lindenii

Dracaena fragrans massangeana

TYPES

Dracaena fragrans is a solid-looking plant. On top of the stout trunk there is a crown of glossy leaves which are about 4 in. wide. Several varieties such as **lindenii** and **Victoria** (broad yellow stripe) are available, but **massangeana** with its corn-colour central band outsells all the others.

Dracaena fragrans lindenii

CORDYLINE

leaf 1 ft long

green, splashed with red, pink and cream

C. terminalis tricolor

leaf 9 in. long

green, streaked with red

C. terminalis Rededge

leaf 1 ft long

plain green

C. terminalis Ti

Cordyline terminalis Kiwi

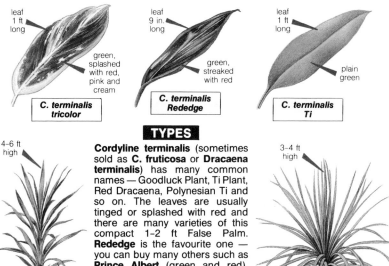

4-6 ft high

dull, rough-edged leaves

C. stricta (C. congesta)

TYPES

Cordyline terminalis (sometimes sold as **C. fruticosa** or **Dracaena terminalis**) has many common names — Goodluck Plant, Ti Plant, Red Dracaena, Polynesian Ti and so on. The leaves are usually tinged or splashed with red and there are many varieties of this compact 1–2 ft False Palm. **Rededge** is the favourite one — you can buy many others such as **Prince Albert** (green and red), **Firebrand** (bronze), **amabilis** (green and white) and **baptistii** (green, pink and yellow). **Ti** is all-green and is the 'grass' used for hula skirts in Hawaii. New varieties of C. terminalis continue to appear —look for **Atom** and **Kiwi**. The larger Cordylines are grown as specimen plants in tubs — examples are **C. stricta** (sometimes called **C. congesta**) and **C. australis**.

3-4 ft high

long, narrow and arching leaves

C. australis (Draceana indivisa)

Cabbage Tree (Grass Palm)

EPISCIA

FLOWERING HOUSE PLANT
page 55

Episcia cupreata

leaf 1–2 in. long, covered with downy hairs

tubular flower 1½ in. across — white with feathered edges

surface green and velvety — veins purple or brown

E. dianthiflora
Lace Flower

Episcia is an attractive trailing plant which has never enjoyed the popularity of its well-known relative, the African Violet. Because it requires high air humidity it is often difficult to grow as an isolated specimen plant or in a hanging basket, but it makes an excellent ground cover between taller plants where it can benefit from the increased humidity in the enclosed environment. There are two types — the Flame Violet and the delicate Lace Flower. The Flame Violet has the more eye-catching leaves — large and quilted with silvery or pale green veins. The trailing stems grow about 1½ ft long — with the Lace Flower the small leaves are borne in groups along thread-like runners. Both bloom throughout the summer and the runners root in surrounding compost, forming plantlets for propagation. Shorten stems after flowering.

TYPES

Episcia is grown for its attractive foliage and pretty, if rather small, flowers. The two most popular species are shown here. **Episcia cupreata** (Flame Violet) bears tubular orange-red flowers which are yellow-eyed and about ¾ in. across. It has produced many hybrids and sports — **Amazon, Metallica, Acajou, Cleopatra** and **Harlequin** are examples. **E. dianthiflora** produces larger flowers — white and deeply fringed. Other species are hard to find. **E. reptans** is rather like some of the E. cupreata varieties, bearing silver-veined leaves and bright red flowers. On the other hand **E. lilacina** is easy to recognise — the flowers have lilac lobes and a yellow throat.

SECRETS OF SUCCESS

Temperature: Average warmth — minimum 55°F in winter.

Light: Bright light, away from direct sunlight in summer.

Water: Keep compost moist at all times during the growing season. Reduce watering in winter.

Air Humidity: Mist leaves frequently. Surround pot with damp peat.

Repotting: Repot in spring every year.

Propagation: Layer runners in spring or summer.

ERICA

FLOWERING POT PLANT
page 57

Erica hyemalis

globular flower ⅛ in. across

plant 1½ ft tall

needle-like leaf ¼ in. long

E. gracilis
Cape Heath

The Ericas are small shrubby plants which are bought in flower during the winter months. Their tiny leaves and masses of bell-shaped flowers are attractive, but these plants will give disappointing results in a centrally heated room. In hot, dry air the leaves drop very rapidly, so only choose an Erica for display in winter if you can provide a cool and well-lit spot. Pay careful attention to watering — never use hard water and make sure that the compost is never allowed to dry out. There are two popular varieties to choose from — E. gracilis bears tiny globular pink or pale purple flowers and E. hyemalis which bears larger tubular pink flowers with white tips. Even under cool conditions and with the compost kept suitably moist you cannot expect an Erica to survive for long in the home.

TYPES

The Cape Heath and its close relatives are bought in bloom and are then discarded once the flowering period is over. There are needle-like leaves and masses of small flowers — **Erica gracilis** is the favourite one and is in flower during autumn and winter. **E. hyemalis** is also widely grown — it produces its blooms at the same time as E. gracilis but the flowers are larger — ¾ in. long pink tubes with white mouths. The Christmas Heather (**E. canaliculata**) bears tiny white blooms with black centres. There is a midsummer-flowering Heather — the white or mauve **E. ventricosa** (2 ft). The popular garden species E. carnea is not suitable for indoor cultivation.

SECRETS OF SUCCESS

Temperature: Cool — must be kept at 40°–55°F when in flower.

Light: Bright light. Some direct sun is beneficial.

Water: Keep compost moist at all times — frequent watering may be necessary. Use soft water.

Air Humidity: Mist leaves frequently.

Care After Flowering: Plant is usually discarded. To keep for a second year, trim back shoots after flowering and stand pot outdoors during summer.

Propagation: Not easy. Take stem cuttings in late summer — use a rooting hormone.

Eucalyptus gunnii

leaf
2 in.
long

aromatic
leaves

E. globulus
Blue Gum

TYPES

Eucalyptus globulus (Blue Gum) grows too tall for indoor cultivation — it is better to choose either the slower-growing **E. gunnii** (Cedar Gum) or **E. citriodora** (Lemon-Scented Gum).

EUCALYPTUS

FOLIAGE HOUSE PLANT page 51

Young plants have attractive grey-green leaves which produce a distinctive aroma when crushed. They will flourish under ordinary room conditions if kept well-lit and cool. Pots can be stood outdoors in summer. Pinch out tips to keep growth in check and to maintain the production of juvenile foliage — old leaves are much less attractive. Plants are usually discarded after a couple of years.

SECRETS OF SUCCESS

Temperature: Cool or average warmth. Keep cool (45°-55°F) in winter.

Light: Bright light. Some direct sun is beneficial.

Water: Water regularly from spring to autumn. Water sparingly in winter.

Air Humidity: Misting is not essential.

Repotting: Repot in spring every year.

Propagation: Sow seeds in spring — germinate at 65°F.

Eucharis grandiflora

fragrant
flower
3 in.
across

oval
leaf
8 in.
long

E. grandiflora
Amazon Lily

TYPE

Eucharis grandiflora flowers in late summer, and again a few months later if conditions are favourable. Each bloom looks like a spiky trumpet, and 3–6 are borne on a 2 ft stalk.

EUCHARIS

FLOWERING HOUSE PLANT page 55

It seems strange that this bulbous plant should be missing from the house plant bestseller lists. The problem is that it does not like cold nights — a minimum of 60°F is required, even in mid winter. If you start with a bulb rather than a potted specimen, plant in spring or autumn and keep warm until growth starts. Water sparingly at this stage.

SECRETS OF SUCCESS

Temperature: Average warmth — minimum 60°F in winter.

Light: Bright light or semi-shade — not direct sun.

Water: Water liberally from spring to autumn. Water moderately in winter.

Air Humidity: Sponge leaves occasionally.

Repotting: Repot in spring every 3–4 years.

Propagation: Detach offsets from mature plants in summer.

Euonymus japonica microphyllus

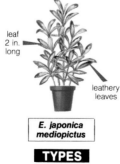

leaf
2 in.
long

leathery
leaves

E. japonica
mediopictus

TYPES

Euonymus japonica is the house plant species. There are several varieties, differing in the distribution of green and yellow (or white) on the leaves. Grow **microphyllus** where space is limited.

EUONYMUS

FOLIAGE HOUSE PLANT page 51

Several variegated types are available — two popular varieties are illustrated here. These shrubby plants have oval, leathery foliage — E. japonica microphyllus leaves are less than 1 in. long. Small white flowers may appear in late spring. Euonymus is a useful specimen for a bright unheated room — in a heated place, it will probably shed its leaves in winter. Keep in check by pruning in spring.

SECRETS OF SUCCESS

Temperature: Average warmth. Keep cool in winter.

Light: Bright, indirect light or some sun.

Water: Water regularly from spring to autumn. Water sparingly in winter.

Air Humidity: Mist leaves occasionally.

Repotting: Repot in spring every year.

Propagation: Take stem cuttings in summer.

EUPHORBIA

FLOWERING HOUSE PLANT page 55

grooved stems covered with sharp thorns

leaf 2 in. long

E. milii
Crown of Thorns

Euphorbia fulgens

Listed here are the non-succulent flowering Euphorbias with the exception of Poinsettia (E. pulcherrima) which is described separately on page 195. The Crown of Thorns is an old favourite which remains an excellent and undemanding choice for a sunny window. It does not need misting, will withstand some neglect and does not have to be moved to an unheated room in winter. Leaves may drop during this resting season but new leaf buds will appear within a month or two. Scarlet Plume is much less common and its growth habit is quite different. Long arching branches bear Willow-like leaves, and in winter the flower-heads appear — coloured bracts surround tiny true flowers. The colour is orange or white with a yellow eye. Keep cool and rather dry for a month after flowering.

SECRETS OF SUCCESS

Temperature: Average warmth — minimum 55°F in winter.

Light: As much light as possible, but shade from summer sun.

Water: Water moderately from spring to autumn. Water sparingly in winter. Let compost surface dry between waterings.

Air Humidity: Mist E. fulgens occasionally in spring and summer.

Repotting: Repot in spring every 2 years.

Propagation: Take stem cuttings in spring or summer. Let milky sap dry before placing in compost.

TYPES

The most popular one is **Euphorbia milii (E. splendens)**. Its 3 ft stems bear tiny flowers which are surrounded by showy bracts — red is the usual flower-head colour but both salmon and yellow types are available. The length of the flowering season depends on the light intensity. E. milii is normally in bloom from early spring to midsummer, but in a brightly-lit spot it can flower almost all year round. The sap is poisonous. **E. fulgens** (Scarlet Plume) is not often seen and is more difficult to care for. The stems are arched and thornless — quite unlike those of E. milii, but the flower-heads have the same structure.

FATSIA

FOLIAGE HOUSE PLANT page 51

leaf 1 ft across

shiny surface

pointed tip

F. japonica
(Aralia sieboldii)
Japanese Aralia
(Castor Oil Plant)

Fatsia japonica

An excellent specimen plant, reaching a height of 4 ft or more. It prefers a cool, well-ventilated and bright situation but it is extremely durable, accepting a wide range of conditions. For economy buy a small plant — it will grow quickly, especially if it is fed regularly and repotted annually — it will reach 3 ft in a couple of years. Fatsia has been a popular specimen foliage plant since Victorian times — flower-heads rarely appear. Cut back the growing tips each spring to keep it bushy. Wash the leaves occasionally.

SECRETS OF SUCCESS

Temperature: Average warmth — if possible keep cool in winter. Avoid temperatures above 70°F.

Light: Bright or light shade. Keep well-lit in winter.

Water: Water regularly from spring to autumn. Water sparingly in winter.

Air Humidity: Mist leaves frequently.

Repotting: Repot in spring every year.

Propagation: Take stem cuttings in summer, or sow seeds in spring.

TYPES

Fatsia japonica is an old favourite with a tough constitution. There are several varieties, including **variegata** (cream-edged foliage) and **moseri** (compact growth habit).

SPECIAL PROBLEMS

LEAVES TURN YELLOW AND THEN DROP
Cause: Two separate culprits can cause this trouble. If leaves are wilted and soft — overwatering is the reason. If leaves are brittle — too much heat is the cause.

LEAVES SHRIVELLED
Cause: The air is too dry or the leaves have been exposed to hot summer sun. Remember to provide some shade in summer.

LEAVES PALE & SPOTTED, LEAF EDGES BROWN & BRITTLE
Cause: Underwatering. A large plant will need frequent watering in summer.

fragrant gold-centred flower ½ in. across

shiny leaf 1 in. long

E. affine
Arabian Violet

EXACUM

FLOWERING POT PLANT
page 57

Exacum is a small and neat plant which is only a few inches high when offered for sale. Its flowers, pale purple with a yellow centre, are also small, but this plant still has several points in its favour. The blooms are abundant and fragrant, and the flowering season extends from midsummer to late autumn. Keep reasonably cool and in good light. To ensure the maximum flowering period, pick a plant which is mainly in bud and not in full flower.

TYPE

Raise **Exacum affine** from seed or buy as a pot plant. An easy-to-care-for plant but it does dislike draughts. Remove dead flowers regularly to prolong display.

SECRETS OF SUCCESS

Temperature: Cool or average warmth — keep at 50°–70°F.
Light: Bright light — protect from hot summer sun.
Water: Keep compost moist at all times.
Air Humidity: Mist leaves frequently.
Care After Flowering: Plant should be discarded.
Propagation: Sow seeds in late summer.

Exacum affine Starlight Fragrance

shiny surface

leaf 7 in. long

F. lizei
Ivy Tree

FATSHEDERA

FOLIAGE HOUSE PLANT
page 51

This easy-to-grow hybrid of Hedera and Fatsia deserves its popularity. It prefers cool conditions, but it can be grown in a heated room as long as the winter temperature is kept below 70°F and the light is reasonably bright. It can be grown as a shrub, like its Castor Oil Plant parent — pinch out the growing tips each spring. Or you can grow it as a climber like its Ivy parent — train it to a stake or trellis.

TYPES

Fatshedera lizei can reach 6 ft or more. Support is needed, or you can pinch out the tips and grow it as a bush. The white-blotched form (**variegata**) is more difficult to grow.

SECRETS OF SUCCESS

Temperature: Average warmth — minimum 35°F in winter.
Light: Bright or light shade — keep well-lit in winter.
Water: Water regularly from spring to autumn. Water sparingly in winter.
Air Humidity: Mist leaves frequently.
Repotting: Repot in spring every year.
Propagation: Take stem cuttings in summer.

Fatshedera lizei variegata

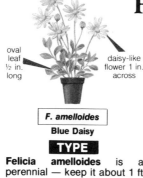

oval leaf ½ in. long

daisy-like flower 1 in. across

F. amelloides
Blue Daisy

FELICIA

FLOWERING HOUSE PLANT
page 55

Felicia is worth looking for if you like out-of-the-ordinary plants. This undemanding mini-shrub will produce a floral display almost the whole year round if you follow the Secrets of Success. Pinch back regularly to keep the plant bushy, but be careful not to cut off stems bearing buds. Avoid the two pet hates — low light intensity and dry soil.

TYPE

Felicia amelloides is a perennial — keep it about 1 ft high by pruning the growing tips. Midsummer is the main flowering season — blue Daisies with yellow centres which open only in sunlight.

SECRETS OF SUCCESS

Temperature: Average warmth — minimum 50°F in winter.
Light: Brightly lit spot, but shade from hot summer sun.
Water: Keep compost moist at all times.
Air Humidity: Mist leaves occasionally.
Repotting: Repot, if necessary, in spring.
Propagation: Take stem cuttings in spring or sow seeds in summer.

Felicia amelloides

FERNS

FOLIAGE HOUSE PLANT
page 51

Ferns are making a comeback. In Victorian times they were extremely popular and large collections were grown in conservatories and in specially constructed glass cases. But very few varieties were grown as ordinary living room plants, because gas fumes and coal fire smoke are extremely toxic to nearly all ferns. It was the advent of central heating with its freedom from fumes which led to the revival of interest, but radiators in turn have their problems. Few ferns can tolerate hot dry air, so air humidity has to be artificially increased (see Secrets of Success).

Most ferns are not really difficult to grow in the modern home, but they will not tolerate neglect. The compost must never be allowed to dry out, and the surrounding air needs to be kept moist.

There is a bewildering choice of varieties. Nearly two thousand are suitable for growing indoors, but comparatively few are available commercially. The classical picture of a fern is a rosette of much divided, arching leaves (correctly referred to as 'fronds') but there are also ferns with spear-shaped leaves, holly-like leaflets and button-like leaflets. There is also a wide choice of ways to display your collection. Many of them are ideal for a hanging basket and some, such as Boston Fern and Bird's Nest Fern, are large enough and bold enough to be displayed as specimen plants on their own. Delicate ferns, such as Delta Maidenhair, are best planted in a terrarium. When grouping ferns with other plants make sure that they are not crushed — the fronds are fragile and need room to develop. In addition ensure that all dead and damaged fronds are removed so that new ones can grow.

FERN LEAF LANGUAGE

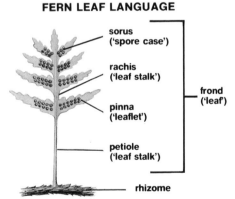

sorus ('spore case')

rachis ('leaf stalk')

pinna ('leaflet')

petiole ('leaf stalk')

frond ('leaf')

rhizome

HOW TO CHOOSE A FERN

Easiest to grow	**Cyrtomium** **Davallia** **Pteris cretica** **Nephrolepis** **Asplenium nidus** **Pellaea rotundifolia**
For hanging baskets	**Nephrolepis** **Adiantum**
For bold display as a specimen plant	**Nephrolepis** **Asplenium nidus** **Blechnum gibbum**

SECRETS OF SUCCESS

Temperature: Average warmth — cool but not cold nights are desirable. The best temperature range is 60°–70°F — the minimum for most types is about 50°F and ferns may suffer at more than 75°F.

Light: Despite popular opinion, ferns are not shade lovers indoors as most varieties originated in the dappled brightness of tropical woodland. Good indirect light is the proper location — an east- or north-facing windowsill is ideal.

Water: Compost must be kept moist at all times and never allowed to dry out. This does not mean constantly soggy compost — waterlogging will lead to rotting. Reduce watering in winter.

Air Humidity: Moist air is necessary for nearly all ferns. Mist fronds regularly and use one or other of the techniques described on page 232.

Repotting: Repot in spring when the roots fill the pot — most young specimens will probably require annual repotting. Do not bury the crown of the plant.

Propagation: The simplest way is to divide the plant into 2 or 3 pieces in early spring if it produces rhizomes. Some ferns produce young plants at the ends of runners (example — Boston Fern) or on fronds (example — Mother Fern). It is possible, but not always easy, to raise plants from spores obtained from the underside of mature fronds — see page 240.

SPECIAL PROBLEMS

BROWN DOTS OR LINES REGULARLY ARRANGED ON UNDERSIDE OF FRONDS
Cause: These are spore cases — an indication that the frond is mature and healthy. The spores produced inside these spore cases can be used for propagation — see page 240.

BROWN SHELLS IRREGULARLY SCATTERED ON FRONDS
Cause: Scale — the Bird's Nest Fern is particularly susceptible to this pest. For control, see page 244.

YELLOWING FRONDS, BEGINNING AT BASE OF PLANT. MATURE FRONDS DEVELOP BROWN SPOTS AND FALL
Cause: Air too warm — a common complaint when ferns are stood too close to radiators. Few ferns can tolerate very high temperatures. If the plant is also limp and wilting, then the cause is incorrect watering.

YELLOWING FRONDS, BROWN TIPS. NO NEW GROWTH
Cause: Air too dry. See Secrets of Success.

PALE FRONDS, SCORCH MARKS ON SURFACE
Cause: Too much sun. Ferns must be protected from midday sunshine in summer.

PALE FRONDS, WEAK GROWTH
Cause: Not enough fertilizer. Ferns need feeding, little and often, during the growing season.

FRONDS DYING BACK
Cause: Two most likely culprits are dry air and dry compost.

TYPES

ADIANTUM

leaflets ½ in. long

young fronds coppery-pink

black stems

filmy leaflets

fronds forked at base

A. raddianum
(A. cuneatum)

**Maidenhair Fern
(Delta Maidenhair)**

A. hispidulum

**Australian Maidenhair
(Rose Maidenhair)**

The Maidenhair Ferns have wiry stems, delicate leaves and a delicate constitution. They need moist air, warmth and shade — plants for the terrarium or shaded conservatory rather than the living room. **Adiantum raddianum** is perhaps the easiest to grow — the arching **A. tenerum farleyense** is the most attractive. **A. hispidulum** is quite distinctive and **A. capillus-veneris** grows wild in Britain.

Adiantum raddianum

Adiantum capillus-veneris

AGLAOMORPHA

narrow leaflets

broad leaflets

paw-like rhizome

A. meyeniana

Bear's Paw Fern

Aglaomorpha meyeniana is a fern you will find in few homes — it's one for the specialist. It has 2 unusual features — a creeping furry rhizome and fronds with both narrow and broad leaflets.

BLECHNUM

large palm-like crown of stiff fronds; trunk develops with age

B. gibbum

A distinct trunk develops with age — the crown has a 3 ft spread. The most popular species is **Blechnum gibbum** — in a large collection you might find the Brazilian Tree Fern (**B. braziliense**).

CIBOTIUM

pale green lacy fronds

C. schiedei

Mexican Tree Fern

Cibotium is much more likely to be seen in the U.S than in Britain. **Cibotium schiedei** is extremely graceful with arching fronds and capable of producing an 8 ft tall trunk.

CYRTOMIUM

holly-shaped leaflets, glossy dark green

C. falcatum rochfordianum

Holly Fern

An excellent fern to buy — it can withstand dry air and draughts. **Cyrtomium falcatum** (Fishtail Fern) has smooth-edged leaflets — the variety **rochfordianum** is Holly-like.

ASPLENIUM

leaf 2 ft long

brown midrib

wavy margin

feathery fronds

frond 2 ft long

dark wiry stalks

A. nidus

Bird's Nest Fern

A. bulbiferum

**Mother Fern
(Hen-and-Chicken Fern)**

The Aspleniums or Spleenworts need shade and a moist atmosphere. There are 2 basic types which are cultivated as house plants, and they look nothing like each other. Firstly there is the Bird's Nest Fern — **Asplenium nidus**. Its spear-like leaves surround the fibrous 'nest' at the centre. Not difficult, but you must not handle the young fronds. The other type of Asplenium is the Mother Fern. The fronds are finely divided and when mature bear numerous tiny plantlets. **A. bulbiferum** is the usual one — **A. viviparum** is smaller and the fronds more arching.

Asplenium nidus

Asplenium bulbiferum

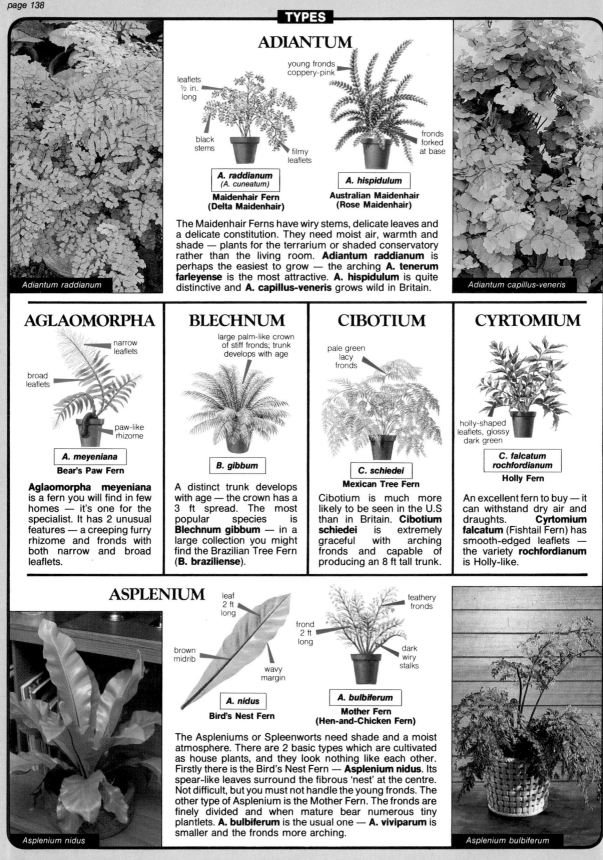

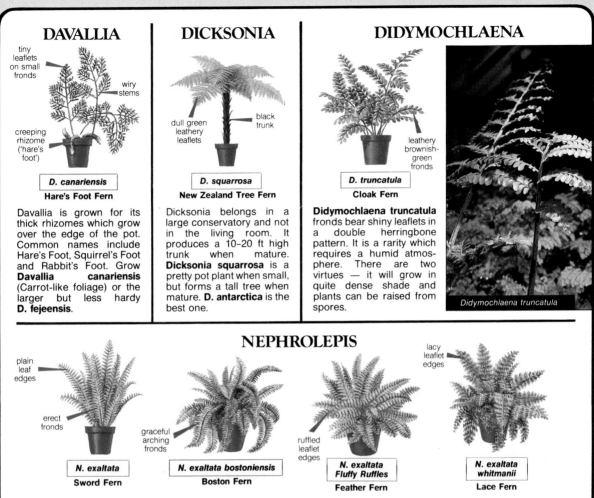

DAVALLIA

tiny leaflets on small fronds

wiry stems

creeping rhizome ('hare's foot')

D. canariensis

Hare's Foot Fern

Davallia is grown for its thick rhizomes which grow over the edge of the pot. Common names include Hare's Foot, Squirrel's Foot and Rabbit's Foot. Grow **Davallia canariensis** (Carrot-like foliage) or the larger but less hardy **D. fejeensis**.

DICKSONIA

dull green leathery leaflets

black trunk

D. squarrosa

New Zealand Tree Fern

Dicksonia belongs in a large conservatory and not in the living room. It produces a 10–20 ft high trunk when mature. **Dicksonia squarrosa** is a pretty pot plant when small, but forms a tall tree when mature. **D. antarctica** is the best one.

DIDYMOCHLAENA

leathery brownish-green fronds

D. truncatula

Cloak Fern

Didymochlaena truncatula fronds bear shiny leaflets in a double herringbone pattern. It is a rarity which requires a humid atmosphere. There are two virtues — it will grow in quite dense shade and plants can be raised from spores.

Didymochlaena truncatula

NEPHROLEPIS

plain leaf edges

erect fronds

N. exaltata

Sword Fern

graceful arching fronds

N. exaltata bostoniensis

Boston Fern

ruffled leaflet edges

N. exaltata Fluffy Ruffles

Feather Fern

lacy leaflet edges

N. exaltata whitmanii

Lace Fern

If you can only have one fern, choose a variety of Nephrolepis. In Victorian times **Nephrolepis cordifolia** with its 1–2 ft erect fronds and the larger **N. exaltata** were very popular. These stiff species are now not often grown — about a hundred years ago a gracefully drooping mutation was discovered in Boston — **N. exaltata bostoniensis**. This has become the popular variety on both sides of the Atlantic and there are now scores of different types. Examples are **rooseveltii** (large with wavy leaflets), **maassii** (compact with wavy leaflets) and **scottii** (compact with rolled leaflets). There are varieties with a double herringbone pattern — each leaflet being divided up like a herringbone. The leaflets are sometimes divided even further, to give a feathery or lacy effect. Examples are **Fluffy Ruffles** (feathery leaflets in a double herringbone pattern), **whitmanii** (lacy leaflets in a triple herringbone pattern) and **smithii** (fine lacy leaflets in a quadruple herringbone pattern).

Nephrolepis cordifolia

Nephrolepis exaltata bostoniensis

Nephrolepis exaltata Gloriosa

PELLAEA

Pellaea rotundifolia

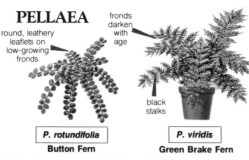

round, leathery leaflets on low-growing fronds

fronds darken with age

black stalks

P. rotundifolia
Button Fern

P. viridis
Green Brake Fern

Pellaea viridis macrophylla

Pellaea has an unusual feature for a fern — it prefers dry surroundings to the moist conditions required by the vast majority of the group. **Pellaea rotundifolia** is easy to grow — foot long arching fronds arise from a creeping rootstock. Pairs of shiny leaflets grow along the wiry stalk. These ½ in. leaflets are round at first — later oval. **P. viridis** is also easy to grow but is much more fern-like — its variety **macrophylla** has paler and much larger leaflets.

HOW TO MAKE A FERN PLAQUE

Chain or cord attachment

Piece of cork or log

Staghorn Fern. Remove plant from pot, cover root ball with damp sphagnum moss and then attach to cork or log with plastic-covered wire

Watering is simple. Once a week immerse plant and plaque in a bucket of water for a few minutes. Allow it to drain before rehanging

PHYLLITIS

leaf 1 ft long

wavy margin

base eared around brown stalk

P. scolopendrium
Hart's Tongue Fern

Phyllitis scolopendrium undulatum

The strap-shaped fronds of **Phyllitis scolopendrium** are erect at first and then arch with age. The frond edges are wavy — the varieties **crispum** and **undulatum** have frilly margins.

PLATYCERIUM

Platycerium bifurcatum

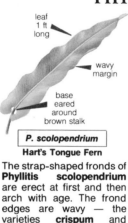

sterile frond (4 ft across) pale green — fan-shaped and upturned

P. grande
Regal Elkhorn Fern

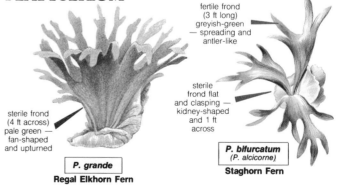

fertile frond (3 ft long) greyish-green — spreading and antler-like

sterile frond flat and clasping — kidney-shaped and 1 ft across

P. bifurcatum
(P. alcicorne)
Staghorn Fern

The Staghorn and Elkhorn Ferns bear large and spectacular fronds, usually divided at their ends into antler-like lobes. The fronds are of two distinct types — there are sterile fronds at the base and spore-bearing fertile fronds above. **Platycerium bifurcatum** is the popular and easy-to-grow species — the fertile fronds are the showy ones. **P. grande** is larger, and here it is the sterile fronds rather than the fertile ones which provide the display.

POLYSTICHUM

Polystichum tsus-simense

upright. pointed fronds

P. auriculatum

Prickly Shield Fern

The most popular species is **Polystichum tsus-simense**, the Tsus-sima Holly Fern. It is a small plant, less than 1 ft high. An excellent house fern because it does not mind dry air — the larger **P. auriculatum** needs a humid atmosphere.

POLYPODIUM

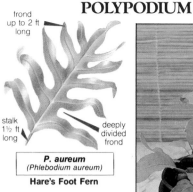

frond up to 2 ft long

stalk 1½ ft long

deeply divided frond

P. aureum
(Phlebodium aureum)

Hare's Foot Fern

Polypodium aureum has deeply cut leaves on thin stalks. There are unusual features — the rhizome creeps along the surface and it will grow in dry air. The most attractive variety is **mandaianum** — blue-green leaflets with wavy edges.

Polypodium aureum mandaianum

PTERIS

Pteris ensiformis victoriae

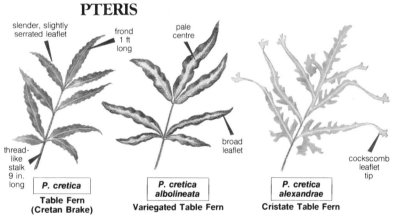

slender, slightly serrated leaflet

frond 1 ft long

thread-like stalk 9 in. long

P. cretica

Table Fern
(Cretan Brake)

pale centre

broad leaflet

P. cretica albolineata

Variegated Table Fern

cockscomb leaflet tip

P. cretica alexandrae

Cristate Table Fern

Most types of Pteris are easy to grow, producing handsome fronds in a range of shapes and sizes. The most popular types are varieties of **Pteris cretica** which are available in an assortment of leaflet colours and forms — all-green or variegated, plain or crested. These varieties include **albolineata**, **wilsonii** (compact with feathery leaflet tips) and the cockscomb-tipped **alexandrae** and **wimsettii**. **P. ensiformis** is similar to P. cretica, but the leaves are darker. Its variety **victoriae** (silver band along the midrib) is the prettiest of all the Table Ferns. **P. tremula** (Australian Brake Fern) is quite different. The 3 ft long fronds are borne on upright stalks, each leaflet being much divided to produce a feathery effect. The third type of Pteris (**P. vittata**) is not often seen —its common name (Ladder Fern) aptly describes its shape. Long leaflets are borne like the rungs of a ladder on either side of the midrib of each frond. It is a large plant, with arching fronds growing 2-3 ft long.

Pteris tremula

Pteris vittata

FICUS

**FOLIAGE
HOUSE PLANT**
page 51

In the Ficus or Ornamental Fig family are found house plants which vary from stately trees to lowly creepers, and since Victorian times the unchallenged head of the family has been the Rubber Plant. Once only the narrow-leaved F. elastica was grown, but this old-fashioned variety has now been replaced by the much more attractive F. elastica decora and F. elastica robusta. The all-green Rubber Plants are much easier to grow than the variegated ones, and by far the most important danger is overwatering. Wash leaves occasionally.

The Weeping Fig is increasing in popularity because it is a splendid specimen plant for the modern home. Its leaves are not large, but it is so much more tree-like and graceful than the Rubber Plant.

At the other end of the scale are the trailing types, which are much smaller ... and more difficult to grow. This is because they need moist air and are fussy about their requirement for evenly moist compost.

SECRETS OF SUCCESS

Temperature: Average warmth — minimum 55°F in winter.

Light: Bright spot for tree types, partially shaded site for others. A Rubber Plant will adapt to a few hours' sunshine each morning, but this would be fatal to a Creeping Fig.

Water: Water with care. With tree types the compost must dry out to some extent between waterings. The trailing types require more frequent watering. Use tepid water and apply very little in the winter months.

Air Humidity: Mist leaves occasionally in summer. Misting is essential for trailing types.

Repotting: Avoid frequent repotting. Repot in spring every 2 years until the plant is too large to handle.

Propagation: Take stem cuttings in summer if stems are non-woody. Use a rooting hormone and provide bottom heat. Air layer woody varieties. (See page 240).

SPECIAL PROBLEMS

SUDDEN LOSS OF LEAVES
Cause: The most likely reason depends on the type of Ficus. Rubber Plant — overwatering is the usual culprit — carry out standard remedial treatment (see page 246). Other possibilities are low winter temperatures, too little light, too much fertilizer and cold draughts. Weeping Fig — most likely cause is too little light or movement of the plant from one environment to another.

LOSS OF LOWEST LEAF
Cause: The bottom leaf of tree types will turn yellow and drop with age — this is a natural process and some degree of legginess is usual after a few years.

YELLOWING LEAF EDGES, SOME LOSS OF LOWER FOLIAGE
Cause: An early sign of more serious trouble, or the effect of underfeeding. Feed at the recommended rate throughout the growing season.

DRY SHRIVELLED LEAVES
Cause: A common problem with trailing types — the most likely reasons are exposure to direct sunlight, failure to mist the leaves regularly and allowing the compost to dry out.

TYPES

BUSHY TYPE

small olive-like berries
leathery, dark green leaves
F. diversifolia
Mistletoe Fig

Ficus diversifolia (**F. deltoidea**) is a slow-growing bush, eventually reaching a height of about 3 ft. The leaves bear small brown spots and the pea-sized fruits appear all year round — quite attractive but inedible.

Ficus diversifolia

TRAILING TYPES

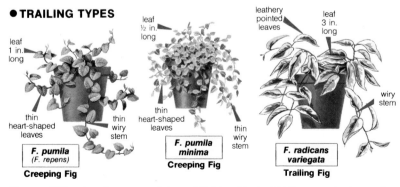
leaf 1 in. long
thin heart-shaped leaves
thin wiry stem
F. pumila (F. repens)
Creeping Fig

leaf ½ in. long
thin heart-shaped leaves
F. pumila minima
Creeping Fig

leathery pointed leaves
leaf 3 in. long
thin wiry stem
wiry stem
F. radicans variegata
Trailing Fig

Ficus Sunny

The word 'Ficus' conjures up a picture of Rubber Plants, but there are lowly species which are useful as trailers or climbers. **Ficus pumila** produces a dense green carpet and is one of the best of all indoor ground covers — the stems will cling to any damp surface and so it is an excellent climbing subject for a moss stick (see page 223). The variety **minima** has smaller leaves and **variegata** has white-spotted foliage. Newer varieties include **Rikki** and the cream-edged **Sunny**. **F. radicans** (**F. sagittata**) has larger leaves with wavy edges — the popular type is the cream-edged **variegata**.

● TREE TYPES

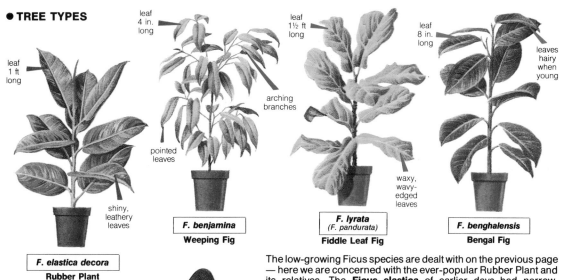

leaf 1 ft long

shiny, leathery leaves

leaf 4 in. long

pointed leaves

arching branches

F. benjamina
Weeping Fig

leaf 1½ ft long

waxy, wavy-edged leaves

F. lyrata
(F. pandurata)
Fiddle Leaf Fig

leaf 8 in. long

leaves hairy when young

F. benghalensis
Bengal Fig

F. elastica decora
Rubber Plant

F. triangularis

**F. elastica
Black Prince**

**F. rubiginosa
variegata**
Rusty Fig

**F. elastica
tricolor**

F. religiosa
Bo Tree

The low-growing Ficus species are dealt with on the previous page — here we are concerned with the ever-popular Rubber Plant and its relatives. The **Ficus elastica** of earlier days had narrow, drooping leaves and a rather fussy nature — it has been replaced by a number of varieties. **Decora** is the favourite one, **robusta** has even larger, wider leaves and **Black Prince** is just like robusta but with near-black foliage. There are also variegated types with yellow- or cream-splashed leaves — look for the pink midrib of **doescheri**, the complicated marbling of **schrijvereana**, the pink flush of **tricolor** and the cream edges of **variegata**. **F. benjamina** is increasing in popularity because it is a splendid specimen plant for the modern home. The variety **nuda** has narrow leaves — other varieties include **Hawaii**, **Natasha**, **variegata**, **Starlight** and **Gold Princess**. F. benjamina is a weeping tree growing about 6 ft high — **F. rubiginosa** (**F. australis**) is a low-spreading tree with 4 in. long leaves. Its common name (Rusty Fig) is derived from the brown colouration of the underside of the leaves. Other species with 3–4 in. leaves include **F. triangularis** (triangular), **F. retusa** (oval) and **F. religiosa** (heart-shaped with a tail-like tip). Even smaller is the foliage of the shrub-like **F. buxifolia** — the brown stems bear 1 in. triangular leaves. But the spectacular species are the large-leaved ones — **F. benghalensis** (the Banyan Tree of India) bears leaves of the standard Rubber Plant type but which are hairy when young. The largest-leaved popular Ficus is **F. lyrata** — violin-like foliage in both shape and size. For something new look for the tall-growing **F. Ali** which bears long and narrow leaves.

Ficus elastica robusta

Ficus benjamina variegata

Ficus benjamina Starlight

FITTONIA

**FOLIAGE
HOUSE PLANT**
page 51

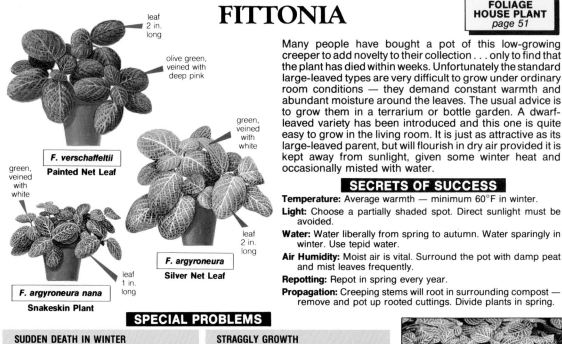

leaf 2 in. long

olive green, veined with deep pink

F. verschaffeltii
Painted Net Leaf

green, veined with white

green, veined with white

F. argyroneura
Silver Net Leaf

leaf 2 in. long

F. argyroneura nana
Snakeskin Plant

leaf 1 in. long

Many people have bought a pot of this low-growing creeper to add novelty to their collection . . . only to find that the plant has died within weeks. Unfortunately the standard large-leaved types are very difficult to grow under ordinary room conditions — they demand constant warmth and abundant moisture around the leaves. The usual advice is to grow them in a terrarium or bottle garden. A dwarf-leaved variety has been introduced and this one is quite easy to grow in the living room. It is just as attractive as its large-leaved parent, but will flourish in dry air provided it is kept away from sunlight, given some winter heat and occasionally misted with water.

SECRETS OF SUCCESS

Temperature: Average warmth — minimum 60°F in winter.

Light: Choose a partially shaded spot. Direct sunlight must be avoided.

Water: Water liberally from spring to autumn. Water sparingly in winter. Use tepid water.

Air Humidity: Moist air is vital. Surround the pot with damp peat and mist leaves frequently.

Repotting: Repot in spring every year.

Propagation: Creeping stems will root in surrounding compost — remove and pot up rooted cuttings. Divide plants in spring.

SPECIAL PROBLEMS

SUDDEN DEATH IN WINTER
Cause: Cold and wet conditions are always fatal. It needs warmth and slightly moist compost in winter.

STRAGGLY GROWTH
Cause: Fittonia is a creeping plant and straggly growth is natural. Cut back stems in spring.

SHRIVELLED LEAVES
Cause: Air too dry or too much light. See Secrets of Success.

YELLOWING, WILTING LEAVES
Cause: Overwatering. Carry out standard remedial treatment (see page 246).

TYPES

Fittonia is easily recognised — the leaves bear a network of white, pink or red veins. This pattern is responsible for all the common names — Net Plant, Lace Leaf, Snakeskin Plant and so on. The large-leaved **Fittonia verschaffeltii** has pink veins — for bright red veins grow the variety **pearcei**. The white-veined **F. argyroneura** is even more distinctive, but both are difficult to grow under ordinary room conditions. Choose instead the less-demanding dwarf **F. argyroneura nana**.

Fittonia argyroneura nana

GARDENIA

**FLOWERING
HOUSE PLANT**
page 55

Gardenia jasminoides

glossy leaf 4 in. long

fragrant flower 3 in. across

G. jasminoides
Gardenia

TYPE

The blooms of **Gardenia jasminoides** are semi-double or double and the petals are waxy. The plant grows about 1½ ft high and several varieties are available.

Sadly Gardenia is often a disappointment because it is extremely demanding. For flower buds to form a night temperature of 60°–65°F is required, and during the day it should be about 10°F higher. An even temperature and careful watering are needed to prevent bud drop.

SECRETS OF SUCCESS

Temperature: Average warmth — minimum 60°F in winter.

Light: Bright light is essential, but avoid direct midday sun in summer.

Water: Keep compost moist at all times — reduce watering in winter. Use soft, tepid water.

Air Humidity: Mist leaves frequently.

Repotting: Repot in spring every 2–3 years.

Propagation: Take stem cuttings in spring. Use a rooting hormone and provide bottom heat.

FOOD PLANTS

FOLIAGE HOUSE PLANT *page 51*	FLOWERING HOUSE PLANT *page 55*	FLOWERING POT PLANT *page 57*

House plants are not usually regarded as a source of food for the kitchen, but a surprisingly large number of culinary types can be grown.

Mustard and Cress are, of course, by far the most popular indoor food crops — an almost universal introduction for children to the world of plants. But there are several other leaf vegetables which can be raised on the kitchen windowsill — see page 147 for examples. Growing fruit indoors is possible, but don't expect too much. Some textbooks paint far too rosy a picture of the living room as a growing area for fresh fruit for the table. In the average room Pineapples rarely ripen, Oranges remain small and bitter, Pomegranates fall off the plant shortly after the fruits have formed and ripe Bananas remain just a dream. Still, a number of other plants will bear edible fruit if grown on a large windowsill and these are described below and overleaf.

The range of vegetables is strictly limited. Lettuce can be grown, but it is not really worthwhile and they do attract insects. Chives are a much better idea, and so are Spring Onions grown from seed. Pots of herbs on the kitchen windowsill in winter are a good idea — it saves the walk to the vegetable garden in mid winter to gather Mint, Thyme etc.

● FRUITS

TYPES

TOMATO

Tomato Minibel

Once the idea of growing the Tomato (**Lycopersicon esculentum**) as a house plant was unthinkable, but the introduction of bushy dwarfs such as **Florida Petit**, **Minibel** and **Tiny Tim** now make it possible. An even more recent introduction is the hanging basket Tomato such as **Tumbler** — see the illustration at the top of the page. Follow the standard rules — water daily when necessary, feed regularly, stake if required and tap the stems to aid pollination. Clusters of cherry-sized fruit will be your reward.

CUCUMBER

Cucumber Fembaby

Cucumber (**Cucumis sativus**) sounds even less like a house plant than Tomato, but the F_1 hybrid **Fembaby** has brought this greenhouse crop into the home. Not a thing of beauty, of course, but the plants grow no more than 3 ft high and are easily trained. The yellow flowers are all-female and each one should produce a Cucumber. Stand the pot on a windowsill in a saucer and keep topped up with water. Mist leaves daily. Whitefly can be a problem — hang a Bio Friendly Greenhouse Fly Catcher nearby.

AUBERGINE

Aubergine Long Purple

The Aubergine (**Solanum melongena ovigerum**) makes an interesting windowsill plant, growing about 1 ft high and bearing large leaves and shiny fruits. Pinch out the tips if the stems exceed this height — stake as necessary and mist the leaves regularly. Grow **Easter Egg** for white fruits, **Long Purple** for the standard Eggplant of the supermarket or **Black Enorma** (1 lb. or more) to impress the neighbours. As with Cucumbers whitefly can be a problem — avoid trouble in the same way.

● FRUITS continued

PEANUT

Peanut

The Peanut or Groundnut (**Arachis hypogaea**) is an annual grown by planting unshelled and unroasted peanuts. The result is a rather plain 1 ft high plant with oval leaflets and short-lived yellow flowers borne just above soil level. Nothing special — but after the flowers have faded there is the extraordinary growth habit of stalks which curve downwards and drive the developing fruits into the compost. Warm conditions are essential.

STRAWBERRY

Strawberry

You can grow ordinary Straw-berries in tubs or clay strawberry pots indoors, but it is usually better to choose the more compact Alpine Strawberry (**Fragaria vesca sempervirens**). It is easily raised from seed and the small plant (there are no runners) will produce its first fruits about 4 or 5 months after the seeds have germinated. Choose the variety **Alexandria** for the largest berries.

SWEET PEPPER

Sweet Pepper

The varieties of Capsicum grown indoors are nearly always the small-fruited Christmas Pepper (page 112) used to brighten up the winter windowsill. But there are also the large-fruited Sweet Peppers (**Capsicum grossum**) which are picked at the green or red stage for cooking. You will need a large well-lit area — they grow 2–3 ft high. Insects such as whitefly love them, which can make them a poor indoor plant. Suitable varieties include **Canape** and **Gypsy**.

MUSHROOM

Mushroom

The Mushroom (**Psalliota campestris**) may seem a strange choice for a book on indoor plants, but it is a/ fruit-bearing plant which is easily grown in an ordinary room and so earns its place here. Buy a Mushroom Tub — they are readily available and everything will have been done for you. No special care is needed — the upper surface or casing is kept moist and the first buttons will appear in 4–6 weeks.

OKRA

Okra

Okra (**Hibiscus esculentus**) has begun to appear in the supermarkets — 4 in. long pods used in soups, stews and curries. Seeds are now sold by large nurseries and it is generally grown in the green-house. Although you won't find it in the house plant books you can grow it in a sunny spot indoors. You will need space — the plants grow about 3 ft high, but there are no pests to worry about and the pretty yellow flowers and erect pods provide a conversation piece.

KUMQUAT

Kumquat

The Kumquat is the one member of the Citrus family which can be relied upon to bear edible fruit under well-lit but ordinary room conditions. **Fortunella margarita** (Nagami Kumquat) bears oval orange fruits which are about 1½ in. long and are eaten whole. The glossy leaves are about 4 in. long — the spring and summer sweetly-scented white flowers are followed by the fruit in autumn.

● LEAVES

PARSLEY

Parsley

Sow Parsley (**Petroselinum crispum**) between spring and midsummer and have patience — it takes a long time to germinate. Pot up the seedlings in ordinary pots or plant in the holes in the sides of a parsley pot. Place the pots on a sunny windowsill and water regularly. Parsley is never really happy indoors — try to stand the pots outdoors on fine days and raise new plants each year to replace the old stock.

MINT

Mint

There is always a need for a plentiful supply of fresh Mint (**Mentha spicata**) in the kitchen. Many varieties are available. Lift a clump from the garden in autumn or spring and plant in a 5 in. pot, or buy a pot from your local garden shop. Stand the pot in a saucer of water during the summer months — remove the water and keep rather dry in winter. Keep the pot on a windowsill and cut regularly.

OTHER HERBS

Basil

A windowsill in a cool room can be used to grow several varieties of herbs. Grow them in separate pots and the best plan is to buy the pots from your local garden shop rather than trying to raise the plants from seed. Some are annuals — the suitable ones for indoors are Basil (**Ocimum basilicum**) and Sweet Marjoram (**Origanum marjorana**). Others are perennials — the house plant ones are Sage (**Salvia officinalis**) and Thyme (**Thymus vulgaris**).

LETTUCE

Lettuce

Growing Lettuce (**Lactuca sativa**) on the windowsill is certainly not a way to save money, nor is it really satisfactory as the plants tend to be leggy. Still, it can be fun if you don't have a garden. Sow a forcing variety such as **Kloek**, **Dandie** or **Kwiek** — prick out the seedlings into 5 in. pots filled with potting compost. Place on a windowsill and keep the compost moist at all times. The plants will be ready to cut in 2-3 months.

MUSTARD & CRESS

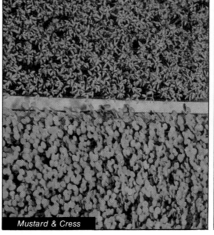

Mustard & Cress

The favourite edible indoor plants are Mustard (**Sinapis alba**) and Cress (**Lepidium sativum**). No description is really necessary for the millions who gained their first horticultural experience with them. Sow Cress seed evenly and thickly on damp kitchen paper in a tray. Sprinkle Mustard seed amongst or alongside the Cress 3 days later — move to a well-lit spot when the leaves start to unfold. Cut when the seedlings are 2 in. high — this will take 10-15 days.

CHIVES

Chives

Chives (**Allium schoenoprasum**) will grow happily on a sunny windowsill if the compost is kept moist at all times and the grassy leaves are cut regularly for use in omelettes, potato salad etc. You can start with seed but it is easier to buy a pot from a garden centre or dig up a clump from the garden. With seed-sown Chives trim off tips when they are about 2 in. high — do not let the plants flower.

FUCHSIA

FLOWERING POT PLANT
page 57

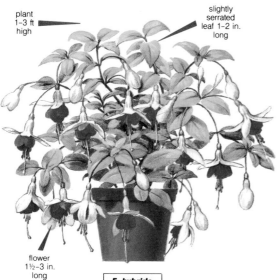

plant 1–3 ft high

slightly serrated leaf 1–2 in. long

flower 1½–3 in. long

F. hybrida

BUSH   TRAILER   STANDARD

Fuchsias occur in a wide range of colours, shapes and sizes. There are hundreds of named varieties of F. hybrida, with the familiar bell-shaped flowers hanging from the stems. These blooms may be single, semi-double or double, with colour combinations of white, pink, red or purple. A collection of these hybrids can provide blooms from spring to autumn, and some experts regard the Fuchsia as the most satisfactory of all flowering house plants.

Unfortunately nearly all of the plants bought for home decoration or as gifts are consigned to the dustbin once flowering stops and the leaves begin to fall. It is, however, quite easy to overwinter the plant in a cool room. The leaves will fall but growth begins again in the spring and with proper care the plant can be kept for many years. Flowers are borne on new growth, so cut back the stems in early spring just before growth begins.

Regular training and pruning are necessary to keep the plant free-flowering and shapely. With young plants pinch out the stem tips to promote bushy growth, and with flowering plants remove dead blooms to induce bud formation.

SECRETS OF SUCCESS

Temperature: Cool or average warmth — plant may suffer if temperature exceeds 70°F. Keep at 50°–60°F in winter.

Light: Bright light away from direct sunshine.

Water: Keep compost moist at all times from spring to autumn. Water sparingly in winter.

Air Humidity: Mist leaves occasionally during the growing season.

Repotting: Repot in spring every year.

Propagation: Take stem cuttings in spring or summer. Use a rooting hormone.

SPECIAL PROBLEMS

LOSS OF LEAVES
Cause: Hot dry atmosphere is the usual reason for general leaf fall; mist leaves occasionally and stand the plant outdoors in hot weather. The common causes of the progressive loss of lower leaves are underwatering and lack of light.

FLOWER BUDS DROP
Cause: Poor watering (too much or too little) is the common cause. Other possibilities are too little light, too much heat and moving or turning the pot.

POOR FLOWERING
Cause: Many factors can shorten the flowering period. Keeping the plant moist and warm in winter will certainly have this effect; so will too little food or water and too little light during the growing season.

BROWN SPOTS WITH YELLOW MARGINS ON LEAVES
Cause: Leaf spot disease, encouraged by over-watering in cold weather.

INSECTS
Both red spider mite and whitefly can be serious in hot and dry conditions — see page 244.

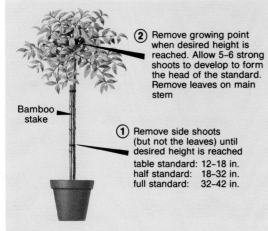

HOW TO MAKE A FLOWERING STANDARD
Choose a vigorous upright variety. Use a rooted cutting and keep the plant well-lit in winter.

② Remove growing point when desired height is reached. Allow 5–6 strong shoots to develop to form the head of the standard. Remove leaves on main stem

Bamboo stake

① Remove side shoots (but not the leaves) until desired height is reached

table standard: 12–18 in.
half standard: 18–32 in.
full standard: 32–42 in.

TYPES

Fuchsia hybrida is deservedly a popular house plant. There are hundreds of named hybrids — in nearly all cases the colour is derived from both the showy sepals and petals, which may or may not be the same colour. These are the familiar Fuchsia flowers — single, semi-double or double bells on soft-stemmed bushes. To induce bushiness, pinch out the tip after 3 sets of leaves have formed. When each of the resulting side shoots has developed 3 sets of leaves, repeat the pinching-out operation. Remove dead flowers to promote bud formation.

In addition to the familiar hooped-skirt types, there are the Clustered Hybrids or Honeysuckle Fuchsias, generally derived from **F. triphylla**. Here the colour of the bloom comes from the sepals — the petals are either insignificant or absent.

Fuchsias are usually grown as bushes, although the trailing types are widely used in hanging baskets. Examples of Trailing Fuchsias include **Marinka** (red), **Golden Marinka** (red, variegated foliage), **Red Ribbons** (white and red) and **Pink Galore** (pink).

It is possible to train a vigorous upright variety as a standard (see page 148), but this will take several seasons and is more suited to the conservatory than to the living room.

Fuchsia Pink Galore

SINGLE HYBRIDS	SEMI-DOUBLE HYBRIDS	DOUBLE HYBRIDS	CLUSTERED HYBRIDS

Winston Churchill
(pink sepals, purple petals)
Aintree
(white sepals, red petals)
Bon Accord
(white sepals, lilac petals)
Checkerboard
(red and white sepals, red petals)
Brutus
(red sepals, purple petals)

Snowcap
(red sepals, white petals)
Tennessee Waltz
(pink sepals, lilac petals)
Texas Longhorn
(red sepals, white petals)
Whirlaway
(white sepals, white petals)
Satellite
(red sepals, white petals)

Swingtime
(red sepals, white petals)
Fascination
(pink sepals, pink petals)
Midge
(rose sepals, pink petals)
Alice Hoffman
(red sepals, white petals)
Brigadoon
(red sepals, purple petals)

Gartenmeister Bonstedt
(salmon-orange sepals)
Swanley Yellow
(orange sepals)
Leverkusen
(red sepals)
Thalia
(deep pink sepals)
Traudchen Bonstedt
(pale salmon sepals)

Fuchsia Winston Churchill

Fuchsia Texas Longhorn

Fuchsia Traudchen Bonstedt

FUN PLANTS

**FOLIAGE
HOUSE PLANT**
page 51

There is no clear-cut definition of a Fun Plant — the only feature they all have in common is that these indoor plants cost nothing to buy. They are obtained by sowing or planting seeds, pips or plant tops from a wide variety of vegetables and fruits bought for the kitchen.

Growing Carrot (Daucus carota) tops is something we usually do with the children on a rainy day, but the plants produced bear attractive feathery foliage which fits in well with a small Pot Group or Indoor Garden. Cut off the top inch from a well-grown Carrot and trim off the outer leaves. Push the cut end into compost in a 5 in. pot and leave just the crown exposed. It will take about a month for the foliage display to develop fully as in the illustration on the right. Keep in a cool and partially shaded spot.

Not all plant top types are projects for children — Bromeliads are expensive to buy and you can get one for nothing by using the top of a fresh Pineapple (Ananas comosus). Choose a fruit with a healthy crown of leaves and cut off the top inch of the Pineapple. Pare away the outer soft flesh so that you are left with a leafy crown attached to a cylindrical fibrous core. Leave this to dry for a couple of days and then plant in compost in a 5 in. pot. See page 85 for cultural details.

The most popular Fun Plants are those grown from pips and stones. The choice is extensive — Almond, Pomegranate, Lychee, Coffee, Peach, Plum, Apple etc. Try any of these, but the best results are usually obtained by choosing one of the popular trio described below.

TYPES

AVOCADO

Avocado

An Avocado tree (**Persea americana**) can be grown quite easily from the large stone within the fruit — after a few years you will have a large-leaved plant about 3 ft tall — grown from scratch with your own hands. Push the blunt end of the stone into a pot containing a multi-purpose compost — leave the pointed end exposed. Keep warm (65°F) until the leaves appear — keep cool in winter. Repot annually — pinch out tips to encourage bushiness.

DATE

Date

The Dates you buy are the fruit of **Phoenix dactylifera**, an attractive Palm with stiff leaves and narrow leaflets. Plant the stone vertically in compost so that the top is about ½ in. below the surface. Keep it warm (70°F) until germination takes place — be patient, you may have to wait for 3 months. Keep the plant fairly cool in winter (50°–55°F) and repot every year. With care the Date stone will produce a stately 5 ft tree.

CITRUS

Citrus

The pips of citrus fruits germinate quite readily — choose Lemon (**Citrus limon**), Orange (**C. sinensis**) or Grapefruit (**C. paradisi**). Soak the pips overnight and then press each one down to a depth of ½ in. into compost in a 3½ in. pot. Keep in a warm and dark place until the shoots appear, then move to a sunny spot. Your plants will need to spend the summer months outdoors and the winter in a fairly cool room (50°–60°F).

Geogenanthus undatus

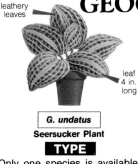
leathery leaves

leaf 4 in. long

G. undatus
Seersucker Plant

TYPE

Only one species is available for indoors — **Geogenanthus undatus**. A compact plant, rarely exceeding 1 ft. The stems are unbranched — the leaves dark green with silvery stripes.

GEOGENANTHUS

FOLIAGE HOUSE PLANT
page 51

Geogenanthus produces frilly-edged mauve flowers in summer, but it is grown for its unusual foliage rather than for the short-lived blooms. Each leaf is striped from base to tip and the surface is puckered — hence the common name. Geogenanthus is neither an easy plant to find nor an easy type to care for — it needs both warmth and moist air.

SECRETS OF SUCCESS

Temperature: Warm — minimum 65°F at all times.

Light: Brightly lit spot, away from direct summer sun.

Water: Keep compost moist at all times — reduce watering in winter.

Air Humidity: Mist leaves frequently in spring and summer.

Repotting: Repot, if necessary, in spring.

Propagation: Take stem cuttings in spring. Use a rooting hormone and provide bottom heat.

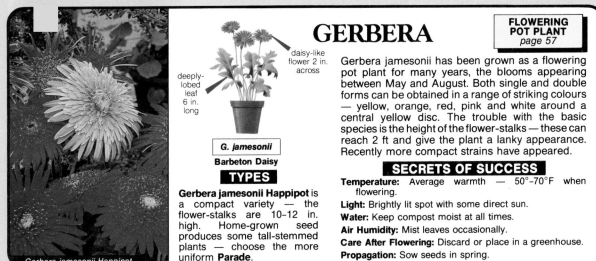
Gerbera jamesonii Happipot

deeply-lobed leaf 6 in. long

daisy-like flower 2 in. across

G. jamesonii
Barbeton Daisy

TYPES

Gerbera jamesonii Happipot is a compact variety — the flower-stalks are 10–12 in. high. Home-grown seed produces some tall-stemmed plants — choose the more uniform **Parade**.

GERBERA

FLOWERING POT PLANT
page 57

Gerbera jamesonii has been grown as a flowering pot plant for many years, the blooms appearing between May and August. Both single and double forms can be obtained in a range of striking colours — yellow, orange, red, pink and white around a central yellow disc. The trouble with the basic species is the height of the flower-stalks — these can reach 2 ft and give the plant a lanky appearance. Recently more compact strains have appeared.

SECRETS OF SUCCESS

Temperature: Average warmth — 50°–70°F when flowering.

Light: Brightly lit spot with some direct sun.

Water: Keep compost moist at all times.

Air Humidity: Mist leaves occasionally.

Care After Flowering: Discard or place in a greenhouse.

Propagation: Sow seeds in spring.

Glechoma hederacea variegata

pale green leaf, blotched or edged with white

hairy surface

G. hederacea variegata
Ground Ivy

TYPE

It is **Glechoma hederacea variegata** (sometimes sold as **Nepeta hederacea**) which is grown as a house plant. Use it for ground cover or in a hanging basket — the stems must be cut back drastically each winter.

GLECHOMA

FOLIAGE HOUSE PLANT
page 51

Glechoma is an excellent trailing plant — quick growing, easy to propagate, undemanding and with the added bonuses of pale blue flowers and fragrant 1 in. leaves. It does have a major drawback — hardly any house plant suppliers in Britain offer it for sale. Like Ivy it is one of the few house plants which originated in Europe and is hardy outdoors. This means that cool winter conditions are required.

SECRETS OF SUCCESS

Temperature: Average warmth — if possible keep cool in winter.

Light: Well-lit but away from direct sunlight.

Water: Water liberally from spring to autumn. Water sparingly in winter.

Air Humidity: Mist leaves occasionally in summer.

Repotting: Repot in spring, but not usually necessary.

Propagation: Use trimmings as stem cuttings.

Gloriosa superba

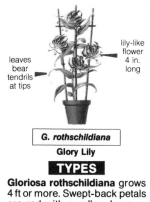

leaves bear tendrils at tips

lily-like flower 4 in. long

G. rothschildiana

Glory Lily

GLORIOSA

FLOWERING POT PLANT
page 57

The Glory Lily bears large flowers in midsummer. The stems are weak and some form of support must be provided. At flowering time keep warm and well-lit. It is either bought in flower or raised at home from a tuber. Plant the tuber upright in a 6 in. pot in spring with the tip 1 in. below the surface. Water sparingly at first, then more freely as the stems start to grow.

TYPES

Gloriosa rothschildiana grows 4 ft or more. Swept-back petals are red with a yellow base — **G. superba** is similar but petals change from green to orange and finally to red.

SECRETS OF SUCCESS

Temperature: Warm or average warmth — minimum 60°F in the growing season.

Light: Brightly lit spot, but shade from hot summer sun.

Water: Water liberally during the growing season.

Air Humidity: Mist leaves occasionally.

Care After Flowering: Reduce and then stop watering. Store tuber in its pot at 50°–55°F. Repot in spring.

Propagation: Remove and plant offsets at repotting time.

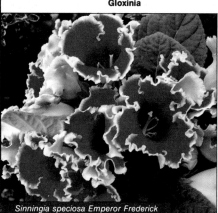

upturned bell-shaped flower 3 in. across

oval, velvety leaf 8 in. long

Sinningia speciosa

Gloxinia

Sinningia speciosa Emperor Frederick

GLOXINIA

FLOWERING POT PLANT
page 57

Gloxinia (proper name Sinningia speciosa) is usually bought in flower during summer. Choose a plant with plenty of unopened buds and with proper care it should continue to bloom for 2 months or more. Tubers for potting up are available in spring — for details of planting see Secrets of Success. The velvety blooms are 3 in. or more in diameter — white, pink, red, blue and purple varieties can be purchased. Gloxinia, unlike so many gift plants, can be kept for growing again next season but it is not a particularly easy plant for the novice. It needs moist air, freedom from draughts, regular feeding and careful watering.

SECRETS OF SUCCESS

Temperature: Average warmth — minimum 60°F.

Light: Bright light away from direct sunlight.

Water: Keep compost moist at all times. Use tepid water — keep off leaves and flowers.

Air Humidity: Stand pot on a pebble tray (see page 19) or surround with damp peat. Occasionally mist air around the plant.

Care After Flowering: Reduce watering and stop feeding. Allow to dry out when leaves turn yellow — store pot at about 50°F. Repot tuber in fresh compost in spring — plant hollow side up with top of tuber level with compost surface. Keep warm and rather dry until leaves appear, then provide the recommended temperature, light and watering conditions described above.

Propagation: Sow seeds in spring or take leaf cuttings in early summer.

TYPES

The petal edges of **Sinningia speciosa** are either plain or ruffled. Multi-lobed (double) varieties are available. There are 2 groups which are an improvement on the species — the **maxima** group with somewhat nodding flowers and the **fyfiana** group which bears extra-large and upright blooms. A number of named varieties are available — examples include **Gregor Mendel** (double, red with white edge), **Emperor Frederick** (single, red with white edge), **Duchess of York** (single, violet with white edge), **Mont Blanc** (single, white) and **Champers** (single, pale pink with mauve spots). The large foliage is sometimes a disadvantage — the **Brocade** strain has relatively small leaves and double flowers in blue or red.

SPECIAL PROBLEMS

CURLED LEAVES WITH BROWN TIPS
Cause: Hot, dry air is the usual reason. During flowering it is essential to increase the humidity around the plant.

PLANT COLLAPSE, TUBER SOFT & ROTTEN
Cause: Waterlogging due to overwatering or poor drainage. Another possible cause is the use of cold instead of tepid water.

PALE ELONGATED LEAVES WITH BROWN EDGES
Cause: Not enough light. Gloxinia needs protection from hot summer sun but it will not tolerate dark places.

FLOWER BUDS FAIL TO OPEN
Cause: Several possibilities — most usual reasons are dry air and cold draughts.

GREVILLEA

FOLIAGE HOUSE PLANT page 51

Grevillea robusta

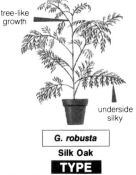

tree-like growth

underside silky

G. robusta

Silk Oak

TYPE

Grevillea robusta is the only type grown. The lacy, Fern-like effect of the foliage tends to disappear with age, so it is usual to cut back or discard plants once they reach 2–3 ft.

Large indoor trees are expensive to buy, but with nearly all suitable varieties buying a seedling will mean a wait of several years before it becomes a specimen tree. Grevillea may be the answer for a cool and bright spot — it can be grown easily from seed and will be 1 ft high in the first season — it may reach the ceiling in four or five years.

SECRETS OF SUCCESS

Temperature: Cool or average warmth — minimum 45°F in winter.

Light: Brightly lit spot — protect from midday summer sun.

Water: Water liberally from spring to autumn. Water sparingly in winter.

Air Humidity: Mist leaves occasionally.

Repotting: Repot in spring every year.

Propagation: Sow seeds in spring or summer.

GYNURA

FOLIAGE HOUSE PLANT page 51

Gynura sarmentosa

leaf 3 in. long

dark green, covered with purple hairs

G. sarmentosa

Velvet Plant

TYPES

Gynura sarmentosa is a popular trailer. The foliage has a velvety look — gleaming purple in bright light. **G. aurantiaca** has larger leaves, but it is more upright and less attractive.

Gynura grows quickly, it has no special needs and the foliage is covered with shiny purple hairs. This attractive colouring requires good light for development. Gynura produces small Dandelion-like flowers in spring — these should be removed at the bud stage as the aroma is offensive. Pinch out the tips occasionally.

SECRETS OF SUCCESS

Temperature: Average warmth — minimum 50°F in winter.

Light: Brightly lit spot — some direct sunlight is beneficial.

Water: Water liberally from spring to autumn. Water sparingly in winter.

Air Humidity: Mist leaves occasionally.

Repotting: Repot, if necessary, in spring.

Propagation: Stem cuttings root very easily.

HAEMANTHUS

FLOWERING HOUSE PLANT page 55

Haemanthus katharinae

ball-like flower-head 8 in. across

wavy leaf 1 ft long

H. katharinae

Blood Lily

TYPES

Haemanthus katharinae is the most popular evergreen. The red flowers appear in summer — offsets are not produced. The flower-head of **H. albiflos** is white and much smaller — offsets are formed.

A stout stalk bears the giant flower-head above the few large leaves at the base. The species of Haemanthus differ in more than flower colour and size — the one you choose may be either evergreen or devoid of leaves for part of the year, and it may or may not produce offsets at the base. The bulb is planted with the tip above the compost.

SECRETS OF SUCCESS

Temperature: Average warmth — minimum 50°F in winter.

Light: Bright light with some direct sun.

Water: Keep compost moist at all times. Water sparingly in winter.

Air Humidity: Sponge leaves occasionally.

Repotting: Repot in spring every 4–5 years.

Propagation: Detach offsets and pot up in summer. Sow seeds in spring.

HEDERA

FOLIAGE HOUSE PLANT
page 51

stems not self supporting

leaves not succulent

There are several types of Ivy — German Ivy, Swedish Ivy, Ground Ivy etc. Here we are dealing with the 'True' Ivies which are all varieties of Hedera. These Ivies thoroughly deserve their good reputation as decorative plants, and have long been a basic feature of Pot Groups. As climbers they can quickly clothe bare surroundings, provided you choose a vigorous Hedera helix variety. The stems bear aerial roots which cling to wallpaper, woodwork etc. The larger leaved, slower growing Canary Island Ivy does not possess these clinging aerial roots, so adequate support is necessary.

Ivies are not only climbers. They are just as useful as trailers in hanging baskets or as ground cover between larger plants, and it is here that the smaller bushy varieties come into their own. Examples of suitable types are Eva, Glacier and Needlepoint Ivy.

Very popular and useful, but the Ivies do not deserve their reputation as easy plants. They flourished in the unheated rooms of yesterday, but they do suffer in the hot, dry air of the centrally heated homes of today. Regular misting of the leaves is necessary when the radiators are switched on in winter. Expect brown leaf tips if you don't.

SECRETS OF SUCCESS

Temperature: Cool but frost-free. Ideally the room should be unheated in winter. Night temperatures above 60°F can lead to problems.

Light: Bright conditions in winter. Avoid direct sunlight in summer.

Water: Keep compost moist in summer by regular watering. In winter water sparingly, but never let the compost dry out.

Air Humidity: Mist leaves frequently in summer, especially if the room is warm and dry. Mist leaves in winter if the room is heated. Wash leaves occasionally.

Repotting: Transfer to a larger pot in spring every 2 years.

Propagation: Occasional removal of tips is necessary to promote bushiness. Use these trimmings as stem cuttings.

HOW TO MAKE AN IVY TREE

Cut the side shoots from a specimen of Fatshedera lizei and stake the stem. When it has reached 3 ft high remove the top growth with a horizontal cut. Make crossed cuts on stem top as shown below.

4 Ivy cuttings inserted into cut stem and bound with raffia

1 inch-deep cuts

SPECIAL PROBLEMS

LEAVES UNDERSIZED. BARE SPINDLY GROWTH
Cause: Too little light, although it is natural for mature leaves at stem base to drop with age. Cut back bare stems.

LEAF EDGES BROWN & DRY. BARE SPINDLY GROWTH
Cause: Too warm. Look for red spider mite (see page 244). Cut back bare stems. Move to a cooler site.

LEAVES ALL GREEN
Cause: Too little light. Variegated types revert to all-green habit in shady conditions. Another possibility is the need for repotting.

LEAF TIPS BROWN & DRY. STUNTED GROWTH
Cause: Air too dry. Look for red spider mite (see page 244). Remove dead growth. Mist leaves regularly.

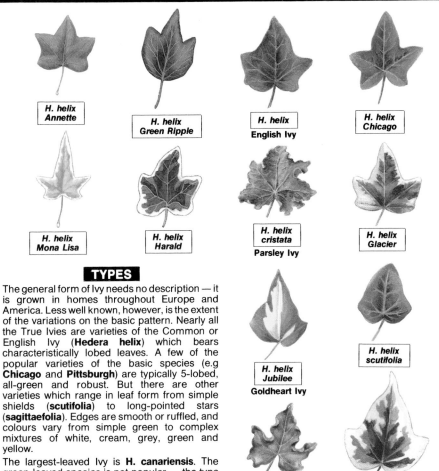

H. helix
Annette

H. helix
Green Ripple

H. helix
English Ivy

H. helix
Chicago

H. helix
Eva

H. helix
Mona Lisa

H. helix
Harald

H. helix
cristata
Parsley Ivy

H. helix
Glacier

H. helix
lutzii

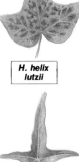

H. helix
Jubilee
Goldheart Ivy

H. helix
scutifolia

H. helix
sagittaefolia
Needlepoint Ivy

H. helix
Ivalace
Lacyleaf Ivy

H. canariensis
Gloire de Marengo
Canary Island Ivy

H. helix
marmorata

TYPES

The general form of Ivy needs no description — it is grown in homes throughout Europe and America. Less well known, however, is the extent of the variations on the basic pattern. Nearly all the True Ivies are varieties of the Common or English Ivy (**Hedera helix**) which bears characteristically lobed leaves. A few of the popular varieties of the basic species (e.g **Chicago** and **Pittsburgh**) are typically 5-lobed, all-green and robust. But there are other varieties which range in leaf form from simple shields (**scutifolia**) to long-pointed stars (**sagittaefolia**). Edges are smooth or ruffled, and colours vary from simple green to complex mixtures of white, cream, grey, green and yellow.

The largest-leaved Ivy is **H. canariensis**. The green-leaved species is not popular — the type seen everywhere is the variegated **Gloire de Marengo**. Most True Ivies can be grown as either climbers or trailers — for a compact ground cover choose a small-leaved variety and pinch out the growing tips 2 or 3 times each year.

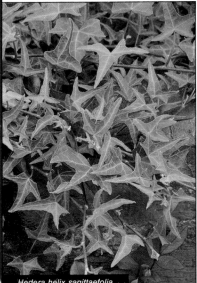

Hedera helix sagittaefolia

Hedera helix Kholibra

Hedera canariensis Gloire de Marengo

Hebe andersonii variegata

flower-head 4 in. long

leaf 4 in. long

H. andersonii

HEBE

FLOWERING HOUSE PLANT page 55

This shrub can be seen in flower in some supermarkets and garden centres in July or August — a plant for the conservatory although it can be kept in a large room for a few years. The problem is that it flowers from summer to early autumn and this is the time it should spend outdoors. The floral spikes are made up of tiny flowers which fade to white with age.

SECRETS OF SUCCESS

Temperature: Average warmth. Keep cool (50°-60°F) in winter.

Light: Bright light or semi-shade — protect from direct sunshine.

Water: Water liberally from spring to autumn — reduce watering in winter.

Air Humidity: Mist leaves occasionally.

Repotting: Repot, if necessary, in spring.

Propagation: Take stem cuttings in spring or summer.

TYPES

Hebe andersonii is an evergreen flowering shrub growing about 3 ft high — leaves are oblong and leathery. Flowers are pink or mauve. The variety **variegata** has cream-edged foliage.

Heliconia indica

leaf 9 in.-1 ft long

H. indica

HELICONIA

FOLIAGE HOUSE PLANT page 51

Heliconia in a large hot-house or in the wild is a real stunner. The large paddle-shaped leaves indicate its relationship to the Banana and the pendant 1-2 ft long flower-heads ('lobster claws') show its kinship to Strelitzia. As a house plant it has a much more modest use — the colourful foliage species are grown for their leafy display. Definitely not easy to grow and not easy to find — maybe not worth the trouble.

SECRETS OF SUCCESS

Temperature: Warm — minimum 65°F in winter.

Light: Brightly lit spot — some direct sun is beneficial.

Water: Water liberally from spring to autumn. Do not water in winter.

Air Humidity: Mist leaves daily during the growing season.

Repotting: Repot in spring every year.

Propagation: Divide plants in spring.

TYPES

Heliconia indica bears large pink leaves. **H. illustris aureostriata** is even more striking — each green leaf is covered with narrow yellow streaks at right angles to the main vein.

Heliotropium hybridum Mrs Lowther

fragrant flower-head 4-6 in. across

deeply-veined leaf 3 in. long

H. hybridum

Heliotrope

HELIOTROPIUM

FLOWERING HOUSE PLANT page 55

A good choice if you are looking for an easy-to-grow flowering plant with a strong fragrance. Purple, blue and white varieties are available. The plant can be trained as a standard — see page 148 for instructions. Heliotrope can be kept for years as a house plant but the ability to produce attractive flower-heads rapidly deteriorates with age.

SECRETS OF SUCCESS

Temperature: Cool or average warmth — keep at 40°-50°F in winter.

Light: Bright light — protect from hot summer sun.

Water: Keep compost moist at all times. Reduce watering in winter.

Air Humidity: Mist leaves occasionally.

Repotting: Repot in spring every year.

Propagation: Take stem cuttings in summer. Use a rooting hormone. Sow seeds in spring.

TYPE

Heliotropium hybridum is an excellent but little-used shrub for indoor decoration — the large heads of tiny flowers will perfume a room throughout the summer months.

HELXINE

FOLIAGE HOUSE PLANT page 51

round leaves on pinkish stems

leaf ⅓ in. long

H. soleirolii
Mind Your Own Business (Baby's Tears)

TYPES

The mossy mounds of **Helxine soleirolii (Soleirolia soleirolii)** were used for ground cover in conservatories long before the start of the present boom in house plants. The variety **argentea** has silvery leaves.

New pots of Helxine are raised at home rather than on professional nurseries. A small clump is removed from an established plant and placed on the surface of moist compost in a pot — in a short time tiny green leaves cover the surface. Helxine is excellent in hanging baskets or for covering the soil around tall plants. But a word of warning — in an indoor garden it can easily smother low-growing plants.

SECRETS OF SUCCESS

Temperature: Average warmth — minimum 45°F in winter.
Light: Bright indirect light is best but will survive almost anywhere.
Water: Keep compost moist at all times.
Air Humidity: Mist leaves frequently.
Repotting: Repot, if necessary, in spring.
Propagation: Very easy — pot up small clumps at any time of the year.

Helxine soleirolii argentea

HEMIGRAPHIS

FOLIAGE HOUSE PLANT page 51

purple metallic sheen

stalk and underside wine red

H. alternata
(H. colorata)
Red Ivy

TYPES

Hemigraphis alternata is the usual one offered for sale. Despite its name, this plant is quite different from a True Ivy —growth is limited to 1–1½ ft and the 3 in. leaves are oval. **H. exotica** (Waffle Plant) has puckered leaves.

A climbing plant, popular in the U.S for hanging baskets but a rarity in Britain. Red Ivy has coloured leaves — silvery in the shade, metallic purple when exposed to a few hours' sunshine. Hemigraphis is not an easy plant to grow, but it is not quite as difficult as indicated by some textbooks. It needs winter warmth, moist air, and pruning when stems become straggly.

SECRETS OF SUCCESS

Temperature: Average warmth — minimum 55°F in winter.
Light: Bright light or semi-shade. Some direct sun will enhance colour.
Water: Water liberally from spring to autumn. Water sparingly in winter.
Air Humidity: Mist leaves regularly.
Repotting: Repot in spring every year.
Propagation: Take stem cuttings in late spring or summer.

Hemigraphis alternata

HEPTAPLEURUM

FOLIAGE HOUSE PLANT page 51

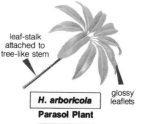

leaf-stalk attached to tree-like stem

glossy leaflets

H. arboricola
Parasol Plant

TYPES

Stake **Heptapleurum arboricola** to produce a 6 ft unbranched tree. Named varieties are available — **Hayata** (greyish leaves), **Geisha Girl** (rounded leaf tips) and **variegata** (yellow-splashed leaves).

A fast-growing tree-like plant with about ten leaflets radiating from each leaf-stalk. Its main advantage over its close relative Schefflera is that it will happily grow as a bush if the growing point of the main stem is removed. Heptapleurum is quite easy if you provide winter warmth, good light and moist air. Leaf fall may occur if there is a sudden change in conditions — blackened tips indicate overwatering.

SECRETS OF SUCCESS

Temperature: Average warmth — minimum 60°F in winter.
Light: Bright light — not direct sun.
Water: Water liberally from spring to autumn. Water sparingly in winter.
Air Humidity: Mist leaves frequently. Wash leaves occasionally.
Repotting: Repot in spring every year.
Propagation: Take stem cuttings or sow seeds in spring.

Heptapleurum arboricola variegata

prominent central column

double or single flower 4–5 in. across

saw-edged leaf 3 in. long

H. rosa-sinensis
Rose of China

Hibiscus rosa-sinensis cooperi

HIBISCUS

FLOWERING HOUSE PLANT page 55

Hibiscus is an excellent specimen plant for the sunny windowsill. Its large papery flowers last for only a day or two, but with proper care there will be a succession of blooms from spring to autumn. A Hibiscus bush can live for 20 years or more, and may be kept small by regular pruning — cut back stems in late winter to induce bushiness. It can also be trained as a standard (see page 148).

SECRETS OF SUCCESS

Temperature: Average warmth — minimum 55°F in winter.

Light: As much light as possible, but shade from hot sun.

Water: Keep compost moist at all times — reduce watering in winter.

Air Humidity: Mist leaves occasionally.

Repotting: Repot in spring every year.

Propagation: Take stem cuttings in late spring.

TYPES

Hibiscus rosa-sinensis has numerous named varieties in white, yellow, orange, pink and red. The variety **cooperi** has variegated foliage. **H. schizopetalus** stems require support — its petals are frilly edged, tubular and pendant.

SPECIAL PROBLEMS

BUD DROP
Cause: Dry compost is the usual reason. Other causes are underfeeding or a sudden change in temperature.

LOSS OF LEAVES
Cause: Dry compost is the usual reason. Other possibilities are draughts and overwatering.

CURLING OF LEAVES
Cause: Air too dry. Mist leaves in spring and summer.

INSECTS
Aphid and red spider mite can be problems.

Hoya bella

single flower

fragrant white flower with reddish-purple centre — approximately 10 per cluster

non-glossy leaf 1 in. long

H. bella
Miniature Wax Plant

glossy leaf 3 in. long

fragrant pale pink flower with red centre — approximately 20 per cluster

single flower

H. carnosa variegata
Variegated Wax Plant

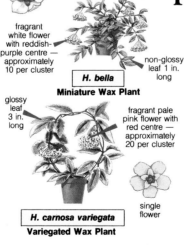

HOYA

FLOWERING HOUSE PLANT page 55

The Wax Plant (H. carnosa) is an easy-to-grow flowering climber. Its vigorous twining stems can reach 15 ft or more, and they must be trained on wires, trellis work or on a moss stick. New stems are bare — the leaves which later appear are fleshy and green, or green-and-cream on the Variegated Wax Plant. The fragrant flower-heads appear between late spring and early autumn. The Miniature Wax Plant (H. bella) needs more heat and humidity but less light — it is best planted in a hanging basket. There are several 'do nots' for growing Hoyas — do not disturb the plant once buds appear, do not remove the dead flowers and do not repot until it is unavoidable.

SECRETS OF SUCCESS

Temperature: Average warmth. Keep cool (50°–55°F) in winter.

Light: Bright light — some direct sun is beneficial.

Water: Water liberally from spring to autumn. Water sparingly in winter.

Air Humidity: Mist leaves regularly, but not when plant is in bloom.

Repotting: Repot, if necessary, in spring.

Propagation: Take stem cuttings, using mature shoots, in spring.

TYPES

The Hoyas are climbers or trailers with fleshy leaves and clusters of waxy, star-shaped flowers which appear from May to September. **Hoya carnosa** is the basic species. Several varieties are available, including **variegata** (cream-edged leaves), **exotica** (yellow-centred leaves) and **Krimson Princess** (red-coloured young foliage). **H. australis** is quite similar, but its leaves are almost round. **H. bella** is a trailer and is much more difficult to grow under room conditions than H. carnosa. **H. multiflora** is another species which is commercially available — pale yellow flowers are its claim to fame.

HYDRANGEA

FLOWERING POT PLANT page 57

Hydrangea macrophylla

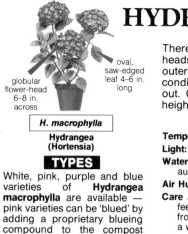

globular flower-head 6–8 in. across

oval, saw-edged leaf 4–6 in. long

H. macrophylla

Hydrangea (Hortensia)

TYPES

White, pink, purple and blue varieties of **Hydrangea macrophylla** are available — pink varieties can be 'blued' by adding a proprietary blueing compound to the compost before the flowers open.

There are the *Mop Heads* (see drawing) with round heads and the *Lacecaps* (see photograph) with an outer ring of open flowers. Two basic needs — cool conditions and compost which is not allowed to dry out. Cut back stems after flowering to half their height.

SECRETS OF SUCCESS

Temperature: Cool — minimum 45°F in winter.

Light: Bright light away from direct sunlight.

Water: Keep compost moist at all times from spring to autumn. Use rainwater if tap water is hard.

Air Humidity: Mist leaves occasionally.

Care After Flowering: Repot and continue to water and feed — stand outdoors during summer. Overwinter in a frost-free room. Water sparingly. In mid winter move to a warmer, brighter room and increase watering.

Propagation: Not practical in the home.

HYPOCYRTA

FLOWERING HOUSE PLANT page 55

Hypocyrta glabra

pouch-like flower 1 in. long

glossy leaf 1½ in. long

H. glabra

Clog Plant

TYPES

Hypocyrta glabra needs moist air. The branches are erect or gracefully arching, and the orange blooms (midsummer) are waxy. **H. nummularia** is a trailing relative.

The Clog Plant produces large numbers of orange flowers which look like tiny goldfish. When not in bloom it is an attractive foliage plant with shiny, dark green succulent leaves. In the growing season the main needs of the Clog Plant are careful watering and frequent misting — in winter place the plant in a cool, sunlit spot and cut the stems back to encourage flowering growth next spring.

SECRETS OF SUCCESS

Temperature: Average warmth — minimum 50°F in winter.

Light: Bright or light shade — some direct sun in winter.

Water: Water moderately from spring to autumn. Water sparingly in winter.

Air Humidity: Mist leaves regularly.

Repotting: Repot in spring every 2 years.

Propagation: Take stem cuttings in spring or summer.

HYPOESTES

FOLIAGE HOUSE PLANT page 51

Hypoestes sanguinolenta Splash

pink spots

leaf 2 in. long

H. sanguinolenta
(H. phyllostachya)

Freckle Face (Polka Dot Plant)

TYPES

The leaves of **Hypoestes sanguinolenta** are covered with pale pink spots — they are at their showiest in the variety **Splash**. Pinch out tips to maintain bushiness.

Hypoestes is grown for its spotted leaves. In a well-lit place with some direct sunshine the leaf colouring will be vivid — in a shady site the foliage will be all-green. Young plants make attractive small bushes — prune regularly to keep them 1–2 ft high. The lavender flowers should be pinched out. After flowering, the plant sometimes becomes dormant. Reduce watering until new growth starts.

SECRETS OF SUCCESS

Temperature: Average warmth — minimum 55°F in winter.

Light: Bright light — some direct sun will enhance colour.

Water: Keep compost evenly moist. Water liberally from spring to autumn — more sparingly in winter.

Air Humidity: Mist leaves frequently.

Repotting: Repot in spring every year.

Propagation: Sow seeds in spring or take stem cuttings in spring or summer.

IMPATIENS

FLOWERING HOUSE PLANT
page 55

green leaf, usually tinged brown. Reddish stems; plant 2 ft or more tall

I. holstii

purplish-bronze leaf. Red stems; plant 2 ft or more tall

I. petersiana

green stems; plant 1–2 ft tall

I. sultani

I. sultani variegata

New Guinea Hybrids. Multicoloured leaf. Plant 1–3 ft tall

I. linearifolia

I. hawkeri

Impatiens has been extremely popular as a house plant for generations. Cuttings root very easily and the plants will, with proper care, bloom almost all year round. This non-stop blooming habit is the reason for its common name — Busy Lizzie.

There are three basic groups. Until recently only the *Traditional* types were grown — spreading, succulent stems bearing white, red or pink flowers amongst the leaves. In recent years breeders and plant hunters have been responsible for hundreds of new varieties. One of the new groups is the *F₁ Hybrid* — a range of small and compact plants with a mass of blooms which partly or almost entirely cover the leaves. The standard colours of white, pink and red have been joined by orange and lilac. The third group is made up of the *New Guinea Hybrids* which generally bear multicoloured leaves.

Busy Lizzies are not difficult to grow but they do need regular care. Pinch out the tips of young plants several times to ensure bushy plants — prune mature plants each spring. The stems of the Traditional types are brittle — tall plants may require staking. Feed regularly during the growing season and provide ventilation on hot days. Above all, remember to water frequently in summer.

SECRETS OF SUCCESS

Temperature: Average warmth — minimum 55°F in winter. Keep at 60°F or more to ensure flowering during winter.

Light: Bright light is necessary, but avoid direct sunlight in summer. A few hours of sun are necessary in winter if the plant is to continue flowering.

Water: Keep compost moist at all times — daily watering may be necessary in summer. Reduce watering in winter.

Air Humidity: Mist leaves occasionally, but avoid open blooms.

Repotting: The pot must be filled with roots before the plant will flower freely. Repot, if necessary, in spring.

Propagation: Stem cuttings root readily at any time of the year. Sow seeds in spring.

SPECIAL PROBLEMS

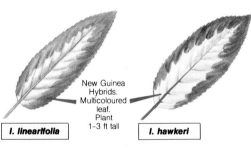

LOSS OF LEAVES
Cause: Usual reason for sudden leaf fall is prolonged exposure to low temperatures. Irregular watering and severe insect attack are other common causes.

LEAVES WILTED
Cause: Underwatering. Wilting can occur the day after watering in summer. Frequent watering is the only answer — do not keep the plant standing in a saucer of water.

POOR FLOWERING
Cause: Many possibilities — the five most common causes are too little light, too little food, too much food, too cold or repotting too early.

INSECTS
Red spider mite is a menace in hot, dry weather; leaves become bronzed and mottled. Both aphid and whitefly can be serious nuisances, disfiguring and weakening the plant. See Chapter 7 for methods of insect control.

SPINDLY GROWTH
Cause: Too much warmth coupled with too little light will certainly produce this condition, but some older varieties soon become lanky with age even when well grown. Choose a modern compact hybrid — take cuttings and discard old plants.

NO FLOWERS
Cause: Repotting is the usual reason why a mature plant fails to flower. Busy Lizzie must be kept somewhat pot-bound.

ROTTING STEMS
Cause: This is always caused by overwatering, especially in cool, shady conditions. Always reduce watering in winter; water very sparingly if plant is kept below 60°F.

LOSS OF FLOWERS
Cause: Too little light is the usual reason. Other possibilities are dry air, dry compost or red spider mite attack.

flat-faced flower
1–2 in. across —
long spur at rear

leaf
3 in.
long

stems brittle
and succulent,
1–3 ft long

I. wallerana
Busy Lizzie
(Patient Lucy)

TYPES

The Traditional types of Impatiens have long been grown on both sides of the Atlantic — the well known Busy Lizzie in British homes and Patient Lucy in American ones. There is much confusion over naming, and the best plan is to group the various popular species together as **Impatiens wallerana**. Included here are the green-leaved **I. holstii** and **I. sultani** plus the red-leaved **I. petersiana**. A typical specimen grows about 2 ft high and stays in bloom almost all year round if the temperature is kept at 60°F or above. The stems are straggly and fleshy with oval leaves which may be all-green, bronze, red, mahogany or green edged with white. Nowadays it is much more usual to grow one of the many F$_1$ Hybrids — plants are much more compact and the floral display is more impressive. Plants can be raised from seed but this is not easy — it is better to buy small seedlings if you require a lot of them or pot-grown plants in bloom if you need just one or two. The choice is extensive — the **Super Elfin** strain grows 8–10 in. tall with single flowers. The **Imp** strain is taller and the flowers are larger — **Blitz** is even more impressive with 2 in. wide blooms which are borne freely. A number of bicolours with white stripes or centres are available — look for **Cinderella**, **Novette Star**, **Zig-Zag**, **Sparkles** and **Rose Star**. Doubles are less popular than the single varieties, but you can try **Rosette**, **Double Duet** or **Confection** if you would like something different. Even more different than the old-fashioned varieties are the New Guinea Hybrids. These plants have evolved from **I. hawkeri**, **I. linearifolia** and **I. schlechteri**, the complex crosses producing eye-catching specimens growing 1–2 ft high. The long leaves are nearly always bicoloured or multicoloured although there are a number of all-red and bronzy types. The blooms are often very large, and these new Busy Lizzies are well worth growing although the floral season is generally limited to the summer months. Examples include **Tango** (leaves bronze — flowers orange), **Fanfare** (leaves yellow/green — flowers pink) and **Arabesque** (leaves yellow/green/red — flowers pink).

Impatiens Blitz

I. Super Elfin
Single bloom

I. Novette Star
Bicolour bloom

I. Rosette
Double bloom

Impatiens sultani variegata

Impatiens Zig-Zag

Impatiens Fanfare

INSECTIVORES

FOLIAGE HOUSE PLANT
page 51

FLOWERING HOUSE PLANT
page 55

Some plants live in situations where their roots cannot obtain sufficient nutrients, and so they have evolved mechanisms to trap insects and then digest the contents of their bodies. There are three groups of these insectivorous plants — the *Fly Traps* with spiny-edged leaves which are hinged in the middle, the *Sticky-leaved Plants* with hairs which secrete insect-catching fluid, and the *Pitcher Plants* with leaves which are water-filled funnels. These plants are very difficult to grow indoors — water with rainwater, keep the compost constantly moist and the surrounding air humid, and feed very occasionally with tiny bits of meat or dead flies. But even if you follow these rules their life span in the average living room will be quite short. Don't be put off — they will arouse more interest during this limited period than some plants you have had for many years!

TYPES

FLY TRAPS

Dionaea muscipula

Dionaea muscipula (Venus Fly Trap) is the most spectacular insectivore in its action. There is a rosette of heart-shaped leaves, each one fringed with teeth. When touched by an insect the two halves close immediately.

STICKY-LEAVED PLANTS

Drosera capensis

Drosera (Sundew) bears a rosette of leaves covered with red hairs. These hairs secrete the juices which both trap and digest the insects. **Drosera binata** is an Australian Sundew which bears long and deeply-lobed leaves — the American **D. capensis** has undivided leaves.

PITCHER PLANTS

Nepenthes coccinea

Darlingtonia californica

There are two types of Pitcher Plants — the lidded varieties and the hooded ones. **Nepenthes coccinea** is one of the lidded Pitcher Plants — insects are attracted by the brightly-coloured pitcher. Once inside this container they drown in the pepsin solution at the base. There are other lidded Pitcher Plants — **Sarracenia drummondii** has pale green tubes streaked with purple. **Darlingtonia californica** is a hooded Pitcher Plant. Its snake's-head appearance is responsible for the common name — Cobra Plant. The pale green pitcher will grow to 2 ft or more under ideal conditions — the heavily-veined head and dark forked tongue making this one of the strangest of plants.

Iresine herbstii aureoreticulata

leaf 3 in. long

wine red leaves

I. herbstii

Bloodleaf

TYPES

Iresine herbstii grows about 2 ft high, its red stems bearing notched leaves. The variety **aureoreticulata** (Chicken Gizzard) is more colourful — red stems, green leaves and yellow veins.

IRESINE

FOLIAGE HOUSE PLANT page 51

The Iresines are colourful plants. Chicken Gizzard has a most unusual common name and Bloodleaf has remarkable wine red leaves and stems. They are rarities in Britain but are quite widely grown in the U.S. Iresines are sun-lovers — away from a south-facing window the colours tend to fade and growth becomes lank and straggly. Nip out growing tips occasionally to maintain bushiness.

SECRETS OF SUCCESS

Temperature: Average warmth — minimum 55°F in winter.

Light: As much light as possible, but shade from summer noonday sun.

Water: Keep compost moist at all times — reduce watering in winter.

Air Humidity: Mist leaves regularly.

Repotting: Repot, if necessary, in spring.

Propagation: Take stem cuttings in spring or summer.

Ixora coccinea

flower-head 4 in. across

tubular flower ½ in. across

glossy, leathery leaf 3-4 in. long

I. coccinea

Flame of the Woods

TYPE

Ixora coccinea is a difficult shrub — with care the large flower-heads in white, yellow, salmon, pink or red will last throughout the summer months.

IXORA

FLOWERING HOUSE PLANT page 55

A 3–4 ft shrub with glossy leathery leaves. From late spring to autumn it bears large clusters of flowers. This is not a plant for the novice — leaves drop if exposed to cool air for even a short time — flower buds drop if it is moved from one spot to another. Humid air is essential. After flowering keep rather dry for a month, then resume normal watering.

SECRETS OF SUCCESS

Temperature: Warm or average warmth — minimum 60°F in winter.

Light: Bright light — avoid direct sun in summer.

Water: Keep compost moist at all times — reduce watering in winter. Use soft water.

Air Humidity: Mist leaves regularly.

Repotting: Repot, if necessary, in spring.

Propagation: Difficult. Take stem cuttings in spring. Use a rooting hormone and provide bottom heat.

Jacaranda mimosifolia

ferny foliage

J. mimosifolia

Jacaranda

TYPE

Only one species is grown indoors — **Jacaranda mimosifolia**. It will not flower, but the delicate leaves make Jacaranda an attractive house plant. Plants lose their lower leaves with age.

JACARANDA

FOLIAGE HOUSE PLANT page 51

An elegant plant but specimens are not easy to obtain. Under good conditions it grows rapidly and will reach 3 ft high, but Jacaranda cannot be expected to produce its beautiful blooms indoors. It is therefore grown as a foliage house plant, and despite its rarity it is not difficult to grow in a heated sunny room. Remember to use tepid soft water.

SECRETS OF SUCCESS

Temperature: Average or above average warmth — minimum 55°F in winter.

Light: Bright light — some direct sun is beneficial.

Water: Water moderately from spring to autumn. Water sparingly in winter.

Air Humidity: Mist leaves frequently.

Repotting: Repot, if necessary, in spring.

Propagation: Take stem cuttings in summer. Sow seeds in spring.

JACOBINIA

FLOWERING HOUSE PLANT
page 55

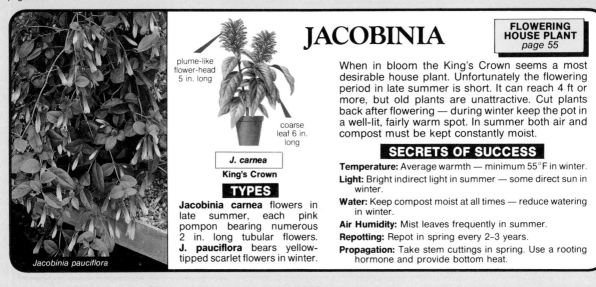

plume-like flower-head 5 in. long

coarse leaf 6 in. long

J. carnea
King's Crown

When in bloom the King's Crown seems a most desirable house plant. Unfortunately the flowering period in late summer is short. It can reach 4 ft or more, but old plants are unattractive. Cut plants back after flowering — during winter keep the pot in a well-lit, fairly warm spot. In summer both air and compost must be kept constantly moist.

SECRETS OF SUCCESS

Temperature: Average warmth — minimum 55°F in winter.

Light: Bright indirect light in summer — some direct sun in winter.

Water: Keep compost moist at all times — reduce watering in winter.

Air Humidity: Mist leaves frequently in summer.

Repotting: Repot in spring every 2–3 years.

Propagation: Take stem cuttings in spring. Use a rooting hormone and provide bottom heat.

TYPES

Jacobinia carnea flowers in late summer, each pink pompon bearing numerous 2 in. long tubular flowers. **J. pauciflora** bears yellow-tipped scarlet flowers in winter.

Jacobinia pauciflora

JASMINUM

FLOWERING HOUSE PLANT
page 55

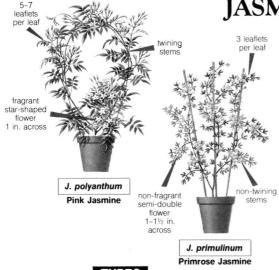

5–7 leaflets per leaf

twining stems

3 leaflets per leaf

fragrant star-shaped flower 1 in. across

J. polyanthum
Pink Jasmine

non-fragrant semi-double flower 1–1½ in. across

non-twining stems

J. primulinum
Primrose Jasmine

There are several Jasmines which can be grown as house plants — all are climbers which bear flowers in clusters. The most popular ones have white blooms with a delicious fragrance, but not all follow this familiar pattern. The easiest to grow is the Pink Jasmine, the pale rosy buds opening into starry white flowers which are borne in groups of 20 or more. There are other white-flowered Jasmines which open in winter or summer, and there is the Primrose Jasmine which is the odd one out. It is yellow, non-fragrant and the stems do not twine. The basic rules for success with Jasmine are to keep the plant cool in winter, stand the pot outdoors in summer, give it plenty of light and provide some form of support for the stems. The compost should never be allowed to dry out.

SECRETS OF SUCCESS

Temperature: Average warmth — minimum 45°F in winter.

Light: Bright light with some direct sun.

Water: Keep compost moist at all times.

Air Humidity: Mist leaves frequently.

Repotting: Repot, if necessary, in spring.

Propagation: Take stem cuttings in spring — use a rooting hormone.

TYPES

The favourite one is **Jasminum polyanthum** with pink buds which open into white tubular flowers in spring. It is a vigorous climber and the stems can reach 10 ft if left unchecked. Annual pruning is necessary to stop the plant becoming too straggly. **J. officinale** (White Jasmine) is similar in appearance — twining stems, much-divided leaves and long-tubed white flowers with a strong fragrance. There are, however, important differences — the flowers appear from summer to early autumn and they do not have a rosy tinge on the reverse. Another difference is that the blooms do not appear until the plant is mature. The showiest of the white-flowering types is **J. rex** which has long oval leaves and winter flowers which measure 2–3 in. across. The drawbacks are the lack of fragrance and the difficulty in finding a supplier. **J. primulinum** (**J. mesnyi**) has semi-double flowers with 6 or more petals. They appear in spring and summer — bright yellow without any perfume. The stems must be tied to supports.

Jasminum primulinum

Jasminum officinale grandiflora

JATROPHA

FLOWERING POT PLANT
page 57

Jatropha podagrica

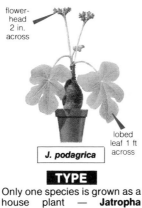

flower-head 2 in. across

lobed leaf 1 ft across

J. podagrica

TYPE

Only one species is grown as a house plant — **Jatropha podagrica**. The flower-stalk is about 2 ft tall and the flowers are coral red. The blooms remain for most of the year.

Jatropha once belonged in the textbook rather than the garden centre, but it is now widely available. It is a remarkable oddity — the tall bottle stem remains bare throughout the winter, and then in early spring the flower-stalks appear with a crown of small red blooms. Later the long-stalked leaves appear — a conversation piece rather than a thing of beauty. Few plants are easier to grow — hardly any watering is required and it has no special needs.

SECRETS OF SUCCESS

Temperature: Average warmth — minimum 50°F in winter.

Light: Bright light — avoid hot summer sun.

Water: Water sparingly from spring to summer — hardly at all in winter.

Air Humidity: Misting is not necessary.

Repotting: Repot, if necessary, in spring.

Propagation: Sow seeds in spring.

JUANULLOA

FLOWERING HOUSE PLANT
page 55

Juanulloa aurantiaca

trumpet-shaped orange flowers

leaf 3 in. long, felted below

J. aurantiaca
Goldfinger

TYPE

Just one species — **Juanulloa aurantiaca**. This member of the Potato family will grow up to 5 ft high if left unpruned. The drooping flowers are borne in small groups.

A new one for the 1990s with a tongue-twisting latin name but a simple common one — Goldfinger. It is offered as a house plant, but it is quite a large shrub which is much happier in a conservatory than in the living room. Waxy buds open into bright orange flowers which last for several weeks. If the shrub gets out of hand prune back in spring. Good drainage is essential.

SECRETS OF SUCCESS

Temperature: Average warmth — minimum 55°F in winter.

Light: Brightly lit spot with morning or afternoon sun.

Water: Water moderately from spring to autumn. Water sparingly in winter.

Air Humidity: Mist leaves occasionally.

Repotting: Repot in spring every 2 years.

Propagation: Take stem cuttings in summer. Use a rooting hormone and provide bottom heat.

KOHLERIA

FLOWERING HOUSE PLANT
page 55

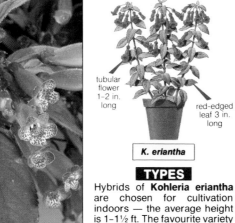

Kohleria eriantha

tubular flower 1-2 in. long

red-edged leaf 3 in. long

K. eriantha

TYPES

Hybrids of **Kohleria eriantha** are chosen for cultivation indoors — the average height is 1-1½ ft. The favourite variety is **K. Rongo** — red flowers with white-veined mouths.

Kohleria is related to the better-known Smithiantha (page 208) but unlike its more popular cousin does not lose its leaves in winter. Plant the rhizomes about ½ in. below the surface and keep fairly dry until growth appears. The plants produce flowers which are orange or red with yellow-speckled mouths. The blooming period is usually spring or summer, but flowers can appear almost all year round.

SECRETS OF SUCCESS

Temperature: Average warmth — minimum 55°F in winter.

Light: Bright light — protect from hot summer sun.

Water: Water moderately from spring to autumn. Water sparingly in winter.

Air Humidity: Mist frequently around the plant but do not wet leaves.

Repotting: Repot in spring every year.

Propagation: Divide plants at repotting time.

KALANCHOE

FLOWERING HOUSE PLANT page 55

FLOWERING POT PLANT page 57

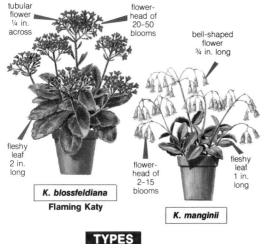

- tubular flower ¼ in. across
- flower-head of 20–50 blooms
- bell-shaped flower ¾ in. long
- fleshy leaf 2 in. long
- flower-head of 2–15 blooms
- fleshy leaf 1 in. long

K. blossfeldiana
Flaming Katy

K. manginii

It is surprising that more pots of flowering Kalanchoe are sold at the Dutch plant auctions each year than any other house plant. Once it was just a Christmas-flowering gift plant, but now Kalanchoe is sold in flower all year round.

There are two basic types — Kalanchoe blossfeldiana and K. manginii hybrids. K. blossfeldiana is by far the more popular, and this is the one which growers are able to induce to flower at any season although it is naturally a spring-flowering plant. The leaves turn reddish in sunlight and the large flower-heads last for many weeks. After flowering prune the tops and place the pot on a shady windowsill. Keep the compost nearly dry for a month and then put in a well-lit spot and water normally.

K. manginii has fleshy leaves like its more popular relative, but it bears large and pendant bell-like flowers.

SECRETS OF SUCCESS

Temperature: Average warmth — minimum 50°F in winter.
Light: East- or west-facing windowsill from spring to autumn — a south-facing windowsill in winter.
Water: Water thoroughly — let surface dry between waterings.
Air Humidity: Misting is not necessary with K. blossfeldiana.
Repotting: Repot every year after spring rest period.
Propagation: See Propagation of Succulents, page 212.

TYPES

Kalanchoe blossfeldiana is a bushy plant which can be bought in flower at any season of the year. Hybrids are available with white, yellow, orange, lilac, pink or red blooms borne in large heads on 1–1½ ft high plants. There are many named varieties, including **Bali** (red), **Fortyniner** (yellow), **Mistral** (lilac), **Tarantella** (orange) and **Vesuvius** (red). Miniatures are also available — these compact varieties grow about 6 in. high and bear glowing red flowers — look for **Tom Thumb**, **Compact Lilliput** and **Margarethe**. At least one (**Vulcan**) can be raised at home from seed. Most plants are thrown away after flowering but it is possible to keep them to produce a repeat display. Hybrids of **K. manginii** are now widely available and you can find examples such as **Tessa**, **Wendy** and **Shinano**. Spring is the usual flowering time for these pendant-flowered types — they need regular misting as moist air is essential for prolonged flowering. The Kalanchoes in this section are the flowering ones — see the Succulents section (page 217) for the types grown for their foliage.

Kalanchoe manginii Wendy

Kalanchoe blossfeldiana

LACHENALIA

FLOWERING POT PLANT page 57

Lachenalia aloides

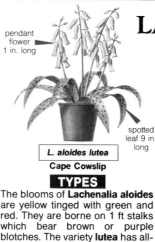

- pendant flower 1 in. long
- spotted leaf 9 in. long

L. aloides lutea
Cape Cowslip

TYPES

The blooms of **Lachenalia aloides** are yellow tinged with green and red. They are borne on 1 ft stalks which bear brown or purple blotches. The variety **lutea** has all-yellow flowers.

An attractive plant, providing a host of tubular flowers in winter. Despite its novel appearance, Lachenalia has never been popular because of its inability to live in a heated room. In late summer plant 6–8 bulbs in a 6 in. pot with the tips just below the surface. Keep in a cool bright room, water once and then leave until shoots appear. At this stage water and feed regularly.

SECRETS OF SUCCESS

Temperature: Cool — minimum 40°F in winter.
Light: Bright light with some direct sun.
Water: Keep compost moist at all times during the flowering season.
Air Humidity: Mist leaves occasionally.
Care After Flowering: Continue watering for several weeks, then reduce and stop. Keep dry — repot in autumn.
Propagation: Remove and plant offsets at repotting time.

LANTANA

FLOWERING HOUSE PLANT page 55

flower-head 1-2 in. across

rough leaf 2 in. long

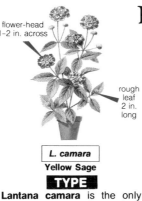

L. camara
Yellow Sage

TYPE

Lantana camara is the only species grown indoors. It is usually kept trimmed to 1-2 ft. The flowering season lasts from spring to late summer.

Lantana camara

When not in bloom this shrub is unimpressive with coarse wrinkled leaves and prickly stems. However, in summer it is eye-catching — the globular flower-heads change colour from pale yellow to red as the tiny flowers mature. Keep watch for whitefly. Cut back the stems after flowering and raise new plants every 2 or 3 years.

SECRETS OF SUCCESS

Temperature: Average warmth — minimum 55°F in winter.

Light: Give as much light as possible, but shade from summer noonday sun.

Water: Water regularly from spring to autumn. Water sparingly in winter.

Air Humidity: Mist leaves occasionally.

Repotting: Repot, if necessary, in spring.

Propagation: Sow seeds in spring. Take stem cuttings at any time of the year.

LAURUS

FOLIAGE HOUSE PLANT page 51

leaf 3 in. long

aromatic leaves

L. nobilis
Bay Tree

TYPE

The leaves of **Laurus nobilis** are the 'bay leaves' sold for kitchen use. The plant can be trimmed into a geometric or fanciful shape — an excellent choice in some settings.

Laurus nobilis

The Laurel is not often referred to in house plant books, but it was first grown inside Roman villas more than 2,000 years ago. It will thrive under ordinary room conditions if it is kept in a sunny spot, given plenty of fresh air (it doesn't mind draughts) and watered with care. Overwatering in winter is the usual cause of failure. Keep the shrub trimmed to 3-4 ft high and place outdoors in summer.

SECRETS OF SUCCESS

Temperature: Cool or average warmth — keep cool but frost-free in winter.

Light: Bright light — some direct sunlight is beneficial.

Water: Water moderately from spring to autumn. Water sparingly in winter.

Air Humidity: Mist leaves regularly.

Repotting: Repot, if necessary, in spring.

Propagation: Take stem cuttings in spring or autumn.

LEEA

FOLIAGE HOUSE PLANT page 51

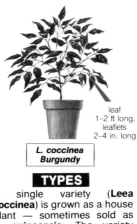

leaf 1-2 ft long, leaflets 2-4 in. long

L. coccinea
Burgundy

TYPES

A single variety (**Leea coccinea**) is grown as a house plant — sometimes sold as **L. guineensis**. The variety **Burgundy** maintains the red foliage colour in good light.

Leea coccinea Burgundy

Leea is not in many textbooks but it can be found in garden centres and large stores. It is a shrubby plant bearing large leaves — each leaf being divided into numerous pointed leaflets. This foliage is bronzy red when young but usually turns green when mature. Feed regularly during the growing season and keep away from draughts. Try this one as an alternative specimen plant to its better-known relative Fatsia japonica (page 135).

SECRETS OF SUCCESS

Temperature: Average warmth — if possible keep cool in winter.

Light: Bright or light shade. Keep well-lit in winter.

Water: Water regularly from spring to autumn. Water sparingly in winter.

Air Humidity: Mist leaves frequently.

Repotting: Repot in spring every year.

Propagation: Take stem cuttings in summer.

LILIUM

FLOWERING POT PLANT
page 57

average height of plant 2½–4 ft

waxy flower 2–10 in. across, depending on variety

leaf generally lance-shaped and arching

The most popular Lilium species for growing indoors is the Easter Lily. The tall stems grow 3 ft high and the white 6 in. long trumpet-shaped blooms are heavily scented. The main requirements are space and cold nights. In the U.S millions are forced by nurserymen for sale in bloom at Easter; in Britain it is an unusual summer-flowering plant grown at home from a bulb. Make sure that the bulb is plump and not shrivelled. In autumn plant it in a 6 in. pot immediately after purchase, covering the tip with 1½–2 in. of compost. Keep cold, dark and moist. When shoots appear move to a brightly lit spot.

SECRETS OF SUCCESS

Temperature: Cool — minimum 35°F. Night temperature should not exceed 50°F during the growing season.

Light: Bright light away from direct sunlight.

Water: Keep compost moist at all times during the growing season.

Air Humidity: Mist leaves occasionally.

Care After Flowering: Reduce watering as leaves turn yellow and stems die down. Keep the compost just moist and repot bulb in autumn. Unfortunately growth will be less vigorous and the flowers smaller than on plants raised from newly-purchased bulbs.

TYPES

BOWL SHAPED
The petals flare open to produce a wide bowl. The flowers are usually large.

L. auratum (Golden-rayed Lily) Height 4–5 ft. Flowers 8–10 in. across. White with yellow stripes and brown spots. Fragrant. Flowering period late summer.
L. speciosum (Japanese Lily) Height 3–4 ft. Flowers 3–5 in. across. White with red markings. Fragrant. Flowering period summer.
   Grand Commander — the best variety, petals deep red with paler edges.
L. Empress of China Height 3–4 ft. Flowers 8 in. across. White with dark red spots. Fragrant. Flowering period summer.

TRUMPET SHAPED
The petals are grouped together for part of the length of the flower to produce a basal tube.

L. longiflorum (Easter Lily) Height 3 ft. Flowers 5 in. across. White. Fragrant. Flowering period summer.
   Mount Everest — giant (6 ft) variety with large flowers.
L. regale (Regal Lily) Height 4 ft. Flowers 5 in. across. White with yellow throat. Fragrant. Flowering period summer.
   Royal Gold — all-yellow.
L. Mid-Century Hybrids Height 2–4 ft. Flowers 4–5 in. across. Yellow, orange or red — all spotted. Flowering period early summer.

Enchantment — orange-red, very popular	**Brandywine** — apricot
Destiny — lemon-yellow	**Prosperity** — pale yellow
Cinnabar — maroon-red	**Connecticut King** — gold
Paprika — crimson	**Chinook** — orange
Sterling Silver — cream	**Tabasco** — dark red

L. Golden Splendor Height 4 ft. Flowers 6 in. across. Gold; maroon-striped on reverse. Flowering period summer.

TURK'S-CAP SHAPED
The petals are rolled and swept back. The flowers are usually small.

L. pumilum Height 1–2 ft. Flowers 2 in. across. Red. Flowering period early summer.
L. Fiesta Hybrids Height 3–4 ft. Flowers 3 in. across. Various colours. Flowering period summer.
L. Citronella Height 3 ft. Flowers 3 in. across. Yellow with black dots. Flowering period summer.

Lilium longiflorum

Lilium Destiny

LIVING STONES

FOLIAGE HOUSE PLANT page 51

FLOWERING HOUSE PLANT page 55

The Living Stones are interesting rather than beautiful, as they mimic the pebbles which abound in their natural habitat. All are members of the Mesembryanthemum family and each plant consists of a pair of extremely thick leaves. These are fused together to produce a stem-like body with a slit at the top. This slit may be as small as a tiny hole or it may extend right down to ground level, depending upon the species. The sizes of the various types available do not differ very much — the range is a height of ½–2 in. Colours and patterns, however, present a bewildering array and collecting a comprehensive range of Living Stones can be a hobby in itself.

All are extremely slow growing and must be kept dry throughout the winter. Below ground there is a short stem and a long tap root — above ground white, pink or yellow daisy-like flowers appear in autumn, and after many years a clump of 'stones' will fill the pot.

Scores of different Living Stones are available. Nearly all belong to two genera — Lithops and Conophytum, and identification of individual species can be extremely difficult. In some cases leaf colour is affected by the soil type.

TYPES

1 in. high, olive-green with brown markings — **Lithops pseudotruncatella**

1½ in. high, grey-green with mottled top — **Lithops fulleri**

1½ in. high, grey with green mottled top — **Lithops salicola**

1 in. high, greenish-white — **Argyroderma testiculare**

1½ in. high, blue-grey — **Lapidaria margaretae**

1 in. high, green with translucent top — **Conophytum friedrichae**

The most popular Living Stones are species of Lithops. Three are illustrated above — others which are offered for sale include **Lithops turbiniformis** (brown, wrinkled), **L. bella** (pale brown with dark markings), **L. lesliei** (brown with lighter markings) and **L. optica** (grey-green with translucent 'windows' on upper surface). The cleft between the two leaves in Lithops may be shallow or deep, depending on the species, but the cleft between the leaves of Conophytum is reduced to a small fissure through which the flower-stalk appears. Several species are available, including **Conophytum bilobum** (grey-green tinged with red) and **C. calculus** (pale green).

Lithops bella

Lithops lesliei

Conophytum pearsonii nana

LISIANTHUS

FLOWERING POT PLANT
page 57

Lisianthus russelianus

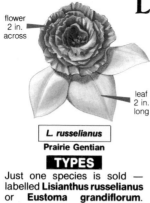

flower 2 in. across

leaf 2 in. long

L. russelianus
Prairie Gentian

TYPES

Just one species is sold — labelled **Lisianthus russelianus** or **Eustoma grandiflorum**. Compact varieties 1–1½ ft high rather than the tall-growing species are the types on offer.

A new one for the 1990s. These pot plants are offered for sale in flower during the summer months —double and single varieties are available in blue, purple, mauve and white. Technically the erect bushy plants are perennials, but they are grown as annuals or biennials indoors. The Poppy-like blooms appear in clusters. Not an easy plant to keep from one season to the next.

SECRETS OF SUCCESS

Temperature: Average warmth — keep cool in winter.

Light: Brightly lit spot — some sun is beneficial.

Water: Water thoroughly, then leave until compost is moderately dry.

Air Humidity: Mist leaves frequently.

Care After Flowering: Plants are usually discarded.

Propagation: Sow seeds in spring or divide plants in autumn.

MANETTIA

FLOWERING HOUSE PLANT
page 55

Manettia inflata

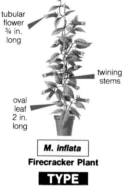

tubular flower ¾ in. long

twining stems

oval leaf 2 in. long

M. inflata
Firecracker Plant

TYPE

Manettia inflata (M. bicolor) is the only species grown as a house plant. In good light it will bloom for most of the year — the flowers are small but plentiful.

The Firecracker Plant should be more popular. The twining stems will quickly cover a wire support or trellis, or they can be left to trail from a hanging basket. The yellow-tipped flowers sometimes almost cover the dark green, pointed leaves. Pinch out the tips occasionally to stop the plant becoming straggly. In winter keep at 50°–60°F.

SECRETS OF SUCCESS

Temperature: Average warmth — minimum 50°F in winter.

Light: Brightly lit spot — some direct sun is essential.

Water: Keep compost moist at all times — reduce watering in winter.

Air Humidity: Mist leaves regularly.

Repotting: Repot in spring every year.

Propagation: Take stem cuttings in summer — use a rooting hormone.

MEDINILLA

FLOWERING HOUSE PLANT
page 55

Medinilla magnifica

large bracts in tiers

individual flower ½ in. long

pendant flower-head 1½ ft long

M. magnifica
Rose Grape

TYPE

Medinilla magnifica is the only species grown. The oval leaves are prominently veined, the stems are winged and the flowers are as spectacular as anything to be seen indoors.

The pride of any collection, but you will need a warm greenhouse or conservatory. The leathery leaves of this 4 ft tropical shrub are borne in pairs and in late spring the magnificent flower-heads appear. Temperature must be carefully controlled and the air must be kept constantly moist.

SECRETS OF SUCCESS

Temperature: Warm — 65°–75°F in summer and 60°–65°F in winter.

Light: Brightly lit spot screened from direct sun.

Water: Water moderately from spring to autumn. Water sparingly in winter.

Air Humidity: Mist leaves frequently — stand pot on a pebble tray (see page 19).

Repotting: Repot in spring every 1–2 years.

Propagation: Very difficult. Take stem cuttings in spring. Use a rooting hormone and provide bottom heat.

The MARANTA Group

FOLIAGE HOUSE PLANT *page 51*

The Maranta group contains four closely-related members — Maranta, Calathea, Ctenanthe and Stromanthe. The outstanding feature is their spectacular foliage, bearing coloured veins or prominent blotches on a background which ranges from near white to almost black. The plants in the Maranta group have a number of requirements in common — protection from the direct rays of the sun, a need for high air humidity, a hatred of cold draughts and a vital need for warmth in winter.

The Marantas are low-growing, rarely exceeding 8 in. high. The popular varieties are not particularly difficult to grow, although in general Maranta is not for the beginner. The common name of Prayer Plant describes their curious habit of folding and raising their leaves at night. The Calatheas are generally taller and more difficult to care for. In expert hands they can be grown as uncovered specimens but they are much more suitable for the terrarium or bottle garden.

oblong leaves

underside usually purple

SECRETS OF SUCCESS

Temperature: Average warmth — sudden fluctuations can harm delicate varieties. Maintain minimum winter temperature of 50°F for Maranta, 60°F for Calathea.

Light: Partial shade — colours fade in bright light. Do not expose to direct sunlight. Move to a well-lit but sunless spot in winter.

Water: Keep compost moist at all times — reduce watering in winter. Use soft, tepid water.

Air Humidity: Mist leaves regularly. Surround pot with damp peat.

Repotting: Repot in spring every 2 years.

Propagation: Divide plants at repotting time. Cover pots with polythene and keep warm until new plants are established.

SPECIAL PROBLEMS

LEAF TIPS BROWN & DRY. STUNTED GROWTH
Cause: Air too dry. Look for red spider mite (see page 244). Remove dead growth. Mist leaves regularly.

LEAVES CURLED & SPOTTED. LOWER LEAVES YELLOW
Cause: Underwatering. Compost should be kept moist at all times — unlike many house plants it should not be allowed to dry out slightly between waterings when the plant is actively growing.

LEAF FALL
Cause: Air too dry. The plant is particularly sensitive to low air humidity and should be surrounded with damp peat or planted in a bottle garden.

LIMP, ROTTING STEMS
Cause: Air too cool and compost too wet in winter. See Secrets of Success.

LEAVES DISCOLOURED OR SCORCHED
Cause: Too much light, especially direct sunlight. The plant should be moved immediately; delay could be fatal.

TYPES
MARANTA

Maranta tricolor

M. tricolor
(M. leuconeura erythrophylla)
Herringbone Plant

prominent red veins

M. leuconeura kerchoveana
Prayer Plant (Rabbit's Tracks)

brown blotches turning green with age

blackish-green leaf with silvery veins

M. leuconeura massangeana

Maranta leaves are about 6 in. long. All the popular varieties belong to the species **Maranta leuconeura**. The basic species is rarely grown — the usual choice is a colourful variety. For bold red veins pick **erythrophylla** (sold as **M. tricolor**) or **Fascinator**. The white-veined variety is **massangeana** — more eye-catching but less popular than **kerchoveana** which has plain green leaves with 2 rows of brown patches ('rabbit's tracks'). The uncommon **M. bicolor** is rather similar in appearance to M. leuconeura kerchoveana, but it does not form tubers below the surface.

CALATHEA

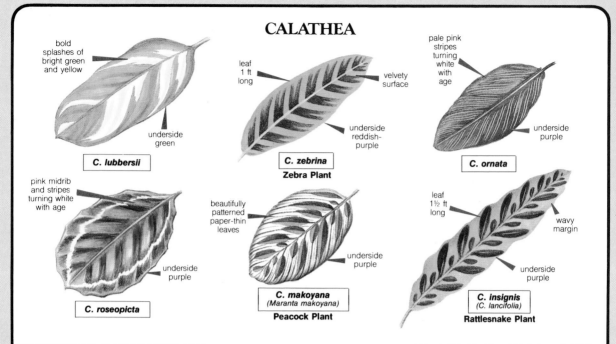

bold splashes of bright green and yellow

underside green

C. lubbersii

leaf 1 ft long

velvety surface

underside reddish-purple

C. zebrina
Zebra Plant

pale pink stripes turning white with age

underside purple

C. ornata

pink midrib and stripes turning white with age

underside purple

C. roseopicta

beautifully patterned paper-thin leaves

underside purple

C. makoyana
(Maranta makoyana)
Peacock Plant

leaf 1½ ft long

wavy margin

underside purple

C. insignis
(C. lancifolia)
Rattlesnake Plant

Calathea makoyana

The Calatheas are grown for their ornately patterned leaves, but there is an exception. **Calathea crocata** has quite plain foliage and is bought for its display of erect orange-red flowers. Undoubtedly the showiest of the foliage types is **C. makoyana**. With 1 ft long papery leaves borne upright on long stalks, the decorative tracery gives rise to one of its common names — Cathedral Windows. The leaves of **C. ornata** are smaller and bear pink veins — choose one of the varieties such as **roseolineata** or **sanderiana**. The pink colouring of **C. roseopicta** is more spectacular — for interesting combinations of pale and dark green look for **C. picturata**, **C. veitchiana** and **C. Maui Queen**. The boldest blend of yellow and green occurs on **C. lubbersii** foliage. Not all Calathea species have oval leaves — some are spear-shaped. **C. insignis** and the smaller **C. lindeniana** bear their long leaves upright — the foliage of **C. zebrina** and the smaller **C. bachemiana** is held horizontally.

Calathea crocata

CTENANTHE

velvety surface

leaf 1½ ft long

underside reddish-purple

C. oppenheimiana tricolor
Never Never Plant

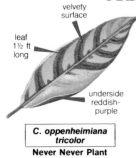

The Ctenanthes are closely related to the Calatheas — both are eye-catching and difficult to grow. They have a long list of hates — direct sunlight, temperatures below 60°F, cold or hard water and feeding after repotting. There are several species, but the only one you are likely to find is **Ctenanthe oppenheimiana tricolor** with cream-coloured blotches covering a large part of the leaf surface.

STROMANTHE

Stromanthe is compact and low-growing like Maranta, but the foliage is marked with the distinct tracery of Calathea with which it is easily confused. The usual species is **Stromanthe amabilis**, but it is hard to find a supplier and even harder to grow. Don't waste your money unless you have a heated greenhouse or terrarium — it needs a minimum temperature of 65°F and the air must be moist.

underside grey-green

S. amabilis

MIKANIA

FOLIAGE HOUSE PLANT *page 51*

leaflet 1–2 in. long

underside purple

M. ternata
Plush Vine

A quick-growing trailing plant which is one of the new generation of house plants — it entered the shops in the 1980s. It is colourful — the veins are purple and the leaf surface is distinctly red or purple when the plant is kept in a brightly lit spot. Mikania is not really happy in the living room — it needs moist air, but misting can damage the leaves.

SECRETS OF SUCCESS

Temperature: Average warmth — minimum 50°-55°F in winter.

Light: Bright light with some direct sunlight.

Water: Keep compost moist at all times — reduce watering in winter.

Air Humidity: Mist with care — tepid water, very fine spray and keep misted plants away from sunshine.

Repotting: Repot, if necessary, in spring.

Propagation: Take stem cuttings in spring.

TYPE

There is a single species sold as a house plant — **Mikania ternata**. The palmate leaves are green with a purplish sheen, slightly hairy above and densely hairy below.

Mikania ternata

MIMOSA

FOLIAGE HOUSE PLANT *page 51* **FLOWERING HOUSE PLANT** *page 55*

fluffy pink flower-head

leaves fold when touched

M. pudica
Sensitive Plant

Although this plant makes an attractive feature, its main claim to fame is its peculiar habit of rapidly folding up its leaves and drooping its branches when touched during the day — at night the leaves fold naturally. It is an easy plant to raise and to care for, with the added benefit of bearing ball-like pink flower-heads during the summer months.

SECRETS OF SUCCESS

Temperature: Average warmth — minimum 60°F in winter.

Light: Bright light — some direct sunlight is beneficial.

Water: Keep compost moist at all times — reduce watering in winter.

Air Humidity: Mist leaves regularly.

Repotting: Not usually necessary.

Propagation: Take stem cuttings in spring or summer. Sow seeds in early spring — pour hot water over seeds before sowing.

TYPE

Mimosa pudica is a 2 ft plant bearing delicate branches and feathery leaves. The stems are spiny and the sensitive leaves take about ½–1 hour to recover after being touched.

Mimosa pudica

MUSA

FOLIAGE HOUSE PLANT *page 51* **FLOWERING HOUSE PLANT** *page 55*

yellow flowers within red bracts

velvety reddish fruits

leaf 2 ft long

M. velutina
Banana

The Victorians gave pride of place to the Banana Plant in their conservatories, but only recently has there been a revival of interest. Few other leaves give such a tropical look to an indoor collection, but this plant is much more suited to the greenhouse than the living room. Even under glass you have to choose the variety with care. Bananas are best regarded as decorative rather than fruit-producing plants indoors.

SECRETS OF SUCCESS

Temperature: Warm — minimum 60°F in winter.

Light: Bright light with some direct sun.

Water: Keep compost very moist at all times.

Air Humidity: Mist leaves frequently.

Repotting: Repot, if necessary, in spring or summer.

Propagation: Not practical in the home.

TYPES

Musa velutina grows about 4 ft high — the yellow flowers are followed by attractive but inedible fruit. Even smaller is the 3 ft Flowering Banana (**M. coccinea**).

Musa coccinea

MONSTERA

FOLIAGE HOUSE PLANT page 51

moss stick: tube of rolled plastic netting filled with damp moss or peat (see page 223)

aerial roots

foliage on young plant undivided — later cut and often perforated

M. deliciosa *(Philodendron pertusum)*

Swiss Cheese Plant (Splitleaf Philodendron)

Monstera deliciosa has been a favourite for many years. With proper care young specimens (sometimes mistakenly sold as Philodendron pertusum) soon develop large adult leaves which are perforated and deeply cut. Sturdy support is essential, and stems can reach a height of 20 ft or more. If your aim is to grow a tall plant with giant leaves you must care for the aerial roots — push them into the compost or use a moss stick. Winter brightness is essential — Monstera produces small leaves and spindly leaf-stalks when there is not enough light. The plant stops growing altogether in deep shade.

The Monsteras are easy to grow and have no special requirements. However, the white Lily-like flowers and edible fruits are only likely to appear on conservatory or greenhouse plants.

TYPES

Monstera deliciosa is the species grown as a house plant. With proper care giant leaves 1½ ft or more across will be produced. The form **variegata** has white and cream lines or patches on the leaves — more colourful but not necessarily more attractive. Where space is limited grow the compact variety **borsigiana** or **Mini**.

Monstera deliciosa variegata

SECRETS OF SUCCESS

Temperature: Average warmth — minimum 50°F in winter. Active growth starts at 65°F.

Light: Keep out of direct sunlight. Choose a spot in light shade or moderate brightness.

Water: During winter keep the soil just moist — make sure it is not waterlogged. For the rest of the year water thoroughly, but allow compost to become dryish between waterings.

Air Humidity: Mist leaves if room is heated. Occasionally wash and polish mature leaves.

Repotting: Transfer to a larger pot in spring every 2 years.

Propagation: When too tall remove tip in summer at a point just below an aerial root. Plant the cutting — the severed parent will continue to grow. Air layer as an alternative.

SPECIAL PROBLEMS

LEAVES WEEPING AT EDGES
Cause: Compost too wet. Allow to dry out and increase time between waterings.

ROTTING STEMS
Cause: Stem rot disease. This is usually a winter problem as the fungus is encouraged by too much moisture and too little heat. It may be possible to save the plant by repotting and keeping the compost dry and warm.

YELLOWING LEAVES
Cause: Overwatering is the most likely reason if many leaves are affected and if there are signs of wilting and rotting. If there is no wilting or rotting, underfeeding is the probable cause. If only lower leaves are affected, look for brown spots and for small and dark new leaves — the signs of underwatering. Pale leaves with straw-coloured patches indicate too much sunlight.

LOSS OF LEAVES
Cause: It is normal for the lowest leaves to drop with age. If there is abnormal leaf fall then any serious upset in conditions could be the cause — always look for other symptoms on upper leaves. If the leaves turn brown and dry before falling then too much warmth is the cause. This is a common winter problem when the pot is kept near a radiator.

LEGGY GROWTH, SMALL PALE LEAVES
Cause: Too little light is the first thing to look for. Monstera will not thrive in deep shade.

BROWN SPOTS ON UNDERSIDE OF LEAVES
Cause: Red spider mite — see page 244.

LEAVES WITH BROWN, PAPERY TIPS AND EDGES
Cause: Dry air is the most probable cause. Mist the leaves or surround the pot with damp peat. A pot-bound plant will show similar symptoms. Brown tips are a symptom of overwatering, but general yellowing will also be present if waterlogging is the cause.

NO HOLES IN LEAVES
Cause: It is normal for the leaves of young plants to be uncut and not perforated. In mature leaves the most likely causes are lack of light, cold air, too little water and underfeeding. In tall plants the most likely reason is failure of water and food to reach the uppermost leaves. Aerial roots should be pushed into the compost or allowed to grow into a moist support.

MYRTUS

FLOWERING HOUSE PLANT
page 55

oval leaf 2 in. long

fragrant flower ¾ in. across

M. communis
Myrtle

Myrtle has been grown as a decorative plant for thousands of years and yet it is still a rarity indoors in Britain. The small oval leaves are shiny and aromatic — the white flowers appear in large numbers in summer. In autumn the purple berries appear. The shrub will grow about 2 ft tall if left untrimmed and can be stood outdoors during the summer months.

SECRETS OF SUCCESS

Temperature: Cool or average warmth — minimum 40°F in winter.

Light: Bright with some direct sunlight, but protect from midday summer sun.

Water: Water regularly from spring to autumn. Water sparingly in winter. Use soft water.

Air Humidity: Mist leaves frequently.

Repotting: Repot, if necessary, in spring.

Propagation: Take stem cuttings in summer.

TYPES

Myrtus communis bears bowl-shaped blooms, each with a prominent central boss of golden stamens. Where space is limited choose the small-leaved variety **microphylla**.

Myrtus communis

NERIUM

FLOWERING HOUSE PLANT
page 55

fragrant flower 2 in. across

willow-like leaf 6–8 in. long

N. oleander
Oleander

Oleander needs a large room or conservatory. The fragrant blooms appear in summer and are borne in clusters above the Willow-like foliage. The wood and sap are poisonous. Oleander is not an easy plant to care for when it is large — the pot or tub must be moved to an unheated room in winter and it benefits from a summer vacation in the garden. In autumn cut back the stems which have flowered.

SECRETS OF SUCCESS

Temperature: Average warmth — minimum 45°F in winter.

Light: Choose sunniest spot available.

Water: Water liberally in spring and summer. Water sparingly in winter. Use tepid water.

Air Humidity: Do not mist leaves.

Repotting: Repot, if necessary, in spring.

Propagation: Take stem cuttings in spring or summer.

TYPES

Nerium oleander may look compact in the garden centre, but remember that it will grow into a spreading shrub about 6 ft tall. White, pink, red and yellow varieties are available.

Nerium oleander La Aitana

NERTERA

FLOWERING POT PLANT
page 57

creeping stems with tiny leaves. Glassy orange berries cover surface in autumn

N. depressa
Bead Plant

Tiny white flowers in late spring are followed by berries which should last throughout the autumn and winter. Provide plenty of water, fresh air and bright light. Nearly all of them are discarded once the display of berries is finished. With care, however, this plant can be kept for several years.

SECRETS OF SUCCESS

Temperature: Cool — minimum 40°F in winter.

Light: Bright light with some direct sun.

Water: Keep compost moist at all times — water sparingly in winter.

Air Humidity: Mist leaves occasionally.

Care After Flowering: Keep cool and rather dry during winter — increase watering when new growth appears. Place outdoors from late spring until the berries have appeared. Bring indoors for display.

Propagation: Divide plants in spring before placing outdoors.

TYPE

The mat of creeping stems and ¼ in. leaves of **Nertera depressa** might be mistaken for Helxine at first glance, but it is immediately recognisable once the pea-sized berries appear.

Nertera depressa

Nicodemia diversifolia

oak-like leaves 1-2 in. long

N. diversifolia
Indoor Oak

TYPE

There is a single species — **Nicodemia diversifolia**, also called **Buddleia indica**. This leafy shrub grows about 1½ ft high. It needs to rest in winter — water sparingly and do not feed.

NICODEMIA

FOLIAGE HOUSE PLANT page 51

The Indoor Oak is a rarity in Europe, but it is gaining popularity in the U.S. Nicodemia foliage is dark green and glossy with a quilted surface — the growth habit is shrubby and definitely not tree-like. This indoor plant would add an unusual note, but it is no more attractive than many of the popular shrubs described elsewhere in this book. It is not difficult to care for, but winter warmth is essential.

SECRETS OF SUCCESS

Temperature: Average warmth — minimum 55°F in winter.

Light: Bright light or semi-shade — avoid direct sun in summer.

Water: Keep compost moist at all times — reduce watering in winter.

Air Humidity: Mist leaves occasionally.

Repotting: Repot, if necessary, in spring.

Propagation: Take stem cuttings in spring or summer.

Ophiopogon jaburan variegata

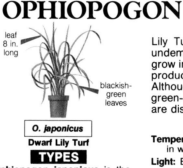

leaf 8 in. long

blackish-green leaves

O. japonicus
Dwarf Lily Turf

TYPES

Ophiopogon japonicus is the Dwarf Lily Turf, bearing short leaves and insignificant mauve flowers. **O. jaburan** or White Lily Turf is taller (2 ft) and the white summer flowers are more prominent.

OPHIOPOGON

FOLIAGE HOUSE PLANT page 51   FLOWERING HOUSE PLANT page 55

Lily Turf is not often seen indoors, but it is an undemanding plant for an unheated room. It will grow in sun or shade and has the added benefit of producing small white or mauve flowers in summer. Although a member of the Lily family its long green, green-and-white striped, or purplish-black leaves are distinctly grass-like and spread to form a turf.

SECRETS OF SUCCESS

Temperature: Average warmth — keep cool but frost-free in winter.

Light: Bright light or semi-shade — avoid direct sun in summer.

Water: Keep compost moist at all times — reduce watering in winter.

Air Humidity: Mist leaves frequently.

Repotting: Repot in spring every year.

Propagation: Divide plants at repotting time.

Oplismenus hirtellus variegatus

narrow leaves with wavy edges

O. hirtellus
Basket Grass

TYPES

The house plant species is **Oplismenus hirtellus**. The variety you are most likely to see is **variegatus (Panicum variegatum)**. Its 3-4 in. leaves on branching stems are striped with white and pink.

OPLISMENUS

FOLIAGE HOUSE PLANT page 51

Basket Grass is an excellent alternative to Tradescantia. Its slender stems spread rapidly and trail gracefully. Oplismenus is sometimes recommended as a ground cover for use between other plants, but it can be a menace if allowed to get out of hand. One of its blessings is the simplicity of raising new plants.

SECRETS OF SUCCESS

Temperature: Average warmth — minimum 45°F in winter.

Light: Bright light — avoid direct sun.

Water: Water liberally from spring to autumn. Water sparingly in winter.

Air Humidity: Mist leaves occasionally.

Repotting: Not usually necessary. If plant is to be retained, repot in spring.

Propagation: Very easy. Divide plants or take stem cuttings between spring and autumn.

ORCHIDS

**FLOWERING
HOUSE PLANT**
page 55

ANATOMY OF AN ORCHID PLANT

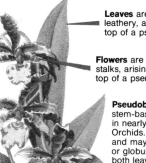

Leaves are long and leathery, arising from the top of a pseudobulb

Flowers are borne on stalks, arising from the top of a pseudobulb

Pseudobulb is a thickened stem-base which is present in nearly all house plant Orchids. It is a storage organ, and may be oval, cylindrical or globular. From it arise both leaves and flower-stalk. A few Orchids (e.g Vanda) are **single-stemmed** — no pseudobulb is present and flowers appear at the top of the single stem

Backbulb is a pseudobulb after the flowers have died down. It may remain on the plant for several years

Rhizome is the thickened stem-base which joins the pseudobulbs together

ANATOMY OF AN ORCHID FLOWER

There is a simple basic pattern for all Orchids, but with innumerable variations in the size, shape and colour of the individual parts.

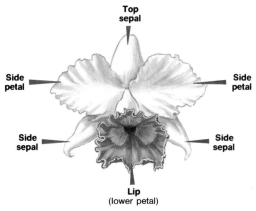

Top sepal

Side petal

Side petal

Side sepal

Side sepal

Lip
(lower petal)

Not too many years ago the idea of growing Orchids in the living room was unthinkable. Since then it has been found that a number will grow quite happily in the home . . . . provided you take a little time to learn about their needs.

Firstly, it is essential to remember that only a tiny fraction of the 100,000 known types are suitable — choose from the 'house plant' group described on the next page and pick an easy one if you are a beginner. You will find specimens in garden centres, department stores etc — look for a well-grown plant which is free from obvious blemishes. It will be pricey as it takes more than 5 years to reach the ready-for-sale stage.

Each type has its own special needs, but there are a number of general rules. You can't just place the plant anywhere. Miniature varieties can be grown in a terrarium (pages 26–28) but the usual home for a potted Orchid is on a pebble tray (page 19). Good light is essential and an east- or west-facing windowsill is ideal if net curtains or other form of sun screen is used — you must protect the plants from unfiltered sunshine. Turn the pot occasionally and move the tray away from the window on frosty nights.

House plant Orchids cannot tolerate hot and stuffy conditions so good ventilation is required even in winter — don't be afraid to stand the pot outdoors on warm and sunny days. Indoors, however, you must avoid cold draughts which can be fatal.

Feed during the summer months. Orchids appreciate being pot-bound but after a few years repotting and division may be necessary. You will require a special Orchid Compost.

SECRETS OF SUCCESS

Temperature: Individual types vary, but the general rule is a day temperature of about 70°F in summer, 60°F in winter and a drop at night of 10°F. Cool nights are important.

Light: Good light, shaded from direct sunlight. Orchids need 10–15 hours of light each day — in winter supplement daylight with artificial light.

Water: Keep compost moist — reduce watering in winter. Use soft, tepid water. With Cattleya and Miltonia let surface dry between waterings.

Air Humidity: Moist air is essential. Mist leaves occasionally.

Repotting: Do not worry if a few roots grow outside the pot. Repot only when growth begins to suffer.

Propagation: Divide plants at repotting time. Leave at least 3 shoots on each division. Stake each newly potted plant.

SPECIAL PROBLEMS

BROWN SPOTS ON LEAVES
Cause: If the spots are hard and dry, the plant has been scorched by the sun. Provide shade; there is no need to remove the spots. If the spots are soft, then a fungus disease is present and the affected parts should be removed immediately.

HORIZONTAL OR DROOPING GROWTH
Cause: Lack of light is the common reason; Orchids need good illumination. If the growth is limp and the light is good then incorrect watering may be the cause of loss of vigour.

MOULD ON LEAVES
Cause: Mildew may develop if the leaves are thoroughly misted under cool conditions and the water does not quickly evaporate.

NO FLOWERS
Cause: When growth is unhealthy any incorrect cultural condition can be the reason. If growth appears healthy then insufficient light is the probable cause.

The old idea that Orchids are only for skilled growers with a conservatory is not true, but you must choose one of the house plant varieties to stand any chance of success in living room conditions. Ten popular types are illustrated here, and 5 of them are generally regarded as 'easy'. Miniature **Cymbidium** is regarded as the beginner's Orchid — plants need a short resting period in autumn. **Coelogyne cristata** and **Odontoglossum grande** are also reliable if given a short rest period in winter. **Phalaenopsis** is becoming increasingly popular because a well-grown specimen can stay in flower almost all year round — it has no resting period so keep the compost moist at all times. **Paphiopedilum** is another so-called easy one which does not need a period of rest. Not all the house plant Orchids are shown here — others include **Brassavola**, **Dendrobium**, **Laelia**, **Oncidium**, **Pleione**, **Stanhopea** and **Zygopetalum**.

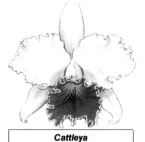

Cattleya
Corsage Orchid
Waxy, beautiful flowers 4–6 in. across. A terrarium plant as it needs high humidity and a fairly constant temperature.

Coelogyne
Fragrant flower 2–4 in. across. **C. cristata** (illustrated above) is the easy one. Winter rest needed.

Cymbidium
The miniature Cymbidium hybrids are popular house plant Orchids. Waxy flower 1½ in. across.

Lycaste
Flowers are borne singly. **L. aromatica** is a popular species — highly fragrant yellow blooms (2 in. across) appear in spring.

Miltonia
Pansy Orchid
Velvety, Pansy-like flower 2–4 in. across. Not easy under room conditions — dislikes temperature changes.

Odontoglossum
Tiger Orchid
O. grande (flower 6 in. across) is the popular one — not difficult if good light, high humidity and winter rest are provided.

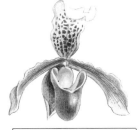

Paphiopedilum
Slipper Orchid
Many hybrids available — sometimes listed as **Cypripedium**. Prominently-pouched flower 2–4 in. across — suitable for room cultivation.

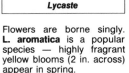

Phalaenopsis
Moth Orchid
Flat-faced flower 2 in. across — numerous blooms borne on arching stalks. Very popular — needs steady temperature and high humidity.

Vanda
Tall, single-stemmed Orchid with aerial roots. Horizontal flower-stalks bear 5–10 blooms, each one 3 in. across, waxy and fragrant.

Vuylstekeara
Popular man-made hybrid. Flower about 4 in. across — has the same requirements as Odontoglossum, one of its parents.

Cymbidium Rievaulx Hamsey

Paphiopedilum Hybriden

Phalaenopsis Happy Rose

OSMANTHUS

FOLIAGE HOUSE PLANT *page 51*

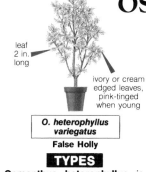

leaf 2 in. long

ivory or cream edged leaves, pink-tinged when young

O. heterophyllus variegatus

False Holly

TYPES

Osmanthus heterophyllus is the species grown, and **variegatus** is the most popular variety. The plant grows about 3 ft high. The variety **purpureus** has near-black leaves.

Osmanthus heterophyllus variegatus

If you like the idea of having Holly growing in your home at Christmas, then choose Osmanthus (False Holly) rather than Ilex — the True Holly. Osmanthus will flourish quite happily indoors all year round, provided that you keep it in an unheated room and let it receive some direct sunlight. The bush is slow growing and the leaves are hard and prickly. Flowers rarely appear when the plant is grown indoors.

SECRETS OF SUCCESS

Temperature: Cool but frost-free. Night temperatures above 60°F can lead to problems.

Light: Brightly lit spot — some direct sun is beneficial.

Water: Water moderately from spring to autumn. Water sparingly in winter.

Air Humidity: Mist leaves occasionally.

Repotting: Repot, if necessary, in spring.

Propagation: Take stem cuttings in spring.

PACHYSTACHYS

FLOWERING HOUSE PLANT *page 55*

golden flower-head 5 in. long

oval leaf 4 in. long

P. lutea

Lollipop Plant

TYPE

Pachystachys lutea grows about 1½ ft high, with flower-heads made up of golden bracts and white blooms peeping through. The leaves are prominently veined.

Pachystachys lutea

The Lollipop Plant bears cone-shaped flower-heads above the oval leaves. The main appeal is the long flowering season — from late spring until autumn if the plant is liberally watered and fed regularly. Leaf fall is a sign of dryness at the roots. This shrubby plant can get out of hand if it is not pruned in the spring. The stem tips which are removed can be used as cuttings.

SECRETS OF SUCCESS

Temperature: Average warmth — minimum 55°F in winter.

Light: Brightly lit spot away from direct sun in summer.

Water: Water liberally from spring to late autumn. Water sparingly in winter.

Air Humidity: Mist leaves in summer.

Repotting: Repot in spring every year.

Propagation: Take stem cuttings in spring or summer.

PANDANUS

FOLIAGE HOUSE PLANT *page 51*

leaf 2-3 ft long

leaves spirally arranged on stem

saw-edged leaves

P. veitchii

Screw Pine

TYPES

Pandanus veitchii is wide-spreading and reaches a height of about 4 ft. The serrated leaf edges are sharp — grow the variety **compacta** to keep the foliage out of harm's way. **P. baptistii** has smooth-edged leaves.

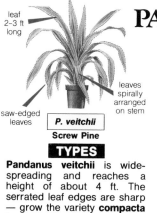

Pandanus veitchii

The spiny-edged narrow leaves are quite similar to those of the Pineapple plant and they are arranged spirally around the stem — hence the common name Screw Pine. It is a slow-growing plant, but it develops into a showy false palm several feet high, with a corkscrew-like trunk and long, arching leaves. Thick aerial roots will appear; these should not be removed.

SECRETS OF SUCCESS

Temperature: Average warmth — minimum 55°F in winter.

Light: Brightly lit spot away from direct sun in summer.

Water: Water liberally from spring to autumn. Water very sparingly in winter. Use tepid water.

Air Humidity: Mist leaves frequently.

Repotting: Repot in spring every 2-3 years.

Propagation: Remove basal suckers when they are about 6 in. long and treat as stem cuttings. Use a rooting hormone and provide bottom heat.

PALMS

FOLIAGE HOUSE PLANT
page 51

SPECIAL PROBLEMS

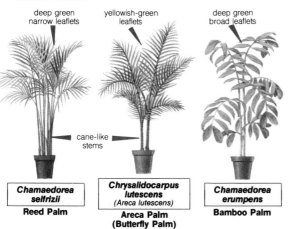

LEAVES WITH BROWN TIPS
Cause: Dry air is the most likely reason. Mist the plants regularly during hot weather. Other possibilities are underwatering, cold air and damage by touching.

LEAVES WITH BROWN SPOTS
Cause: Usual reason is leaf spot disease, due to overwatering or sudden chilling. Remove affected foliage and improve growing conditions. Another possible cause is use of very hard water.

YELLOWING LEAVES
Cause: Underwatering. Roots should not be allowed to dry out during the summer months.

BROWN LEAVES
Cause: It is natural for the lowest leaves to turn brown and droop. Remove by cutting, not pulling. If browning is general and accompanied by rotting, the problem is overwatering. Carry out standard remedial treatment (see page 246).

INSECTS
Red spider mite, scale and mealy bug can be troublesome (see page 244).

Palms are attractive, but a mature specimen is expensive. They are still well worth the investment. For a bottle garden or terrarium the Parlour Palm is unrivalled as a centrepiece, and the old 'Palm Court' favourite, the Kentia Palm, is ideal if you want an elegant specimen plant with a cast-iron constitution.

Both of these well-known Palms are remarkably easy to look after in an average room, provided you don't regard them as lovers of tropical sunshine and desert-dry air. In fact they require cool winters, moist summers and protection from direct sunlight. The Parlour Palm produces tiny ball-like flowers while the plant is still quite small.

Palms come in a range of leaf types and sizes, but there is a basic common feature. The only growing point is at the tip of each stem. If you try to cut a stem back you will kill it.

SECRETS OF SUCCESS

Temperature: Average warmth — minimum 50°F in winter. Winter night temperature should not exceed 60°F for Parlour and Kentia Palms.

Light: A few delicate Palms revel in sunshine, but the popular varieties should be kept in partial shade. Both Parlour and Kentia Palms can thrive in low light conditions.

Water: The first need is for good drainage — all Palms detest stagnant water at the roots. During winter keep the soil slightly moist. Water more liberally in spring and summer.

Air Humidity: Mist leaves if room is heated. Occasionally sponge mature leaves. Avoid draughts.

Repotting: Only repot when the plant is thoroughly pot-bound, as Palms dislike disturbance. Compact the compost around the soil ball.

Propagation: From seed. A temperature of 80°F is required, so propagation is difficult.

TYPES

● **CANE PALMS**

deep green narrow leaflets

yellowish-green leaflets

deep green broad leaflets

cane-like stems

Chamaedorea seifrizii
Reed Palm

Chrysalidocarpus lutescens
(Areca lutescens)
Areca Palm (Butterfly Palm)

Chamaedorea erumpens
Bamboo Palm

A small group of Palms produce tall reed-like stems which look rather like bamboo canes when mature. These plants are popular with interior decorators in the U.S, providing bold focal points for large rooms. **Chamaedorea seifrizii** and **C. erumpens** can grow 6–10 ft tall under good conditions and the fronds of the Areca Palm (**Chrysalidocarpus lutescens**), may reach 3 ft or more. **Rhapis excelsa** (page 182) and the closely related **R. humilis** are sometimes called Bamboo Palms as their slender stems can grow 5–7 ft high.

Chrysalidocarpus lutescens

● FEATHER PALMS

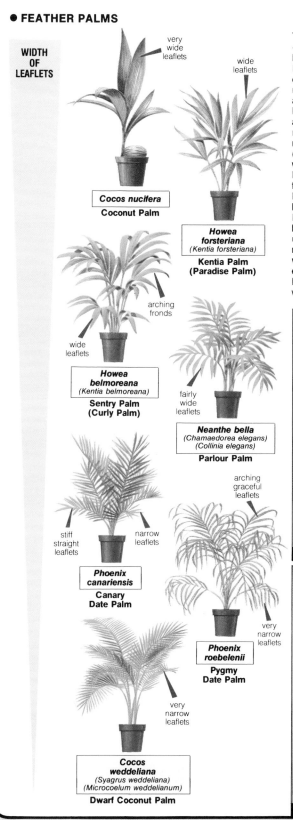

WIDTH OF LEAFLETS

very wide leaflets

Cocos nucifera
Coconut Palm

wide leaflets

Howea forsteriana
(Kentia forsteriana)
Kentia Palm
(Paradise Palm)

arching fronds

wide leaflets

Howea belmoreana
(Kentia belmoreana)
Sentry Palm
(Curly Palm)

fairly wide leaflets

Neanthe bella
(Chamaedorea elegans)
(Collinia elegans)
Parlour Palm

stiff straight leaflets

narrow leaflets

Phoenix canariensis
Canary Date Palm

arching graceful leaflets

very narrow leaflets

Phoenix roebelenii
Pygmy Date Palm

very narrow leaflets

Cocos weddeliana
(Syagrus weddeliana)
(Microcoelum weddelianum)
Dwarf Coconut Palm

The fronds are divided on either side of the midrib into leaflets — these leaflets may be soft and drooping or stiff and erect. **Neanthe bella**, the most widely grown of all indoor Palms, belongs to this group. It may be listed as **Collinia elegans** or **Chamaedorea elegans** in the textbooks, but all these names refer to the old favourite Parlour Palm which is usually bought as a 6–12 in. specimen. After a few years it will reach its adult height of about 2 ft and tiny yellow flowers and small fruit appear if grown in good light. The dwarf nature of Neanthe makes it ideal for small rooms and bottle gardens — for a much bolder display the usual choice is one of the Howea (Kentia) Palms. These are the traditional Palm Court plants which grow up to 8 ft tall. It is not too easy to distinguish between the 2 species — **Howea forsteriana** is the British favourite and is quicker growing but less arching than **H. belmoreana**. The true Date Palm (**Phoenix dactylifera**) is less attractive though quicker growing than the species of Phoenix sold as house plants — **P. canariensis** (6 ft) and **P. roebelenii** (3 ft). The true Coconut Palm (**Cocos nucifera**) unfortunately dies after a couple of years indoors. Its near relative **Cocos weddeliana** (more correctly **Syagrus weddeliana**) is sold as a house plant and is thought by some experts to be the most attractive of all the indoor Palms. But it has none of the hardiness of the popular types and needs the warmth and humidity of a conservatory.

Howea belmoreana

Phoenix canariensis

● FAN PALMS

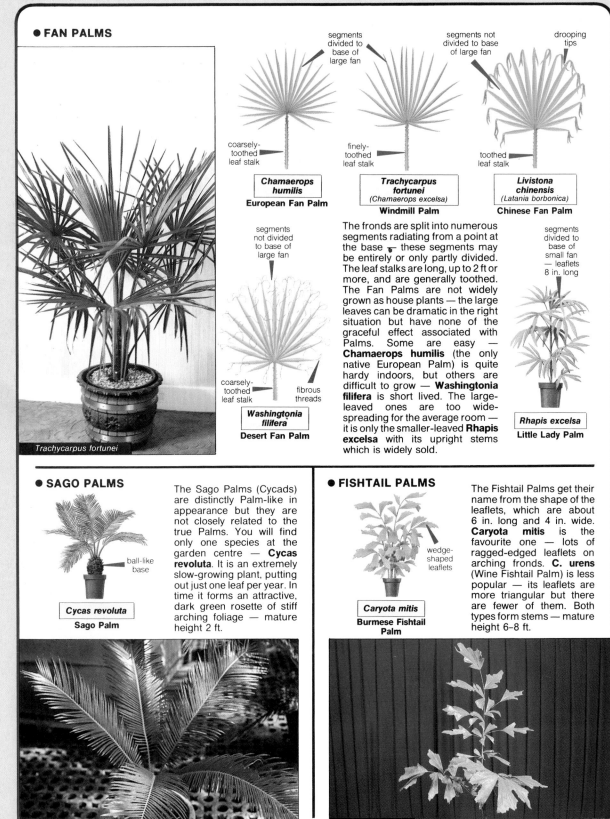

Trachycarpus fortunei

segments divided to base of large fan

segments not divided to base of large fan

drooping tips

coarsely-toothed leaf stalk

Chamaerops humilis
European Fan Palm

finely-toothed leaf stalk

Trachycarpus fortunei
(Chamaerops excelsa)
Windmill Palm

toothed leaf stalk

Livistona chinensis
(Latania borbonica)
Chinese Fan Palm

segments not divided to base of large fan

coarsely-toothed leaf stalk

fibrous threads

Washingtonia filifera
Desert Fan Palm

segments divided to base of small fan — leaflets 8 in. long

Rhapis excelsa
Little Lady Palm

The fronds are split into numerous segments radiating from a point at the base — these segments may be entirely or only partly divided. The leaf stalks are long, up to 2 ft or more, and are generally toothed. The Fan Palms are not widely grown as house plants — the large leaves can be dramatic in the right situation but have none of the graceful effect associated with Palms. Some are easy — **Chamaerops humilis** (the only native European Palm) is quite hardy indoors, but others are difficult to grow — **Washingtonia filifera** is short lived. The large-leaved ones are too wide-spreading for the average room — it is only the smaller-leaved **Rhapis excelsa** with its upright stems which is widely sold.

● SAGO PALMS

The Sago Palms (Cycads) are distinctly Palm-like in appearance but they are not closely related to the true Palms. You will find only one species at the garden centre — **Cycas revoluta**. It is an extremely slow-growing plant, putting out just one leaf per year. In time it forms an attractive, dark green rosette of stiff arching foliage — mature height 2 ft.

ball-like base

Cycas revoluta
Sago Palm

Cycas revoluta

● FISHTAIL PALMS

The Fishtail Palms get their name from the shape of the leaflets, which are about 6 in. long and 4 in. wide. **Caryota mitis** is the favourite one — lots of ragged-edged leaflets on arching fronds. **C. urens** (Wine Fishtail Palm) is less popular — its leaflets are more triangular but there are fewer of them. Both types form stems — mature height 6–8 ft.

wedge-shaped leaflets

Caryota mitis
Burmese Fishtail Palm

Caryota urens

PELARGONIUM (GERANIUM)

FOLIAGE HOUSE PLANT *page 51*

FLOWERING HOUSE PLANT *page 55*

SPECIAL PROBLEMS

YELLOWING OF LOWER LEAVES
Cause: If the leaves remain firm or are crisp with scorched edges then underwatering is the reason. If the leaves wilt or rot then overwatering is the cause. In both cases leaf fall may occur.

REDDENING OF LEAF EDGES
Cause: Temperature too low. Move pot away from window on frosty nights.

BLACKENING OF STEM BASE
Cause: Black leg disease. Destroy infected plant; in future use sterile compost and avoid overwatering.

SPINDLY GROWTH; LOSS OF LOWER LEAVES
Cause: Too little light; Pelargoniums will not grow in shade.

WATER-SOAKED CORKY PATCHES ON LEAVES
Cause: Oedema disease, associated with over-moist conditions. Non-infectious — reduce watering.

GREY MOULD ON LEAVES
Cause: Botrytis, associated with over-wet conditions. Infectious — remove diseased leaves, spray with a systemic fungicide, improve ventilation and reduce watering.

NO FLOWERS ON REGAL PELARGONIUM
Cause: If the plant is healthy the likely reason is too much heat in winter.

INSECTS
Whitefly, aphid and vine weevil can be troublesome — see page 244.

It is not surprising that the Pelargoniums are one of the world's favourite house plants. They are easy to grow and propagate, they have a long flowering period and the clusters of blooms are large and colourful. These are the plants popularly known as *Flowering Geraniums*. There is also a much smaller group which are grown for their aromatic foliage rather than for their small flowers — the *Scented-leaved Geraniums*.

By far the most popular flowering type is the Common or Zonal Pelargonium. It will bloom almost all year round if kept on a sunny windowsill at 55°F or more. Keep the compost rather dry — overwatering is the main enemy of Pelargoniums. The Regal Pelargonium is the glamorous member of the Group. Unfortunately it has a shorter flowering season and it is not as easy to grow. Overwinter at 45°–50°F. The Trailing Pelargonium is becoming increasingly popular. Its long brittle stems bear long-stalked flower clusters throughout summer and autumn if the plant is kept in a sunny spot.

There are a few general rules for all Pelargoniums. Pinch back young plants to induce bushiness. Do not repot until it is essential. Provide plenty of fresh air and not much humidity. Remove dead flowers and prune in early spring (Regal Pelargonium in autumn).

SECRETS OF SUCCESS

Temperature: Average warmth with cool nights — minimum 45°F in winter (50°F for Trailing Pelargonium).

Light: Provide as much light as possible. Direct sunlight is essential.

Water: Water thoroughly, then leave until compost is moderately dry. Avoid overwatering. Reduce watering frequency in winter — compost should be barely moist if plant is not in bloom.

Air Humidity: Do not mist the leaves.

Repotting: Repot, if necessary, in spring.

Propagation: Take stem cuttings in summer. Do not use a rooting hormone and do not cover. Sow seed in spring.

TYPES

SCENTED-LEAVED GERANIUMS

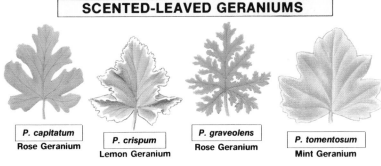

P. capitatum
Rose Geranium

P. crispum
Lemon Geranium

P. graveolens
Rose Geranium

P. tomentosum
Mint Geranium

The common names of the Scented-leaved Geraniums describe the aroma when the leaves are gently crushed. Rose, citrus and mint aromas are amply covered. The foliage can be used in all the standard roles for fragrant leaves — pot-pourri, scented pillows, linen bags etc. In addition the foliage can be used in the kitchen to add zest to a wide variety of dishes. Make sure that the plants have not been recently treated with a pesticide, and wash the leaves before use. Some examples are shown here — **Pelargonium capitatum** (3 ft, pink flowers), **P. crispum** (2 ft, pink flowers), **P. graveolens** (3 ft, pink flowers) and **P. tomentosum** (2 ft, white flowers). There are other aromas, such as **P. fragrans** (nutmeg), **P. Prince of Orange** (orange) and **P. odoratissimum** (apple). Keep the plants cool and fairly dry in winter and prune back the stems in spring to maintain bushiness.

Pelargonium graveolens variegatum

FLOWERING GERANIUMS

● ZONAL PELARGONIUM

The Zonal (or Common) Pelargonium is the type you are most likely to see. The bushy plants are usually 1–2 ft high, but some varieties can reach 4 ft or more. Buy plants which show no sign of wilting and have plenty of buds rather than open flowers. Once plants were raised exclusively from cuttings but nowadays there are many excellent varieties which can be raised from seed. With care the flowering season can last nearly all year round. They must receive some direct sunlight and the compost should be kept on the dry side. Feed with a high-potash fertilizer at regular intervals and do not repot unless the plant is clearly pot-bound.

brittle, thick stems

rounded leaf 3–4 in. across. Most varieties have a horseshoe marking or 'zone'

P. hortorum
(P. zonale)

flower ½–1½ in. across. Single, semi-double and double are the usual forms. Colours — white, pink, orange, red and purple

SINGLE

DOUBLE

STELLAR

CACTUS

Verona

Happy Thought

Black Cox

Marechal MacMahon

Distinction

Mrs Pollock

Mrs Henry Cox

STANDARD VARIETIES: All the old favourites belong here — the bright flowering ones such as Paul Crampel and the fancy-leaved ones such as Mrs Henry Cox. They grow 1–2 ft high and are propagated from cuttings taken in late summer — allow these cuttings to dry for a day before inserting in the compost.

P. Paul Crampel Bright red, single
P. King of Denmark Rose, semi-double
P. Gustave Emich Bright red, double
P. Jane Campbell Orange, single
P. Queen of the Whites White, single
P. Vera Dillon Purple, single
P. Hermione White, double
P. Festiva Maxima Purple, double
P. Distinction Red, single
P. Mrs Pollock Vermilion, single
P. Mrs Henry Cox Rose, single
P. Pandora Red, single
P. Elaine Pink, single
P. Josephine Red, double
P. Mrs Lawrence Pink, double

F₁ HYBRIDS: Nowadays many shop-bought plants are raised from seed, and you will find a large selection in the catalogues. Germination is straightforward, but a temperature of 70°–75°F must be maintained until the shoots break through. Move to a cooler spot after germination.

P. Ringo Deep Scarlet Red
P. Red Elite Red
P. Cheerio Scarlet Red
P. Sprinter Red
P. Bright Eyes White-eyed red
P. Hollywood Star White-eyed pink
P. Cherie Salmon
P. Appeal Orange
P. Hollywood White White
P. Breakaway series — spreading growth habit
P. Sensation series — large number of flower-heads

IRENES: The plants are vigorous and free-flowering. The flower-heads are larger than those borne by the Standard varieties and a key feature of these American Pelargoniums is the semi-double nature of their blooms.

P. Springtime Salmon-pink
P. Modesty White
P. Surprise Pink
P. Electra Red with blue overtones

DEACONS: The growth habit is compact and the flowers are small. Their virtues are that the flower-heads are unusually numerous and the blooms of the ones listed are double.

P. Deacon Fireball Bright red
P. Mandarin Orange
P. Deacon Bonanza Bright pink

ROSEBUDS: The centre petals of the small flowers remain unopened which gives a rosebud-like appearance.

P. Red Rambler Red
P. Appleblossom Rosebud Pink
P. Rosebud Supreme Red

CACTUS: The petals of the single or double blooms are narrow and twisted.

P. Fire Dragon Red
P. Noel White
P. Attraction Salmon
P. Spitfire Red

MINIATURES & DWARFS: The basic feature of these plants is their compact growth — height is 6–9 in. Nearly all are raised from cuttings, but the Video series are available as seed.

P. Video Various colours
P. Red Black Vesuvius Red
P. Waveney Red
P. Blakesdorf Red
P. Goblin Red
P. Miranda Red
P. Pauline Pink

Pelargonium Red Elite

Pelargonium Mrs Henry Cox

● REGAL PELARGONIUM

The Regal (or Martha Washington) Pelargoniums have more eye-catching blooms than the ordinary Zonal types — each flower is larger, frillier and more colourful. An added advantage is that these showy varieties are less prone to disease — whitefly is the only pest problem which is a serious nuisance. But the Regals do have their drawbacks — there are fewer blooms and there is a limited flowering season which stretches from early spring to midsummer. The normal height is 1–2 ft and they are propagated from cuttings taken in late summer. As with the Zonals the cuttings should be allowed to dry for about a day before inserting in the compost.

scalloped leaf with serrated edge 3 in. across

brittle, thin stems

P. domesticum
(P. grandiflorum)

flower 1½–2½ in. across. Petals are usually frilled, with splashes or lines of a second colour. Prominent eye often present. Colours — white, pink, orange, red and purple

Pelargonium Carisbrooke

P. Easter Greetings Rose with brown blotches
P. Aztec White with pink blotches
P. Grand Slam Red with purple blotches
P. Blythwood Mauve with purple blotches
P. Doris Frith White with red blotches, frilled
P. Lavender Grand Slam Lavender with purple blotches
P. Grandma Fischer Orange with brown blotches
P. Snowbank White, frilled
P. Geronimo Red, frilled
P. Applause Pink, frilled
P. Gay Nineties White with purple blotches
P. Elsie Hickman Vermilion, pink and white
P. Georgia Peach Peach, frilled
P. Carisbrooke Rose-pink
P. Sue Jarrett Salmon-pink with maroon blotches
P. Swabian Maid Carmine-rose

Pelargonium Lavender Grand Slam

● TRAILING PELARGONIUM

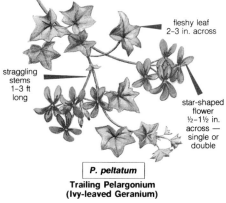

fleshy leaf 2–3 in. across

straggling stems 1–3 ft long

star-shaped flower ½–1½ in. across — single or double

P. peltatum

Trailing Pelargonium (Ivy-leaved Geranium)

The Ivy-leaved Geranium (**Pelargonium peltatum**) is widely used in hanging baskets. The flowers are available in a range of colours — **Madame Margot** (white), **Charles Turner** (pink), **Apricot Queen** (salmon), **La France** (lilac) and **Madame Crousse** (red). Some varieties are grown for their decorative foliage as well as their flowers — e.g **L'Elégante** (white-edged leaves) and **Sussex Lace** (creamy-veined leaves). One (**Summer Showers**) can be raised from seed.

Pelargonium peltatum roulettii

Pelargonium peltatum La France

PASSIFLORA

FLOWERING HOUSE PLANT
page 55

ornate flower 3 in. across

hand-like leaf 4 in. across

P. caerulea
Passion Flower

The Passiflora flower has an intricate structure — despite the delicacy of the flower there is nothing delicate about the plant. It is a rampant climber which will outgrow its welcome if it is not cut back hard each spring. The stems bear deeply-lobed leaves, tendrils and short-lived flowers all summer long.

SECRETS OF SUCCESS

Temperature: Average warmth. Keep at 40°–50°F in winter.

Light: Choose sunniest spot available.

Water: Keep compost moist at all times — may need daily watering in summer. Reduce watering in winter.

Air Humidity: Mist leaves occasionally.

Repotting: Repot in spring every year.

Propagation: Take stem cuttings in summer. Sow seeds in spring.

TYPES

There are several Passifloras, including the Granadilla (**Passiflora quadrangularis**) which bears large yellow fruit, but only **P. caerulea** is grown as a house plant.

Passiflora caerulea

PELLIONIA

FOLIAGE HOUSE PLANT
page 51

oval, green leaf with pale central area

P. daveauana

The two types of Pellionia make useful additions to the terrarium or bottle garden, but when used in a hanging basket or as ground cover between other plants they are more demanding than easy trailers like Tradescantia. The Pellionias require moist air and winter warmth. They are not too fussy about the amount of light they receive but they are unusually sensitive to draughts.

SECRETS OF SUCCESS

Temperature: Average warmth — minimum 55°F in winter.

Light: Semi-shade or bright indirect light.

Water: Keep compost moist at all times — reduce watering in winter. Use soft water.

Air Humidity: Mist leaves frequently.

Repotting: Repot in spring every 2 years.

Propagation: Divide plants at repotting time. Stem cuttings root easily.

TYPES

Trailing **Pellionia daveauana** (Watermelon Pellionia) bears a pale central band on each leaf — the outer margin may be olive or bronzy-green. **P. pulchra** (Satin Pellionia) has very dark veins on the upper surface and is purple below.

Pellionia pulchra

PENTAS

FLOWERING HOUSE PLANT
page 55

flower-head 3–4 in. across

hairy leaf 2–3 in. long

P. lanceolata
Egyptian Star Cluster

Not a plant you are likely to find in your local garden shop, but it is well worth growing in a sunny window if you can obtain one. The growth becomes straggly if you fail to pinch out the stem tips regularly. Keep the plant about 18 in. high. The flowers may appear at any time of the year — winter is the most usual. Pentas is easy to grow — keep the plant at about 60°F in winter.

SECRETS OF SUCCESS

Temperature: Average warmth — minimum 50°F in winter.

Light: Bright light with some direct sun.

Water: Keep compost moist at all times — reduce watering in winter.

Air Humidity: Mist leaves occasionally.

Repotting: Repot in spring every year.

Propagation: Take stem cuttings in spring — use a rooting hormone.

TYPES

Pentas lanceolata (**P. carnea**) is the basic species. The flower-head bears numerous tubular starry blooms — there are named varieties in white, pink, red and mauve.

Pentas lanceolata K. Schum

PEPEROMIA

FOLIAGE
HOUSE PLANT
page 51

SPECIAL PROBLEMS

LEAVES WITH BROWN TIPS & EDGES
Cause: Sudden drop in temperature.
Remove all damaged leaves; keep plants out of draughts and away from cold windowsills.

SUDDEN LOSS OF LEAVES FROM SUCCULENT VARIETIES
Cause: Foliage has been allowed to wilt before watering. Remember to water when the compost is dryish but *before* leaves wilt.

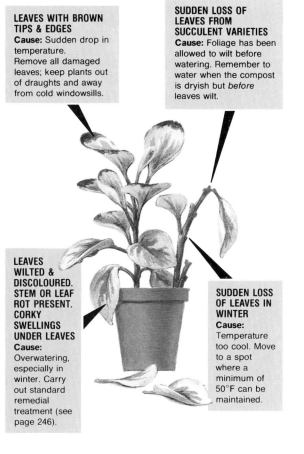

LEAVES WILTED & DISCOLOURED. STEM OR LEAF ROT PRESENT. CORKY SWELLINGS UNDER LEAVES
Cause: Overwatering, especially in winter. Carry out standard remedial treatment (see page 246).

SUDDEN LOSS OF LEAVES IN WINTER
Cause: Temperature too cool. Move to a spot where a minimum of 50°F can be maintained.

Peperomias are widely used in dish gardens, bottle gardens and other situations where space is limited. They are slow growing, compact and some species produce curious 'rat-tail' flower-heads made up of tiny greenish flowers on an upright spike. Despite these common characteristics, there really is no way of knowing whether an unknown plant in a house plant display is a Peperomia. There are three which have been popular favourites for many years — P. caperata, P. hederaefolia and P. magnoliaefolia. The experienced indoor gardener will have no difficulty in recognising that trio, but there are scores of other species. Trailing, bushy and upright types are available, and the foliage may be fleshy, quilted, corrugated, smooth or hairy, green or variegated ... or even striped like a watermelon.

The Peperomias are easy to care for under average room conditions, but do remember that their natural home is either the tree trunks or mossy floor of the tropical rain-forests in America. Use a peat-based compost rather than soil. The leaves will fall if allowed to wilt through lack of water. Despite their jungle home, however, Peperomias do not need a constantly moist atmosphere for success and will grow in a centrally-heated room.

SECRETS OF SUCCESS

Temperature: Average warmth — minimum 50°–55°F in winter.

Light: A bright or semi-shady spot, away from direct sunlight. Peperomias will thrive in fluorescent light.

Water: Water with care. The compost must dry out to some extent between waterings, but never wait until the leaves wilt. Use tepid water and apply very little in the winter months.

Air Humidity: Mist leaves occasionally in summer — never in winter.

Repotting: Avoid frequent repotting. If necessary after several years transfer to a slightly larger pot in spring.

Propagation: Cuttings root easily. Between spring and late summer take stem cuttings from upright and trailing varieties — use leaf cuttings from bushy varieties.

TYPES

● **TRAILING TYPES**

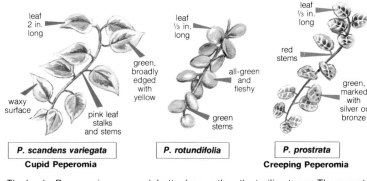

leaf 2 in. long

green, broadly edged with yellow

waxy surface

pink leaf stalks and stems

P. scandens variegata
Cupid Peperomia

leaf ⅓ in. long

all-green and fleshy

green stems

P. rotundifolia

leaf ⅓ in. long

red stems

green, marked with silver or bronze

P. prostrata
Creeping Peperomia

Peperomia scandens variegata

The bushy Peperomias are much better known than the trailing types. There are two species which bear large waxy and oval leaves. **Peperomia glabella** (Wax Privet) foliage has short stems (6–9 in.) which are spreading rather than trailing and the leaves are blunt at the tip. **P. scandens** has pointed leaves and the stems grow 3–4 ft long. This plant can be used as a climber by tying the stems to supports and its yellow-edged variety (**variegata**) is the only trailing Peperomia you are likely to find at the garden centre. Both **P. prostrata** and **P. rotundifolia** have tiny leaves and there is much confusion over their naming and identification.

● BUSHY TYPES

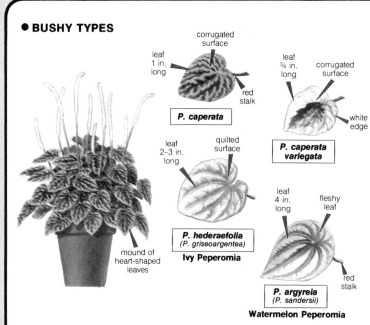

P. caperata

leaf 1 in. long · corrugated surface · red stalk

P. caperata variegata

leaf ¾ in. long · corrugated surface · white edge

P. hederaefolia
(P. griseoargentea)
Ivy Peperomia

leaf 2-3 in. long · quilted surface

P. argyreia
(P. sandersii)
Watermelon Peperomia

leaf 4 in. long · fleshy leaf · red stalk

mound of heart-shaped leaves

Peperomia caperata variegata

Peperomia argyreia

The bushy Peperomias grow about 4-6 in. high, and the familiar small-leaved species is **Peperomia caperata**. Dwarf varieties such as **Little Fantasy** and the white-edged **variegata** are available. There are several out-of-the-ordinary small-leaved bushes — **P. orba Astrid** bears pale green, spoon-shaped leaves and **P. fraseri** stands out from other Peperomias by producing round and sweetly-scented flower-heads. The large-leaved bushes are more popular — you will have no trouble finding the metallic-leaved **P. hederaefolia**, but the striped-leaved **P. argyreia** is harder to find in the shops than in the books.

● UPRIGHT TYPES

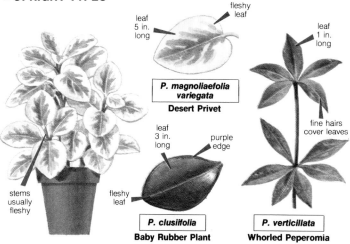

P. magnoliaefolia variegata
Desert Privet

leaf 5 in. long · fleshy leaf

P. clusiifolia
Baby Rubber Plant

leaf 3 in. long · purple edge · fleshy leaf

P. verticillata
Whorled Peperomia

leaf 1 in. long · fine hairs cover leaves

stems usually fleshy

The upright Peperomias have more distinct stems which grow vertically for part or all of the plant's life. Unfortunately there is much confusion over naming — the textbooks and the plant labels rarely agree! The most popular one is the large-leaved **Peperomia magnoliaefolia**. The all-green species is rarely seen — the favourite one is the gold-edged and -splashed variety **variegata**. This species is labelled as **P. obtusifolia** in the U.S and some European countries. A number of varieties are offered — the large-leaved **Green Gold**, the almost all-gold **Sensation** etc. **P. clusiifolia** has all-green leaves edged with purple. **P. verticillata** is unmistakable (1 ft stems and whorls of leaves) and so is **P. pereskiaefolia** — look for the zig-zagged stems.

Peperomia magnoliaefolia variegata

PHILODENDRON

FOLIAGE HOUSE PLANT
page 51

Philodendrons have been used as house plants since Victorian times, and their popularity has increased in recent years. The conditions they need for healthy growth are those which they enjoyed in their ancestral home within the American tropical forests — no direct sunlight and moist surroundings when the air is warm.

There are two basic types of Philodendron. The first group, the climbers, are well suited to the average room, as long as you provide firm support for the stems. The Sweetheart Plant is the smallest and it is also the easiest to look after, with its ability to withstand both neglect and poor conditions. A feature of many climbing Philodendrons is the production of aerial roots from the stems, and these roots have an important part to play. Push them into the compost to provide moisture for the upper leaves. Flowers and fruits rarely appear under home conditions.

Most of the second group, the non-climbers, are capable of growing into immense plants with large, deeply-lobed leaves. They are therefore more suitable for public buildings than for the average home.

SECRETS OF SUCCESS

Temperature: Average warmth — minimum 55°F in winter. P. scandens will endure lower temperatures (minimum 50°F) but P. melanochrysum needs higher than average warmth (minimum 65°F).

Light: All Philodendrons should be kept out of direct sunlight. P. scandens will succeed in shady conditions, but the usual requirement is light shade or moderate brightness. Both P. melanochrysum and variegated-leaved forms should be kept in a well-lit spot.

Water: During winter keep the compost just moist — make sure it is not waterlogged. For the rest of the year water thoroughly and regularly.

Air Humidity: Keep the air moist in summer and in heated rooms in winter — surround pots with damp peat or mist leaves regularly.

Repotting: Transfer to a larger pot in spring every 2–3 years.

Propagation: Cuttings require warm conditions. In summer take stem cuttings or air layer the climbing varieties. With a non-climbing variety, shoots taken from the base of the stem should be used as cuttings.

SPECIAL PROBLEMS

See Monstera, page 174.

TYPES

● **CLIMBING TYPES**

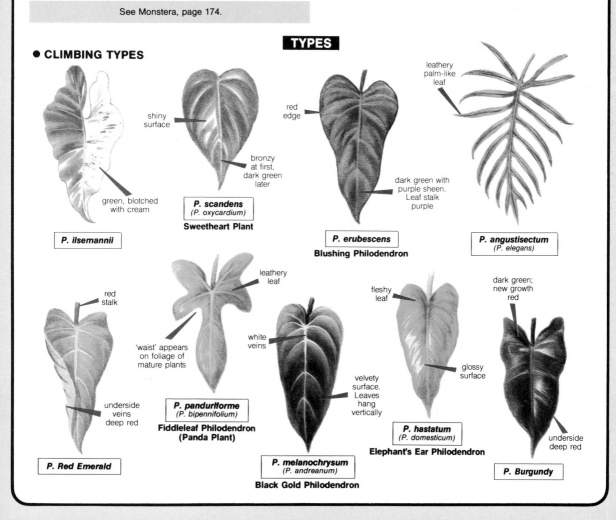

green, blotched with cream

P. ilsemannii

shiny surface

bronzy at first, dark green later

P. scandens
(P. oxycardium)
Sweetheart Plant

red edge

dark green with purple sheen. Leaf stalk purple

P. erubescens
Blushing Philodendron

leathery palm-like leaf

P. angustisectum
(P. elegans)

red stalk

underside veins deep red

P. Red Emerald

leathery leaf

'waist' appears on foliage of mature plants

P. panduriforme
(P. bipennifolium)
Fiddleleaf Philodendron
(Panda Plant)

white veins

velvety surface. Leaves hang vertically

P. melanochrysum
(P. andreanum)
Black Gold Philodendron

fleshy leaf

glossy surface

P. hastatum
(P. domesticum)
Elephant's Ear Philodendron

dark green; new growth red

underside deep red

P. Burgundy

● CLIMBING TYPES continued

The Philodendrons and closely-related Monsteras live in the tropical rain-forests of America. In their native home they grow 60 ft or more, clinging to the trunks of trees by means of aerial roots. Indoors they will grow 6–15 ft if the aerial roots are not removed. These plants are the most spectacular of all the house plant climbers. A moss stick (see page 223) is the ideal support and the leaves of some varieties exceed 2 ft in length. The leathery foliage varies widely in shape (entire to deeply cut), colour (pale green to rich red) and texture (glossy to velvety). Some grow quickly — **Philodendron imbe** can increase by 7 ft in 2–3 years, whereas **P. Burgundy** will grow less than 1 ft in the same length of time. **P. scandens** (the Sweetheart Plant or Heart-leaf Philodendron) is extremely popular and is one of the easiest plants to grow. Thin stems bear 3–5 in. shiny leaves. Grow as a trailer — pinch out tips to keep plant bushy. Or grow as a climber — retain aerial roots and use a moss stick for maximum effect. The general foliage pattern for the large-leaved Philodendrons is a 6–15 in. arrow-shaped leaf with a glossy surface. Popular varieties include **P. hastatum** and its more branching hybrid **P. Tuxla**. **P. erubescens** and its hybrids such as **Red Emerald** and **Burgundy** are more colourful, and the dramatic two are the velvety **P. melanochrysum** and the variegated **P. ilsemannii**.

Philodendron melanochrysum

Philodendron scandens

Philodendron Red Emerald

● NON-CLIMBING TYPES

leaf 2 ft long on 2 ft long arching stalk

ruffled edge

P. selloum
Lacy Tree Philodendron

leaf 1½ ft long on 1½ ft long stalk

mature leaf deeply indented

P. bipinnatifidum
Tree Philodendron

Philodendron bipinnatifidum

The non-climbing Tree Philodendrons are large plants which may spread to 8 ft or more. Not for a small room, of course, but most impressive in a spacious hall. The two types are quite similar — large, deeply-cut leaves on long stalks with stems which become trunk-like with age. **Philodendron selloum** is the one seen in the U.S — **P. bipinnatifidum** is shorter (mature height 4 ft) and is the species sold in Britain.

PILEA

FOLIAGE HOUSE PLANT
page 51

A wide variety of bushy and trailing Pileas are available, and they are generally quite easy to grow, even for the beginner. Easiest of all is the popular Aluminium Plant with its white-splashed leaves. The list of rules is a small one — move pots off windowsills on frosty nights, pinch out growing tips occasionally to keep plants bushy, and keep pots away from draughts. Even in expert hands the bushy Pileas tend to become leggy and unattractive with age. As cuttings root easily it is a good idea to start new plants each spring rather than retaining old specimens. Except for the Artillery Plant all of the bushy varieties are grown for the beauty of their individual leaves.

SECRETS OF SUCCESS

Temperature: Average warmth — minimum 50°F in winter.

Light: Bright light or semi-shade — protect from direct sun in summer.

Water: Water liberally from spring to autumn, allowing compost to dry out slightly between waterings. Water sparingly in winter. Use tepid water.

Air Humidity: Mist leaves regularly.

Repotting: Repot in spring if the plant is to be retained.

Propagation: Take stem cuttings in late spring or summer.

SPECIAL PROBLEMS

INSECTS
Red spider mite can be troublesome — see page 244.

LEAF FALL IN WINTER
Cause: Cold air and wet compost can cause serious leaf fall, but even a healthy plant may shed a few leaves in winter. Cut back affected stems in spring to induce new healthy growth.

LEAVES WILTED & DISCOLOURED. STEM ROT PRESENT. SOME LEAF FALL
Cause: Overwatering, especially in winter. Carry out standard remedial treatment (see page 246).

LEAVES DISCOLOURED WITH BROWN TIPS & EDGES
Cause: Too much shade is the most likely reason. Move to a brighter spot. If the plant is well-lit, the probable cause is a sudden drop in temperature.

TYPES

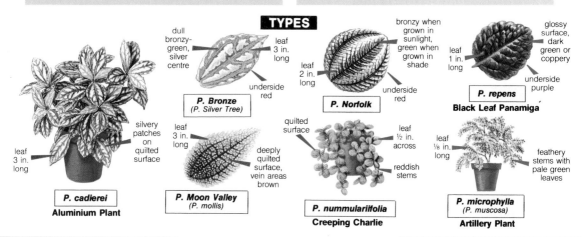

P. Bronze (P. Silver Tree) — dull bronzy-green, silver centre, leaf 3 in. long, underside red

P. Norfolk — bronzy when grown in sunlight, green when grown in shade, leaf 2 in. long, underside red

P. repens — glossy surface, dark green or coppery, leaf 1 in. long, underside purple
Black Leaf Panamiga

P. cadierei — silvery patches on quilted surface, leaf 3 in. long
Aluminium Plant

P. Moon Valley (P. mollis) — leaf 3 in. long, deeply quilted surface, vein areas brown

P. nummulariifolia — quilted surface, leaf ½ in. across, reddish stems
Creeping Charlie

P. microphylla (P. muscosa) — leaf ⅛ in. long, feathery stems with pale green leaves
Artillery Plant

Pilea Norfolk

The small-leaved Pileas include the trailing **Pilea nummulariifolia** (Creeping Charlie) and **P. depressa** (Creeping Jenny) and the fern-like **P. microphylla** which puffs out smoke-like pollen when tapped in summer.

Over the years the naming of the large-leaved Pileas has become quite confused. There is no problem with either recognising or naming the most popular species — **P. cadierei** grows about 1 ft tall and becomes leggy and unattractive with age. The variety **minima** is more compact. The species **P. spruceana** has given rise to two popular varieties — **P. Norfolk** and **P. Bronze**, with oval or rounded leaves in which bronze and silver dominate the quilted surface when grown in bright light. **P. involucrata**, the original Pan-American Friendship Plant, is not sold as such — the popular form is **P. Moon Valley**. **P. repens** is smaller than the popular varieties, a low and spreading plant with coppery leaves.

Pilea Moon Valley

Piper crocatum

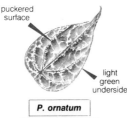

puckered surface

light green underside

P. ornatum
Ornamental Pepper

TYPES

The waxy, dappled leaves (3–5 in. long) make Piper more eye-catching than the Sweetheart Plant (page 189). Two varieties are available — **Piper crocatum** (underside dark red) and **P. ornatum** (underside light green).

PIPER

FOLIAGE HOUSE PLANT page 51

Ornamental Pepper plants are not easy to obtain. They are climbers, and with support they will reach 5 ft high. Their leaves are highly decorative, but the plants do not bear fruit. Growing Piper should not be too much of a problem if the winter temperature can be maintained at 55°F or more and if you mist the leaves regularly. Leaf fall is the sign that conditions are wrong.

SECRETS OF SUCCESS

Temperature: Average warmth — minimum 55°F in winter.

Light: Bright light — not direct sun.

Water: Keep compost moist at all times — reduce watering in winter.

Air Humidity: Mist leaves regularly.

Repotting: Repot in spring every 2 years.

Propagation: Take stem cuttings in spring or summer. Use a rooting hormone and provide bottom heat.

Pisonia umbellifera variegata

leaf 1 ft long

white-edged leaves

P. umbellifera variegata
Birdcatcher Tree

TYPES

Pisonia umbellifera is all-green — the variety offered for sale as a house plant is **variegata**. The large leaves have a creamy margin shot with pink.

PISONIA

FOLIAGE HOUSE PLANT page 51

At first sight this unusual indoor tree looks like a Rubber Plant — glossy oval leaves are borne on the upright stems and the foliage texture is leathery. The growth habit, however, is rather different. The stems branch readily and the leaves bear a sticky resin — hence the common name. Tiny flowers may appear — whitish tubular blooms followed by sticky fruits.

SECRETS OF SUCCESS

Temperature: Average warmth — minimum 55°F in winter.

Light: Good light — not direct sun.

Water: Water with care — allow the compost to dry out to some extent between waterings.

Air Humidity: Mist leaves occasionally in summer.

Repotting: Repot in spring every 2 years.

Propagation: Take stem cuttings in summer. Use a rooting hormone and provide bottom heat.

Pittosporum tobira

PITTOSPORUM

fragrant flower ½ in. across

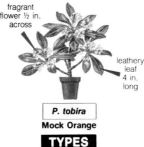

leathery leaf 4 in. long

P. tobira
Mock Orange

TYPES

Pittosporum tobira is a flat-topped tree with dark leaves — in spring the branches are crowned with clusters of tubular star-faced flowers. **Variegatum** leaves have white blotches.

FOLIAGE HOUSE PLANT page 51   **FLOWERING HOUSE PLANT** page 55

Pittosporum is popular with American interior decorators who require a glossy-leaved tree which will grow under poor conditions. In Britain it has never found favour. There are a few problems — the creamy flowers appear only under good light conditions, and cool winter quarters are needed.

SECRETS OF SUCCESS

Temperature: Average warmth — keep at 40°–50°F in winter.

Light: Brightly lit spot away from direct sun in summer.

Water: Water thoroughly when compost begins to dry out. Water sparingly in winter.

Air Humidity: Mist leaves occasionally.

Repotting: Repot, if necessary, in spring.

Propagation: Take stem cuttings in spring. Use a rooting hormone and provide bottom heat.

PLECTRANTHUS

FOLIAGE HOUSE PLANT page 51

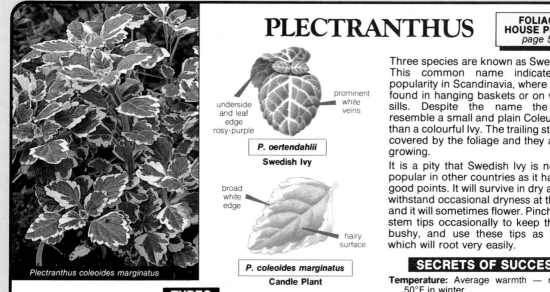

underside and leaf edge rosy-purple

prominent white veins

P. oertendahlii
Swedish Ivy

broad white edge

hairy surface

P. coleoides marginatus
Candle Plant

Plectranthus coleoides marginatus

Three species are known as Swedish Ivy. This common name indicates their popularity in Scandinavia, where they are found in hanging baskets or on window-sills. Despite the name the leaves resemble a small and plain Coleus rather than a colourful Ivy. The trailing stems are covered by the foliage and they are fast-growing.

It is a pity that Swedish Ivy is not more popular in other countries as it has many good points. It will survive in dry air, it will withstand occasional dryness at the roots and it will sometimes flower. Pinch out the stem tips occasionally to keep the plant bushy, and use these tips as cuttings which will root very easily.

TYPES

The advantages of these creeping plants as ground cover and for clothing the edges of pots and hanging baskets are well known in Scandinavia. They flourish in dry air where True Ivies would fail, and there is the added bonus of occasional flowers. The foliage of the most popular type (**Plectranthus oertendahlii**) is especially colourful. Its leaves measure 1 in. across — the largest are borne by **P. coleoides marginatus** (2–2½ in.). You will have to search to find **P. australis** (**P. parviflorus**). The leaves are thicker and glossier than the other species, but they are also plainer as the colour is all-green.

SECRETS OF SUCCESS

Temperature: Average warmth — minimum 50°F in winter.

Light: Bright light or semi-shade — avoid direct sunlight.

Water: Keep compost moist at all times — reduce watering in winter.

Air Humidity: Mist leaves occasionally.

Repotting: Repot in spring every 2–3 years, but best grown as an annual.

Propagation: Very easy. Take stem cuttings in spring or summer.

POLYSCIAS

FOLIAGE HOUSE PLANT page 51

leaflet 3 in. across

leathery leaves

leaf 8 in. long

P. balfouriana
Dinner Plate Aralia

feathery leaves

P. fruticosa
Ming Aralia

Polyscias balfouriana marginata

Varieties of Polyscias are oriental trees with twisted stems and attractive foliage. They make excellent specimen plants when placed in decorative containers, but large plants are prohibitively expensive. Buy a small plant if you can and look after it carefully. The leaves are usually ferny, but the most popular Polyscias is the Dinner Plate Aralia with large rounded leaflets. Unfortunately Polyscias is not easy to grow under room conditions, and it will readily drop its leaves if the environment is wrong. It will need good light, even moisture at the roots, and warmth in winter. The main problem is air humidity — Polyscias is distinctly unhappy in situations where the atmosphere is dry.

SECRETS OF SUCCESS

Temperature: Warm or average warmth — minimum 55°–60°F in winter.

Light: Bright, but away from direct sun. Will adapt to light shade.

Water: Water moderately from spring to autumn. Water sparingly in winter.

Air Humidity: Mist leaves frequently.

Repotting: Repot in spring every 2 years.

Propagation: Not easy. Take stem cuttings in spring. Use a rooting hormone and provide bottom heat.

TYPES

Polyscias balfouriana bears dark green, rounded leaflets which are speckled with grey or pale green. The variety **pennockii** is yellow-veined — **marginata** has white-bordered foliage. **P. fruticosa** is quite different — the leaves are longer and are divided into irregular and saw-edged leaflets. This tree with its twisted stems and ferny foliage is popular with American interior decorators when an oriental look is required. **P. guilfoylei victoriae** (Wild Coffee, Lace Aralia) has feathery white-edged leaves.

PLUMBAGO

FLOWERING HOUSE PLANT page 55

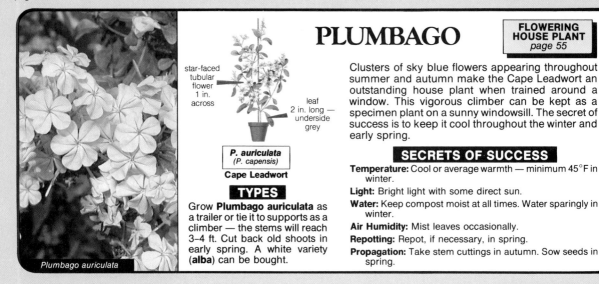

star-faced tubular flower 1 in. across

leaf 2 in. long — underside grey

P. auriculata (P. capensis)
Cape Leadwort

Clusters of sky blue flowers appearing throughout summer and autumn make the Cape Leadwort an outstanding house plant when trained around a window. This vigorous climber can be kept as a specimen plant on a sunny windowsill. The secret of success is to keep it cool throughout the winter and early spring.

TYPES

Grow **Plumbago auriculata** as a trailer or tie it to supports as a climber — the stems will reach 3–4 ft. Cut back old shoots in early spring. A white variety (**alba**) can be bought.

SECRETS OF SUCCESS

Temperature: Cool or average warmth — minimum 45°F in winter.

Light: Bright light with some direct sun.

Water: Keep compost moist at all times. Water sparingly in winter.

Air Humidity: Mist leaves occasionally.

Repotting: Repot, if necessary, in spring.

Propagation: Take stem cuttings in autumn. Sow seeds in spring.

Plumbago auriculata

PLUMERIA

FLOWERING HOUSE PLANT page 55

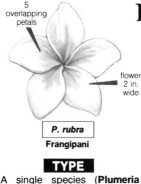

5 overlapping petals

flower 2 in. wide

P. rubra
Frangipani

Frangipani is a popular shrub in sub-tropical regions but it is a rarity indoors in temperate countries. It is sometimes recommended as a house plant, but it grows 6 ft or more in a tub and is better suited to the conservatory. The glory of the plant is the large clusters of flowers borne at the ends of the branches.

TYPE

A single species (**Plumeria rubra**) is grown as a house plant. The pointed leaves are long and oval and the heavily scented flowers are white or pink.

SECRETS OF SUCCESS

Temperature: Average warmth — minimum 50°F in winter.

Light: Bright light with some direct sun.

Water: Water liberally from spring to autumn. Water very sparingly in winter.

Air Humidity: Mist leaves occasionally.

Repotting: Repot in spring every 2 years.

Propagation: Take stem cuttings in spring. Use a rooting hormone and provide bottom heat.

Plumeria rubra

PODOCARPUS

FOLIAGE HOUSE PLANT page 51

leaf 3 in. long

strap-like leaves

P. macrophyllus
Buddhist Pine

Podocarpus demands an unheated room if it is to live successfully for many years indoors. This durable plant does not mind a draughty situation, and there are few better trees for a cold hallway. The upright stems bear narrow and glossy leaves. Buddhist Pine can be kept as a compact shrub by regular pruning, but its slow-growing habit means that it requires little attention.

TYPES

In its oriental home **Podocarpus macrophyllus** grows 30–40 ft high — indoors it will reach about 6 ft. The house plant variety is **Maki** (Southern Yew) — leaves are small and growth is compact.

SECRETS OF SUCCESS

Temperature: Cool — minimum 40°F in winter.

Light: Brightly lit spot — some sun is beneficial.

Water: Keep compost fairly moist at all times — reduce watering in winter.

Air Humidity: Mist leaves occasionally.

Repotting: Repot, if necessary, in spring.

Propagation: Take stem cuttings in summer. Use a rooting hormone and provide bottom heat.

Podocarpus macrophyllus

POINSETTIA

FLOWERING POT PLANT page 57

red, pink or white flower-head up to 1 ft across

lobed leaf 5 in. long

Euphorbia pulcherrima
Poinsettia

The symbol of Christmas outdoors is the Holly with its bright red berries. Indoors it is now the Poinsettia (proper name Euphorbia pulcherrima) with its large, scarlet flower-heads. This was not always so — in the early 1960s it was a tall-growing shrub which was distinctly difficult to keep in leaf or flower in the average home. Things have changed — modern varieties are bushier, more attractive and much less delicate — in addition modern chemicals are used to keep the plants small. The result is that the Poinsettia of today is compact (1–1½ ft high) and the flowers (which are really coloured bracts) should last for 2–6 months. When buying a plant look at the true flowers (yellow and tiny in the centre of the flower-head); they should be unopened for maximum flower life. Also the plant should not have been stood outdoors or in an icy shop. Once in your living room put it in a well-lit spot away from draughts and keep it reasonably warm.

SECRETS OF SUCCESS

Temperature: Average warmth — minimum 55°–60°F during the flowering season.

Light: Maximum light during winter — protect from hot summer sun if plant is to be kept for next Christmas.

Water: Water thoroughly — wait until compost is moderately dry before watering again. Water immediately if leaves begin to wilt. Water more liberally in summer.

Air Humidity: Mist leaves frequently during the flowering season.

Care After Flowering: Plant should be discarded, but if you like a challenge it can be kept and will bloom again next Christmas. The lighting will have to be very carefully controlled in autumn — see detailed instructions on this page.

Propagation: Take stem cuttings in early summer. Use a rooting hormone.

HOW TO MAKE A POINSETTIA BLOOM AGAIN NEXT CHRISTMAS

When the leaves have fallen cut back the stems to leave stumps 4 in. high. The compost should be kept almost dry and the pot placed in a mild, shady position. In early May water and repot the plant, removing some of the old compost. Continue watering and shoots will soon appear. Feed regularly and remove some of the new growth to leave 4–5 strong new stems. The prunings can be used as cuttings.

From the end of September careful light control is essential. Cover with a black polythene bag from early evening and remove next morning so that the plant is kept in total darkness for 14 hours. Continue daily for 8 weeks, then treat normally. Your Poinsettia will again be in bloom at Christmas time, but it will be taller than the plant you bought.

SPECIAL PROBLEMS

LOSS OF FLOWER-HEADS; LEAF MARGINS YELLOW OR BROWN
Cause: The usual reason is dry air in a warm room. Poinsettia needs moist air — mist leaves frequently.

INSECTS
Red spider mite and mealy bug are the main pests — see page 244.

LOSS OF LEAVES FOLLOWING WILTING
Cause: Overwatering is the likely culprit; the surface of the compost must be dry before water is applied. Of course, failure to water when the compost around the roots is dry will also cause leaves to wilt and fall.

LOSS OF LEAVES WITHOUT WILTING
Cause: If the temperature is too low or if the plant has been subjected to hot or freezing draughts then the leaves will suddenly fall.
Another cause of leaf fall is poor light.

Euphorbia pulcherrima

TYPES

All Poinsettias are varieties of **Euphorbia pulcherrima**. Red is the favourite colour — types include **Barbara Ecke Supreme**, **Mrs Paul Ecke** and **Angelica**. Pinks such as **Dorothe** are not very popular but the whites and pale creams (**Regina**, **Ecke's White**) are widely available. The most unusual Poinsettia is **Marble** — the bracts are deep cream with a rosy-red heart.

PRIMULA

FLOWERING POT PLANT
page 57

The Primula group contains some of the best of all winter- and spring-flowering pot plants. The plants bear large numbers of flowers, clustered in the centre of the leaf rosette (the stalkless varieties) or on long, erect flower stems (the stalked varieties).

The Primrose and Polyanthus which grow in the garden make pretty pot plants — the blooms are large and colourful and after flowering they can be planted in the garden.

It is usually the tender species which are grown indoors. The flowers are smaller and are borne on stalks. The Fairy Primrose is the daintiest, the Chinese Primrose has frilly leaves and flowers, and the Poison Primrose is the one not to touch if you have sensitive skin.

Do not plant too deeply — the crown should be just above the compost surface. Keep your plant well-lit, free from draughts, away from heat and protected from direct sun. Remove dead flowers and feed regularly.

SECRETS OF SUCCESS

Temperature: Cool — keep at 55°-60°F during the flowering season.

Light: Maximum light, but protect from direct sunlight.

Water: Keep compost moist at all times during flowering season.

Air Humidity: Mist leaves occasionally. Place on a pebble tray (see page 19) if conditions are rather warm.

Care After Flowering: Plant P. acaulis in the garden; other types are generally discarded. P. obconica and P. sinensis can be kept — repot and provide cool airy conditions in light shade throughout summer. Water very sparingly — in autumn remove yellowed leaves and resume normal watering.

Propagation: Sow seeds in midsummer.

TYPES

● TENDER TYPES

flower-stalk 1½ ft long

yellow-eyed flower ½ in. across

oval, toothed leaf

P. malacoides
Fairy Primrose

green-eyed flower 1–1½ in. across

flower-stalk 1 ft long

heart-shaped, coarse leaf

P. obconica
Poison Primrose

frilly flower 1–1½ in. across

flower-stalk 1 ft long

lobed, toothed leaf

P. sinensis
Chinese Primrose

fragrant flower ¾ in. across

flower-stalk 1 ft long

powdery, toothed leaf

P. kewensis

Primulas bear large numbers of flowers during the winter months. Two garden types are grown indoors to brighten up the winter windowsill — the Common Primrose (**Primula vulgaris** or **P. acaulis**) with its large flowers in white, yellow, red or blue clustered in a rosette of leaves, and the Polyanthus (**P. variabilis**) with its bright and often bicoloured flowers clustered on stout 1 ft stalks. **P. malacoides** is the most popular of the tender types which are grown as temporary pot plants. The fragrant, small flowers in white, pink, purple or red are arranged in tiers on slender stalks. The flowers of **P. obconica** are large, fragrant and available in a wide range of colours, but the leaves can cause a rash on sensitive skins. The yellow-eyed **P. sinensis** is available in white, pink, red, orange and purple — the popular varieties have red, frilly-edged petals. **P. kewensis** is unmistakable — it is the only yellow-flowering tender Primula.

● GARDEN TYPES

showy flower 1–1½ in. across

flower-stalk 3 in. long

oblong, wrinkled leaf

P. acaulis
Common Primrose

Primula malacoides

Primula obconica

Primula kewensis

PSEUDERANTHEMUM

FOLIAGE HOUSE PLANT
page 51

Pseuderanthemum atropurpureum tricolor

4 ft shrub

leaf 5 in. long

glossy variegated leaves

P. atropurpureum
(Eranthemum atropurpureum)

TYPES

Pseuderanthemum atropurpureum is marked with purple. Varieties **tricolor** and **variegatum** are splashed with cream, purple and pink.

Pseuderanthemum is primarily grown for its brightly-coloured foliage, but if the conditions are right mature plants produce purple-eyed white flowers in late spring and summer. The problem with this plant is its need for high humidity — it belongs in a conservatory or plant window rather than in the living room. The upright stems bear oval leaves.

SECRETS OF SUCCESS

Temperature: Warm — minimum 60°F in winter.

Light: Semi-shade or bright light. Keep away from direct sunlight.

Water: Water thoroughly, but let compost become dryish between waterings.

Air Humidity: Mist leaves frequently.

Repotting: Repot, if necessary, in spring.

Propagation: Take stem cuttings in spring. Use a rooting hormone and provide bottom heat.

PUNICA

FLOWERING POT PLANT
page 57

Punica granatum nana

leaf 1 in. long

red tubular flowers followed by orange fruit

P. granatum nana

Dwarf Pomegranate

TYPE

Punica granatum nana grows about 3 ft high. The leaves are glossy and bright scarlet flowers appear in summer. Ball-like fruit develop . . . if you are lucky.

The ordinary Pomegranate is not suitable for the living room but the Dwarf Pomegranate makes an excellent pot plant for a sunny window. The flowers may be followed by bright orange fruit, but they will not ripen. In summer the pot can be stood outdoors and in winter a cool spot is required. During the dormant period the leaves will drop.

SECRETS OF SUCCESS

Temperature: Average warmth — minimum 40°F in winter.

Light: Bright light — some direct sun is essential.

Water: Water liberally from spring to autumn. Water very sparingly in winter.

Air Humidity: Mist leaves occasionally in summer.

Repotting: Repot, if necessary, in spring.

Propagation: Take stem cuttings in summer. Use a rooting hormone and provide bottom heat.

RADERMACHERA

FOLIAGE HOUSE PLANT
page 51

Radermachera sinica

leaflet 1 in. long

R. sinica

TYPES

There is much confusion over the naming of the Radermachera grown as a house plant. It may be labelled as **Radermachera sinica**, **R. Danielle** or **Stereospermum suaveolens**. A variegated form is available.

A house plant of the eighties — it was introduced to Europe from Taiwan at the beginning of the decade, and its popularity as a specimen indoor tree has increased. It may be labelled simply as 'foliage plant', but you can't mistake the large compound leaves bearing shiny, deeply-veined leaflets with long tapering points. Central heating is no problem because it tolerates dry air.

SECRETS OF SUCCESS

Temperature: Average warmth — minimum 50°–55°F in winter.

Light: Bright, but protect from midday summer sun.

Water: Keep compost moist at all times — avoid waterlogging.

Air Humidity: Misting is not necessary.

Repotting: Repot, if necessary, in spring.

Propagation: Take stem cuttings in summer.

RECHSTEINERIA

FLOWERING POT PLANT
page 57

tubular flower 2 in. long

velvety leaf 4 in. long

R. cardinalis
(Gesneria cardinalis)
Cardinal Flower

TYPES

The hooded, bright red blooms of **Rechsteineria cardinalis** are borne horizontally at the top of the 1 ft stems. **R. leucotricha** has woolly silvery-grey leaves and pink flowers.

Rechsteineria cardinalis

The Cardinal Flower is closely related to Gloxinia, and the treatment required is very similar. The shape of the flowers, however, is completely different — R. cardinalis bears tubular blooms quite unlike the open bells of Gloxinia. The bright red flowers appear in summer.

SECRETS OF SUCCESS

Temperature: Average warmth — minimum 60°F.

Light: Bright light — protect from summer sun.

Water: Keep compost moist at all times. Use tepid water and keep it off the leaves and flowers.

Air Humidity: Mist around plants frequently.

Care After Flowering: Water sparingly — stop when leaves turn yellow. Keep at 50°-60°F. Repot in early spring.

Propagation: Take stem cuttings in early summer or plant tubers in winter.

RHOEO

FOLIAGE HOUSE PLANT
page 51

leaf 1 ft long

underside purple

boat-shaped bracts containing tiny flowers

R. discolor
Boat Lily

TYPES

Rhoeo discolor is the only species — the popular variety is **vittata** which bears green leaves with bold yellow stripes. The 'boat' flowers are responsible for one of the common names — Moses in the Cradle.

Rhoeo discolor vittata

The short stem bears fleshy, lance-shaped leaves. Their colouring is unusual — glossy green or green-and-yellow above, purple below. An added feature of interest is the presence of small white flowers in purple 'boats' at the base of the lower leaves. Remove side shoots if grown as a specimen plant. It needs winter warmth and freedom from draughts.

SECRETS OF SUCCESS

Temperature: Average warmth — minimum 50°-55°F in winter.

Light: Bright or semi-shade — no direct sun in summer.

Water: Keep compost moist at all times — reduce watering in winter.

Air Humidity: Mist leaves frequently.

Repotting: Repot in spring every year.

Propagation: Use side shoots as cuttings in spring or summer. Bushy plants can be divided.

ROCHEA

FLOWERING HOUSE PLANT
page 55

leathery leaf 1 in. long

fragrant flower 1 in. long

R. coccinea
Crassula

TYPES

Rochea coccinea is usually bought in flower. It is a neat plant, 1-1½ ft high, with clusters of red tubular flowers. The varieties are more popular — **alba** (white) and **bicolor** (red and white).

Rochea coccinea

The proper name of the plant sold as 'Crassula' is Rochea coccinea. The stems are clothed with leathery triangular leaves and showy clusters of flowers appear in summer. Rochea needs standard succulent treatment — plenty of light and water in summer and a period outdoors in sunny weather. Good ventilation is important.

SECRETS OF SUCCESS

Temperature: Cool or average warmth — minimum 45°F in winter.

Light: Brightly lit spot with some direct sunshine.

Water: Water thoroughly when compost begins to dry out. Water sparingly in winter.

Air Humidity: Misting is not necessary.

Repotting: Repot, if necessary, in spring.

Propagation: Take stem cuttings in spring or summer. Allow cuttings to dry for 2-3 days before inserting in compost.

ROSA

FLOWERING POT PLANT
page 57

It may seem surprising that Roses are found in nearly all gardens but very few homes possess an indoor Rose. This cannot be due to a lack of appeal — Miniature Roses bear lovely ½–1½ in. blooms which are similar to their larger outdoor relatives. There are fragrance, a wide array of colours and a variety of shapes including bushes (6–12 in. high), climbers and standards. The reason for the lack of popularity is their inability to flourish in the average room, but with care they can be grown successfully, providing blooms from early spring to late summer. The secret is to treat it as an outdoor plant which is brought indoors for flowering. Outdoors it needs little care — keep pests and diseases at bay and prune in winter. Indoors it needs abundant light, airy conditions, high humidity and plenty of water. Remove faded blooms to prolong the flowering season.

SECRETS OF SUCCESS

Temperature: Average warmth — keep at 50°–70°F during the growing season.

Light: Maximum light — a sunny windowsill is ideal. In the short-day months extra light will be needed — place the pot near a fluorescent lamp at night.

Water: Water liberally when indoors. Allow to dry out slightly between waterings.

Air Humidity: Stand pot on a pebble tray (see page 19) if the room is warm. Mist leaves frequently.

Care After Flowering: Repot in autumn and transfer outdoors — bury the pot in soil if you can. Bring indoors in mid winter and remove top half of stems — move into an unheated spot for a week or two before placing it in a heated room.

Propagation: Take stem cuttings in early spring — use a rooting hormone.

TYPES

flowers single, semi-double or double

plant 6–12 in. high

flower ½–1½ in. across

R. chinensis minima
Miniature Rose
(Fairy Rose)

You will have no difficulty at all in recognising a Miniature Rose in bloom. It looks just like an ordinary garden variety scaled down to size — the same leaves, the same wide range of colours and flower-shapes, the same range of fragrance. These hybrids of **Rosa chinensis minima (R. roulettii)** do make excellent pot plants for summer display if you follow the rules. Make sure you choose a variety listed as 12 in. tall or less, pick a plant grown from a cutting or micro-cutting rather than a grafted Rose, and treat as an indoor/outdoor plant as described above.

Baby Darling (double, orange and pink, no fragrance, 12 in.)

Judy Fischer (double, pink, no fragrance, 9 in.)

Yellow Doll (double, pale yellow, fragrant, 10 in.)

Starina (double, vermilion, fragrant, 10 in.)

New Penny (double, coppery-pink, no fragrance, 9 in.)

Cinderella (double, silvery-pink, slight fragrance, 10 in.)

Scarlet Gem (double, bright red, no fragrance, 10 in.)

Angela Rippon (double, carmine pink, fragrant, 12 in.)

SINGLE less than 8 petals

SEMI-DOUBLE 8–20 petals

DOUBLE more than 20 petals

Rosa Starina

Rosa Judy Fischer

Rosa Baby Darling

RUELLIA

FLOWERING HOUSE PLANT
page 55

trumpet-shaped flower 1½ in. across

oval leaf 3 in. long

purple underside

R. makoyana
Monkey Plant

Ruellia macrantha

You would expect a plant with the appeal of the Monkey Plant to be more popular. The velvety leaves are tinged with purple and veined in silver, the flowers are 2 in. long flared trumpets. The stems droop gracefully, making it suitable for hanging baskets. The problem is its constitution — it needs an atmosphere which is warm and moist.

TYPES

Ruellia makoyana produces weak stems about 2 ft long — leave to trail or tie to a support. Pinch out tips to induce bushiness. **R. macrantha** is larger with plain green leaves.

SECRETS OF SUCCESS

Temperature: Warm or average warmth — minimum 55°F in winter.

Light: Brightly lit spot away from direct sun in summer.

Water: Keep compost very moist when growing and flowering. Reduce watering after flowering.

Air Humidity: Use a pebble tray — mist leaves frequently.

Repotting: Repot, if necessary, in spring.

Propagation: Take stem cuttings in summer. Use a rooting hormone and provide bottom heat.

SALPIGLOSSIS

FLOWERING POT PLANT
page 57

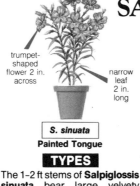

trumpet-shaped flower 2 in. across

narrow leaf 2 in. long

S. sinuata
Painted Tongue

Salpiglossis sinuata

You will not find Salpiglossis in many house plant books, but it is an outstanding pot plant. As a garden annual the beauty of the individual flowers is often lost — indoors the yellow, orange, red or lilac flowers provide an eye-catching display. Raise from seed — sow in early spring for summer flowering or sow in autumn for an early spring display. Transfer each seedling to a 5 in. pot — stake the tall stems.

TYPES

The 1–2 ft stems of **Salpiglossis sinuata** bear large velvety blooms in a wide range of colours, the petals dark veined and regularly arranged to form a 5-pointed star.

SECRETS OF SUCCESS

Temperature: Cool or average warmth — keep at 50°–65°F.

Light: Bright light with some direct sun.

Water: Keep compost moist at all times.

Air Humidity: Mist leaves occasionally.

Care After Flowering: Plant should be discarded.

Propagation: Sow seeds in spring or autumn.

SANCHEZIA

FOLIAGE HOUSE PLANT
page 51

FLOWERING HOUSE PLANT
page 55

tubular flower 2 in. long

prominently-veined leaf 1 ft long

S. nobilis

Sanchezia nobilis

This striking greenhouse shrub can be grown as a house plant if its requirement for high air humidity is met; stand the pot on a pebble tray (page 19) and mist the leaves frequently. The yellow flowers are borne in upright clusters above the foliage. These blooms are attractive, but the large leaves, up to 12 in. long, provide the main display with their yellow or ivory veins. Prune each spring.

TYPE

Sanchezia nobilis (S. speciosa) is a larger but much less popular relative of the Zebra Plant (page 67). The bush grows about 3 ft high and the flowers appear in early summer.

SECRETS OF SUCCESS

Temperature: Average warmth — minimum 55°F in winter.

Light: Brightly lit spot away from direct sun in summer.

Water: Keep compost moist at all times — reduce watering in winter.

Air Humidity: Use a pebble tray — mist leaves frequently.

Repotting: Repot in spring every year.

Propagation: Take stem cuttings in summer. Use a rooting hormone and provide bottom heat.

SAINTPAULIA

FLOWERING HOUSE PLANT
page 55

It is less than 70 years since the first African Violet was sold as a house plant, but in that time it has become a world-wide favourite. Its main attraction is the ability to flower at almost any time of the year and its compact size means it can fit on a narrow windowsill.

The original African Violet was notoriously difficult to grow, but modern varieties are much more robust and freer flowering. A beginner cannot expect to match the expert in keeping the plant in bloom continually for 10 months or more, but there should be no difficulty in producing several flushes each year.

There are five basic needs — steady warmth, careful watering, good light, high air humidity and regular feeding. Note these few extra tips from the experts: Keep the leaves off the windowpane. Remove dead flowers and damaged leaves immediately — do not leave a stalk. Remove side shoots on older plants as they develop. Keep the plant moderately root-bound. Use a plastic pot when repotting is essential.

SECRETS OF SUCCESS

Temperature: Average warmth— minimum 60°F in winter. Avoid cold draughts and sudden changes in temperature.

Light: Bright light — ideally an east or south window in winter, and a west window in summer. Always protect from strong sunlight. For winter blooming provide some artificial light at night. To grow entirely by artificial light use two 40 W fluorescent tubes about 12 in. above the plants for 14 hours each day.

Water: Keep compost moist — wait until the surface is dry before watering. Use tepid water. Push the spout below the foliage. Use immersion method occasionally.

Air Humidity: High humidity is essential. Surround the pot with damp peat or place on a pebble tray (see page 19). Mist with care — tepid water, plant not in flower, very fine spray and keep misted plant away from sunshine.

Repotting: Repot, if necessary, in spring.

Propagation: Take leaf cuttings or sow seeds in spring.

SPECIAL PROBLEMS

STRAW-COLOURED PATCHES ON LEAVES
Cause: Too much direct sun in summer. Leaf edges may turn yellow and holes may develop.

BROWN SPOTS ON LEAVES
Cause: Cold water has been used for watering. Always use tepid water.

YELLOWING LEAVES
Cause: There are several possible reasons. Dry air is a frequent cause, so are too much sun and incorrect watering. Overfeeding can result in yellowing; make sure you follow the instructions.

PALE GREEN LEAVES WITH LONG STALKS; LEAF EDGES CURLED
Cause: The plant has been chilled. The minimum temperature should be 60°F, although it will survive short periods at 50°–60°F if the compost is fairly dry. Move pots away from the window on frosty nights.

LIMP LEAVES; CENTRE CROWN ROTTEN
Cause: Crown rot disease, caused by overwatering and wide fluctuations in temperature. This is a difficult disease to control and it is infectious; the best plan is to remove and destroy the plant as soon as possible.

NO FLOWERS
Cause: There are many possible reasons. The most likely cause is insufficient light, especially in winter. Other possibilities are dry air, cold air, too frequent repotting and failure to remove side shoots. Moving the pot to a new location can cause the plant to cease blooming for some time.

MOULDY LEAVES & FLOWERS
Cause: Botrytis or powdery mildew disease. Stop misting the leaves. Pick off and destroy diseased parts. Spray the plant with systemic fungicide; use tepid water and keep out of sun until the spray deposit has dried.

INSECTS
Whitefly, mealy bug and cyclamen mite can be troublesome. See page 244.

TYPES

● TRAILING TYPES

The trailing types are officially defined as African Violets with a main stem which divides into a multicrown plant. The leaves are more widely spaced than the foliage of standard varieties. In popular language the trailers have long drooping stems which often form small plants at their tips. All are hybrids — the most important parent is **Saintpaulia magungensis**. The flowers borne by Trailing African Violets are usually smaller than those produced by the Standard African Violets — the plants may be miniature or standard-sized. Several varieties are available from specialist growers:

rounded leaf 2 in. across

violet-like flower 1 in. across

S. hybrida
Trailing African Violet

Star Trail Star-shaped flowers — blue with white edge. Miniature-sized plant.

Jet Trail Double flowers — dark lavender. Miniature-sized plant — semi-trailing habit.

Trail Along Double flowers — bright pink. Miniature-sized plant.

Snowy Trail Double flowers — white. Miniature-sized plant.

Breezy Blue Double flowers — bright blue/lavender. Standard-sized plant.

Sweetheart Trail Double flowers — bicolour pink. Standard-sized plant.

Saintpaulia Breezy Blue

● STANDARD & MINIATURE TYPES

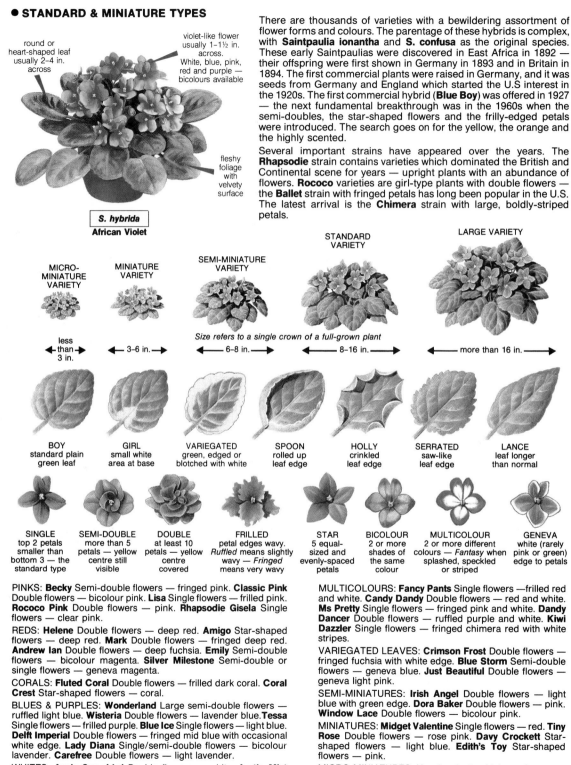

round or heart-shaped leaf usually 2–4 in. across

violet-like flower usually 1–1½ in. across. White, blue, pink, red and purple — bicolours available

fleshy foliage with velvety surface

S. hybrida
African Violet

There are thousands of varieties with a bewildering assortment of flower forms and colours. The parentage of these hybrids is complex, with **Saintpaulia ionantha** and **S. confusa** as the original species. These early Saintpaulias were discovered in East Africa in 1892 — their offspring were first shown in Germany in 1893 and in Britain in 1894. The first commercial plants were raised in Germany, and it was seeds from Germany and England which started the U.S interest in the 1920s. The first commercial hybrid (**Blue Boy**) was offered in 1927 — the next fundamental breakthrough was in the 1960s when the semi-doubles, the star-shaped flowers and the frilly-edged petals were introduced. The search goes on for the yellow, the orange and the highly scented.

Several important strains have appeared over the years. The **Rhapsodie** strain contains varieties which dominated the British and Continental scene for years — upright plants with an abundance of flowers. **Rococo** varieties are girl-type plants with double flowers — the **Ballet** strain with fringed petals has long been popular in the U.S. The latest arrival is the **Chimera** strain with large, boldly-striped petals.

MICRO-MINIATURE VARIETY	MINIATURE VARIETY	SEMI-MINIATURE VARIETY	STANDARD VARIETY	LARGE VARIETY
less than 3 in.	3–6 in.	6–8 in.	8–16 in.	more than 16 in.

Size refers to a single crown of a full-grown plant

BOY standard plain green leaf	GIRL small white area at base	VARIEGATED green, edged or blotched with white	SPOON rolled up leaf edge	HOLLY crinkled leaf edge	SERRATED saw-like leaf edge	LANCE leaf longer than normal

SINGLE top 2 petals smaller than bottom 3 — the standard type	SEMI-DOUBLE more than 5 petals — yellow centre still visible	DOUBLE at least 10 petals — yellow centre covered	FRILLED petal edges wavy. *Ruffled* means slightly wavy *Fringed* means very wavy	STAR 5 equal-sized and evenly-spaced petals	BICOLOUR 2 or more shades of the same colour	MULTICOLOUR 2 or more different colours — *Fantasy* when splashed, speckled or striped	GENEVA white (rarely pink or green) edge to petals

PINKS: Becky Semi-double flowers — fringed pink. **Classic Pink** Double flowers — bicolour pink. **Lisa** Single flowers — frilled pink. **Rococo Pink** Double flowers — pink. **Rhapsodie Gisela** Single flowers — clear pink.

REDS: Helene Double flowers — deep red. **Amigo** Star-shaped flowers — deep red. **Mark** Double flowers — fringed deep red. **Andrew Ian** Double flowers — deep fuchsia. **Emily** Semi-double flowers — bicolour magenta. **Silver Milestone** Semi-double or single flowers — geneva magenta.

CORALS: Fluted Coral Double flowers — frilled dark coral. **Coral Crest** Star-shaped flowers — coral.

BLUES & PURPLES: Wonderland Large semi-double flowers — ruffled light blue. **Wisteria** Double flowers — lavender blue. **Tessa** Single flowers — frilled purple. **Blue Ice** Single flowers — light blue. **Delft Imperial** Double flowers — fringed mid blue with occasional white edge. **Lady Diana** Single/semi-double flowers — bicolour lavender. **Carefree** Double flowers — light lavender.

WHITES: Aca's Snowbird Double flowers — white. **Arctic Mist** Double flowers — white. **White Kathleen** Single flowers — white. **Lily White** Double flowers — white. **Snow Ballet** Double flowers — white.

MULTICOLOURS: Fancy Pants Single flowers —frilled red and white. **Candy Dandy** Double flowers — red and white. **Ms Pretty** Single flowers — fringed pink and white. **Dandy Dancer** Double flowers — ruffled purple and white. **Kiwi Dazzler** Single flowers — fringed chimera red with white stripes.

VARIEGATED LEAVES: Crimson Frost Double flowers — fringed fuchsia with white edge. **Blue Storm** Semi-double flowers — geneva blue. **Just Beautiful** Double flowers — geneva light pink.

SEMI-MINIATURES: Irish Angel Double flowers — light blue with green edge. **Dora Baker** Double flowers — pink. **Window Lace** Double flowers — bicolour pink.

MINIATURES: Midget Valentine Single flowers — red. **Tiny Rose** Double flowers — rose pink. **Davy Crockett** Star-shaped flowers — light blue. **Edith's Toy** Star-shaped flowers — pink.

MICRO-MINIATURES: Novelty plants which can be grown in a wine glass. **Twinkle** Star-shaped flowers — pink. **Pip Squeek** Single bell-like flowers — light pink. **Blue Imp** Star-shaped flowers — blue.

Saintpaulia Silver Milestone

Saintpaulia Blue Storm

Saintpaulia Kiwi Dazzler

Saintpaulia Diana Blue

Saintpaulia Rhapsodie Gisela

Saintpaulia Rhapsodie No. 3

Saintpaulia Rococo Pink

Saintpaulia Fancy Pants

Saintpaulia Pip Squeek

SANSEVIERIA

**FOLIAGE
HOUSE PLANT**
page 51

sword-
like
foliage

golden-
edged
leaves

S. trifasciata laurentii
Mother-in-Law's Tongue

S. trifasciata
Snake Plant

broad
yellow
stripes

sharp
tips

S. hahnii

S. Golden hahnii
Golden Bird's Nest

If all else fails, grow Sansevieria. This tough plant, known as Mother-in-Law's Tongue in Britain and Snakeskin Plant in the U.S, deserves its reputation for near-indestructibility. It will grow in bright sunshine or shade, withstand dry air, draughts and periods without water, and it rarely needs repotting. It can, however, be quite easily killed by prolonged overwatering in winter and prolonged exposure to near freezing temperatures.

The best-known variety is S. trifasciata laurentii. Its erect, fleshy, sword-like leaves, cross-banded with distinct golden edges, are a common sight everywhere. This bold foliage provides an excellent background for plants with ferny foliage or small flowers — Mother-in-Law's Tongue is an almost essential ingredient for the Pot Group. Grow this plant in a clay pot and treat it properly — under good conditions sprays of small, fragrant flowers will appear. The low-growing rosette varieties are much less popular, but are useful for a windowsill.

SECRETS OF SUCCESS

Temperature: Average warmth — minimum 50°F in winter.

Light: Bright light with some sun preferred, but will grow in shade.

Water: Water moderately from spring to autumn, allowing compost to dry out slightly between waterings. In winter water every 1–2 months. Avoid wetting the heart of the plant.

Air Humidity: Misting is not necessary.

Repotting: Seldom required — repot when growth cracks the pot.

Propagation: Remove offset by cutting off at base — allow to dry before inserting in compost. Alternatively divide up plant. Leaf cuttings can be used for all-green varieties (see page 238).

SPECIAL PROBLEMS

ROT AT BASE. LEAVES YELLOW AND DYING BACK
Cause: Basal rot disease. The cause is generally overwatering in winter. If the whole of the base is affected, use the upper foliage as leaf cuttings and then discard the plant. If only part of the plant is affected, remove it from the pot and chop off the diseased section. Dust cut surface with sulphur and repot. Keep dry and move to a warmer spot.

ROT AT BASE IN WINTER; NOT OVERWATERED
Cause: Cold damage. Sansevieria can be quickly damaged at 40°F or below; 50°F is the minimum temperature for safe winter care.

BROWN BLOTCHES ON LEAVES
Cause: A non-infectious disorder which starts at the tips and works downwards along the leaf. The cause is unknown and there is no cure.

TYPES

Sansevierias are one of the most popular of all house plants, and the favourite one is **Sansevieria trifasciata laurentii**. Its leaves can reach 3 ft or more, but the usual height is 1–1½ ft. The basic species **S. trifasciata** (sometimes wrongly sold as **S. zeylanica**) is smaller, plainer and much less popular, but there are other colourful varieties in addition to the overworked Mother-in-Law's Tongue. **Moonshine** is small and finely modelled in light and dark green, **Bantel's Sensation** is cross-banded with cream and **craigii** is broadly-edged with cream. The tall one (5 ft) is **S. cylindrica**. Not all species of Sansevieria are tall and upright — there is the compact **S. hahnii** which produces a rosette of fleshy leaves. These leaves are about 4 in. long with pale horizontal stripes. **Golden hahnii** has vertical yellow bands along the leaf margins — **Silver hahnii** has silvery-green leaves with darker stripes. For something really unusual grow the trailing **S. grandis** in a hanging basket.

Sansevieria trifasciata laurentii

Sansevieria Golden hahnii

SAXIFRAGA

FOLIAGE HOUSE PLANT page 51

green, edged with white and pink

leaf 1½ in. across

underside red

S. sarmentosa tricolor
Mother of Thousands (Magic Carpet)

Saxifraga sarmentosa

TYPES

Saxifraga sarmentosa (S. stolonifera) bears olive green leaves with silvery veins. These plants grow about 9 in. high, and the pendant runners can reach 2–3 ft. The colourful variety **tricolor** is smaller.

The outstanding feature is the production of long, slender red runners which bear miniature plants at their ends. Clusters of insignificant flowers appear in summer. You can choose from two varieties: S. sarmentosa is easy to care for — S. sarmentosa tricolor is more attractive, but it is unfortunately slow growing and more tender.

SECRETS OF SUCCESS

Temperature: Cool or average warmth — minimum 40°–45°F in winter.

Light: Brightly lit spot, away from direct sunshine.

Water: Water liberally from spring to autumn. Water sparingly in winter.

Air Humidity: Mist leaves occasionally.

Repotting: Repot in spring every year.

Propagation: Very easy. Peg down plantlets in compost — cut stem when rooted.

SCHEFFLERA

FOLIAGE HOUSE PLANT page 51

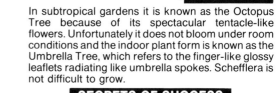

leathery, glossy leaflets

leaf-stalk attached to tree-like stem

S. actinophylla
(Brassaia actinophylla)
Umbrella Tree

Schefflera actinophylla

TYPES

Schefflera actinophylla is an attractive bush when young — a 6–8 ft tree when mature. The number of leaflets per stalk increases from 4 to 12 with age. Less easy to find are the smaller **S. digitata** and the distinctly-veined **S. octophyllum.**

In subtropical gardens it is known as the Octopus Tree because of its spectacular tentacle-like flowers. Unfortunately it does not bloom under room conditions and the indoor plant form is known as the Umbrella Tree, which refers to the finger-like glossy leaflets radiating like umbrella spokes. Schefflera is not difficult to grow.

SECRETS OF SUCCESS

Temperature: Average warmth — minimum 55°F in winter. If possible avoid temperatures above 70°F.

Light: Bright light, away from direct sunshine.

Water: Water liberally from spring to autumn. Water sparingly in winter.

Air Humidity: Mist leaves frequently.

Repotting: Repot in spring every 2 years.

Propagation: Difficult. Take stem cuttings in summer. Use a rooting hormone and provide bottom heat.

SCHIZANTHUS

FLOWERING POT PLANT page 57

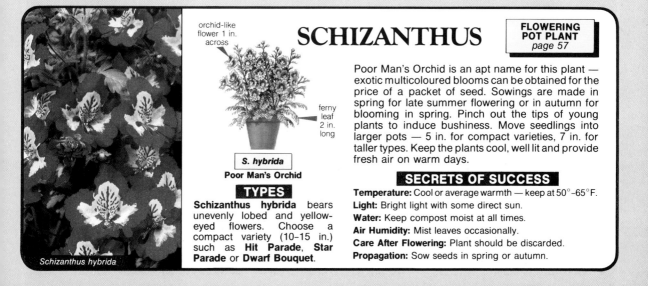

orchid-like flower 1 in. across

ferny leaf 2 in. long

S. hybrida
Poor Man's Orchid

Schizanthus hybrida

TYPES

Schizanthus hybrida bears unevenly lobed and yellow-eyed flowers. Choose a compact variety (10–15 in.) such as **Hit Parade**, **Star Parade** or **Dwarf Bouquet**.

Poor Man's Orchid is an apt name for this plant — exotic multicoloured blooms can be obtained for the price of a packet of seed. Sowings are made in spring for late summer flowering or in autumn for blooming in spring. Pinch out the tips of young plants to induce bushiness. Move seedlings into larger pots — 5 in. for compact varieties, 7 in. for taller types. Keep the plants cool, well lit and provide fresh air on warm days.

SECRETS OF SUCCESS

Temperature: Cool or average warmth — keep at 50°–65°F.

Light: Bright light with some direct sun.

Water: Keep compost moist at all times.

Air Humidity: Mist leaves occasionally.

Care After Flowering: Plant should be discarded.

Propagation: Sow seeds in spring or autumn.

SCINDAPSUS (POTHOS)

FOLIAGE HOUSE PLANT *page 51*

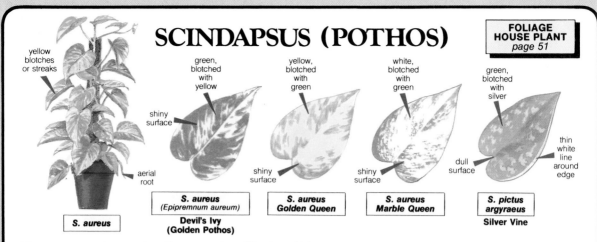

yellow blotches or streaks

green, blotched with yellow

shiny surface

aerial root

S. aureus

S. aureus *(Epipremnum aureum)* **Devil's Ivy (Golden Pothos)**

yellow, blotched with green

shiny surface

S. aureus Golden Queen

white, blotched with green

shiny surface

S. aureus Marble Queen

green, blotched with silver

dull surface

thin white line around edge

S. pictus argyraeus Silver Vine

The most popular species illustrates the difficulty which sometimes occurs over the naming of plants. You will find it in the garden centre with a 'Scindapsus aureus' label. The common name in Britain is Devil's Ivy, but it's Golden Pothos in the U.S and to the botanist it is Epipremnum aureum! Although it is sometimes described as a difficult plant to grow there is no reason why it should not do well if you follow the Secrets of Success. In some varieties the yellow or white variegation takes up more leaf area than the green background — such varieties are difficult indoors and are best confined to the conservatory or greenhouse.

Scindapsus is a climber with aerial roots — a moss stick makes an ideal support. The stems are sometimes allowed to trail from a hanging basket or wall display. Pinch out tips to induce bushiness — keep the plant well away from draughts.

SECRETS OF SUCCESS

Temperature: Average warmth — minimum 50°–55°F in winter (60°F for S. pictus argyraeus).

Light: Well-lit but sunless spot. Variegation will fade in poor light.

Water: Water liberally from spring to autumn — let compost dry out slightly between waterings. Water sparingly in winter.

Air Humidity: Mist leaves frequently.

Repotting: Repot, if necessary, in spring.

Propagation: Take stem cuttings in spring or summer — use a rooting hormone. Keep compost rather dry and leave in dark until rooted.

SPECIAL PROBLEMS

YELLOWING & FALLING LEAVES; ROTTING STEMS
Cause: Overwatering, especially in winter. Scindapsus cannot survive in waterlogged soil. Carry out standard remedial treatment (see page 246).

BROWN & SHRIVELLED LEAF TIPS
Cause: Air too dry. Mist the leaves regularly.

BROWN LEAF EDGES; BROWN SPOTS ON LEAF SURFACE
Cause: Underwatering during the growing season. Surface of compost should become dry between waterings, but root ball must not be allowed to dry out.

CURLED LIMP LEAVES; ROTTING STEMS
Cause: Cold air damage. Scindapsus is extremely sensitive to a sudden drop in temperature below 50°F.

TYPES

Scindapsus aureus

The easiest one to grow is the species **Scindapsus aureus** — it can be treated as a trailer or climber, reaching 6 ft or more under good conditions. The leaves are similar to but more colourful than Philodendron scandens, the Sweetheart Plant. The glossy green leaves are splashed with yellow, and the varieties of the basic species are even more colourful but are also more difficult to grow. **Golden Queen** is more yellow than green, and **Marble Queen** is near white. **Tricolor** leaves are a mixture of dark green, pale green, yellow and pale cream. **S. pictus argyraeus (Pothos argyraeus)** is a smaller-leaved plant which bears white-edged leaves. Its most prominent feature is the large splashes of silver which occur on the upper surface of the foliage — small white flowers sometimes appear on this variety. **S. siamense** is an uncommon species which bears silver-marked leaves.

Scindapsus aureus Marble Queen

SELAGINELLA

FOLIAGE HOUSE PLANT page 51

Selaginella, or Creeping Moss, was a Victorian favourite. Today it has lost much of this early popularity, but it is still an excellent choice for the bottle garden or terrarium. It is much less happy away from this protection, the tiny leaves shrivelling in hot rooms, draughty rooms or in dry air. To increase your chance of success grow it in a shallow, well-drained pot in semi-shade some distance away from the window. Surround the pot with damp peat and use soft water for watering and misting.

SECRETS OF SUCCESS

Temperature: Average warmth — minimum 55°F in winter.

Light: Semi-shade.

Water: Keep compost moist at all times — reduce watering in winter. Use soft water.

Air Humidity: Moist air is essential. Mist leaves regularly — avoid soaking leaves.

Repotting: Repot, if necessary, in spring.

Propagation: Take stem cuttings in spring or summer.

leaves blue-green

leaves pale green

S. uncinata

S. martensii

Selaginella emmeliana

Selaginella martensii watsoniana

TYPES

Trailing Selaginellas include **Selaginella uncinata** (the blue-green Peacock Fern), **S. apoda** (pale green and moss-like) and **S. kraussiana aurea** (the yellow-green Spreading Clubmoss). The Resurrection Plant (**S. lepidophylla**) is bought as a dried-up ball and is restored to life by soaking in water. Not all Selaginellas trail — **S. martensii** has 1 ft high upright stems and aerial roots grow down from the stems into the compost — the variety **watsoniana** has silvery tips. **S. emmeliana** is another erect species with 6 in. high stems and lacy leaves.

SENECIO

FOLIAGE HOUSE PLANT page 51

Senecio is a confusing genus. It includes the Cinerarias (page 116), several succulents (page 218) and the Ivy-like climbers described here. At first glance both the Cape Ivy and German Ivy can be mistaken for one of the True Ivies described on page 154. The leaves are lobed and the stems either trail or are trained up canes. On closer inspection the lobes of Senecio leaves are found to be fleshier and generally more pointed, and if the small flowers appear the difference is immediately obvious.

SECRETS OF SUCCESS

Temperature: Average warmth — minimum 50°F in winter.

Light: Bright light — some direct sun is beneficial in winter. Will tolerate semi-shade.

Water: Keep compost moist at all times — reduce watering in winter.

Air Humidity: Mist leaves occasionally.

Repotting: Repot in spring every 2 years.

Propagation: Easy. Take stem cuttings in spring or summer.

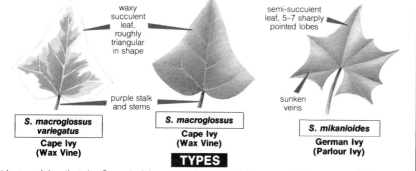

waxy succulent leaf, roughly triangular in shape

purple stalk and stems

semi-succulent leaf, 5–7 sharply pointed lobes

sunken veins

S. macroglossus variegatus
Cape Ivy (Wax Vine)

S. macroglossus
Cape Ivy (Wax Vine)

S. mikanioides
German Ivy (Parlour Ivy)

Senecio macroglossus variegatus

TYPES

It is surprising that the Senecio Ivies are not more widely grown. They are more vigorous than the True Ivies and are less affected by the warm and dry conditions in a centrally-heated room in winter. Small Daisy-like flowers appear if kept in a well-lit spot. They are tall growing — pinch out tips to induce bushiness. **Senecio macroglossus** is rarely grown — you are more likely to find the yellow-edged form (**variegatus**). The leaves of **S. mikanioides** have several pointed lobes.

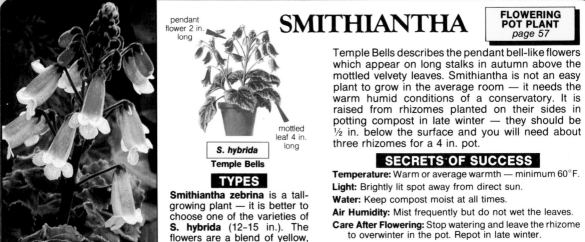

SMITHIANTHA

FLOWERING
POT PLANT
page 57

pendant flower 2 in. long

mottled leaf 4 in. long

S. hybrida
Temple Bells

Smithiantha hybrida Cathedral

Temple Bells describes the pendant bell-like flowers which appear on long stalks in autumn above the mottled velvety leaves. Smithiantha is not an easy plant to grow in the average room — it needs the warm humid conditions of a conservatory. It is raised from rhizomes planted on their sides in potting compost in late winter — they should be ½ in. below the surface and you will need about three rhizomes for a 4 in. pot.

SECRETS OF SUCCESS

Temperature: Warm or average warmth — minimum 60°F.
Light: Brightly lit spot away from direct sun.
Water: Keep compost moist at all times.
Air Humidity: Mist frequently but do not wet the leaves.
Care After Flowering: Stop watering and leave the rhizome to overwinter in the pot. Repot in late winter.
Propagation: Divide rhizomes at repotting time.

TYPES

Smithiantha zebrina is a tall-growing plant — it is better to choose one of the varieties of **S. hybrida** (12–15 in.). The flowers are a blend of yellow, orange and/or pink.

SOLANUM

FLOWERING
POT PLANT
page 57

leaf 2 in. long with wavy edges

star-shaped flowers followed by roundish-oval berries

downy stems

S. capsicastrum
Winter Cherry

Solanum plants bear tiny flowers in summer and these are followed in autumn by green berries which change colour as winter approaches. The Winter Cherry is a familiar sight at Christmas. The orange or red berries among the dark green leaves provide a festive touch, and if this small shrubby plant is placed on a sunny windowsill in a cool room then the berries will last for months. A closely related species, Jerusalem Cherry (S. pseudocapsicum) bears larger berries. A word of warning — these fruits can be poisonous. The Winter Cherry should last until February. Early leaf fall usually means overwatering — dropping berries indicate too little light or hot, dry air.

SECRETS OF SUCCESS

Temperature: Cool — keep at 50°–60°F in winter.
Light: Bright light with some direct sun.
Water: Keep compost moist at all times.
Air Humidity: Mist leaves frequently.
Care After Flowering: Prune back stems to half their length in late winter. Keep compost almost dry until spring, then repot. Stand the pot outdoors during the summer months — spray the plants when in flower. Bring back indoors in autumn.
Propagation: Sow seeds or take stem cuttings in spring.

TYPES

Solanum capsicastrum is sold in vast quantities every Christmas from supermarkets, garden centres and market stalls. The dark green leaves are narrowly oval and the white flowers form berries which are about ½ in. in diameter when mature. The plants are usually bought when the fruits have changed from green to orange-red and these will remain on the plants for months if kept in a cool place. There are several varieties, such as **Cherry Ripe** (bright red berries) and **variegatum** (cream-splashed leaves). The Jerusalem Cherry (**S. pseudocapsicum**) is also popular, especially in the U.S, and is quite similar. If you look closely, however, you will see that the stems are smooth. Also the berries are larger, the leaves shorter and the colours generally brighter. The species is quite tall (1½–2½ ft) but 1 ft dwarf varieties (**nanum, Tom Thumb**, etc) are the favourite types.

Solanum capsicastrum

Solanum pseudocapsicum

Sonerila margaritacea

SONERILA

FOLIAGE HOUSE PLANT page 51

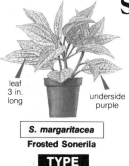

leaf 3 in. long

underside purple

S. margaritacea
Frosted Sonerila

TYPE

Sonerila margaritacea is a low-growing plant with beautifully marked leaves. The surface is green or coppery green lined and spotted with silver — pink flowers appear in summer.

This bushy, colourful plant from Java will grow quite happily in a terrarium, but Sonerila is a real challenge to your skill under ordinary room conditions. It is a hot house plant needing warmth, constant humidity around the leaves and careful watering. Surround the pot with damp peat and mist the leaves each day with tepid water.

SECRETS OF SUCCESS

Temperature: Warm or average warmth — minimum 60°F in winter.

Light: Semi-shade — keep away from direct sunlight.

Water: Keep compost moist at all times — reduce watering in winter. Avoid overwatering.

Air Humidity: Mist leaves regularly.

Repotting: Repot in spring every 2 years.

Propagation: Take stem cuttings in spring or summer. Use a rooting hormone and provide bottom heat.

Sparmannia africana

SPARMANNIA

FLOWERING HOUSE PLANT page 55

golden-centred flower 1½ in. across

downy leaf 9 in. long

S. africana
House Lime

TYPE

Sparmannia africana is tree-like, quickly growing several feet high. The flowers appear in long-stalked clusters. Cut back after blooming has finished — repeat flowering may occur.

The pale downy leaves make a pleasant contrast to the dark leathery foliage of Philodendron or Ficus. It grows quickly and may need repotting more than once a year. Keep growth in check by pinching out the stem tips of young plants. Sparmannia blooms in early spring if it has been kept in direct sunlight during winter.

SECRETS OF SUCCESS

Temperature: Average warmth — minimum 45°F in winter.

Light: Brightly lit spot away from direct sun in summer.

Water: Keep compost moist at all times — may require daily watering in summer. Water more sparingly in winter.

Air Humidity: Mist leaves occasionally in summer.

Repotting: Repot in spring every year.

Propagation: Stem cuttings root easily in spring or summer.

Spathiphyllum wallisii

SPATHIPHYLLUM

FLOWERING HOUSE PLANT page 55

arum-like flower 3 in. long

lance-shaped leaf 6 in. long

S. wallisii
Peace Lily

TYPES

Spathiphyllum wallisii grows about 1 ft high — a dwarf variety (**Petite**) is available. **S. Mauna Loa** is larger (2 ft) and less hardy. White flowers turn pale green with age.

The Peace Lily is a good choice if it can be kept out of direct sunlight in a room which is reasonably warm in winter. There must be no cold draughts and the pot should be surrounded by moist peat or stood on a pebble tray (page 19). The glossy leaves grow directly out of the compost; in spring and sometimes again in autumn the flowers appear.

SECRETS OF SUCCESS

Temperature: Warm or average warmth — minimum 55°F in winter.

Light: Semi-shade in summer — bright light in winter. Strong sunlight will damage the leaves.

Water: Keep compost moist at all times — reduce watering in winter.

Air Humidity: Mist leaves very frequently.

Repotting: Repot in spring every year.

Propagation: Divide plants at repotting time.

Stapelia variegata

STAPELIA

FLOWERING HOUSE PLANT page 55

fleshy erect stem 6 in. long

grey-green blotched with purple

star-shaped flower 2–3 in. across

S. variegata
Carrion Flower

TYPES

Stapelia variegata bears uniquely-patterned blooms at the base of the stems during the summer. For maximum display choose the odourless **S. gigantea** (blooms 10–12 in. across).

The smell of the blooms of the Carrion Flower has been described as 'disagreeable', 'offensive', and 'disgusting'. It is therefore not surprising that these flowering succulents have never been popular, although some types produce flowers which have little or no smell. All Stapelias have spectacular flowers. By far the most popular type is S. variegata. Unfortunately it is a strong-smelling species.

SECRETS OF SUCCESS

Temperature: Average warmth — minimum 50°F in winter.

Light: Brightly lit spot, away from direct sun in summer.

Water: Water moderately, then leave until compost surface is dry. Water sparingly in winter.

Air Humidity: Misting is not necessary.

Repotting: Repot, if necessary, in spring.

Propagation: See Propagation of Succulents, page 212.

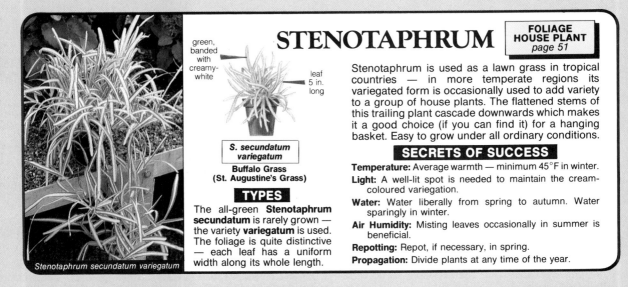

Stenotaphrum secundatum variegatum

STENOTAPHRUM

FOLIAGE HOUSE PLANT page 51

green, banded with creamy-white

leaf 5 in. long

S. secundatum variegatum
Buffalo Grass
(St. Augustine's Grass)

TYPES

The all-green **Stenotaphrum secundatum** is rarely grown — the variety **variegatum** is used. The foliage is quite distinctive — each leaf has a uniform width along its whole length.

Stenotaphrum is used as a lawn grass in tropical countries — in more temperate regions its variegated form is occasionally used to add variety to a group of house plants. The flattened stems of this trailing plant cascade downwards which makes it a good choice (if you can find it) for a hanging basket. Easy to grow under all ordinary conditions.

SECRETS OF SUCCESS

Temperature: Average warmth — minimum 45°F in winter.

Light: A well-lit spot is needed to maintain the cream-coloured variegation.

Water: Water liberally from spring to autumn. Water sparingly in winter.

Air Humidity: Misting leaves occasionally in summer is beneficial.

Repotting: Repot, if necessary, in spring.

Propagation: Divide plants at any time of the year.

Stephanotis floribunda

STEPHANOTIS

FLOWERING HOUSE PLANT page 55

glossy leaf 4 in. long

star-shaped tubular flower 1 in. across

S. floribunda
Wax Flower
(Madagascar Jasmine)

TYPE

The stems of **Stephanotis floribunda** can reach 10 ft or more, but is usually sold twined around a wire hoop. The heavily-scented waxy flowers appear in summer.

Stephanotis is usually associated with bridal bouquets, but it can also be grown as a free-flowering house plant. Its vigorous climbing stems must be trained on a support. A beautiful but difficult plant — it hates sudden changes in temperature, needs constant cool conditions in winter and is attractive to scale and mealy bug.

SECRETS OF SUCCESS

Temperature: Average warmth — keep at 55°–60°F in winter.

Light: Brightly lit spot, away from direct sun in summer.

Water: Keep compost moist at all times. Water sparingly in winter.

Air Humidity: Mist leaves occasionally.

Repotting: Repot in spring every 2 years.

Propagation: Take stem cuttings in summer. Use a rooting hormone and provide bottom heat.

Strelitzia reginae

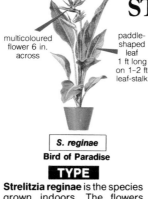

multicoloured flower 6 in. across

paddle-shaped leaf 1 ft long on 1-2 ft leaf-stalk

S. reginae
Bird of Paradise

STRELITZIA

FLOWERING HOUSE PLANT
page 55

Surely the most spectacular of all the flowers which can be grown in the home. The vivid flowers last for several weeks on top of tall stalks, surrounded by large leaves. It needs patience (new plants take 4–6 years before flowering starts) and space (mature plants in a 10 in. pot grow 3–4 ft high), but is surprisingly easy to grow.

TYPE

Strelitzia reginae is the species grown indoors. The flowers usually appear in spring, but sometimes occur earlier or later.

SECRETS OF SUCCESS

Temperature: Average warmth — keep at 55°–60°F in winter.

Light: As much light as possible, but shade from hot summer sun.

Water: Water thoroughly, then leave until the compost surface is dry. Water sparingly in winter.

Air Humidity: Mist leaves occasionally.

Repotting: Repot young plants in spring.

Propagation: Divide plants at repotting time.

Streptocarpus Constant Nymph

trumpet-shaped flower 2 in. across

strap-shaped leaf 8–12 in. long

S. hybrida
Cape Primrose

STREPTOCARPUS

FLOWERING HOUSE PLANT
page 55

Many hybrids have appeared but the old favourite Constant Nymph still remains the most popular Streptocarpus. When growing conditions are satisfactory a succession of blooms appear above the rosette of coarse, stemless leaves throughout the summer. It needs a shallow pot, moist air, bright light and freedom from draughts and cold air in winter. Remove flowers as they fade.

TYPES

Flowers are white, blue, purple, pink and red with prominently-veined throats. The blooms of **Streptocarpus Constant Nymph** are lilac with violet veins.

SECRETS OF SUCCESS

Temperature: Average warmth — minimum 55°F in winter.

Light: Brightly lit spot away from direct sun in summer.

Water: Water freely, then leave until the compost surface is dry. Reduce watering in winter.

Air Humidity: Mist occasionally. Do not wet the leaves.

Repotting: Repot in spring every year.

Propagation: Divide plants at repotting time. Seeds may be sown in spring.

Streptosolen jamesonii

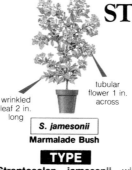

wrinkled leaf 2 in. long

tubular flower 1 in. across

S. jamesonii
Marmalade Bush

STREPTOSOLEN

FLOWERING HOUSE PLANT
page 55

The main feature of Streptosolen is the large clusters of marmalade-coloured flowers borne at the tip of each branch in spring or summer. The stems require some form of support — you can stake the main stem and train it as a standard (page 148). Streptosolen becomes leggy with age — this is most marked when the compost is not kept constantly moist. A well-lit spot is essential, especially in winter.

TYPE

Streptosolen jamesonii will grow 4–6 ft high if left unpruned. The branches are weak — the best way to grow this rambling shrub in a conservatory is to train it against a wall.

SECRETS OF SUCCESS

Temperature: Average warmth — minimum 50°F in winter.

Light: Bright light, away from direct sun in summer.

Water: Keep compost moist at all times.

Air Humidity: Mist leaves occasionally.

Repotting: Repot, if necessary, after flowering.

Propagation: Take stem cuttings in spring or summer.

SUCCULENTS

FOLIAGE
HOUSE PLANT
page 51

Three or four tiny pots of succulents and a small Cactus or two are the usual starting point for a life-long interest in house plants.

The succulents are indeed a good starting point for children as these plants are easy to care for, can withstand a great deal of neglect and mismanagement, and are amongst the easiest of all plant groups to propagate.

Succulents are easily defined as plants with fleshy leaves or stems which can store water — the Cacti (page 101) are a distinct group of succulents. Much less distinct is the dividing line between 'succulents', and 'house plants with fleshy leaves'. Sansevieria and other fleshy-leaved types which have different requirements to other succulents are treated as ordinary house plants in this book. Those succulents which are grown mainly for their blooms (Hoya, Rochea, Kalanchoe blossfeldiana etc) are treated as flowering house plants or flowering pot plants.

Hundreds of succulents with widely differing shapes and sizes are commercially available. Most of them have a rosette shape, as the tightly-packed leaf arrangement helps to conserve water in their desert habitat. With age some of these types become 'rosette trees' with leaf clusters at the ends of woody stems. The remainder grow as trailing or bushy plants.

Despite the wide variety of shapes, the succulents are remarkably consistent in their needs. They evolved in the dry areas of the world and their general requirements are related to this habitat — free-draining compost, sunshine, fresh air, water in the growing season and a cold and dry resting period. Winter dormancy is vital if you want your plants to bloom and last for many years — another requirement for top-quality plants is a period outdoors in summer.

SECRETS OF SUCCESS

Temperature: Average warmth from spring to autumn — succulents (unlike most house plants) relish a marked difference between night and day temperatures. Keep cool in winter; 50°–55°F is ideal but no harm will occur at 40°F.

Light: A windowsill is the right spot, as some sunshine is vital. Choose a south-facing windowsill if you can, but some shade in summer may be necessary. Haworthia and Gasteria need a bright but sunless site.

Water: Treat as an ordinary house plant from spring to autumn, watering thoroughly when the compost begins to dry out. In winter water very infrequently, once every 1–2 months.

Air Humidity: No need to mist the leaves. The main requirement is for fresh air — open windows in summer.

Repotting: Only repot when essential — then transfer to a slightly larger container in spring. Use a shallow pot rather than a deep one.

Propagation: Cuttings root easily. Take stem cuttings, offsets or leaf cuttings in spring or summer. It is vital to let the cuttings dry for a few days (large cuttings for 1–2 weeks) before inserting in compost. Water very sparingly and do not cover with polythene or glass. Another propagation method is seed sowing — germination temperature 70°–80°F.

SPECIAL PROBLEMS

STEM ELONGATED & MISSHAPEN
Cause: Too much water in winter or too little light in summer. Refer to Secrets of Success; turn pots occasionally to ensure even growth.

BROWN DRY SPOTS
Cause: Underwatering. Remember that succulents require generous watering in summer.

BROWN SOFT SPOTS
Cause: Leaf spot disease. Water with systemic fungicide. Improve ventilation.

LEAVES WILTED & DISCOLOURED
Cause: Overwatering, especially in winter. Carry out standard remedial treatment (see page 246).

SUDDEN LOSS OF LEAVES
Cause: Very cold water straight from the tap; use tepid water in future. Another possibility is underwatering in summer.

ROT AT BASE FOLLOWED BY STEM COLLAPSE
Cause: Basal stem rot disease, due to overwet conditions in winter. Use upper stem for propagation. Next time avoid overwatering in winter, and cover compost surface with a layer of stone chippings.

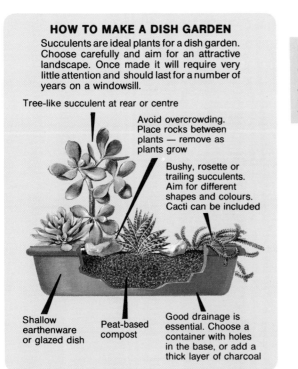

HOW TO MAKE A DISH GARDEN

Succulents are ideal plants for a dish garden. Choose carefully and aim for an attractive landscape. Once made it will require very little attention and should last for a number of years on a windowsill.

Tree-like succulent at rear or centre

Avoid overcrowding. Place rocks between plants — remove as plants grow

Bushy, rosette or trailing succulents. Aim for different shapes and colours. Cacti can be included

Shallow earthenware or glazed dish

Peat-based compost

Good drainage is essential. Choose a container with holes in the base, or add a thick layer of charcoal

TYPES

ADROMISCHUS

fleshy
spoon-like
leaves

A. cooperi

Adromischus cooperi has thick leaves with wavy tips. The grey-green foliage is splashed with purple and the reddish hairs which appear at the base are really aerial roots.

AEONIUM

rosette
of shiny
leaves

tightly-
packed
waxy
leaves

A. arboreum atropurpureum

A. tabulaeforme
Saucer Plant

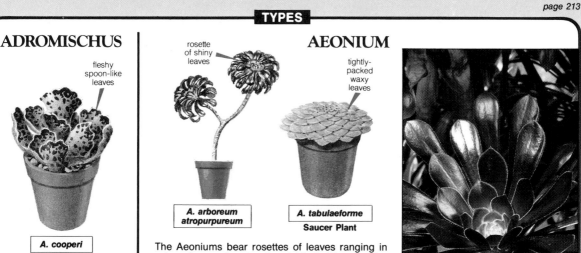

Aeonium arboreum atropurpureum Schwarzkopf

The Aeoniums bear rosettes of leaves ranging in colour from yellow to almost black. The rosettes may be flat saucers of densely-packed leaves, as in **Aeonium tabulaeforme**, or a looser arrangement on top of branched stems as found in **A. arboreum**. The latter species is all-green — more popular is the purple-brown leaved variety **atropurpureum** which can reach 3 ft or more. Even more dramatic is the variety **Schwarzkopf** which has near-black foliage.

AGAVE

saw-edged
leaves

fine
threads

black
spines
at leaf
tips

A. americana
Century Plant

A. americana mediopicta

A. filifera
Thread Agave

A. victoriae-reginae

Agave americana marginata

The most popular Agave is the Century Plant, so-called because of the mistaken belief that it flowers only once every 100 years. There are two colourful varieties — **Agave americana marginata** (green leaves edged with yellow) and **A. americana mediopicta** (cream leaves edged with green). With time these plants produce leaves 3 or 4 ft long, and both size and sharp spines make them unsuitable for a small room. **A. filifera** (upward-turned leaves 1 ft long) is more compact — even smaller is **A. parviflora**, another Agave with filament-bearing leaves. Experts usually recommend **A. victoriae-reginae** as the best choice — its 6 in. triangular leaves are dark green edged with white. Much more colourful but much rarer is **A. parrasana** — blue-grey leaves edged with bright red thorns.

Agave victoriae-reginae

ALOE

A. aristata — white warts on leaves
Lace Aloe

A. humilis — toothed leaves
Hedgehog Aloe

A. variegata — white edges, thick triangular leaves
Partridge-breasted Aloe

A. mitriformis — toothed leaves

Aloe jucunda

Aloes come in all shapes and sizes, and many form stemless rosettes of fleshy leaves. Only two of them are popular as plants for the home. **Aloe variegata** is immediately recognisable — the upright 6 in. leaves are triangular with prominent white banding and edging on the dark green or purplish surface. **A. aristata** is smaller — the 4 in. long leaves form a globular rosette which when mature readily produces a large number of offsets. There are several other attractive Aloes — **A. jucunda** is the small one, forming 3 in. rosettes of spiny, cream-blotched dark leaves. **A. humilis** is another dwarf, with blue-green leaves bearing white teeth. **A. mitriformis** is the thorny one.

Aloes are usually stemless rosettes but there are a few stemmed forms, including the Tree Aloe **A. arborescens** (9 in. spiny leaves on tall trunks) and **A. ferox** (18 in. spiny and warty leaves). Both species are unsuitable for small rooms.

Aloe ferox

BRYOPHYLLUM

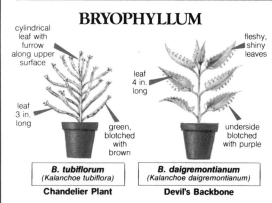

B. tubiflorum
(Kalanchoe tubiflora) — cylindrical leaf with furrow along upper surface, leaf 3 in. long, green, blotched with brown
Chandelier Plant

B. daigremontianum
(Kalanchoe daigremontianum) — fleshy, shiny leaves, leaf 4 in. long, underside blotched with purple
Devil's Backbone

The Bryophyllums belong to the small group of house plants which bear plantlets on their leaves. **Bryophyllum tubiflorum** has a series of tubular leaves encircling the stem, and at the tip of each fleshy leaf a small group of plantlets appear. It grows 3 ft high and in spring bell-shaped orange flowers appear. **B. daigremontianum** is an erect, unbranched 2-3 ft succulent with triangular leaves. These leaves are held stiffly at an angle to the stem with the serrated edges curled inwards. At these edges tiny plantlets develop.

CEROPEGIA

leaf ¾ in. long — heart-shaped and fleshy
dark green, blotched with silver
underside purple

C. woodii
Rosary Vine
(String of Hearts)

Ceropegia woodii is an unusual succulent for a hanging basket. The wiry stems grow about 3 ft long. It is an easy plant to grow, but the foliage is unfortunately sparse and the 1 in. tubular flowers are insignificant.

Ceropegia woodii

CRASSULA

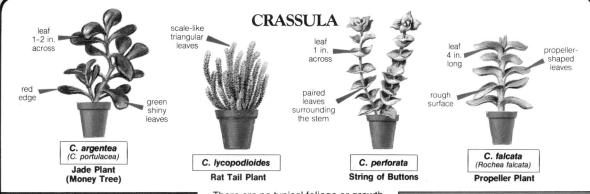

leaf 1–2 in. across

red edge

green shiny leaves

C. argentea
(C. portulacea)
**Jade Plant
(Money Tree)**

scale-like triangular leaves

C. lycopodioides
Rat Tail Plant

leaf 1 in. across

paired leaves surrounding the stem

C. perforata
String of Buttons

leaf 4 in. long

propeller-shaped leaves

rough surface

C. falcata
(Rochea falcata)
Propeller Plant

Crassula ovata Hummel's Sunset

There are no typical foliage or growth characteristics to help you identify a plant as a Crassula. Leaves range from scale-like to several inches long, growth habit from sprawling to stiffly erect and leaf colour from grey to red. One of the most popular species is **Crassula argentea** with its tree-like trunk growing 3 ft or more. **C. arborescens** is rather similar, but the leaves are less rounded and are greyish in colour. There are several Crassulas with stems which seem to grow through the fused leaves — **C. perforata** (2 ft tall) and the very similar **C. rupestris** are the usual ones. **C. falcata** has larger leaves than any other common Crassula — this grey-leaved, red-flowering species is easy to grow. It reaches 2–3 ft — much taller than the upright branching stems of **C. lycopodioides** which are completely clothed with minute fleshy scales. A specialist supplier will offer many others.

Crassula rupestris

COTYLEDON

Cotyledon orbiculata

wavy-edged leaves

silvery surface

C. undulata
Silver Crown

Best known is the popular **Cotyledon undulata** — 1–2 ft stems bearing wavy-edged and bloom-covered leaves. **C. orbiculata** is a larger shrub with spoon-shaped leaves. The tubular flowers of Cotyledon appear in summer.

EUPHORBIA

milky sap

leafless stems

E. tirucalli
**Milk Bush
(Pencil Euphorbia)**

Euphorbias come in many shapes and forms. Some of them (e.g **Euphorbia grandicornis** and **E. resinifera**) are Cactus-like. Thornless succulent ones include the globular **E. obesa** (Turkish Temple) and also the pencil-stemmed **E. tirucalli**.

Euphorbia obesa

ECHEVERIA

brown-tipped pointed leaves

spoon-shaped leaves

waxy leaves

red-tipped leaves

fine white hairs on leaves

E. agavoides

E. derenbergii
Painted Lady

E. glauca
Blue Echeveria

E. setosa
Firecracker Plant

surface covered with fine hairs

pinky-bronze leaves

E. gibbiflora metallica

E. harmsii
(Oliveranthus elegans)
Red Echeveria

Echeveria gibbiflora carunculata

Echeveria elegans

There are two popular Echeverias which grow as rosette-topped trees. The red-tipped leaves of **Echeveria harmsii** form a loose rosette above the branching stems. The stout trunk of **E. gibbiflora** is taller (2 ft or more) and the leaves are larger (4–6 in. long) — varieties include **cristata** (wavy edged) and **metallica** (bronzy lustre). Other Echeverias grow as flattened rosettes — the short and tightly-packed leaves are covered with a white bloom, short hairs or a waxy coating. There is an exception — **E. agavoides** bears plain-surfaced, 2 in. long green leaves. Echeveria leaves are 1–3 in. long and each popular species has its own distinctive feature — the ball-like silvery rosettes of **E. elegans**, the pinkish-tinged leaves of **E. carnicolor**, the waxy, hollow-spoon leaves of **E. glauca**, the furry foliage of **E. setosa** and the silvery-green leaves of **E. derenbergii**.

FAUCARIA

toothed jaw-like leaves

F. tigrina
Tiger Jaws

The fleshy leaves of **Faucaria tigrina** are 2 in. long 'jaws' complete with teeth. These spines are quite soft and so the plant is not as vicious as it looks. Bright yellow blooms appear in summer.

Faucaria tigrina

GASTERIA

white warts on leaves

G. verrucosa
Ox Tongue

The leaves are arranged in two rows — as it gets older an untidy rosette is usually formed. **Gasteria verrucosa** is the warty one — **G. maculata** has leaves of a similar size (5–6 in. long) but they are wart-free.

Gasteria maculata

HAWORTHIA

white warts on leaves

finely-pointed leaves

translucent upper surface

H. margaritifera
Pearl Plant

H. fasciata
Zebra Haworthia

H. tessellata
Star Window Plant

Haworthia attenuata

Haworthias are Aloe-like succulents which bear thick and warty leaves. **Haworthia margaritifera** forms a ball-like rosette about 5 in. across. The white tubercles which cover the backs of the leaves give the plant a pearly appearance — **H. papillosa** is similar. The warts on **H. fasciata** are arranged in horizontal bands — this 'zebra striping' is also a feature of **H. attenuata**. Some Haworthias have semi-transparent 'windows' instead of warts on the upper leaf surface — examples are **H. tessellata** and **H. cuspidata**. Haworthias are generally low-growing rosettes but **H. reinwardtii** (Wart Plant) forms an erect 8 in. stem which is clothed with thick triangular leaves.

KALANCHOE

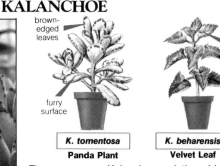

brown-edged leaves

velvety leaves covered with brown hairs

furry surface

K. tomentosa
Panda Plant

K. beharensis
Velvet Leaf

Kalanchoe tomentosa

There are many Kalanchoe varieties which are grown for their flowers and a few for their striking leaves. **Kalanchoe tomentosa** is perhaps the most popular of the foliage ones — 1½ ft tall with woolly leaves. There is also **K. marmorata** (Pen Wiper) with scalloped and brown-blotched leaves, and **K. beharensis** grown for its large velvety foliage.

GRAPTOPETALUM

grey-green leaves

G. paraguayense
Ghost Plant

These plants are grey-leaved, low-growing relatives of Echeveria. **Graptopetalum paraguayense** has 2 in. long leaves on 3 in. stems. **G. pachyphyllum** is a miniature tree with 1 in. high stems — the rosettes are about 1 in. across.

KLEINIA

grey-green stems

K. articulata
(Senecio articulatus)
Candle Plant

Kleinia articulata is grown for its 2 ft bloom-coated stems — pale yellow flowers appear in summer. Even more dramatic is the Cocoon Plant (**K. tomentosa**) with its stems and tubular leaves covered in white wool.

OROSTACHYS

tightly-packed pointed leaves

O. spinosus

Orostachys spinosus is a saucer-like rosette of packed leaves which looks rather like Aeonium tabulaeforme. Look for the differences — this plant has spines at the ends of the leaves, and the centre folds upwards in winter.

PACHYPHYTUM

leaf 1 in. long

silvery-white bloom

P. oviferum
Sugar Almond Plant
(Moonstones)

Pachyphytum is closely related to Echeveria. You can see the family likeness in the mauve-tinged **Pachyphytum amethystinum** but the popular one is quite different — **P. oviferum** bears rosettes of egg-like leaves.

PEDILANTHUS

zig-zag stems

P. tithymaloides
Jacob's Ladder

Pedilanthus tithymaloides is unmistakable — the fleshy stems zig-zag sharply, reaching about 2 ft. The variety **variegatus** is the popular one — waxy leaves edged with white and pink. The milky sap is an irritant, so take care.

SEDUM

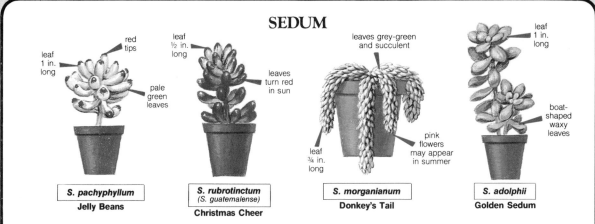

S. pachyphyllum
Jelly Beans

leaf 1 in. long
red tips
pale green leaves

S. rubrotinctum
(S. guatemalense)
Christmas Cheer

leaf ½ in. long
leaves turn red in sun

S. morganianum
Donkey's Tail

leaves grey-green and succulent
leaf ¾ in. long
pink flowers may appear in summer

S. adolphii
Golden Sedum

leaf 1 in. long
boat-shaped waxy leaves

Sedum rubrotinctum

Sedums are generally low growing with branching stems and an abundance of fleshy leaves which are either cylindrical or boat-shaped. There are, of course, exceptions — **Sedum prealtum** is a vigorous 2 ft shrub with shiny 3 in. long leaves. **S. pachyphyllum** is a typical and popular Sedum — the erect, branching stems grow about 1 ft tall and the succulent leaves are cylindrical. The tips are red and so it is easily distinguished from **S. allantoides** (leaves all-green and coated with a greyish bloom) and the compact **S. rubrotinctum** (leaves suffused with red in strong light). Species with boat-shaped leaves include **S. adolphii** and **S. bellum**.

The two trailing Sedums do not look like sisters. **S. morganianum** bears 2–3 ft long stems, completely clothed with cylindrical leaves. The thin stems of **S. sieboldii mediovariegatum** bear leaves in clusters of three. Each ¾ in. leaf is cream-hearted and edged blue-green.

Sedum sieboldii mediovariegatum

SEMPERVIVUM

Sempervivum arachnoideum

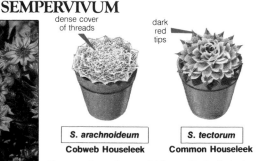

dense cover of threads

dark red tips

S. arachnoideum
Cobweb Houseleek

S. tectorum
Common Houseleek

Sempervivum is an old favourite both indoors and out. They are completely hardy — they seem to thrive on neglect and should not be overwatered, overfed or repotted unnecessarily. The Cobweb Houseleek is the one usually chosen — red flowers appear in summer. Many colourful varieties of both **Sempervivum tectorum** and **S. soboliferum** are available. Offsets form around the base of Sempervivum plants — hence the Hens and Chickens common name.

SENECIO

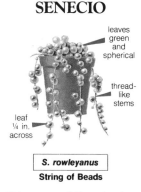

leaves green and spherical
thread-like stems
leaf ¼ in. across

S. rowleyanus
String of Beads

This group of Senecios is strange indeed — pendant threads bearing bead-like leaves. There are **Senecio rowleyanus** (pea-like foliage) **S. herreianus** (oval foliage) **S. citriformis** (lemon-shaped foliage).

STROBILANTHES

FOLIAGE HOUSE PLANT page 51

Strobilanthes dyeranus

underside purple

leaf 5 in. long

S. dyeranus
Persian Shield

TYPE

Only one species is grown — **Strobilanthes dyeranus**. It is an erect shrub bearing finely-toothed leaves which are coloured purple below and with a purple blotch above extending almost to the edges.

Strobilanthes is a lovely foliage plant when it is young. The long, pointed leaves are dark green with a silvery purple sheen. Unfortunately this appearance declines with age — old plants look straggly and the colour fades — the foliage becomes silvery with dark veins. Not an easy plant to grow — a humid atmosphere is needed. Replace them with new stock raised from cuttings.

SECRETS OF SUCCESS

Temperature: Average warmth — minimum 55°F in winter.

Light: Brightly lit spot, away from direct sunlight in summer.

Water: Water moderately from spring to autumn. Water sparingly in winter.

Air Humidity: Mist leaves frequently.

Repotting: Repot, if necessary, in spring.

Propagation: Take stem cuttings in spring or summer.

SYNGONIUM

FOLIAGE HOUSE PLANT page 51

Syngonium requires warmth, moist air and protection from direct sunlight. Aerial roots are produced by the adult plant and a moss stick (see page 223) makes an excellent support for this attractive climbing plant.

An unusual feature of the Goosefoot Plant is the dramatic change in leaf shape which takes place as the plant gets older. The young leaves are arrow-shaped and borne on erect stalks. At this stage the variegation is boldest and brightest. With age the stems acquire a climbing habit and need support — at the same time the leaves become lobed. The juvenile form can be retained by cutting off the climbing stems as they form.

SECRETS OF SUCCESS

Temperature: Average warmth — minimum 60°F in winter.

Light: Well-lit but sunless spot for variegated types, semi-shade for all-green varieties.

Water: Keep compost moist at all times — reduce watering in winter. Avoid overwatering.

Air Humidity: Mist leaves regularly.

Repotting: Repot in spring every 2 years.

Propagation: Take stem cuttings bearing aerial roots in spring or summer. Use a rooting hormone.

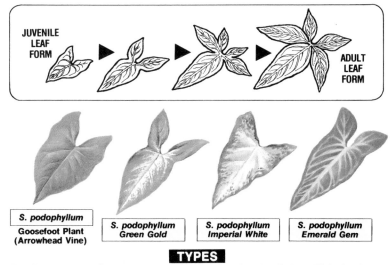

JUVENILE LEAF FORM → → → ADULT LEAF FORM

S. podophyllum
Goosefoot Plant
(Arrowhead Vine)

S. podophyllum
Green Gold

S. podophyllum
Imperial White

S. podophyllum
Emerald Gem

TYPES

The Goosefoots or Syngoniums are closely related to the climbing Philodendrons and require the same growing conditions. The most popular species is **Syngonium podophyllum** — it is sometimes sold under the name **Nephthytis podophyllum**. Many varieties are available — the variegated types are the popular ones, ranging from almost entirely green to practically all-white or yellow. Less frequently seen are the species **S. auritum** and **S. angustatum**.

Syngonium podophyllum Emerald Gem

Thunbergia alata

tubular
flower
2 in.
across

serrated
leaf
2 in.
long

T. alata
Black-eyed Susan

TYPE

Sow seeds or buy a plant of **Thunbergia alata** in spring. Throughout the summer the brown-throated flowers appear, with petals of white, yellow or orange.

THUNBERGIA

FLOWERING POT PLANT
page 57

One of the best pot plants for covering a large area quickly and for providing summer colour. A few seeds sown in early spring will produce enough plants to clothe a screen or trellis with twining stems several feet long. When grown as a climber some form of support is essential — it can also be grown as a trailing plant in a hanging basket. Pinch out tips of young plants. Remove faded flowers before they produce seed.

SECRETS OF SUCCESS

Temperature: Average warmth — minimum 50°F in winter.

Light: Bright light with some direct sun.

Water: Keep compost moist at all times.

Air Humidity: Mist leaves occasionally, especially in hot weather.

Care After Flowering: Plant should be discarded.

Propagation: Sow seeds in early spring.

Tolmiea menziesii

leaf
2 in. across

leaf
stalk
4 in.
long

T. menziesii
Piggyback Plant

TYPE

Tolmiea menziesii is the most popular of the types which bear plantlets on their leaves — it is easy to grow in poor conditions. The long leaf stalks give the plant a trailing appearance.

TOLMIEA

FOLIAGE HOUSE PLANT
page 51

Tolmiea is a compact mound of downy, bright green leaves about 9 in. high. This plant gets its common name from the plantlets which form at the base of mature leaves. It is one of the hardiest of all house plants and actually relishes a cold, well-ventilated and sunless environment. Its enemy is hot, dry air.

SECRETS OF SUCCESS

Temperature: Cool to average warmth — minimum 40°F in winter.

Light: Bright light preferred, but will grow in shade.

Water: Keep compost moist at all times — reduce watering in winter.

Air Humidity: Mist leaves occasionally.

Repotting: Repot in spring every year.

Propagation: Peg down plantlets in compost — cut stems when rooted.

Torenia fournieri

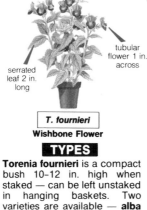

tubular
flower 1 in.
across

serrated
leaf 2 in.
long

T. fournieri
Wishbone Flower

TYPES

Torenia fournieri is a compact bush 10–12 in. high when staked — can be left unstaked in hanging baskets. Two varieties are available — **alba** (all-white) and **grandiflora** (larger and freer-flowering).

TORENIA

FLOWERING POT PLANT
page 57

This summer-flowering annual is raised from seed sown in early spring and is useful for the windowsill. Its growth habit is rather lanky — pinch out the tips to induce bushiness and provide some means of support. The flowers are quite unmistakable. The face of each bloom is violet with a dark purple lower lip and a distinctive yellow blotch. There are no special needs — keep in a well-lit spot, water regularly and avoid draughts.

SECRETS OF SUCCESS

Temperature: Average warmth — keep at 55°–70°F.

Light: Bright light away from direct sun.

Water: Keep compost moist at all times.

Air Humidity: Mist leaves occasionally.

Care After Flowering: Plant should be discarded.

Propagation: Sow seeds in spring.

The TRADESCANTIA Group

FOLIAGE HOUSE PLANT page 51

By far the most important members of this group are the Inch Plants or Wandering Jews — Tradescantia, Zebrina and Callisia. Their leaves clasp the creeping or trailing stems and this group are perhaps the most popular of all hanging basket plants. Pinch out the growing tips regularly to encourage bushiness, and remove all-green shoots as soon as they appear. Winter warmth is not essential.

Setcreasea is also easy to grow and trails like a Wandering Jew, but its leaves are much longer. The Teddy Bear Vine has succulent leaves, densely covered with fur. All members of the Tradescantia family may occasionally flower indoors, but the blooms are generally insignificant. As with most families there is one difficult member. Brown Spiderwort has broad, colourful leaves borne in a rosette and this plant needs skill and a great deal of air humidity.

SECRETS OF SUCCESS

Temperature: Average warmth — minimum 45°-50°F in winter (Siderasis — 55°F).

Light: Bright light is essential. Some direct sunlight is beneficial for Zebrina, Setcreasea and Cyanotis. Grow Siderasis in semi-shade.

Water: Water liberally from spring to autumn. Water sparingly in winter.

Air Humidity: Mist leaves occasionally — Siderasis regularly.

Repotting: Repot, if necessary, in spring.

Propagation: Very easy — take stem cuttings in spring, summer or autumn. Propagate Siderasis by division.

SPECIAL PROBLEMS

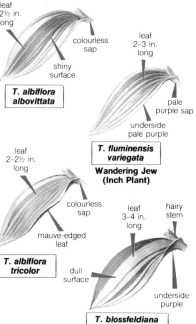

BARE SPINDLY GROWTH
Cause: Too little light, too little water or too little fertilizer. All stems become straggly and bare with age. Cut back spindly growth; replace old plants.

LEAVES ALL-GREEN
Cause: Too little light. Variegated types revert to all-green form in shady conditions.

LEAF TIPS BROWN & SHRIVELLED
Cause: Air too dry. Look for red spider mite (see page 244). Remove dead growth. Mist leaves frequently.

STEMS LIMP, LEAVES YELLOW & SPOTTED
Cause: Underwatering. Water liberally during the growing season; allow surface to dry between waterings.

TYPES

TRADESCANTIA

leaf 2-4 in. long

base of leaf clasps pendant stem

Tradescantia
Wandering Jew (Inch Plant)

Tradescantia fluminensis is perhaps the most popular Tradescantia — the varieties grown are **variegata** (cream striped) and **Quicksilver** (white striped). **T. albiflora** is similar, but neither the sap nor the underside of the foliage is mauve. The usual varieties are **albovittata** (white striped), **tricolor** (white and mauve striped) and **aurea** (yellow with green stripes). **T. blossfeldiana variegata** is the popular large-leaved type.

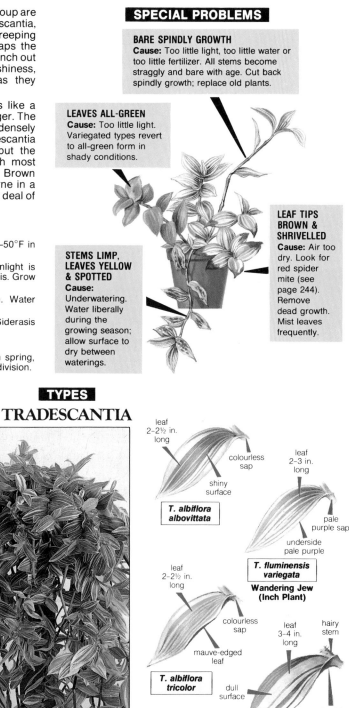

Tradescantia fluminensis Quicksilver

leaf 2-2½ in. long

colourless sap

shiny surface

T. albiflora albovittata

leaf 2-3 in. long

pale purple sap

underside pale purple

T. fluminensis variegata
Wandering Jew (Inch Plant)

leaf 2-2½ in. long

colourless sap

mauve-edged leaf

T. albiflora tricolor

leaf 3-4 in. long

hairy stem

dull surface

underside purple

T. blossfeldiana variegata
Flowering Inch Plant

CALLISIA

leaf 1–1½ in. long

C. elegans
Striped Inch Plant

underside purple

Callisia elegans (sometimes sold as **Setcreasea striata**) has small leaves and long stems — the upper surface of the foliage is dull and boldly striped with white lines. The leaves of **C. fragrans** turn pink in bright light.

Callisia elegans

CYANOTIS

leaf 1 in. long — fleshy and covered with fur

underside purple

C. kewensis
Teddy Bear Vine

Unlike the closely related Tradescantia, Cyanotis bears hairy leaves. **Cyanotis kewensis** foliage has rusty brown hairs — the leaves of **C. somaliensis** (Pussy Ears) are larger and the hairs are pale grey.

Cyanotis somaliensis

SETCREASEA

leaf 5 in. long

leaves and stems purple

S. purpurea
Purple Heart

Setcreasea purpurea is a straggly plant which makes up for its untidiness by its attractive colour — a rich purple when grown in good light. The leaves are slightly hairy and pink flowers appear in summer.

Setcreasea purpurea

SIDERASIS

leaves covered with brown hair

underside red

S. fuscata
Brown Spiderwort

Siderasis differs from its relatives in three distinct ways. The 6–8 in. leaves form a rosette, it needs a terrarium for success and it bears attractive flowers (purple, 1 in. across). One species is grown — **Siderasis fuscata**. A plant for the rarity collector.

Siderasis fuscata

ZEBRINA

leaf 2–2½ in. long

base of leaf clasps pendant stem

underside purple

Zebrina
Wandering Jew (Inch Plant)

green, banded with silver

leaf 2 in. long

glistening surface

underside purple

Z. pendula
Silvery Inch Plant

glistening surface

leaf 2½ in. long

underside purple

Z. pendula quadricolor

glistening surface

leaf 2½ in. long

underside purple

Z. pendula purpusii
Bronze Inch Plant

Zebrina is closely related to Tradescantia but it is more colourful. The leaves are glistening and multicoloured above and purple below. The surface colours may be green and silver edged with pink (**Zebrina pendula**), green and purple (**Z. pendula purpusii**) or green, silver, pink and red (the showy but difficult **Z. pendula quadricolor**). Zebrina bears pink or purplish flowers in spring and summer.

Zebrina pendula quadricolor

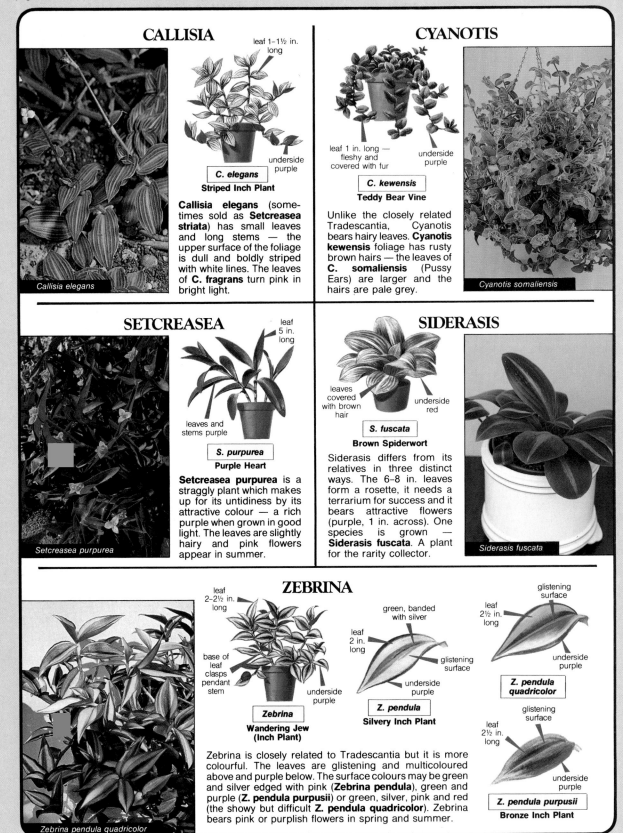

VINES

FOLIAGE HOUSE PLANT
page 51

tendrils
present
which
cling
to
supports

quick-
growing
stems

Many climbers are commonly referred to as 'Vines' but the true Vines are all members of the Grape family. They cling to supports by means of tendrils and two of them (Grape Ivy and Kangaroo Vine) are extremely popular and easy to grow.

The most important use of the popular Vines is to clothe poles, screens and trellis work — Chestnut Vine is useful for covering large areas, Vines can also be employed for hanging baskets and as ground cover. The general requirement is for semi-shade or good light (without direct sunshine), cool conditions and occasional misting; but individual requirements vary. At one end of the scale Grape Ivy is one of the most tolerant of all house plants, surviving sun or shade, hot or cold air, dry or moist surroundings. Kangaroo Vine is a little less tolerant, suffering in bright sun and in hot, stuffy rooms. At the other end of the scale Cissus discolor is a delicate plant needing warmth and constant moisture around the leaves. All Vines need good drainage — pinch out stem tips to induce bushy growth.

SECRETS OF SUCCESS

Temperature: Cool or average warmth — minimum 45°–55°F in winter (Cissus discolor — 60°F).

Light: Brightly lit spot away from direct sunlight. Semi-shade for Cissus discolor and Rhoicissus capensis.

Water: Water liberally from spring to autumn. Water sparingly in winter.

Air Humidity: Mist leaves occasionally.

Repotting: Repot, if necessary, in spring.

Propagation: Take stem cuttings in spring or summer.

SPECIAL PROBLEMS

GLASSY BLOTCHES ON LEAVES WHICH LATER FALL
Cause: Direct sunlight; move plant away from the window.

LEAF TIPS BROWN & SHRIVELLED
Cause: Air too dry; mist leaves occasionally. If other symptoms (wilting, rotting, leaf fall) are present, the cause is overwatering.

SPOTTED & CURLED LOWER LEAVES WHICH LATER FALL
Cause: Underwatering. Compost must not be allowed to dry out.

MILDEW ON LEAVES
Cause: Poor drainage. Remove diseased leaves, spray with systemic fungicide and repot into a container with adequate drainage. Improve ventilation.

WILTING LEAVES
Cause: Too cold; move to a warmer part of the house. If leaf fall occurs the cause is usually too little water or too much sunlight.

SLOW GROWTH
Cause: Starvation; Vines are vigorous plants which need regular feeding with a liquid fertilizer.

HOW TO MAKE A MOSS STICK

A moss stick (U.S name — totem pole) is a valuable aid for growing Vines, Monstera, Philodendron and Ivies. It serves a double purpose for plants with aerial roots such as Monstera — it provides support for the weak stem and it provides moisture through the aerial roots to the upper leaves.

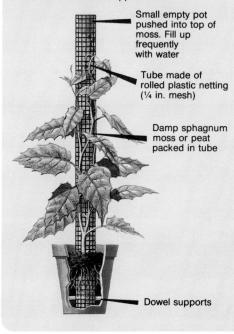

Small empty pot pushed into top of moss. Fill up frequently with water

Tube made of rolled plastic netting (¼ in. mesh)

Damp sphagnum moss or peat packed in tube

Dowel supports

TYPES

CISSUS

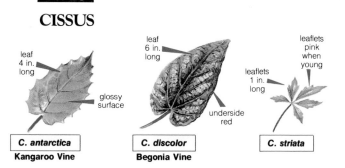

leaf 4 in. long	leaf 6 in. long	leaflets 1 in. long — leaflets pink when young
glossy surface	underside red	
C. antarctica	**C. discolor**	**C. striata**
Kangaroo Vine	Begonia Vine	

Cissus antarctica

Cissus antarctica is a great favourite for covering screens and other large areas, growing about 10 ft tall and clothing the supports with its leathery leaves. Where space is limited, grow the variety **minima**. The smallest-leaved Cissus is the dainty **C. striata** — red-stemmed, quick-growing and best grown as a trailer. The tender Cissus is **C. discolor** — its green leaves are blotched with silver and pale purple. Unusual ones include **C. gongylodes** which bears red aerial roots, the fleshy leaved **C. quadrangularis** and the brownish-green **C. hypoglauca** which has leaves divided up into 5 leaflets.

RHOICISSUS

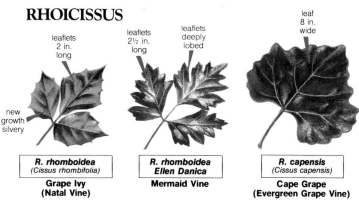

leaflets 2 in. long	leaflets 2½ in. long	leaflets deeply lobed	leaf 8 in. wide
new growth silvery			
R. rhomboidea (Cissus rhombifolia)	**R. rhomboidea** Ellen Danica		**R. capensis** (Cissus capensis)
Grape Ivy (Natal Vine)	Mermaid Vine		Cape Grape (Evergreen Grape Vine)

Rhoicissus rhomboidea

The popular Grape Ivy usually sold as **Rhoicissus rhomboidea** should be called **Cissus rhombifolia** according to the botanists. Each leaf is made up of 3 leaflets, silvery at first and dark green and glossy when mature. It is extremely tolerant of poor conditions, and its only drawback is that it has become commonplace. For something a little different choose the variety **Ellen Danica** (lobed leaflets) or **Jubilee** (large, dark green leaflets). **R. capensis** is quite different to Grape Ivy and its varieties. Each large leaf is undivided — the surface is glossy and brown-edged, the underside brown and furry.

TETRASTIGMA

Tetrastigma voinierianum

The Chestnut Vine (**Tetrastigma voinierianum**) is the giant of the group. Each leaf measures more than 1 ft across when mature — the 5 leaflets which make up each leaf are glossy and saw-edged. This plant is a rampant grower in the greenhouse or conservatory — useful if you want to cover a bare wall but a menace if delicate plants are nearby. It has never become really popular as a house plant as it is too large for most situations and is too unpredictable under room conditions. It is distinctly unhappy in warm, dry air — keep it in a cool place if you want to grow it indoors. Stout supports are necessary and so is space — it can grow 5–8 ft in a year.

leaflets 6 in. long

underside furry

T. voinierianum (Vitis voinieriana)

Chestnut Vine (Lizard Plant)

Vallota speciosa

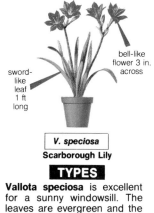

bell-like
flower 3 in.
across

sword-
like
leaf
1 ft
long

V. speciosa
Scarborough Lily

TYPES

Vallota speciosa is excellent for a sunny windowsill. The leaves are evergreen and the red flowers are borne on 1–2 ft flower-stalks. White and salmon varieties are available.

VALLOTA

FLOWERING HOUSE PLANT
page 55

In spring plant the bulb firmly in a 5 in. pot — leave the top half uncovered. Vallota is an easy plant — keep it cool during winter, remove dead flowers and leaves, and let the compost dry out slightly between waterings. In late summer clusters of flowers appear. Don't repot until the clump of bulbs becomes overcrowded.

SECRETS OF SUCCESS

Temperature: Average warmth — keep at 50°–55°F in winter.

Light: Bright light with some direct sun.

Water: Water thoroughly when the compost begins to dry out. Water sparingly in winter.

Air Humidity: Sponge leaves occasionally.

Repotting: Repot in spring every 3–4 years.

Propagation: Divide plants at repotting time, or detach offsets from mature plants and pot up in summer.

Viburnum tinus variegatum

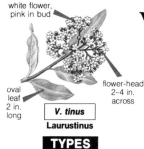

white flower,
pink in bud

oval
leaf
2 in.
long

flower-head
2–4 in.
across

V. tinus
Laurustinus

TYPES

The usual choice is **Viburnum tinus** — an evergreen shrub with dark green leaves. You will find it in the outdoor plants section of your garden centre. Varieties include **purpureum** (purple-tinged leaves) and **variegatum** (cream-edged leaves).

VIBURNUM

FLOWERING HOUSE PLANT
page 55

Several Viburnums are popular garden shrubs, but their use as house plants is virtually unknown. Try one if you want a winter-flowering evergreen. Several summer-flowering types such as V. odoratissimum and V. cinnamomifolium can be grown, but the best choice is V. tinus which blooms from early winter until spring. Stand outdoors in summer.

SECRETS OF SUCCESS

Temperature: Average or below average warmth — keep cool in winter.

Light: Bright light or semi-shade.

Water: Water freely during the growing season. Water sparingly in winter.

Air Humidity: Mist leaves occasionally.

Repotting: Repot, if necessary, in spring.

Propagation: Take stem cuttings in summer. Use a rooting hormone and provide bottom heat.

Yucca elephantipes

leaf
3 ft
long

rough-
edged
leaves

swollen
base

Y. elephantipes
Spineless Yucca

TYPES

The 3–5 ft woody trunk bears a crown of long, leathery leaves. Choose **Yucca elephantipes** — safer than **Y. aloifolia** (Spanish Bayonet) with sword-like leaves.

YUCCA

FOLIAGE HOUSE PLANT
page 51

A mature Yucca is a fine False Palm for a hallway or large room. A large Yucca is expensive and should be treated properly. It will need a deep, well-drained container which can be moved outdoors in summer. In winter it will require an unheated and well-lit spot. White bell-shaped flowers may appear after a number of years.

SECRETS OF SUCCESS

Temperature: Average warmth — keep cool in winter (minimum 45°F).

Light: Provide as much light as possible.

Water: Water liberally from spring to autumn. Water sparingly in winter.

Air Humidity: Misting is not necessary.

Repotting: Repot in spring every 2 years.

Propagation: Remove and pot up offsets, or root cane cuttings.

CHAPTER 5

PLANT CARE

Plants growing in the garden rely to a large extent on the natural elements for their needs. All house plants, however, must depend entirely on you to provide them with their essential requirements. Leave them in deep shade or forget to water them and they will die. Without food they will steadily deteriorate. Virtually all varieties must be kept frost-free and the tender types require a minimum temperature of 60° F. Many plants find the air too dry in heated rooms, and you will have to increase the humidity around them to prevent browning and withering of the foliage. The least important requirement is fresh air, but some varieties demand adequate ventilation. Not all plant care techniques are life-saving exercises — the grooming procedures such as cleaning, training and trimming are designed to make the plant look better.

Warmth, light, water, humidity, food, rest, fresh air, grooming . . . a long list of needs but success calls for neither hard work nor great skill. It is simply a matter of satisfying the particular basic requirements of each plant and not trying to treat all plants in the same way. Remember that excesses can be fatal — too much sun and too much water are common mistakes, and feeding more than the fertilizer manufacturer recommends is foolhardy. Also remember that there is a resting period, usually in winter, when much less water, food and heat are required.

Talk to your plants if you wish, but there is no scientific evidence that it will have any effect at all. What your plants do need is for you to spend a few minutes looking carefully at the leaves, stems and compost. This should be done daily, if possible, during the growing season. You will soon learn to tell when things are wrong. The appearance and feel of the compost will tell you when water is required. The appearance of the foliage will tell you when the water, temperature, light, food or humidity level is wrong. Pick off withered leaves and dead flowers; look for pests and diseases. Some people grow indoor plants for years without ever *really* looking at them or bothering to learn what the leaves have to tell.

Give them the WARMTH they need	*page 227*
Give them the LIGHT they need	*pages 228–229*
Give them the WATER they need	*pages 230–231*
Give them the HUMIDITY they need	*page 232*
Give them the FOOD they need	*page 233*
Give them the REST they need	*page 234*
Give them the FRESH AIR they need	*page 234*
Give them the GROOMING they need	*pages 235–236*

Give them the WARMTH they need

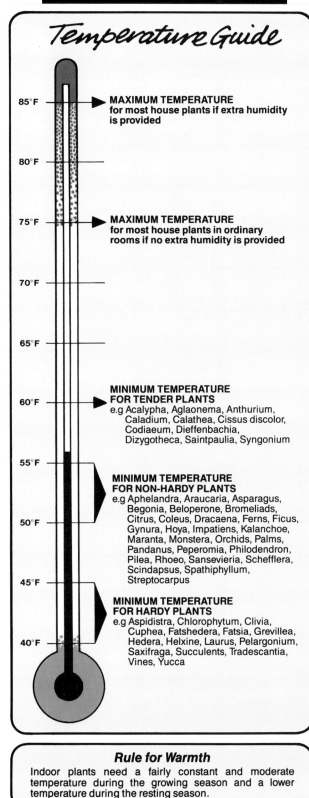

Temperature Guide

85°F — **MAXIMUM TEMPERATURE**
for most house plants if extra humidity
is provided

80°F

75°F — **MAXIMUM TEMPERATURE**
for most house plants in ordinary
rooms if no extra humidity is provided

70°F

65°F

60°F — **MINIMUM TEMPERATURE**
FOR TENDER PLANTS
e.g Acalypha, Aglaonema, Anthurium,
Caladium, Calathea, Cissus discolor,
Codiaeum, Dieffenbachia,
Dizygotheca, Saintpaulia, Syngonium

55°F

MINIMUM TEMPERATURE
FOR NON-HARDY PLANTS
e.g Aphelandra, Araucaria, Asparagus,
Begonia, Beloperone, Bromeliads,
Citrus, Coleus, Dracaena, Ferns, Ficus,
50°F — Gynura, Hoya, Impatiens, Kalanchoe,
Maranta, Monstera, Orchids, Palms,
Pandanus, Peperomia, Philodendron,
Pilea, Rhoeo, Sansevieria, Schefflera,
Scindapsus, Spathiphyllum,
Streptocarpus

45°F

MINIMUM TEMPERATURE
FOR HARDY PLANTS
e.g Aspidistra, Chlorophytum, Clivia,
Cuphea, Fatshedera, Fatsia, Grevillea,
Hedera, Helxine, Laurus, Pelargonium,
40°F — Saxifraga, Succulents, Tradescantia,
Vines, Yucca

Rule for Warmth

Indoor plants need a fairly constant and moderate
temperature during the growing season and a lower
temperature during the resting season.

The natural home of most indoor plants lies in the Tropics. In this country they are raised commercially in glasshouses. These two simple facts have given rise to the widespread belief that high temperatures are essential for the proper cultivation of house plants.

The truth is that very few types will grow satisfactorily at temperatures above 75°F under ordinary room conditions. The reason is that the amount of light falling on the leaves and the amount of moisture in the air are far less in a room than outdoors in the Tropics or under glass in Britain, so the need for heat is correspondingly less.

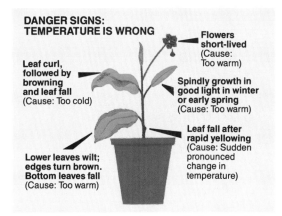

DANGER SIGNS:
TEMPERATURE IS WRONG

Flowers
short-lived
(Cause:
Too warm)

Leaf curl,
followed by
browning
and leaf fall
(Cause: Too cold)

Spindly growth in
good light in winter
or early spring
(Cause: Too warm)

Leaf fall after
rapid yellowing
(Cause: Sudden
pronounced
change in
temperature)

Lower leaves wilt;
edges turn brown.
Bottom leaves fall
(Cause: Too warm)

Nearly all indoor plants will flourish if the temperature is kept within the 55°–75°F range — most types will grow quite happily in rooms which are a little too cool for human comfort. There are exceptions to this general rule — many popular flowering pot plants and some foliage house plants need much cooler conditions with a maximum temperature of 60°F in winter. At the other end of the scale the tender varieties require a minimum of 60°F — with warmth- and moisture-loving plants the pots can be stood in a pebble tray (see page 19) on a wide shelf above a radiator.

Most plants are remarkably tolerant and will survive temperatures slightly above or below the preferred range for short periods. The real enemy is temperature fluctuation. As a rule plants appreciate a drop of 5°–10°F at night but a sudden cooling down by 20°F can be damaging or fatal. Try to minimise the winter night drop in temperature by sealing window cracks and moving pots off windowsills in frosty weather. Cacti and Succulents are an exception — in their desert home they are adapted to hot days and cold nights, and so find the fluctuations in the centrally-heated home no problem at all.

Give them the LIGHT they need

Lighting Guide

▶ **FULL SUN**
Area with as much light as possible, within 2 ft of a south-facing window
Very few house plants can withstand scorching conditions — only the Desert Cacti, Succulents and Pelargonium can be expected to flourish in unshaded continuous sunshine during the summer months. By providing light shade at midday during hot weather a much larger list can be grown — see page 8.

▶ **SOME DIRECT SUN**
Brightly-lit area, with some sunlight falling on the leaves during the day
Examples are a west-facing or an east-facing windowsill, a spot close to but more than 2 ft away from a south-facing windowsill or on a south-facing windowsill which is partly obstructed. This is the ideal site for many flowering and some foliage house plants — see page 8 for a list of examples.

▶ **BRIGHT BUT SUNLESS**
Area close to but not in the zone lit by direct sunlight
Many plants grow best when placed in this region which extends for about 5 ft around a window which is sunlit for part of the day. A large sunless windowsill may provide similar conditions. See page 8 for a list of suitable varieties.

▶ **SEMI-SHADE**
Moderately-lit area, within 5–8 ft of a sunlit window or close to a sunless window
Very few flowering plants will flourish in this part of the room, but many foliage house plants will grow quite happily here — see page 8 for a list of examples. Most of the Bright but Sunless foliage plants will adapt to these conditions.

▶ **SHADE**
Poorly-lit area, but bright enough to allow you to read a newspaper during several hours of the day
Few foliage plants will actually flourish here — Aglaonema, Aspidistra and Asplenium are exceptions. Many Semi-Shade plants, however, will adapt and are capable of surviving in the darker conditions. No flowering plants are suitable.

▶ **DEEP SHADE**
Unsuitable for all indoor plants.

Correct lighting is more than just a matter of giving a plant the brightness it needs — there are two distinct aspects which control growth. The *duration* a plant requires is fairly constant for nearly all types — there must be 12–16 hours of natural light or sufficiently strong artificial illumination in order to maintain active growth. Less light will induce a slowing down in food production, which is why the resting period of foliage plants is not broken by bright days in winter.

The light *intensity* requirement is not constant — it varies enormously from plant to plant. Some types will flourish on a sunny windowsill but quickly deteriorate in a shady corner; others will grow in light shade but cannot survive exposure to sunlight.

The human eye is an extremely poor instrument for measuring light intensity. As you move from a sunny window towards a corner of the room you will pass from Full Sun to Shade in about 8 ft. Walking with your back to the window you may notice little change, yet the light intensity will have dropped by more than 95% over a distance of a few feet.

DANGER SIGNS: TOO LITTLE LIGHT
No growth at all, or spindly growth with abnormally long spaces between leaves
Leaves smaller and paler than normal
Blooms poor or absent in flowering types
Lower leaves turn yellow, then dry up and fall
Variegated leaves turn all-green

DANGER SIGNS: TOO MUCH LIGHT
Leaves have 'washed-out' appearance
Brown or grey scorch patches
Leaves wilt at midday
Leaves of 'sun shy' varieties shrivelled and dead

Natural light

White or cream-coloured walls and ceiling improve plant growth by reflecting light in a poorly-lit room. A white background for a plant grown within the room will reduce the tendency for its stem to bend towards the window.

The leaves and stems of a windowsill plant will bend towards the glass. To prevent lop-sided growth it is necessary to turn the pot occasionally, make only a slight turn each time. Do not turn the pot of a flowering plant when it is in bud.

A flowering plant will suffer if it is moved from the recommended lighting to a shadier spot. The number and quality of the blooms are strictly controlled by both the duration and intensity of the light. Without adequate lighting the foliage may grow perfectly happily but the floral display is bound to disappoint.

If possible move plants closer to the window when winter arrives. This will increase both the duration and intensity of the light falling on the leaves.

Keep the windows clean in winter — removing dust can increase light intensity by up to 10%.

A plant should not be suddenly moved from a shady spot to a sunny windowsill or the open garden. It should be acclimatised for a few days by moving it to a brighter spot each day.

A foliage house plant can be suddenly moved from its ideal location to a shadier spot with no ill-effect. It will survive but not flourish — try to move it back to a brighter area for about a week every 1–2 months to allow it to recuperate.

Practically all plants must be screened from summer sun at midday. New unfolding leaves will suffer most of all if some form of shade is not provided.

Rules for Lighting

Foliage house plants require bright light without direct sunlight; most of them will adapt to semi-shade. Plants with variegated leaves need more light than all-green ones, and flowering plants generally need some direct sunlight. Cacti and Succulents have the highest light requirement of all. There are many exceptions to these rules so consult the A–Z guide for details of specific needs.

Artificial light

REFLECTOR
Used to direct light downwards on to the plants and away from the eyes of the viewer

FLUORESCENT TUBES
Usually 2×40 watts. Use either 1 'daylight' and 1 'cool white' or use 2 Gro-Lux tubes

Flowering plants: 6–12 in.

Foliage plants: 12–24 in.

PEBBLE TRAY
see page 19 for details

Indoor gardening under lights adds two new dimensions. It means that you can grow flowering and foliage house plants in gloomy or even windowless rooms. It also means that you can supplement the duration and intensity of natural light in winter so that the plants remain in active growth — African Violets can be kept in bloom almost all year round.

Ordinary electric bulbs are not suitable for this purpose — the heat generated would scorch the leaves. Fluorescent lighting is used, usually in the form of long tubes. Many types of suitable units can be bought in countries where artificial-light gardening is popular. In Britain it is more usual to make an installation at home.

The basis of the unit is a tube or series of tubes mounted under a reflector. This arrangement may be permanently fixed above the growing surface or it may be suspended so that it can be raised or lowered as required. The plants should be kept in a pebble tray (see page 19). You will need to provide about 20 watts per sq. ft of growing area — if you use a light meter the reading should be the same as for a shady spot outdoors in summer. Look for danger signs. Scorched leaves indicate that the lights are too close — spindly growth and pale leaves indicate that they are not close enough. Change the tubes once a year — do not change all of them at the same time.

The most popular varieties chosen for artificial-light gardening are usually colourful and compact. Examples are Begonia, Bromeliads, Cineraria, Gloxinia, Orchids, Peperomia and Saintpaulia.

Give them the WATER they need

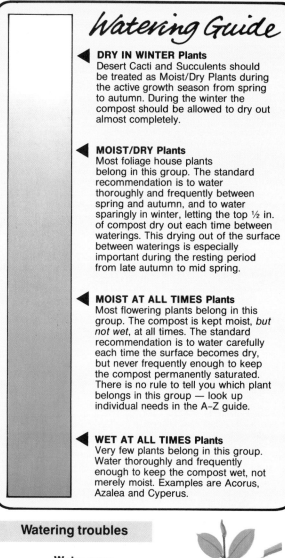

Watering Guide

◄ **DRY IN WINTER Plants**
Desert Cacti and Succulents should be treated as Moist/Dry Plants during the active growth season from spring to autumn. During the winter the compost should be allowed to dry out almost completely.

◄ **MOIST/DRY Plants**
Most foliage house plants belong in this group. The standard recommendation is to water thoroughly and frequently between spring and autumn, and to water sparingly in winter, letting the top ½ in. of compost dry out each time between waterings. This drying out of the surface between waterings is especially important during the resting period from late autumn to mid spring.

◄ **MOIST AT ALL TIMES Plants**
Most flowering plants belong in this group. The compost is kept moist, *but not wet*, at all times. The standard recommendation is to water carefully each time the surface becomes dry, but never frequently enough to keep the compost permanently saturated. There is no rule to tell you which plant belongs in this group — look up individual needs in the A–Z guide.

◄ **WET AT ALL TIMES Plants**
Very few plants belong in this group. Water thoroughly and frequently enough to keep the compost wet, not merely moist. Examples are Acorus, Azalea and Cyperus.

Watering troubles

Water runs straight through

Cause: Shrinkage of compost away from the side of the pot
Cure: Immerse the pot to compost level in a bucket or bath of water

Water not absorbed

Cause: Surface caking
Cure: Prick over the surface with a fork or miniature trowel. Then immerse the pot to compost level in a bucket or bath of water

Without water a house plant must die. This may take place in a single day in the case of a seedling in sandy soil, or it may take months if the plant has fleshy leaves. But in the end the result is always the same.

Because of this obvious fact many beginners give daily dribbles of water, they fail to reduce the frequency of watering once winter arrives and they immediately assume that the plant is thirsty whenever leaves wilt or turn yellow. This produces a soggy mass in which practically no house plant can survive. Waterlogging kills by preventing vital air getting to the roots and by encouraging root-rotting diseases. More plants die through overwatering than any other single cause — they are killed by kindness.

Each plant has its own basic need for water — see the chart on the left. Unfortunately the proper frequency of watering is not a constant feature; it depends on the size of plant, the size of pot, the environment and especially the time of year. Because of this your best guide is observation rather than a moisture meter.

Self-watering pots and devices have a role to play in caring for the Moist At All Times group and for plants when you are on holiday, but they have the distinct disadvantage of not reducing the water supply in winter.

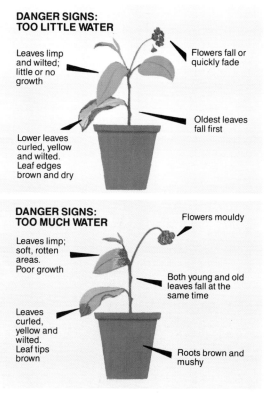

DANGER SIGNS: TOO LITTLE WATER

Leaves limp and wilted; little or no growth

Flowers fall or quickly fade

Lower leaves curled, yellow and wilted. Leaf edges brown and dry

Oldest leaves fall first

DANGER SIGNS: TOO MUCH WATER

Flowers mouldy

Leaves limp; soft, rotten areas. Poor growth

Both young and old leaves fall at the same time

Leaves curled, yellow and wilted. Leaf tips brown

Roots brown and mushy

The water to use

Tap water is suitable for nearly all plants. Ideally the water should be stood overnight in a bowl to allow it to lose some of its chlorine and to reach room temperature. This standing period is not essential for hardy plants but it is necessary for delicate varieties. If you live in a hard water area a white crust may develop in time on the surface of the compost. This crust is harmless, but hard water can be harmful to lime-hating plants which are permanent residents indoors. For lime-haters which last for only a comparatively short time in our rooms (e.g Azalea, Erica) the use of hard water will not really pose a problem.

The standard source of soft water is rainwater. Collect it by standing a large, clean bowl outdoors; never use rainwater from a stagnant water-butt.

When to water

Tapping the pot is useless; measuring water loss by estimating its weight calls for great skill. The simplest way of discovering when to water remains the best. Look at the surface — weekly in winter, daily if possible in midsummer. If the surface is dry and powdery all over, water if the A-Z guide states that the plant should be moist at all times. With the remaining plants insert your forefinger in the compost to the full depth of your fingernail. If your fingertip remains dry then the pot needs watering. The most important exceptions are the Cacti and Succulents in winter — if the room is cool leave them alone unless there are signs of shrivelling.

Rules for Watering

Roots need air as well as water, which means that the compost should be moist but not saturated. Some plants need a partial drying-out period between waterings, others do not. All will need less water during the resting period. Don't guess your plant's watering requirement — look it up in the A-Z guide.

The way to water

Both the watering can and the immersion methods have their devotees, and both have advantages. The best technique for most plants is to use the quick and easy watering can method as the standard routine and to water occasionally by the immersion method where it is practical.

THE WATERING CAN METHOD

Use a watering can with a long, thin spout. Insert the end of the spout under the leaves and pour the water steadily and gently. During the growing season fill up the space between the surface of the compost and the rim of the pot. In the winter stop as soon as water begins to drain from the bottom of the pot. In either case empty the drip tray after about 30 minutes. Never water in full sun as splashed leaves may be scorched. In winter, water in the morning if the room is unheated. Take great care when watering containers without drainage holes — add a little at a time and pour off any free-standing water immediately. Although an occasional droop of the leaves will do no serious harm to most plants, do not make them beg for water in this way, for when this stage is reached the compost is definitely too dry. The leaves of woody plants, such as Azalea, should never be allowed to wilt.

THE IMMERSION METHOD

Plants such as Saintpaulia, Gloxinia and Cyclamen which do not like water on their leaves or crowns can be watered from below. Immerse the pots in water to just below the level of the compost and leave them to soak until the surface glistens. Allow them to drain and then return the pots to their growing quarters.

How often to water

You must never allow watering to become a regular routine whereby the pots are filled up every Sunday. The correct interval will vary greatly — Busy Lizzie may need watering daily in summer, Bishop's Cap may not need watering all winter. The interval between watering for an individual plant also varies with the season and changes in growing conditions.

THE PLANT

Fleshy-leaved plants can tolerate much drier conditions than thin-leaved varieties and a rooted cutting will take up much less water than a mature plant. With any plant, the larger the leaf surface and the more rapidly it is growing the greater will be its need for frequent watering.

THE TIME OF THE YEAR

In winter, growth slows down and may stop; overwatering must be avoided during this resting season. Until new growth starts in the spring, watering one to three times a month is usually sufficient. During the spring and summer, watering will be necessary one to three times a week.

THE ENVIRONMENT

As the temperature and light intensity increase, so does the need for water. Plants in small pots and those which have not been repotted for some time need more frequent watering than those in large containers or ones which have been recently potted on. Plants in clay pots will need watering more often than those in plastic ones; double potted plants (see page 232) will need watering less frequently.

Give them the HUMIDITY they need

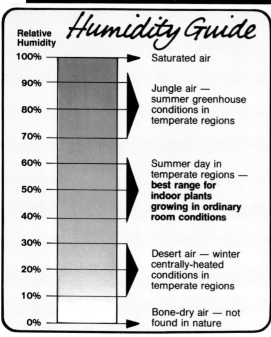

Humidity Guide

Relative Humidity	
100%	Saturated air
90%	
80%	Jungle air — summer greenhouse conditions in temperate regions
70%	
60%	
50%	Summer day in temperate regions — **best range for indoor plants growing in ordinary room conditions**
40%	
30%	
20%	Desert air — winter centrally-heated conditions in temperate regions
10%	
0%	Bone-dry air — not found in nature

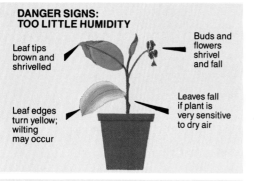

DANGER SIGNS: TOO LITTLE HUMIDITY

Leaf tips brown and shrivelled

Buds and flowers shrivel and fall

Leaf edges turn yellow; wilting may occur

Leaves fall if plant is very sensitive to dry air

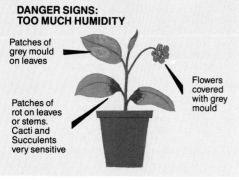

DANGER SIGNS: TOO MUCH HUMIDITY

Patches of grey mould on leaves

Flowers covered with grey mould

Patches of rot on leaves or stems. Cacti and Succulents very sensitive

Rules for Humidity

House plants need less warm air and more moist air than you think; papery leaves generally need more humidity in the air than thick, leathery ones. If your room is centrally heated and you wish to grow more than the dry-air plants listed on page 8, then group the pots together, double-pot specimen plants and mist the foliage as frequently as recommended.

Cold air requires only a small amount of water vapour before it becomes saturated, and so on an average winter day the air is moist. When you turn on a radiator to warm up this cold air, its capacity to hold water vapour is greatly increased. As the room becomes comfortable the amount of water vapour in the air is no longer enough to keep it moist. The air becomes "dry"; in technical terms the Relative Humidity has fallen.

Central heating in the depths of winter can produce air with the Relative Humidity of the Sahara Desert. Very few plants actually like such conditions; many foliage plants and most flowering plants will suffer if you don't do something to increase the humidity around the leaves. You can, of course, avoid the problem by finding a moist home for your plants — the kitchen, bathroom or a terrarium, but the living room atmosphere will be dry. You can use a humidifier to increase the moisture content of the whole room, but it is much more usual to use one or more of the techniques below to produce a moist microclimate around the plant whilst the atmosphere in the rest of the room remains as dry as ever.

Misting

Use a mister to deposit a coating of small droplets over the leaves. It is best to use tepid water and under cool conditions do this job in the morning so that the foliage will be dry before nightfall. Cover all the plant, not just one side, and do not mist when the foliage is exposed to bright sunlight. Misting does more than provide a temporary increase in humidity; it has a cooling effect on hot sunny days, it discourages red spider mite and it reduces the dust deposit on leaves.

Grouping

Plants grown in Pot Groups and Indoor Gardens have the benefit of increased moisture arising from damp compost and the foliage of surrounding plants. The air trapped between them will have an appreciably higher Relative Humidity than the atmosphere around an isolated plant. The best method of raising the humidity is to use a pebble tray — see page 19. There is a danger of too much humidity when grouping plants together — make sure that there is enough space beween them to avoid the onset of Botrytis — see page 245.

Double Potting

Use an outer waterproof container and fill the space between the pot and the container with moist peat. Keep this packing material thoroughly and continually moist so that there will always be a surface layer of moisture to evaporate and raise the Relative Humidity. Double potting does more than raise the humidity — it provides a moisture reservoir below the pot and it insulates the compost inside the pot from sudden changes in temperature.

Give them the FOOD they need

NITROGEN (N)		the **leaf maker**
PHOSPHATES (P_2O_5)		the **root maker**
POTASH (K_2O)		the **flower maker**
TRACE ELEMENTS (Mn, Mg, Fe, Mo, S, B, Zn, Cu)	Present in some house plant foods — derived from humus extracts or added chemicals.	

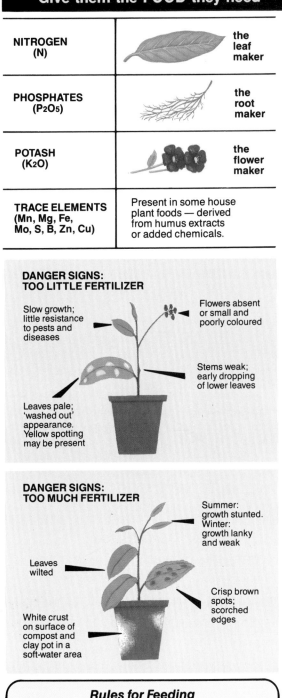

DANGER SIGNS: TOO LITTLE FERTILIZER

Slow growth; little resistance to pests and diseases

Flowers absent or small and poorly coloured

Stems weak; early dropping of lower leaves

Leaves pale; 'washed out' appearance. Yellow spotting may be present

DANGER SIGNS: TOO MUCH FERTILIZER

Summer: growth stunted. Winter: growth lanky and weak

Leaves wilted

Crisp brown spots; scorched edges

White crust on surface of compost and clay pot in a soft-water area

Rules for Feeding

If the plant is growing in soil or compost it is advisable not to use a method of feeding which relies on a reservoir of nutrients. There are times when the plant may not need feeding, and when it is necessary, the amount of nutrients needed will depend on the size of the plant and the size of the pot. The most popular method is to feed each time you water when the plant is growing or flowering. Reduce or stop feeding when the plant is resting.

All plants, indoors and out, need an adequate supply of nitrogen, phosphates and potash together with small amounts of trace elements. Only then will they be capable of producing healthy growth with full-sized flowers and leaves.

In the garden it is usual to apply fertilizers to top up the soil's natural resources, but even in their absence the plant can continue to draw on the soil's supply of nutrients by sending out new roots. Indoors the position is quite different. The soil or compost in the pot contains a strictly limited amount of food, and this is continually depleted by the roots of the plant and by leaching through the drainage holes. Once the nutrient supply is exhausted regular feeding when the plant is actively growing must take place. Cacti can survive for a long time without any feeding, but vigorous foliage plants and flowering plants coming into bloom are seriously affected if not fed.

What to feed

House plant foods are nearly always compound fertilizers containing nitrogen, phosphates and potash. By law the label must state the content of each of these elements; if there is no statement for one of them then you can be sure it is missing. Other plant-feeding ingredients, such as humus extracts, trace elements, etc may be present.

INSOLUBLE POWDERS AND GRANULES
Powder and granular fertilizers are widely used in the garden, but they are of limited use indoors. The plant food is deposited on the surface of the compost and it is not readily taken down to the roots where it is required. Furthermore you cannot cut off the supply when the resting period arrives.

PILLS AND STICKS
Pushing a pill or feeding stick into the pot is certainly labour-saving, but there are important disadvantages. The nutrients are concentrated in one spot which does not promote even root development, and you cannot easily cut off the nutrient supply when the resting period arrives.

LIQUID FEEDS
It is generally agreed that the most effective way to feed plants in pots is to use a liquid fertilizer. Watering and feeding are carried out as a single operation, thus saving an extra job and avoiding the danger of overfeeding. The recommended amount is added to the water, and this is used instead of plain water when watering.

When to feed

Potting composts contain enough plant food for about 2 months after repotting. After this time feeding will be necessary, provided the plant is not dormant. The time to feed regularly is during the growing and flowering seasons — spring to autumn for foliage and most flowering plants, and during winter for winter-flowering types. Feeding should be reduced or stopped during the resting period.

Give them the REST they need

Articles on house plant care always trot out the same list of essential needs — light, water, warmth, humidity, fertilizer but one requirement is often omitted — a period of rest.

Nearly all indoor plants need a dormant or resting period during the year, and this generally takes place in winter. Some plants give unmistakable signs that they are at the end of their growing period and even an absolute beginner can tell that the usual maintenance routine will have to change. The top growth of bulbous and tuberous plants (Hyacinth, Cyclamen, Gloxinia, etc) dies down; the leaves of deciduous woody plants (Punica, Poinsettia, etc) drop off. Watering is greatly reduced or stopped altogether as recommended in the A-Z guide. The *dormant period* has arrived.

Evergreen house plants unfortunately give little or no indication that a period of rest is needed. But as midwinter approaches the duration of natural light is too short to support active growth. The *resting period* has arrived. It is essential to reduce the frequency of watering and feeding; cooler conditions may be required. If the plant is kept warmer than recommended and watered as frequently as in spring then it will certainly suffer.

The appearance of new growth in the spring is a sure sign that the resting period is over. Slowly resume normal watering and feeding and repot the plant if necessary. Some plants, such as African Violet and Busy Lizzie seem to have little need of a resting period, but they do benefit from a period of about a month when watering and feeding are reduced below normal.

There is an important exception to the need for a winter rest period. Winter-flowering pot plants must be fed and watered regularly for as long as they are on display indoors.

Give them the FRESH AIR they need

Plants, unlike pets, do not have to be provided with air to enable them to breathe. Green leaves manufacture oxygen, and some plants will grow quite happily in sealed glass containers. Despite this unique property of plants, fresh air is still an important need of some varieties.

A change of air:

- Lowers the temperature in hot weather.
- Lowers the humidity where overcrowded, moist conditions encourage Botrytis.
- Strengthens the stems and increases disease resistance.
- Removes traces of toxic vapours.

Vapours arising from a number of sources commonly found in rooms have been reported as damaging to house plants or their flowers. These include coke and anthracite fires, coke stoves, dirty oil heaters, fresh paint and ripe apples. Plants with thick leathery leaves are the ones most likely to withstand the effect of these fumes. One menace has disappeared — plant-damaging coal gas has been replaced by natural gas. Tobacco smoke is never present in sufficient amount to be harmful.

Fresh air is provided by *ventilation* — which is the opening of either a door *or* a window in the room in which the plant is growing. Provide summer ventilation for the following plants:

> Araucaria, Cacti, Fatsia, Impatiens,
> Pelargonium, Schizanthus, Succulents, Tolmiea

Guard against *draughts*, which are air currents moving rapidly and directly across the plants. Do not ventilate when the temperature outside is appreciably less than that of the room.

Ventilation is not enough for some plants — they need to be stood outdoors during the summer months. Examples are:

> Acacia, Citrus, Cytisus, Euonymus, Forest Cacti,
> Jasminum, Laurus, Passiflora, Punica, Yucca

Give them the GROOMING they need

CLEANING

Dust is an enemy in several ways:
- It spoils the appearance of the foliage.
- It blocks the leaf pores so that the plant can no longer breathe properly.
- It forms a light-blocking screen so that the full effect of daylight is lost.
- It may contain plant-damaging chemicals. This is more likely to be a problem in industrial areas than in country districts.

It is therefore necessary to remove dust when it becomes obvious on the foliage. Small plants can be immersed in a bucket of water, but it is more usual to syringe or sponge the leaves with clean water. Wash plants early in the day so that they will be dry before nightfall. When the foliage is very dirty it should be lightly dusted with a soft cloth before washing — failure to do this may result in a strongly adhesive mud when the water dries. Remember to support the leaf in your hand when washing, and it is best to syringe and not sponge young leaves. Cacti, Succulents and plants with hairy leaves should not be sprayed or washed; use a soft brush to remove dust.

POLISHING

Foliage, even when clean, tends to become dull and tired-looking as it ages; the glossy sheen of the new leaf is soon lost. Many plant-polishing materials are available, and you should choose with care. Dilute vinegar, milk and beer are sometimes recommended, but they have virtually no shine-producing properties. Olive oil will certainly produce a shine, but it collects dust and can cause damage. Buy a product which is specially made for plants — both wipe-on liquids and aerosol sprays are available. Aerosols are simple to apply and are the preferred method when there are lots of small leaves. Leafshine liquids can be safely used on a wide range of smooth-leaved house plants — apply by gently wiping the foliage with a piece of cotton wool impregnated with the liquid.

There are a few rules when polishing. Do not polish young leaves and never press down on the leaf surface. Read the label on proprietary products before use — you will find a list of plants which should not be treated.

Untreated Rubber Plant leaf —
neither washed nor polished

Leaf polished with
a wax-based leafshine product

TRAINING

Training is the support of stems to ensure maximum display. This method of grooming is, of course, essential for climbing plants. It is also necessary for non-climbers with long, weak stems (e.g Fatshedera), heavy flower-heads (e.g Hydrangea) and brittle stems (e.g Impatiens).

Avoid the single cane wherever possible; use a framework of three or four canes. The canes should reach the bottom of the pot. Many other types of support are available — trellises, moss sticks (page 223) and wire hoops for inserting within the pot and climbing frames of wire and wood outside the pot.

Do not tie stems too tightly to the support. Train new growth before it has become long enough to be untidy and difficult to bend. Vines must be trained frequently or the tendrils will tie the stems together. A few untrained shoots hanging down from a climber can sometimes improve its appearance.

PRUNING

Stopping (Pinching out) is the removal of the growing point of a stem. Use finger and thumb or a pair of scissors.

Pruning (Cutting back) involves more extensive cutting out of excessive growth. Use secateurs, scissors or a knife. Whenever possible cut just above a growth bud.

Trimming is the removal of dead leaves, damaged parts and faded flowers.

The main purpose of stopping is to induce branching in many bushy and trailing plants, such as Coleus, Zebrina, Tradescantia and Pilea. The plants should be actively growing and the stem should have at least three leaves. The result is a plant crowded with stems, but with some climbing plants the opposite effect is desired. Here one or more strong main shoots are selected and trained as required, the weak side shoots being cut out cleanly at their junction with the main stems.

Many plants soon get out of hand and deteriorate if not regularly pruned and trimmed. Some climbing plants, such as Ivy and Philodendron scandens, regularly produce stems bearing abnormally small and pale leaves if kept too warm in winter. This growth should be cut back when spring arrives. Always cut out dead and diseased stems, crowded stems and all-green shoots on variegated plants. Cut back over-long branches and old leafless stems. Trimming of dead flowers (dead-heading) will prolong the flowering period of many species.

Prune flowering plants with care — there are no general rules. Some, such as Fuchsia, Pelargonium, and Hydrangea, bear blooms on new growth. Others, such as Hoya, flower on mature wood. Only prune when the Secrets of Success tell you to do so. Never guess with pruning — some plants will fail to bloom if you prune, others will become overgrown and unattractive if you don't.

Plant care at holiday time

Your time for rest and relaxation away from home is a period of strain for the indoor plants which remain behind, but a little preparation before you leave will ensure that they will be unaffected by your absence.

WINTER HOLIDAYS

Leaving plants for a week or two during the winter months should be a minor problem if you can provide them with the minimum temperature they require. On no account should the plants be left on windowsills; if possible put the pots on a table in the centre of the room and water so that the compost is moist.

SUMMER HOLIDAYS

Leaving plants during the summer months is much more of a problem because the plants will be actively growing and their water requirement will be much greater than during the winter months. If your holiday is for more than a week, the most satisfactory solution is to persuade a friend to call in occasionally and look after them. If your friend has little experience make sure that the perils of overwatering are explained.

When a plant babysitter is not available trim off buds and flowers, move the pots out of the sun and water them thoroughly. If you can, surround the pots with damp peat. This procedure will not be enough for a long holiday in midsummer. A number of automatic watering devices are available; capillary matting soaked by a dripping tap in the kitchen sink is an excellent answer to the problem. Individual pots can be stood on wick waterers or they can be slipped into polythene bags, which are then sealed with self-adhesive tape.

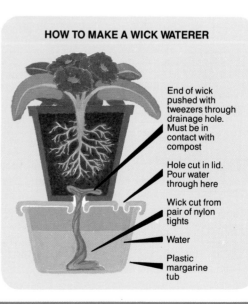

HOW TO MAKE A WICK WATERER

End of wick pushed with tweezers through drainage hole. Must be in contact with compost

Hole cut in lid. Pour water through here

Wick cut from pair of nylon tights

Water

Plastic margarine tub

CHAPTER 6

INCREASING YOUR STOCK

Some indoor plants cannot be raised at home without special equipment — you either have to invest in a thermostatically-controlled propagator or leave it to the nurseryman. But a vast number of different varieties can be propagated quite simply in the kitchen or spare room, and it is strange that there are so many people who grow their own vegetables and paint their own homes and yet are daunted by the idea of raising their own house plants. We now have so many aids which were unknown in grandmother's day — rooting hormone, transparent polythene bags, special composts, rooting bags and so on, yet the Victorians propagated a higher proportion of their own plants than we do.

There are four basic reasons for raising plants at home — to have more plants without having the expense of buying them every time, to replace ageing specimens with vigorous new ones, to have plants which would otherwise be unobtainable and to provide welcome gifts for friends. This final reason is responsible for the term 'friendship plants' given to varieties such as Busy Lizzie and Wandering Jew which are more usually raised at home than bought in a garden shop.

LAYERING

Most climbers and trailers with long, flexible stems can be propagated by layering — the disadvantage of this method is that rooting takes a long time.

Pick a vigorous stem and in spring or early summer pin it down into Seed and Cutting Compost in a small pot, using a hairpin or U-shaped piece of wire. A small nick cut into the underside of the stem will speed up rooting. Several stems arising from the parent plant can be layered at the same time. Once rooting has taken place, fresh growth will appear and the stem can then be cut, thus freeing the new plant.

OFFSETS

Some species produce miniature plants as side shoots from the main stem (e.g Bromeliads, Cacti and Succulents) or as tiny bulbils or bulblets next to the parent bulb (e.g Hippeastrum and Oxalis).

Stem offsets should be cut off as near the main stem as possible — preserve any roots which may be attached. A Bromeliad offset is ready for propagating when it is about a quarter of the size of the parent plant. Pot up each offset in Seed and Cutting Compost and treat as an ordinary cutting — see page 239. Bulb offsets should be separated from the parent bulb and potted up; it will take one or two years before flowering occurs.

PLANTLETS

A few species produce miniature plants at the end of flowering stems (e.g Chlorophytum, Saxifraga sarmentosa and Tolmiea) or on mature leaves (e.g Bryophyllum daigremontianum and Asplenium bulbiferum).

Propagation is easy. If no roots are present on the plantlet, peg it down in moist Seed and Cutting compost — see 'Layering' for details. Sever the plantlet from the parent plant when rooting has taken place. If the plantlet bears roots, it can be propagated by removing it from the parent plant and potting up as a rooted cutting.

CUTTINGS

Cuttings are by far the most usual way to raise indoor plants at home. The chance of success depends on the variety — some woody plants are difficult or impossible to propagate without special equipment, whereas several popular plants, such as Tradescantia, Impatiens and Ivy, will root quite readily in a glass of water. Even with easy-to-root cuttings there can be inexplicable failures so always take several cuttings and do not be disappointed if a few of them fail.

Stem Cuttings

Most house plants can be propagated from stem cuttings. Choose a sturdy and healthy non-flowering shoot. Some non-woody plants will root at any time of the year but woody varieties are generally more reliant on active growing conditions so in this latter case always follow the timing specified in the A-Z guide and always use a rooting hormone. As a general rule spring or early summer is the best time for all plants, but late summer is a popular time for striking Fuchsia and Geranium cuttings.

Stem cuttings should be inserted in the compost as soon as they have been prepared, but a Cactus or Succulent cutting should be left to dry for several days before insertion.

With shrubby plants it is preferable to take heel cuttings rather than the stem-tip cuttings illustrated on the right. Pull off a side shoot with a 'heel' (strip of bark from the main stem) attached. Trim any ragged edges and dip the bottom inch in rooting hormone.

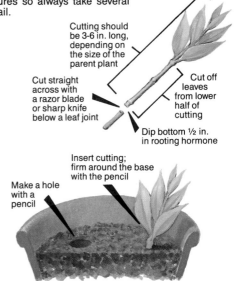

Cutting should be 3-6 in. long, depending on the size of the parent plant

Cut straight across with a razor blade or sharp knife below a leaf joint

Cut off leaves from lower half of cutting

Dip bottom ½ in. in rooting hormone

Make a hole with a pencil

Insert cutting; firm around the base with the pencil

Leaf Cuttings

Some plants do not have stems; the leaves arise directly from the crown of the plant. Obviously stem cuttings are impossible, but leaf cuttings provide an easy way to propagate many of these varieties.

Whole Leaf plus Stalk

Standard method for Saintpaulia, Gloxinia, small-leaved Peperomias and some Begonias.

Mature leaf taken from the base of the plant

Leaf stalk 2 in. long

Dip end into rooting hormone

Cut straight across with a razor blade or sharp knife

Insert cutting with the back of leaf towards the back of the pot. Leaf base should be just above the compost. Firm around the base with the pencil

Make a hole at 45° with a pencil

Whole Leaf

Standard method for Succulents such as Sedum, Echeveria and Crassula.

Mature fleshy leaf. Large leaves should be allowed to dry for a couple of days before planting

Cover surface with sharp sand

Lay small leaves on the surface; press lightly into the compost

Push the ends of large leaves into the compost

Part Leaf

Standard method for Begonia rex, Begonia masoniana, Streptocarpus and Sansevieria.

Begonia
1–1½ in. triangle cut from a mature, healthy leaf

Sansevieria
2–3 in. section cut from a mature, healthy leaf. Note: the plant produced will not be variegated

Streptocarpus
Section of a leaf — an adult leaf will produce 3 or 4 cuttings

Insert cutting and wooden labels for support at 45°. Bury a quarter of the cutting

Insert cutting vertically. Bury half the cutting

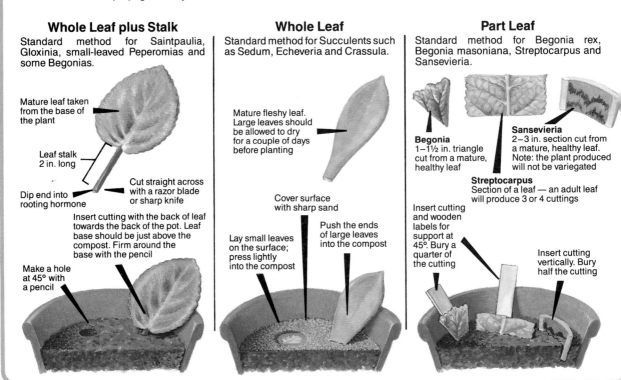

Cane Cuttings

A number of important house plants which produce thick and erect stems are propagated by means of cane cuttings. The best time to do this is when one or more stems have lost their lower leaves and are no longer attractive. The bare trunk is cut into several pieces, and each piece is inserted into Seed and Cutting Compost. The cane cuttings can be placed horizontally, as illustrated, or planted upright. If planted upright, make sure you bury the end which was the lower part on the stem. Cane cuttings can be used for Cordyline, Dracaena and Dieffenbachia; ready-to-plant canes ('Ti-Plants') can be bought in gift shops.

Cutting should be 2–3 in. long, bearing at least 1 node. Leaf buds must point upward. Bury lower half in compost.

How to root Cuttings

The problem your cutting has to face is obvious. It will usually be a severed piece of stem or leaf, and it will steadily lose moisture without having any means of replacing the loss. So it is a race against time — roots must form before the cutting dies through lack of moisture within its cells. Keeping the compost wet is certainly not the answer — use one of the rooting methods described below.

The Rooting Bag Method

A recent innovation is the rooting bag, in which Seed and Cutting Compost is tightly packed and sealed in a stout polythene bag. There are two basic advantages compared to the pot method — the covered compost stays moist much longer and weak cuttings are supported by the polythene. The method consists of cutting fourteen slits in the upper surface and inserting a cutting through each slit. If the cuttings wilt after a few hours, the rooting bag is slipped into a large plastic bag which is blown up and the top tied with a wire tie or self-adhesive tape.

The Propagator Method

A propagator is a useful piece of equipment if you intend to raise a large number of house plants. Basically it consists of a firm tray to hold the compost and a transparent cover which bears air vents. A simple unheated model will meet the needs of the average indoor gardener, but if you plan to raise delicate plants which need a propagating temperature of 70°F or more then you will need a heated propagator. This contains a heating element to raise the temperature of the compost and a thermostat to ensure that the temperature stays constant.

The Pot Method

A 5 in. clay or plastic pot will take three to six average-sized cuttings. The rooting medium must be sterile, free-draining, firm enough to hold the cuttings and contain not too much fertilizer. A specially formulated Seed and Cutting Compost is ideal.

Fill the pot with compost and lightly firm to leave a ½ in. watering space at the top. The cuttings should be inserted close to the side of the pot; make sure that they are properly firmed in as an air space around the cut surface is fatal. Some cuttings are inserted vertically and others at 45°; the instructions on the previous page will tell you when the cutting should be put in at an angle. Water in very gently.

Nearly all cuttings will need a humid atmosphere — in dry air large leaves soon shrivel and die, as there is no root system to replace the rapid loss of moisture. Place four canes in the pot and drape a polythene bag over them; secure with a rubber band. There are three important exceptions to this polythene bag technique — do not cover Cactus, Succulent or Geranium cuttings.

Place the pot in light shade or in a bright spot out of direct sunlight. The temperature should be 65°F or more. Pick off any leaves that turn yellow or start to rot.

The great enemy now is impatience — do not keep lifting the cuttings to see if roots are appearing. In a few weeks the tell-tale signs of success should appear — new growth at the tips of stem cuttings, and tiny plantlets at the base of leaf cuttings.

Potting-on time has arrived. Water the compost and then lift out each rooted stem cutting, taking care not to disturb the compost around the roots. Transfer each cutting to a 2½ or 3½ in. pot — fill with Potting Compost. Firm gently and water to settle the compost around the roots. Put the pots back in the same spot for a week or two; then transfer to their permanent quarters.

The technique with leaf cuttings which produce several plantlets is different. When the new plants are large enough to handle, cut away the parent leaf, gently separate and pot on. Make sure that each plantlet has some roots.

DIVISION

A number of house plants form several clumps or daughter rosettes as they develop, and these plants can be easily propagated by division. Examples are Chlorophytum, Cyperus, Maranta, Saintpaulia, Sansevieria and many Ferns.

Knock the plant out of its pot in spring or early summer and carefully pull off one or more segments. Do this by gently removing some compost so as to expose the connection between the clump and the rest of the plant. Break this join by hand or with a sharp knife. Never divide a plant by simply cutting it in two.

Transplant the segments into pots using Seed and Cutting Compost. Trickle compost between the roots and gently firm to prevent air pockets. Water sparingly until new growth appears.

AIR LAYERING

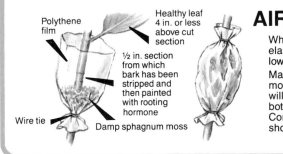

Polythene film

Healthy leaf 4 in. or less above cut section

½ in. section from which bark has been stripped and then painted with rooting hormone

Wire tie

Damp sphagnum moss

When thick-stemmed plants such as Dieffenbachia, Dracaena, Ficus elastica decora or Monstera become leggy due to the loss of their lower leaves, new compact plants can be produced by air layering.

Make the air layer as shown in the illustration; the cut should not be more than 2 ft from the tip of the plant. After a couple of months roots will be seen inside the plastic bag. Sever the stem just below the bottom wire tie, remove the polythene and pot up carefully in Potting Compost. The old plant need not be thrown away; it will produce new shoots on the shortened stem if the compost is kept just moist.

SEED SOWING

Unlike raising plants for the garden, seed sowing is not a popular method of propagating house plants. Nearly all of them require time, skill and heated conditions, but there are special cases where seed sowing is the method to use. Some plants, such as Thunbergia, Exacum and the Bedding Plants have to be raised in this way, and seed sowing allows large numbers of plants such as Coleus to be grown for indoor bedding at very little cost. Lastly, the young (and not-so-young) delight in sowing pips, fruit stones, beans, etc, to produce short-lived foliage plants.

Fill a pot or seed pan with Seed and Cutting Compost; firm lightly with the fingertips or a board and water sparingly. Sow seeds thinly — space out each seed if they are large enough to handle. Cover large seeds with a layer of compost; small seeds not at all. Place a polythene bag over the container and secure with a rubber band.

Stand the pot in a shady place at a temperature of 60°–70°F. As soon as the seeds have germinated move the pot to a bright spot, away from direct sunlight. Remove the plastic cover, keep the compost surface moist and turn the pot regularly to avoid lop-sided growth.

As soon as the seedlings are large enough to handle they should be pricked out into small pots filled with Potting Compost.

SPORE SOWING

Ferns produce dust-like spores, not seeds, and it is always a challenge to try to raise fern plants from these spores at home. Collect them in a paper bag from ripe spore-cases which are found on the underside of the fronds. Leave them to dry for a couple of weeks and then spread them very thinly on the surface of moist Seed and Cutting Compost. The compost should be in a plastic pot which has been sterilised by immersion in boiling water. Cover the pot with a sheet of glass after sowing the spores and place it in a shady spot. When the plants are large enough to handle transplant them into small pots.

CHAPTER 7
PLANT TROUBLES

It is always disappointing when a cherished specimen suddenly looks sickly, and it is so often the more expensive types which succumb first.

There is not going to be much pleasure in growing indoor plants unless you learn how to avoid plant troubles. Specific pests and diseases are not usually to blame; in most cases the cause of ill-health or death is either too much or too little of one or more of the essential growth factors — light, water, warmth, humidity and food.

To keep your plants in perfect condition, your first task is to choose only those types which can be expected to flourish in the conditions you can provide. Then choose carefully and buy healthy specimens, protect them on their way home and finally provide them with the right conditions. Even so, leaf, stem and flower problems can still occur and you should learn to recognise the cause of problems so that you can take immediate action — pages 242–245 will help you. Many troubles can be stopped or cured if tackled quickly enough — delay or the wrong treatment can lead to the death of the plant.

Finally, a word for the beginner. As you will have seen on page 57, not all flowering plants dwell permanently indoors. So there is no need to feel you have failed when Poinsettia, Cineraria, Cyclamen and so on die down once their display is over.

Plant collapse

There are scores of possible reasons which can account for the death of an indoor plant. The seven most common fatal factors are:

● **SOIL DRYNESS** No life can survive without water. Many plants can cope with infrequent watering in winter but failure to provide sufficient water during the growing season soon leads to wilting of the leaves and finally to the death of the plant.

● **OVERWATERING** The most usual cause of plant death in winter is overwatering. The leaves of affected plants droop, and the owner thinks that they are short of water. So the plants are thoroughly watered and collapse soon follows.

It is obviously vital not to confuse the symptoms of drought with those of overwatering. Both cause leaves to wilt and sometimes to drop, but too much water results in yellowing of the foliage, whereas dryness is much more likely to cause shrivelling and browning of the leaves. Also waterlogged clay pots are covered with green slime.

● **COLD NIGHTS** The harmful effects of cold nights are heightened if the plants are kept under warm or hot conditions during the day, as it is the sudden fluctuation in temperature rather than cold air which usually causes the damage.

Frost is generally fatal, and plants standing on windowsills are the ones most likely to suffer. Never leave pots between the windows and drawn curtains on a cold night; if frost is expected and the room is unheated then move the plants away from the window.

● **STRONG SUNSHINE** Some plants will quickly succumb if exposed to direct sunlight even if the air temperature is not unusually high. Some flowering plants, such as Pelargonium, thrive in a sunny window but even these, in common with all other plants, should have the pot and soil surface shaded in the hot summer months. If this is not done, the soil may be baked and the roots killed.

● **HOT DRY AIR** With central heating, and with most forms of artificial heat, the air lacks moisture and conditions are not favourable for most indoor plants. Delicate plants may die under such winter conditions, and it is necessary to increase the Relative Humidity of the surrounding air by one of the techniques on page 232.

● **DRAUGHTS** When a door *and* window are opened in a room, and when the temperature outside the room is lower than within, then a cross-current of air occurs and these draughts are an important cause of plant failure. For this reason, avoid standing plants in a direct line between door and windows.

Another spot which is subject to draughts is the windowsill where there are cracks in the window frame. If delicate plants are to be grown on a windowsill, it is essential to block up all cracks.

● **NO LIGHT** Poor light conditions in an average room do not usually kill; the result is generally pale, weak growth and no flowers. There is a level, however, at which the amount of light is not sufficient to support house plant life and this can occur in dark passages, corners of large rooms, hallways, etc. If you wish to keep plants in such areas, return them at regular intervals to a moderately well-lit spot for a fortnight's holiday.

Cultural faults

UPPER LEAVES FIRM BUT YELLOW

This is generally due to the use of CALCIUM in the compost of lime-hating plants or the use of HARD WATER for watering such plants.

LEAVES DULL AND LIFELESS

TOO MUCH LIGHT is the probable culprit; another possibility is RED SPIDER MITE (see page 244). Even healthy green leaves can be rendered dull and lifeless by dust and grime — follow the cleaning instructions on page 235.

SPOTS OR PATCHES ON LEAVES

If spots or patches are crisp and brown, UNDERWATERING is the most likely cause. If the areas are soft and dark brown, OVERWATERING is the probable reason. If spots or patches are white or straw-coloured, the trouble is due to WATERING WITH COLD WATER, WATER SPLASHES ON LEAVES, AEROSOL DAMAGE, TOO MUCH SUN or PEST/DISEASE DAMAGE (see pages 244 – 245). If spots are moist and blister-like or dry and sunken, the cause is DISEASE (see page 245). Several PESTS can cause speckling of the leaf surface (see page 244).

BROWN TIPS OR EDGES ON LEAVES

If edges remain green, the most likely cause is DRY AIR. Another possible reason is BRUISING — people or pets touching the tips can be the culprit, so can leaf tips pressing against a wall or window. If edges are yellow or brown, the possible causes are many and varied — OVERWATERING, UNDERWATERING, TOO LITTLE LIGHT, TOO MUCH SUN, TOO LITTLE HEAT, TOO MUCH HEAT, OVERFEEDING, DRY AIR or DRAUGHTS. To pinpoint the cause, look for other symptoms.

WILTING LEAVES

The most usual cause is either SOIL DRYNESS (caused by underwatering) or WATERLOGGING (caused by impeded drainage or watering too frequently). Other possible causes are TOO MUCH LIGHT (especially if wilting takes place regularly at midday), DRY AIR, TOO MUCH HEAT, POT-BOUND ROOTS or PEST DAMAGE (see page 244).

LEAVES CURL AND FALL

Curling followed by leaf fall is a sign of TOO LITTLE HEAT, OVERWATERING or COLD DRAUGHTS.

SUDDEN LEAF FALL

Rapid defoliation without a prolonged preliminary period of wilting or discolouration is generally due to a SHOCK to the plant's system. There may have been a large drop or rise in temperature, a sudden increase in daytime light intensity or an intense cold draught. DRYNESS at the roots below the critical level can result in this sudden loss of leaves, especially with woody specimens.

LEAF FALL ON NEW PLANTS

It is quite normal for a newly repotted plant, a new purchase or a plant moved from one room to another, to lose one or two lower leaves. Keep MOVEMENT SHOCK to a minimum by repotting into a pot which is only slightly larger than the previous one, by protecting new plants on the way home from the shop and by never moving a plant from a shady spot to a very bright one without a few days in medium light.

LEAVES TURN YELLOW AND FALL

It is quite normal for an occasional lower leaf on a mature plant to turn yellow and eventually fall. When several leaves turn yellow at the same time and then fall, the most likely cause is OVERWATERING or COLD DRAUGHTS.

LOWER LEAVES DRY UP AND FALL

There are three common causes — TOO LITTLE LIGHT, TOO MUCH HEAT or UNDERWATERING.

PLANT GROWING SLOWLY OR NOT AT ALL

In winter this is normal for nearly all plants, so do not force it to grow. In summer the most likely cause is UNDERFEEDING, OVERWATERING or TOO LITTLE LIGHT. If these factors are not responsible, and the temperature is in the recommended range, then the plant is probably POT-BOUND (see page 13).

SMALL, PALE LEAVES; SPINDLY GROWTH

This occurs in winter and early spring when the plant has been kept too warm and the compost too wet for the limited amount of light available. Where practical, prune off this poor quality growth. If these symptoms appear in the growing season, the most likely cause is either UNDER-FEEDING or TOO LITTLE LIGHT.

FLOWER BUDS FALL

The conditions which cause leaf drop can also lead to loss of buds and flowers. The commonest causes are DRY AIR, UNDERWATERING, TOO LITTLE LIGHT, MOVING THE POT and INSECT DAMAGE (see page 244).

NO FLOWERS

If the plant has reached flowering size and blooms do not appear at the due time of year, several factors can be responsible. The most likely causes are lighting problems — TOO LITTLE LIGHT or WRONG DAYLENGTH. Other possibilities are OVERFEEDING, DRY AIR, THRIPS (see page 244) or REPOTTING (some flowering plants need to be pot-bound before they will flower).

VARIEGATED LEAVES TURN ALL-GREEN

The simple explanation here is that the foliage is receiving TOO LITTLE LIGHT. Remove the all-green branch (if practical) and move the pot closer to the window.

FLOWERS QUICKLY FADE

The commonest culprits are UNDERWATERING, DRY AIR, TOO LITTLE LIGHT and TOO MUCH HEAT.

ROTTING LEAVES AND STEMS

This is due to disease attack where growing conditions are poor. The fault often lies with OVERWATERING in winter or LEAVING WATER ON LEAVES at night.

HOLES AND TEARS IN LEAVES

There are two basic causes — PHYSICAL DAMAGE by pets or people (merely brushing against an opening leaf bud can occasionally be responsible) or INSECT DAMAGE (see page 244).

GREEN SLIME ON CLAY POT

A sure sign of watering problems — OVERWATERING or BLOCKED DRAINAGE is the cause.

WHITE CRUST ON CLAY POT

There are two possible causes — use of excessively HARD WATER or OVERFEEDING.

Pests

Pest attacks are less common indoors than in the garden, but if they do occur and are allowed to get out of hand then serious damage can result. Apply the appropriate remedy as soon as the first signs are seen.

APHID (Greenfly)

Small, sap-sucking insects, usually green but may be black, grey or orange. All plants with soft tissues can be attacked; shoot tips and flower buds are the preferred site. Flowering pot plants are especially susceptible. The plant is weakened and sticky honeydew is deposited. Spray with permethrin — alternatively use malathion or derris. Repeat as necessary.

CATERPILLAR

Caterpillars of many types can infest the plants in a conservatory but these pests are rarely found on specimens in the living room. The tell-tale sign is the presence of holes in the leaves; some species of caterpillar spin leaves together with silken threads. Pick off and destroy individual caterpillars — spraying with fenitrothion or derris is usually not necessary.

CYCLAMEN MITE

Minute mites, looking like a film of dust on the underside of leaves. Cyclamen, Impatiens, Pelargonium and Saintpaulia are susceptible. The infested plant is stunted; leaf edges are curled, stems are twisted, flower buds wither. Unlike red spider mite, this pest will flourish in humid conditions. Spraying with standard insecticides is not effective — destroy infested leaves.

EARWIG

A familiar garden and household pest with a dark brown body and pincer-like tail. It is rarely if ever seen on house plants as it hides during the day, feeding at night on leaves and flower petals. Ragged holes are produced and leaves may be skeletonised. Pick off the insects — look under the leaves and shake the flowers. Spraying with malathion is rarely necessary.

EELWORM

Fortunately these microscopic, soil-living worms are not common house plant pests. If a plant collapses for no apparent reason remove it from its pot — large, corky swellings on the roots are a sure sign of root knot eelworm attack. Destroy the plant immediately — do not put it on the compost heap. In future use sterilised compost and buy plants from a reputable supplier.

FUNGUS GNAT

The small, black, adult insects which fly around the plant are harmless, but they lay eggs on the compost and the tiny, black-headed maggots they produce can be harmful. The maggots normally feed on organic matter in the compost but they will occasionally devour young roots. Fungus gnats can be troublesome in over-damp conditions — water with malathion solution.

MEALY BUG

Small pests covered with white, cottony fluff. Large clusters can occur on the stems and under the leaves of a wide variety of plants. A serious attack leads to wilting, yellowing and leaf fall. A light infestation is easily dealt with — wipe off with a damp cloth or a babycare cotton bud. A severe infestation is difficult to control — spray weekly with malathion or systemic insecticide.

RED SPIDER MITE

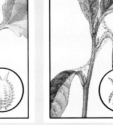

Minute, sap-sucking pests which can infest the underside of leaves of nearly all house plants growing in hot and dry conditions. The upper surface becomes speckled with yellow blotches and the leaves fall prematurely; white webbing is sometimes produced between the leaves and stems. Daily misting will help to prevent attacks; spray with derris, malathion or systemic insecticide as soon as the first signs are seen. Repeat as necessary.

SCALE

Small, brown discs attached to the underside of leaves, especially along the veins. These immobile adults are protected from sprays by the outer waxy shells, but they can be wiped off with a damp cloth or a babycare cotton bud. After removal spray the whole plant with malathion. If a plant is allowed to become badly infested the leaves turn yellow and sticky with honeydew; eradication is difficult or impossible at this stage.

THRIPS

These tiny, black insects are a minor pest of house plants, but Begonia, Codiaeum and Fuchsia are sometimes disfigured. They fly or jump from leaf to leaf, causing tell-tale silvery streaks, but the worst damage is to flowers which are spotted and distorted. Growth is stunted. Control is not difficult — spray with permethrin, malathion or derris at the first sign of attack and repeat as necessary.

VINE WEEVIL

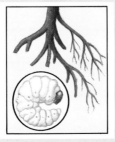

The adult beetles attack leaves, but it is the 1 in. creamy grubs which do the real damage. They live in the compost and rapidly devour roots, bulbs and tubers. Control is difficult or impossible — the root system will have been seriously damaged by the time the plant has started to wilt. Water immediately with lindane (HCH). Use as a precautionary measure if beetles are noticed on Cyclamen or Primula leaves.

WHITEFLY

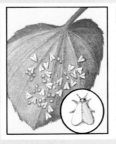

Tiny, white moth-like insects which can be troublesome, especially to Begonia, Fuchsia, Impatiens and Pelargonium. The adult flies are unsightly; the greenish larvae on the underside of the leaves suck sap and deposit sticky honeydew. Badly infested leaves turn yellow and drop. Whitefly can occur in great numbers and rapidly spread from plant to plant. Eradication is difficult — spray with permethrin and repeat at 3-day intervals.

Diseases

The appearance of disease is usually a sign of poor growing conditions. Speedy action is essential — cut out the affected area as soon as it is seen, use a fungicide if one is recommended and correct the cultural fault.

ANTHRACNOSE

Sunken black spots appear on the foliage of Palms, Ficus and other susceptible plants. Dark brown streaks may occur at the leaf tips. This disease is associated with warm and very moist conditions, and it is therefore much more likely in the greenhouse than in the living room. Remove and burn infected leaves, spray the plant with systemic fungicide and keep it on the dry side without misting for several weeks.

BLACK LEG

A disease of stem cuttings, especially Pelargonium. The base of the cutting turns black, due to the invasion of the Botrytis fungus. Remove the infected cutting as soon as possible. The cause is overwatering or overcompaction of the compost which has prevented proper drainage. Make sure that the Seed and Cutting Compost is kept drier next time you take Pelargonium cuttings; do not cover with glass or polythene.

BOTRYTIS (Grey Mould)

Familiar grey, fluffy mould which can cover all parts of the plant — leaves, stems, buds and flowers if the growing conditions are cool, humid and still. All soft-leaved plants can be affected — Begonia, Cyclamen, Gloxinia and Saintpaulia are particularly susceptible. Cut away and destroy all affected parts. Remove mouldy compost. Spray with systemic fungicide. Reduce watering and misting; improve ventilation.

CROWN & STEM ROT

Part of the stem or crown has turned soft and rotten. When the diseased area is at the base of the plant it is known as basal rot. The fungus usually spreads rapidly and kills the plant — the usual course is to throw the pot, compost and plant away. If you have caught the trouble early you can try to save it by cutting away all diseased tissue. In future avoid overwatering, underventilating and keeping the plant too cool.

DAMPING OFF

The damping off fungi attack the root and stem bases of seedlings. Shrinkage and rot occur at ground level and the plants topple over. The golden rules are to use sterilised compost, sow thinly and never overwater. At the first sign of attack remove collapsed seedlings, improve the ventilation and move the seedlings to a cooler spot. Water the remainder with Cheshunt Compound.

LEAF SPOT

Brown, moist spots appear on the foliage of Citrus, Dracaena, Dieffenbachia and other susceptible plants. In a bad attack the small spots enlarge and merge, killing the whole leaf. Both bacteria and fungi can cause this effect — the best general treatment is to remove and burn infected leaves, spray the plant with systemic fungicide and keep it on the dry side without misting for several weeks.

OEDEMA (Corky Scab)

Hard corky growths sometimes appear on the underside of leaves. This disease is not caused by either a fungus or bacterium; it is the plant's response to waterlogged compost coupled with low light intensity. Badly affected leaves will not recover so they should be removed. Transferring the plant to a better lit spot and reducing the frequency of watering will result in healthy new foliage.

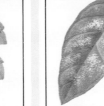

POWDERY MILDEW

A fungus disease which grows on the surface of leaves, spotting or coating them with a white powdery deposit. Unlike Botrytis this complaint is neither common nor fatal, but it is disfiguring and can spread to stems and flowers. Remove badly mildewed leaves and spray the plants with systemic fungicide or dinocap. Alternatively lightly dust the leaves with sulphur. Improve ventilation around the plants.

ROOT ROT (Tuber Rot)

A killer disease to which Cacti, Succulents, Begonia, Palms and Saintpaulia are particularly prone. The first sign is usually the yellowing and wilting of the leaves which is rapidly followed by browning and collapse. The cause is fungal decay of the roots due to waterlogging and you can only save the plant if the trouble is spotted in time and you follow the Root Rot Surgery technique on page 246.

RUST

An uncommon disease which need not concern the ordinary house plant owner. The only plant you are likely to see infected with rust is the Pelargonium — brown concentric rings of spores on the underside of the leaves. It is difficult to control — remove and burn infected leaves, improve the ventilation around the plants and spray with mancozeb. Do not propagate cuttings infected with this disease.

SOOTY MOULD

A black fungus which grows on the sticky honeydew which is deposited by aphid, scale, whitefly and mealy bug. The unsightly mould does not directly harm the plant, but it does reduce growth and vigour by blocking the pores and shading the surface from sunlight. Remove sooty mould by wiping with a damp cloth; rinse with clean warm water. Control future attacks by spraying promptly against the pests which produce honeydew.

VIRUS

There is no single symptom of virus infection. The growth may be severely stunted and stems are often distorted. The usual effect on leaves is the appearance of pale green or yellow spots or small patches. Coloured flowers may bear large white streaks. The infection was brought in by insects or was already present in the plant at the time of purchase. There is no cure — throw away the plant if you are sure of your diagnosis.

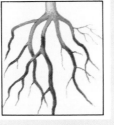

First aid for house plants

House plant varieties have changed over the years, but one would expect their problems to be quite unchanging. This surprisingly is not so — the menace of coal gas fumes has disappeared in recent years but it has been replaced by an equally serious but completely different menace — the hot, desert-dry air of the centrally-heated room. Even pests and diseases change — Pelargonium rust was virtually unknown until a few years ago.

The problems that can occur are many and varied. Inspect the plants regularly, especially under the leaves. You may detect the first signs of rot because you forgot to reduce watering as winter approached, or you may notice symptoms of light deficiency if you have redecorated using much darker wallpaper. Use pages 242–245 to put a name to the problems you see, then take prompt action. The secret of green fingers is to look for and act on the first signs of trouble.

PREVENTION IS BETTER THAN CURE

Don't bring trouble in with the compost
Never use unsterilised soil. Buy a specially-prepared compost, which you can be sure will be pest- and disease-free. Alternatively sterilise soil if you wish to prepare a home-made compost.

Don't bring trouble in with the plants
Inspect new plants carefully and take any remedial action which may be necessary before putting them with the other plants.

Don't put plants in the danger spots:
- Between an open window and a door
- Near an air-conditioning heating duct
- On the TV or radiator unless extra humidity is provided
- On a windowsill with poor-fitting frames
- In an unlit corner or a dark passageway
- Between closed curtains and the window during frosty weather

Remove dead flowers and dying leaves
Hygiene is important. Fallen leaves can become covered in grey mould, and this will spread rapidly to healthy leaves if conditions are cool and humid.

Prevent trouble by following the rules
Look up the plant in the A–Z guide — nearly all problems arise from inadequate care.

Act promptly when there is trouble
Don't wait. Move the plant to a better location or spray the leaves if such treatment is recommended.

GOOD SPRAYING PRACTICE

Use the right product
Make sure that it is recommended for the pest or disease to be controlled, and make sure that there is no warning against spraying the plant to be treated.

Buy a brand recommended for house plants
Where possible obtain a product which is specially recommended for use indoors — check that it will not harm surrounding furnishings or fabrics.

Spray the right way
Before spraying read the instructions — avoid using too little or too much. Cover fish bowls and aquaria before you start. Spray thoroughly both above and below the leaves. Wash out the sprayer after use.

Spray the right plants
With the quick-moving invaders, such as aphid and whitefly, spray all the neighbouring plants. With slow-moving pests, such as scale and mealy bug, only plants which are infested need be sprayed.

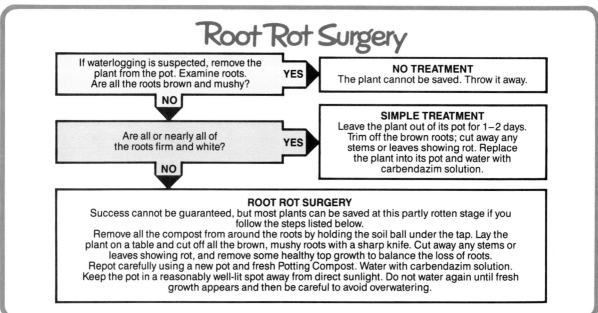

Root Rot Surgery

If waterlogging is suspected, remove the plant from the pot. Examine roots. Are all the roots brown and mushy? — **YES** →

NO TREATMENT
The plant cannot be saved. Throw it away.

NO ↓

Are all or nearly all of the roots firm and white? — **YES** →

SIMPLE TREATMENT
Leave the plant out of its pot for 1–2 days. Trim off the brown roots; cut away any stems or leaves showing rot. Replace the plant into its pot and water with carbendazim solution.

NO ↓

ROOT ROT SURGERY
Success cannot be guaranteed, but most plants can be saved at this partly rotten stage if you follow the steps listed below.
Remove all the compost from around the roots by holding the soil ball under the tap. Lay the plant on a table and cut off all the brown, mushy roots with a sharp knife. Cut away any stems or leaves showing rot, and remove some healthy top growth to balance the loss of roots.
Repot carefully using a new pot and fresh Potting Compost. Water with carbendazim solution. Keep the pot in a reasonably well-lit spot away from direct sunlight. Do not water again until fresh growth appears and then be careful to avoid overwatering.

CHAPTER 8

HOUSE PLANT GROWER'S DICTIONARY

ACID MEDIUM A compost which contains little or no lime and has a pH of less than 6.5.

AERIAL ROOT A root which grows out from the stem above ground level. Aerial roots are commonly seen on mature specimens of Monstera deliciosa.

AIR LAYERING A method of propagating single-stem plants, such as Ficus elastica decora, which have lost their lower leaves. See page 240 for details.

ALTERNATE Leaf form, where the leaves are arranged singly at different heights on the stem. Compare *opposite* and *whorled*.

ANNUAL A plant which completes its life cycle within one year of germination. Compare *biennial* and *perennial*.

ANTHER The part of the flower which produces pollen. It is the upper section of the *stamen*.

APICAL At the tip of a branch.

AQUATIC See Picture Dictionary (page 250).

AREOLE A small well-defined area, usually hairy and cushion-like, found on the stem of cacti. From them arise spines or *glochids*.

AXIL The angle between the upper surface of a leaf or leaf stalk and the stem that carries it. A growth or flower bud ("axillary bud") often appears in the axil.

BEARDED A petal bearing a tuft or row of long hairs.

BICOLOUR A flower with petals which bear two distinctly different colours.

BIENNIAL A plant which completes its life cycle in two seasons. Compare *annual* and *perennial*.

BLADE The expanded part of a leaf or petal.

BLEEDING The loss of sap from plant tissues which have been cut.

BLIND The loss of the growing point, resulting in stoppage of growth. Also, failure to produce flowers or fruit.

BLOOM A natural mealy or waxy coating covering the leaves of some house plants.

BONSAI The art of dwarfing trees by careful root and stem pruning coupled with root restriction.

BOSS A ring of prominent and decorative stamens.

BOTTLE GARDEN A form of *terrarium* in which a large and heavy glass container such as a *carboy* is used.

BOTTOM HEAT Undersurface heat provided in the soil by electric cables or hot water pipes.

BRACT A modified leaf, often highly coloured and sometimes mistaken for a petal. Examples of house plants with showy bracts are Poinsettia, Aphelandra and Bougainvillea.

BREAK Production of a side shoot after removal of the growing point.

BULB A storage organ, usually formed below ground level, used for propagation. A true bulb consists of fleshy scales surrounding the central bud, but the term is often loosely applied to *corms*, *rhizomes* and *tubers*.

BULBIL An immature small bulb formed on the stem of a plant; e.g Lily.

BULBLET An immature small bulb formed at the base of a mature bulb; e.g Hyacinth.

CALYX The outer ring of flower parts, usually green but sometimes coloured.

CAPILLARY ACTION The natural upward movement of water in confined areas, such as the spaces between soil particles.

CARBOY A large and heavy glass vessel, originally designed for the storage of chemicals but now commonly used as a container for bottle gardens.

CHLOROSIS An abnormal yellowing or blanching of the leaves due to lack of chlorophyll. See Chapter 7 for possible causes.

CLADODE A modified stem which has taken on the form of a leaf; e.g the needle-like "leaves" of Asparagus Fern.

COLOURED LEAF See Picture Dictionary (page 250).

COMPOST Usual meaning for the house plant grower is a potting or seed/cutting mixture made from peat ("soilless compost") or sterilised soil ("loam compost") plus other materials such as sand, lime and fertilizer. Compost is also a term for decomposed vegetable matter.

COMPOUND FLOWER A flower made up of many *florets*; e.g Chrysanthemum.

COMPOUND LEAF A leaf made up or two or more *leaflets* attached to the leaf stalk; e.g Schefflera.

CONSERVATORY A structure composed partly or entirely of glass, attached to the house and within which a large number of plants are grown and enjoyed.

CORM A swollen, underground stem base used for propagation; e.g Crocus.

COROLLA The ring of separate or fused petals which is nearly always responsible for the main floral display.

CRESTED Cockscomb-like growth of leaves, stems or flowers. Other name — cristate.

CROCK A piece of broken pot used to help drainage. See page 13.

CROWN The region where shoot and root join, usually at or very near ground level.

CULTIVAR See *The Naming of House Plants*, page 5.

CUTTING A piece of a plant (leaf, stem or root) which can be used to produce a new plant.

DAMPING OFF Decay of young seedlings at ground level following fungal attack. See page 245.

DEAD-HEADING The removal of faded heads of flowers.

DECIDUOUS See Picture Dictionary (page 250).

DISC (DISK) The flat central part of a *compound flower*. It is made up of short, tubular *florets*.

DISTILLED WATER Pure water free from dissolved salts. Formerly made by distillation, now produced chemically by demineralisation.

DIVISION A method of propagating plants by separating each one into two or more sections and then repotting.

DORMANT PERIOD The time when a plant has naturally stopped growing and the leaves have fallen or the top growth has died down. The dormant period is usually, but not always, in winter. Compare *resting period*.

DOUBLE FLOWER See Picture Dictionary (page 250).

DOUBLE POTTING An American term for placing a potted plant in a larger pot with damp peat in between. See page 232.

DRAWN Excessively tall and weak growth, caused by plants being grown in too little light or too closely together.

ENTIRE LEAF An undivided and unserrated leaf.

EPIPHYTE See Picture Dictionary (page 250).

EXOTIC Strictly speaking, a plant which is not native to the area, but popularly any unusual or striking house plant.

EYE Two unrelated meanings — an undeveloped growth bud or the centre of a flower.

F₁ HYBRID A first generation offspring of two pure-bred strains. An F₁ hybrid is generally more vigorous than an ordinary hybrid.

FAMILY See *The Naming of House Plants*, page 5.

FLORET A small flower which is part of a much larger compound flower-head; e.g Cineraria.

FLOWER SPIKE A flower-head made up of a central stem with the flowers growing directly on it.

FORCING The process of making a plant grow or flower before its natural season.

FROND A leaf of a fern or palm.

FUNGICIDE A chemical used to control diseases caused by fungi.

FUNGUS A primitive form of plant life which is known to the house plant grower as the most common cause of infectious disease — powdery mildew, sooty mould and grey mould are examples.

GENUS See *The Naming of House Plants*, page 5.

GERMINATION The first stage in the development of a plant from seed.

GLABROUS Plant surface which is smooth and hairless.

GLAUCOUS Plant surface which is covered with a bluish-grey bloom.

GLOCHID A small hooked hair borne on some cacti.

GRAFTING The process of joining a stem or bud of one plant on to the stem of another.

GROUND COVER A plant used to provide a low-growing carpet between other plants.

GROWING POINT The tip of a stem, which is responsible for extension growth.

HALF HARDY An indoor plant which requires a minimum temperature of 50°-55°F for healthy growth. Compare *hardy* and *tender*.

HARDENING OFF Gradual acclimatisation to colder conditions.

HARDY An indoor plant which can withstand prolonged exposure to temperatures at or below 45°F. Compare *half hardy* and *tender*.

HEEL A strip of bark and wood remaining at the base of a side shoot cutting pulled off a main shoot. Some cuttings root more readily if a heel is attached.

HERB A plant grown for flavouring or medicinal purposes.

HERBACEOUS A plant with a non-woody stem.

HONEYDEW Sticky, sugary secretion deposited on plants by insects such as aphid and whitefly.

HUMIDIFIER A piece of equipment used to raise the humidity of the air in a room.

HYBRID A plant with parents which are genetically distinct. The parent plants may be different *cultivars*, *varieties*, *species* or *genera* but not different *families*.

HYDROPONICS A method of growing a plant in water containing dissolved nutrients.

HYGROMETER An instrument used to measure the Relative Humidity of the air.

INFLORESCENCE The arrangement of flowers on the stem.

INORGANIC A chemical or fertilizer which is not obtained from a source which is or has been alive.

INSECTICIDE A chemical used to control insect pests.

INTERNODE The part of the stem between one *node* and another.

KNOCKING OUT The temporary removal of a plant from its pot in order to check the condition of the root ball.

LATEX Milky sap which exudes from cut surfaces of a few house plants, such as Ficus elastica decora and Euphorbia.

LEAF MOULD Partially decayed leaves used in some potting mixtures. It must be sieved and sterilised before use.

LEAFLET A leaf-like section of a *compound leaf*.

LEGGY Abnormally tall and spindly growth.

LOAM Good quality soil used in preparing compost. Adequate supplies of clay, sand and fibre must be present.

LONG DAY PLANT A plant which requires light for a longer period than it would normally receive from daylight in order to induce flowering; e.g Saintpaulia.

MACRAMÉ Decoratively knotted rope or cord forming a harness-like structure for hanging pots.

MICROCLIMATE The warmth and humidity of the air in close proximity to a plant. It may differ significantly from the general climate of the room.

MICROCUTTING A plant produced by micropropagation — a modern technique using tiny pieces of the parent plant on a sterile nutrient jelly.

MIST PROPAGATION The ideal method of propagation under glass, using automatic mist generators and soil heaters.

MOUTH The open end of a bell-shaped or tubular flower.

MULTICOLOUR A flower with petals which bear at least three distinctly different colours.

MUTATION A sudden change in the genetic make-up of a plant, leading to a new feature. This new feature can be inherited.

NEUTRAL Neither acid nor alkaline; pH 6.5-7.5.

NODE The point on a stem where a leaf or bud is attached.

OFFSET A young plantlet which appears on a mature plant. An offset can generally be detached and used for propagation.

OPPOSITE Leaf form, where the leaves are arranged in opposite pairs along the stem. Compare *alternate* and *whorled*.

ORGANIC A chemical or fertilizer which is obtained from a source which is or has been alive.

OSMUNDA FIBRE The roots of the fern Osmunda regalis, used for making Orchid Compost.

OVER-POTTING Repotting a plant into a pot which is too large to allow successful establishment.

PALMATE LEAF Five or more lobes arising from one point — hand-like.

PEAT (Peat moss in the U.S) Partially decomposed sphagnum moss or sedge used in making composts. Valuable for its pronounced air- and water-holding capacity and its freedom from weeds and disease organisms.

PEBBLE TRAY See *The Pot Group*, page 19.

PENDANT Hanging.

PERENNIAL A plant which will live for three years or more under normal conditions.

PERFOLIATE Paired leaves which fuse around the stem.

PETAL One of the divisions of the *corolla* — generally the showy part of the flower.

PETIOLE A leaf stalk.

pH A measure of acidity and alkalinity. Below pH 6.5 is acid, above pH 7.5 is alkaline.

PHYLLODE A leaf stalk expanded to look like and act like a leaf.

PICOTEE Term applied to a narrow band of colour on a pale ground at the edge of a petal.

PINCHING OUT The removal of the growing point of a stem to induce bushiness or to encourage flowering. Also known as *stopping*.

PINNATE LEAF A series of leaflets arranged on either side of a central stalk.

PIP Two distinct meanings — the seed of some fruits (e.g Orange) and the rootstock of some flowering plants (e.g Convallaria).

PISTIL The female reproductive parts of the flower.

PLANT WINDOW Double window with plants grown in the space between.

PLUG A small but well-rooted seedling raised in a cellular tray and sold for growing on.

PLUNGING The placing of a pot up to its rim outdoors in soil, peat or ashes.

POT-BOUND A plant growing in a pot which is too small to allow proper leaf and stem growth.

POTTING ON The repotting of a plant into a proper-sized larger pot which will allow continued root development.

PRICKING OUT The moving of seedlings from the tray or pot in which they were sown to other receptacles where they can be spaced out individually.

RESTING PERIOD The time when a plant has naturally stopped growing but when there is little or no leaf fall. Compare *dormant period*.

RHIZOME A thickened stem which grows horizontally below or on the soil surface.

ROOT BALL See Picture Dictionary (page 250).

ROOTING HORMONE A chemical in powder or liquid form which promotes the formation of roots at the base of a cutting.

ROSETTE Term applied to a whorl of leaves arising at the base of a plant.

RUNNER See Picture Dictionary (page 250).

SELF-COLOUR A flower with single-coloured petals.

SEPAL One of the divisions of the *calyx*.

SERRATE Saw-edged.

SESSILE A stalkless leaf or flower which is borne directly on the stem.

SHORT DAY PLANT A plant which requires light for a shorter period than it would normally receive from daylight in order to induce flowering; e.g Chrysanthemum and Poinsettia.

SHRUB A woody plant with a framework of branches and little or no central stem. Compare *tree*.

SINGLE FLOWER See Picture Dictionary (page 250).

SPADIX A fleshy flower spike in which tiny *florets* are embedded.

SPATHE A large *bract*, sometimes highly coloured, surrounding or enclosing a *spadix*. The spathe flower is characteristic of the aroids, such as Anthurium and Spathiphyllum.

SPECIES See *The Naming of House Plants*, page 5.

SPORE A reproductive cell of non-flowering plants, such as ferns.

SPORT A plant which shows a marked and inheritable change from its parent; a *mutation*.

STAMEN The male reproductive parts of a flower.

STANDARD A plant which does not normally grow as a tree but is trained into a tree-like form.

STERILISED SOIL A rather misleading term, as steam- or chemically-sterilised soil is only partially sterilised. Harmful organisms have been killed but helpful bacteria have been spared.

STOLON See *runner*.

STOPPING See *pinching out*.

STOVE PLANT A plant which requires warm greenhouse conditions in winter.

STRAIN A selection of a *variety*, *cultivar* or *species* which is raised from seed.

SUCCULENT See Picture Dictionary (page 250).

SUCKER A shoot which arises from an underground shoot or root of a plant.

SYSTEMIC A pesticide which goes inside the plant and travels in the sap stream.

TAP ROOT A strong root, sometimes swollen, which grows vertically into the soil or compost.

TENDER An indoor plant which requires a minimum temperature of 60°F. Occasional short exposure to temperatures below this level may be tolerated. Compare *hardy* and *half hardy*.

TENDRIL A thread-like stem or leaf which clings to any nearby support.

TERMINAL The uppermost bud or flower on a stem.

TERRARIUM A partly or entirely closed glass container used to house a collection of indoor plants.

TERRESTRIAL See Picture Dictionary (page 250).

TOPIARY The art of clipping and training woody plants to form geometric shapes or intricate patterns. Box and Myrtle are suitable types.

TRANSPIRATION The loss of water through the pores of the leaf.

TREE A woody plant with a distinct central trunk. Compare *shrub*.

TUBER A storage organ used for propagation. It may be a fleshy root (e.g Dahlia) or a swollen underground stem.

VARIEGATED LEAF See Picture Dictionary (page 250).

VARIETY See *The Naming of House Plants*, page 5.

WHORLED Leaf form, where three or more leaves radiate from a single *node*.

XEROPHYTE A plant which is able to live under very dry conditions.

Picture Dictionary

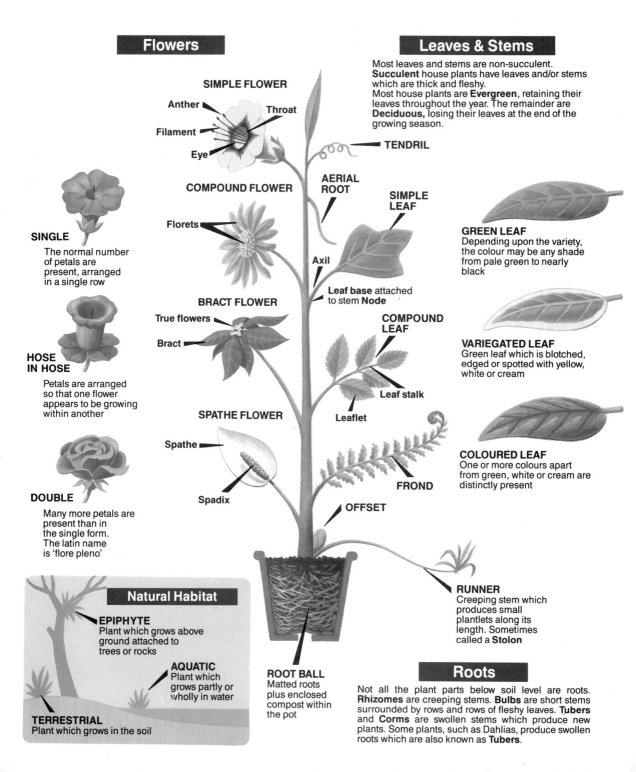

Flowers

SIMPLE FLOWER
- Anther
- Throat
- Filament
- Eye

SINGLE
The normal number of petals are present, arranged in a single row

HOSE IN HOSE
Petals are arranged so that one flower appears to be growing within another

DOUBLE
Many more petals are present than in the single form. The latin name is 'flore pleno'

COMPOUND FLOWER
- Florets

BRACT FLOWER
- True flowers
- Bract

SPATHE FLOWER
- Spathe
- Spadix

- TENDRIL
- AERIAL ROOT
- Axil
- **Leaf base** attached to stem **Node**

SIMPLE LEAF

COMPOUND LEAF
- Leaf stalk
- Leaflet

- FROND
- OFFSET

Leaves & Stems

Most leaves and stems are non-succulent. **Succulent** house plants have leaves and/or stems which are thick and fleshy.
Most house plants are **Evergreen**, retaining their leaves throughout the year. The remainder are **Deciduous,** losing their leaves at the end of the growing season.

GREEN LEAF
Depending upon the variety, the colour may be any shade from pale green to nearly black

VARIEGATED LEAF
Green leaf which is blotched, edged or spotted with yellow, white or cream

COLOURED LEAF
One or more colours apart from green, white or cream are distinctly present

RUNNER
Creeping stem which produces small plantlets along its length. Sometimes called a **Stolon**

Natural Habitat

EPIPHYTE
Plant which grows above ground attached to trees or rocks

AQUATIC
Plant which grows partly or wholly in water

TERRESTRIAL
Plant which grows in the soil

ROOT BALL
Matted roots plus enclosed compost within the pot

Roots

Not all the plant parts below soil level are roots. **Rhizomes** are creeping stems. **Bulbs** are short stems surrounded by rows and rows of fleshy leaves. **Tubers** and **Corms** are swollen stems which produce new plants. Some plants, such as Dahlias, produce swollen roots which are also known as **Tubers**.

CHAPTER 9

PLANT INDEX

A

	page
ABUTILON HYBRIDUM	61
ABUTILON HYBRIDUM SAVITZII	61
ABUTILON MEGAPOTAMICUM	61
ABUTILON MEGAPOTAMICUM VARIEGATA	61
ABUTILON STRIATUM THOMPSONII	61
ACACIA	62, 83
ACACIA ARMATA	62
ACACIA DEALBATA	62
ACACIA PODALYRIIFOLIA	62
ACALYPHA HISPIDA	62
ACALYPHA HISPIDA ALBA	62
ACALYPHA WILKESIANA	62
ACALYPHA WILKESIANA GODSEFFIANA	62
ACALYPHA WILKESIANA MUSAICA	62
ACER PALMATUM	82
ACHIMENES COCCINEA	63
ACHIMENES ERECTA	63
ACHIMENES GRANDIFLORA	63
ACHIMENES HYBRIDA	63
ACHIMENES LONGIFLORA	63
ACHIMENES LONGIFLORA ALBA	63
ACIDANTHERA MURIELAE	98
ACORUS GRAMINEUS VARIEGATUS	64
ADIANTUM CAPILLUS-VENERIS	138
ADIANTUM CUNEATUM	138
ADIANTUM HISPIDULUM	138
ADIANTUM RADDIANUM	138
ADIANTUM TENERUM FARLEYENSE	138
ADROMISCHUS COOPERI	213
AECHMEA CAUDATA	86
AECHMEA CHANTINII	86
AECHMEA FASCIATA	86
AECHMEA FOSTER'S FAVORITE	86
AECHMEA FULGENS DISCOLOR	86
AECHMEA RHODOCYANEA	86
AEONIUM ARBOREUM ATROPURPUREUM	213
AEONIUM ARBOREUM ATROPURPUREUM SCHWARZKOPF	213
AEONIUM TABULAEFORME	213
AESCHYNANTHUS JAVANICUS	63
AESCHYNANTHUS LOBBIANUS	63
AESCHYNANTHUS MARMORATUS	63
AESCHYNANTHUS PULCHER	63
AESCHYNANTHUS RADICANS	63
AESCHYNANTHUS SPECIOSUS	63
AFRICAN CORN LILY	99
AFRICAN MARIGOLD	73
AFRICAN VIOLET	201
AGAPANTHUS AFRICANUS	64
AGAPANTHUS ORIENTALIS	64
AGAPANTHUS ORIENTALIS ALBA	64
AGAVE AMERICANA	213
AGAVE AMERICANA MARGINATA	213
AGAVE AMERICANA MEDIOPICTA	213
AGAVE FILIFERA	213
AGAVE PARRASANA	213
AGAVE PARVIFLORA	213
AGAVE VICTORIAE-REGINAE	213
AGERATUM	72
AGERATUM HOUSTONIANUM	72
ALGAOMORPHA MEYENIANA	138
AGLAONEMA COMMUTATUM	65
AGLAONEMA COMMUTATUM SILVER SPEAR	65
AGLAONEMA MODESTUM	65
AGLAONEMA NITIDUM	65
AGLAONEMA PICTUM	65
AGLAONEMA PSEUDOBRACTEATUM	65
AGLAONEMA SILVER KING	65
AGLAONEMA SILVER QUEEN	65
AIR PLANTS	87
ALLAMANDA	64, 83
ALLAMANDA CATHARTICA	64
ALLAMANDA CATHARTICA GRANDIFLORA	64
ALLAMANDA CATHARTICA HENDERSONII	64
ALLIUM SCHOENOPRASUM	147
ALOCASIA AMAZONICA	66
ALOCASIA SANDERIANA	66
ALOE ARBORESCENS	214
ALOE ARISTATA	214
ALOE FEROX	214
ALOE HUMILIS	214
ALOE JUCUNDA	214
ALOE MITRIFORMIS	214
ALOE VARIEGATA	214

	page
ALPINE STRAWBERRY ALEXANDRIA	146
ALUMINIUM PLANT	191
AMARANTHUS CAUDATUS	67
AMARANTHUS CAUDATUS ATROPURPUREUS	67
AMARANTHUS CAUDATUS VIRIDIS	67
AMARANTHUS TRICOLOR	67
AMARYLLIS	97
AMARYLLIS BELLADONNA	97
AMARYLLIS BELLADONNA ALBA	97
AMAZON LILY	134
AMAZONIAN ZEBRA PLANT	86
ANANAS BRACTEATUS STRIATUS	87
ANANAS COMOSUS	87, 150
ANANAS COMOSUS VARIEGATUS	87
ANANAS SATIVUS	87
ANGEL WING BEGONIA	78
ANGEL'S TRUMPET	126
ANGEL'S WINGS	110
ANNUAL PHLOX	73
ANNUAL PINK	126
ANTHURIUM ANDREANUM	66
ANTHURIUM CRYSTALLINUM	66
ANTHURIUM SCHERZERIANUM	66
ANTHURIUM SCHERZERIANUM ALBUM	66
ANTIRRHINUM MAJUS	72
APHELANDRA AURANTICA	67
APHELANDRA SQUARROSA	67
APOROCACTUS FLAGELLIFORMIS	102
APOROCACTUS MALLISONII	102
ARABIAN VIOLET	136
ARACHIS HYPOGAEA	146
ARALIA ELEGANTISSIMA	128
ARALIA SIEBOLDII	135
ARAUCARIA EXCELSA	68
ARAUCARIA HETEROPHYLLA	68
ARDISIA CRENATA	68
ARDISIA CRISPA	68
ARECA LUTESCENS	180
ARECA PALM	180
ARGYRODERMA TESTICULARE	169
ARROWROOT PLANT	191
ARTILLERY PLANT	191
ARUNDINARIA MURIELAE	68
ARUNDINARIA NITIDA	68
ARUNDINARIA VARIEGATA	68
ASPARAGUS ASPARAGOIDES	69
ASPARAGUS DENSIFLORUS SPRENGERI	69
ASPARAGUS FALCATUS	69
ASPARAGUS FERN	69
ASPARAGUS MEYERI	69
ASPARAGUS PLUMOSUS	69
ASPARAGUS PLUMOSUS NANUS	69
ASPARAGUS SETACEUS	69
ASPIDISTRA ELATIOR	70
ASPIDISTRA ELATIOR VARIEGATA	70
ASPLENIUM BULBIFERUM	138
ASPLENIUM NIDUS	138
ASPLENIUM VIVIPARUM	138
ASTILBE ARENDSII	70
ASTROPHYTUM CAPRICORNE	102
ASTROPHYTUM MYRIOSTIGMA	102
ASTROPHYTUM ORNATUM	102
AUBERGINE BLACK ENORMA	145
AUBERGINE EASTER EGG	145
AUBERGINE LONG PURPLE	145
AUCUBA JAPONICA	70
AUCUBA JAPONICA GOLDIANA	70
AUCUBA JAPONICA VARIEGATA	70
AUSTRALIAN BRAKE FERN	141
AUSTRALIAN MAIDENHAIR	138
AVOCADO	150
AZALEA	71
AZALEA INDICA	71

B

	page
BABIANA STRICTA	98
BABOON ROOT	98
BABY RUBBER PLANT	188
BABY'S TEARS	157
BALL CACTUS	106
BAMBOO	68
BAMBOO PALM	180
BANANA	173
BANYAN TREE	143
BARBETON DAISY	151
BARREL CACTUS	103

	page
BASIL	147
BASKET BEGONIA	74, 75
BASKET GRASS	176
BASKET PLANT	63
BASKET VINE	63
BAY TREE	167
BEAD PLANT	175
BEAR'S PAW FERN	138
BEAUCARNEA RECURVATA	79
BEDDING DAHLIA	126
BEDDING PLANTS	72
BEEFSTEAK BEGONIA	77
BEGONIA ARGENTEO-GUTTATA	78
BEGONIA BARBARA	75
BEGONIA BOWERI	76, 77
BEGONIA CHARISMA	75
BEGONIA CHEIMANTHA	74
BEGONIA CLEOPATRA	76, 77
BEGONIA COCCINEA	78
BEGONIA CORALLINA DE LUCERNA	78
BEGONIA ELATIOR	75
BEGONIA ELFE	75
BEGONIA ERYTHROPHYLLA	77
BEGONIA FEASTII	77
BEGONIA FEASTII BUNCHII	77
BEGONIA FIREGLOW	74, 75
BEGONIA FOLIOSA	77
BEGONIA FUCHSIOIDES	79
BEGONIA GLAUCOPHYLLA	79
BEGONIA GLOIRE DE LORRAINE	75
BEGONIA HAAGEANA	79
BEGONIA HEIDI	75
BEGONIA IMPERIALIS	76, 77
BEGONIA LIMMINGHEIANA	78
BEGONIA LOVE ME	75
BEGONIA LUCERNA	78
BEGONIA MACULATA	76, 77
BEGONIA MANDELA	75
BEGONIA MAPHIL	77
BEGONIA MARCO	75
BEGONIA.MASONIANA	77
BEGONIA METALLICA	76, 77, 79
BEGONIA MULTIFLORA	74, 75
BEGONIA REX	76, 77
BEGONIA SCHWABENLAND	75
BEGONIA SEMPERFLORENS	79
BEGONIA SERRATIPETALA	79
BEGONIA SOLANTHERA	77
BEGONIA SUTHERLANDII	75
BEGONIA TIGER	77
BEGONIA TUBERHYBRIDA	74, 75
BEGONIA TUBERHYBRIDA PENDULA	74, 75
BEGONIA VINE	224
BELLADONNA LILY	97
BELOPERONE GUTTATA	80
BENGAL FIG	143
BERMUDA BUTTERCUP	99
BERTOLONIA MACULATA	80
BERTOLONIA MARMORATA	80
BILLBERGIA NUTANS	88
BILLBERGIA WINDII	88
BIRD OF PARADISE	211
BIRDCATCHER TREE	192
BIRD'S NEST BROMELIAD	89
BIRD'S NEST FERN	138
BISHOP'S CAP	102
BLACK GOLD PHILODENDRON	189
BLACK LEAF PANAMIGA	191
BLACK-EYED SUSAN	220
BLAZING STAR	100
BLECHNUM BRAZILIENSE	138
BLECHNUM GIBBUM	138
BLOOD LILY	153
BLOODLEAF	163
BLUE AFRICAN LILY	64
BLUE DAISY	136
BLUE ECHEVERIA	216
BLUE GUM	134
BLUE MYRTLE CACTUS	105
BLUEBELL	96
BLUE-FLOWERED TORCH	88
BLUSHING BROMELIAD	89
BLUSHING PHILODENDRON	189
BO TREE	143
BOAT LILY	198
BONSAI	81
BOSTON FERN	139
BOTTLEBRUSH PLANT	111
BOUGAINVILLEA	80, 83
BOUGAINVILLEA BUTTIANA MRS BUTT	80
BOUGAINVILLEA GLABRA	80
BOUVARDIA	84
BOUVARDIA DOMESTICA	84
BOWIEA VOLUBILIS	84
BOX	90
BRAIN CACTUS	103
BRASSAIA ACTINOPHYLLA	205
BRAZILIAN TREE FERN	138
BREYNIA NIVOSA ROSEOPICTA	84
BRODIAEA CORONARIA	98
BRODIAEA IDA-MAIA	98
BRODIAEA LAXA	98
BROMELIADS	85
BRONZE INCH PLANT	222
BROOM	125

	page
BROWALLIA SPECIOSA	90
BROWALLIA SPECIOSA ALBA	90
BROWALLIA SPECIOSA MAJOR	90
BROWN SPIDERWORT	222
BRUNFELSIA CALYCINA	90
BRYOPHYLLUM DAIGREMONTIANUM	214
BRYOPHYLLUM TUBIFLORUM	214
BUDDHIST PINE	194
BUDDLEIA INDICA	176
BUFFALO GRASS	210
BUNNY EARS	106
BURMESE FISHTAIL PALM	182
BUSH VIOLET	90
BUSY LIZZIE	160, 161
BUTTERFLY PALM	180
BUTTON FERN	140
BUXUS MICROPHYLLA	90
BUXUS SEMPERVIRENS	90

C

	page
CABBAGE TREE	132
CACTI — DESERT TYPES	101
CACTI — FOREST TYPES	108
CALADIUM BICOLOR	110
CALADIUM HORTULANUM	110
CALADIUM HUMBOLDTII	110
CALADIUM PICTURATUM	110
CALAMONDIN ORANGE	117
CALATHEA BACHEMIANA	172
CALATHEA CROCATA	172
CALATHEA INSIGNIS	172
CALATHEA LANCIFOLIA	172
CALATHEA LINDENIANA	172
CALATHEA LUBBERSII	172
CALATHEA MAKOYANA	172
CALATHEA MAUI QUEEN	172
CALATHEA ORNATA	172
CALATHEA ORNATA ROSEOLINEATA	172
CALATHEA ORNATA SANDERIANA	172
CALATHEA PICTURATA	172
CALATHEA ROSEOPICTA	172
CALATHEA VEITCHIANA	172
CALATHEA ZEBRINA	172
CALCEOLARIA HERBEOHYBRIDA	110
CALENDULA OFFICINALIS	72, 73
CALLA LILY	100
CALLIANDRA INAEQUILATERA	111
CALLIANDRA TWEEDYI	111
CALLISIA ELEGANS	222
CALLISIA FRAGRANS	222
CALLISTEMON CITRINUS	111
CALLISTEMON CITRINUS SPLENDENS	111
CAMELLIA	111
CAMELLIA JAPONICA	111
CAMPANULA FRAGILIS	112
CAMPANULA ISOPHYLLA	112
CAMPANULA ISOPHYLLA ALBA	112
CAMPANULA ISOPHYLLA MAYI	112
CANARY DATE PALM	181
CANARY ISLAND IVY	155
CANDLE PLANT	193, 217
CANDYTUFT	72
CANE PALM	180
CANNA HYBRIDA	98
CAPE COWSLIP	166
CAPE GRAPE	224
CAPE HEATH	133
CAPE IVY	207
CAPE LEADWORT	194
CAPE PRIMROSE	211
CAPSICUM	112, 146
CAPSICUM ANNUUM	112
CAPSICUM GROSSUM	146
CARDINAL FLOWER	198
CAREX MORROWII VARIEGATA	113
CARMONA MICROPHYLLA	83
CARNATION	126
CARPET BEGONIA	76
CARRION FLOWER	210
CARROT	150
CARYOTA MITIS	182
CARYOTA URENS	182
CASCADE CHRYSANTHEMUM	115
CAST IRON PLANT	70
CASTOR OIL PLANT	135
CATHARANTHUS ROSEUS	113
CATHEDRAL WINDOWS	172
CATTLEYA	178
CEDAR GUM	134
CELOSIA CRISTATA	113
CELOSIA PLUMOSA	113
CELOSIA PLUMOSA GOLDEN PLUME	113
CELOSIA PLUMOSA KEWPIE	113
CENTAUREA CYANUS	72
CENTURY PLANT	213
CEPHALOCEREUS SENILIS	102
CEREUS JAMACARU	102
CEREUS PERUVIANUS	102
CEREUS PERUVIANUS MONSTROSUS	102
CEROPEGIA WOODII	214
CESTRUM AURANTICUM	114
CESTRUM ELEGANS	114
CESTRUM NOCTURNUM	114
CESTRUM PARQUI	114

	page
CHAIN CACTUS	108
CHAMAECEREUS SILVESTRII	102
CHAMAECYPARIS PISIFERA	82, 122
CHAMAECYPARIS PISIFERA SQUARROSA INTERMEDIA	122
CHAMAECYPARIS PISIFERA SQUARROSA SULPHUREA	122
CHAMAEDOREA ELEGANS	181
CHAMAEDOREA ERUMPENS	180
CHAMAEDOREA SEIFRIZII	180
CHAMAEROPS EXCELSA	182
CHAMAEROPS HUMILIS	182
CHANDELIER PLANT	214
CHARM CHRYSANTHEMUM	115
CHENILLE PLANT	62
CHESTNUT VINE	224
CHICKEN GIZZARD	163
CHIN CACTUS	104
CHINCHERINCHEE	99
CHINESE EVERGREEN	65
CHINESE FAN PALM	182
CHINESE PRIMROSE	196
CHIONODOXA GIGANTEA	95
CHIONODOXA LUCILIAE	95
CHIONODOXA SARDENSIS	95
CHIVES	147
CHLOROPHYTUM COMOSUM	114
CHLOROPHYTUM COMOSUM MANDAIANUM	114
CHLOROPHYTUM COMOSUM VARIEGATUM	114
CHLOROPHYTUM COMOSUM VITTATUM	114
CHRISTMAS BEGONIA	74
CHRISTMAS CACTUS	109
CHRISTMAS CHEER	218
CHRISTMAS HEATHER	133
CHRISTMAS PEPPER	112
CHRYSALIDOCARPUS LUTESCENS	180
CHRYSANTHEMUM FRUTESCENS	115
CHRYSANTHEMUM MINI-MUM	115
CHRYSANTHEMUM MORIFOLIUM	115
CHRYSANTHEMUM MORIFOLIUM CASCADE	115
CHRYSANTHEMUM MORIFOLIUM CHARM	115
CIBOTIUM SCHIEDEI	138
CIGAR PLANT	123
CINERARIA	116
CISSUS ANTARCTICA	224
CISSUS ANTARCTICA MINIMA	224
CISSUS CAPENSIS	224
CISSUS DISCOLOR	224
CISSUS GONGYLODES	224
CISSUS HYPOGLAUCA	224
CISSUS QUADRANGULARIS	224
CISSUS RHOMBIFOLIA	224
CISSUS STRIATA	224
CITROFORTUNELLA MITIS	117
CITRUS LIMON	117, 150
CITRUS LIMON MEYERI	117
CITRUS LIMON PONDEROSA	117
CITRUS MITIS	117
CITRUS PARADISI	150
CITRUS SINENSIS	117, 150
CITRUS TAITENSIS	117
CLARKIA	72
CLARKIA ELEGANS	72
CLEISTOCACTUS STRAUSSII	103
CLERODENDRUM THOMSONIAE	117
CLEYERA JAPONICA	118
CLEYERA JAPONICA VARIEGATA	118
CLIANTHUS FORMOSUS	118
CLIANTHUS PUNICEUS	118
CLIMBING ONION	84
CLIVIA MINIATA	123
CLOAK FERN	139
CLOG PLANT	159
COBRA PLANT	162
COBWEB HOUSELEEK	218
COCCOLOBA UVIFERA	121
COCONUT PALM	181
COCOON PLANT	217
COCOS NUCIFERA	181
COCOS WEDDELIANA	181
CODIAEUM APPLELEAF	119
CODIAEUM AUCUBIFOLIUM	119
CODIAEUM BRAVO	119
CODIAEUM CRAIGII	119
CODIAEUM EUROPA	119
CODIAEUM EXCELLENT	119
CODIAEUM GOLD FINGER	119
CODIAEUM GOLD MOON	119
CODIAEUM GOLD STAR	119
CODIAEUM GOLD SUN	119
CODIAEUM GOLDEN RING	119
CODIAEUM HOLUFFIANA	119
CODIAEUM JULIETTA	119
CODIAEUM MRS ICETON	119
CODIAEUM NORMA	119
CODIAEUM PETRA	119
CODIAEUM REIDII	119
CODIAEUM VARIEGATUM PICTUM	119
CODIAEUM VULCAN	119
COELOGYNE	178
COELOGYNE CRISTATA	178
COFFEA ARABICA	122
COFFEA ARABICA NANA	122
COFFEE TREE	122
COLEUS BLUMEI	120
COLEUS PUMILUS	120
COLEUS REHNELTIANUS	120
COLEUS VERSCHAFFELTII	120
COLLINIA ELEGANS	181
COLUMN CACTUS	102
COLUMNEA BANKSII	121
COLUMNEA CRASSIFOLIA	121
COLUMNEA GLORIOSA	121
COLUMNEA HIRTA	121
COLUMNEA MICROPHYLLA	121
COLUMNEA STAVANGER	121
COMMON BOX	90
COMMON HOUSELEEK	218
COMMON IVY	155
COMMON PELARGONIUM	184
COMMON PRIMROSE	196
CONIFERS	122
CONOPHYTUM BILOBUM	169
CONOPHYTUM CALCULUS	169
CONOPHYTUM FRIEDRICHAE	169
CONOPHYTUM PEARSONII NANA	169
CONVALLARIA MAJALIS	95
CONVOLVULUS TRICOLOR	72
COPPERLEAF	62
CORAL BERRY	68, 86
CORDYLINE AUSTRALIS	132
CORDYLINE CONGESTA	132
CORDYLINE FRUTICOSA	132
CORDYLINE STRICTA	132
CORDYLINE TERMINALIS	132
CORN PALM	132
CORNFLOWER	72
CORSAGE ORCHID	178
COSTUS IGNEUS	122
COSTUS LUCANUSIANUS	122
COSTUS SPECIOSUS	122
COTYLEDON ORBICULATA	215
COTYLEDON UNDULATA	215
CRASSULA	198
CRASSULA ARBORESCENS	215
CRASSULA ARGENTEA	83, 215
CRASSULA FALCATA	215
CRASSULA LYCOPODIOIDES	215
CRASSULA OVATA HUMMEL'S SUNSET	215
CRASSULA PERFORATA	215
CRASSULA PORTULACEA	215
CRASSULA RUPESTRIS	215
CREEPING CHARLIE	191
CREEPING FIG	142
CREEPING JENNY	191
CREEPING MOSS	207
CREEPING PEPEROMIA	187
CRESS	147
CRETAN BRAKE	141
CRINUM BULBISPERMUM	123
CRINUM POWELLII	123
CRISTATE TABLE FERN	141
CROCUS	95
CROCUS CHRYSANTHUS	95
CROCUS VERNUS	95
CROSSANDRA INFUNDIBULIFORMIS	123
CROSSANDRA UNDULIFOLIA	123
CROTON	119
CROWN OF THORNS	135
CRYPTANTHUS ACAULIS	88
CRYPTANTHUS ACAULIS ROSEO-PICTUS	88
CRYPTANTHUS BIVITTATUS	88
CRYPTANTHUS BROMELIOIDES TRICOLOR	88
CRYPTANTHUS FOSTERIANUS	88
CRYPTANTHUS ZONATUS	88
CRYPTOMERIA JAPONICA	82
CRYSTAL ANTHURIUM	66
CTENANTHE OPPENHEIMIANA TRICOLOR	172
CUCUMBER FEMBABY	145
CUCUMIS SATIVUS	145
CUPHEA IGNEA	123
CUPID PEPEROMIA	187
CUPID'S BOWER	63
CUPRESSUS CASHMERIANA	122
CUPRESSUS MACROCARPA GOLDCREST	122
CURLY PALM	181
CYANOTIS KEWENSIS	222
CYANOTIS SOMALIENSIS	222
CYCAS REVOLUTA	182
CYCLAMEN	124
CYCLAMEN PERSICUM	124
CYCLAMEN PERSICUM DECORA	124
CYCLAMEN PERSICUM GIGANTEUM	124
CYCLAMEN PERSICUM SUTTONS PUPPET	124
CYCLAMINEUS NARCISSUS	93
CYMBIDIUM	178
CYMBIDIUM RIEVAULX HAMSEY	178
CYPERUS ALTERNIFOLIUS	125
CYPERUS ALTERNIFOLIUS GRACILIS	125
CYPERUS ALTERNIFOLIUS VARIEGATUS	125
CYPERUS DIFFUSUS	125
CYPERUS ESCULENTUS	125
CYPERUS HASPAN	125
CYPERUS PAPYRUS	125
CYPRIPEDIUM	178
CYRTOMIUM FALCATUM	138
CYRTOMIUM FALCATUM ROCHFORDIANUM	138
CYTISUS CANARIENSIS	125
CYTISUS RACEMOSUS	125

D

	page
DAFFODIL	93
DAHLIA VARIABILIS	126
DARLINGTONIA CALIFORNICA	162
DARWIN TULIP	94
DATE PALM	150, 181
DATURA CANDIDA	126
DATURA SUAVEOLENS	126
DAUCUS CAROTA	150
DAVALLIA CANARIENSIS	139
DAVALLIA FEJEENSIS	139
DAY JESSAMINE	114
DELTA MAIDENHAIR	138
DESERT FAN PALM	182
DESERT PRIVET	188
DEVIL'S BACKBONE	214
DEVIL'S IVY	206
DIANTHUS CARYOPHYLLUS	126
DIANTHUS CHINENSIS	126
DICKSONIA ANTARCTICA	139
DICKSONIA SQUARROSA	139
DIDYMOCHLAENA TRUNCATULA	139
DIEFFENBACHIA	127
DIEFFENBACHIA AMOENA	127
DIEFFENBACHIA AMOENA TROPIC SNOW	127
DIEFFENBACHIA BAUSEI	127
DIEFFENBACHIA BOWMANNII	127
DIEFFENBACHIA MACULATA	127
DIEFFENBACHIA OERSTEDII	127
DIEFFENBACHIA PICTA	127
DIEFFENBACHIA PICTA CAMILLA	127
DIEFFENBACHIA PICTA EXOTICA	127
DIEFFENBACHIA PICTA MARIANNE	127
DIEFFENBACHIA PICTA RUDOLPH ROEHRS	127
DINNER PLATE ARALIA	193
DIONAEA MUSCIPULA	162
DIPLADENIA SANDERI ROSEA	128
DIPLADENIA SPLENDENS	128
DIZYGOTHECA ELEGANTISSIMA	128
DIZYGOTHECA VEITCHII	128
DONKEY'S TAIL	218
DOUBLE EARLY TULIP	94
DOUBLE NARCISSUS	93
DRACAENA	129
DRACAENA DEREMENSIS	130
DRACAENA DEREMENSIS BAUSEI	130
DRACAENA DEREMENSIS COMPACTA	130
DRACAENA DEREMENSIS GREEN STRIPE	130
DRACAENA DEREMENSIS JANET CRAIG	130
DRACAENA DEREMENSIS RHOERSII	130
DRACAENA DEREMENSIS WARNECKII	130
DRACAENA DEREMENSIS WHITE STRIPE	130
DRACAENA DEREMENSIS YELLOW STRIPE	130
DRACAENA DRACO	131
DRACAENA FRAGRANS	132
DRACAENA FRAGRANS LINDENII	132
DRACAENA FRAGRANS MASSANGEANA	132
DRACAENA FRAGRANS VICTORIA	132
DRACAENA GODSEFFIANA	131
DRACAENA GODSEFFIANA FLORIDA BEAUTY	131
DRACAENA GODSEFFIANA KELLERI	131
DRACAENA INDIVISA	132
DRACAENA MARGINATA	130
DRACAENA MARGINATA COLORAMA	130
DRACAENA MARGINATA TRICOLOR	130
DRACAENA REFLEXA	131
DRACAENA REFLEXA VARIEGATA	131
DRACAENA SANDERIANA	131
DRACAENA SANDERIANA BORINQUENSIS	131
DRACAENA TERMINALIS	132
DRAGON TREE	131
DROSERA BINATA	162
DROSERA CAPENSIS	162
DUCHESNEA INDICA	146
DUMB CANE	127
DUTCH HYACINTH	92
DWARF COCONUT PALM	181
DWARF IRIS	96
DWARF LILY TURF	176
DWARF MORNING GLORY	72
DWARF POMEGRANATE	197

E

	page
EARTH STAR	88
EASTER CACTUS	109
EASTER LILY	168
ECHEVERIA AGAVOIDES	216
ECHEVERIA CARNICOLOR	216
ECHEVERIA DERENBERGII	216
ECHEVERIA ELEGANS	216
ECHEVERIA GIBBIFLORA	216
ECHEVERIA GIBBIFLORA CARUNCULATA	216
ECHEVERIA GIBBIFLORA CRISTATA	216
ECHEVERIA GIBBIFLORA METALLICA	216
ECHEVERIA GLAUCA	216
ECHEVERIA HARMSII	216
ECHEVERIA SETOSA	216
ECHINOCACTUS GRUSONII	103
ECHINOCACTUS HORIZONTHALONIUS	103
ECHINOCEREUS KNIPPELIANUS	103
ECHINOCEREUS PECTINATUS	103
ECHINOCEREUS RIGIDISSIMUS	103
ECHINOCEREUS SALM-DYCKIANUS	103
ECHINOFOSSULOCACTUS HASTATUS	103
ECHINOFOSSULOCACTUS MULTICOSTATUS	103
ECHINOFOSSULOCACTUS ZACATECASENSIS	103
ECHINOPSIS EYRIESII	104
ECHINOPSIS RHODOTRICHA	104
EGGPLANT	145
EGYPTIAN STAR CLUSTER	186
ELEPHANT EAR BEGONIA	79
ELEPHANT FOOT	79
ELEPHANT'S EAR PHILODENDRON	189
ELEPHANT'S EARS	110
ELKHORN FERN	140
EMERALD FERN	69
ENGLISH IVY	155
EPIPHYLLUM ACKERMANNII	109
EPIPHYLLUM COOPERI	109
EPIPHYLLUM GLORIA	109
EPIPHYLLUM LITTLE SISTER	109
EPIPHYLLUM LONDON GLORY	109
EPIPHYLLUM MIDNIGHT	109
EPIPHYLLUM PADRE	109
EPIPHYLLUM REWARD	109
EPIPHYLLUM SABRA	109
EPIPREMNUM AUREUM	206
EPISCIA ACAJOU	133
EPISCIA AMAZON	133
EPISCIA CLEOPATRA	133
EPISCIA CUPREATA	133
EPISCIA DIANTHIFLORA	133
EPISCIA HARLEQUIN	133
EPISCIA LILACINA	133
EPISCIA METALLICA	133
EPISCIA REPTANS	133
ERANTHEMUM ATROPURPUREUM	197
ERANTHIS HYEMALIS	95
ERANTHIS TUBERGENII	95
ERICA CANALICULATA	133
ERICA GRACILIS	133
ERICA HYEMALIS	133
ERICA VENTRICOSA	133
ESPOSTOA LANATA	103
ESPOSTOA MELANOSTELE	103
EUCALYPTUS CITRIODORA	134
EUCALYPTUS GLOBULUS	134
EUCALYPTUS GUNNII	134
EUCHARIS GRANDIFLORA	134
EUCOMIS BICOLOR	98
EUCOMIS COMOSA	98
EUONYMUS JAPONICA	134
EUONYMUS JAPONICA MEDIOPICTUS	134
EUONYMUS JAPONICA MICROPHYLLUS	134
EUPHORBIA FULGENS	135
EUPHORBIA GRANDICORNIS	215
EUPHORBIA MILII	135
EUPHORBIA OBESA	215
EUPHORBIA PULCHERRIMA	195
EUPHORBIA RESINIFERA	215
EUPHORBIA SPLENDENS	135
EUPHORBIA TIRUCALLI	215
EUROPEAN FAN PALM	182
EURYA JAPONICA	118
EURYA JAPONICA VARIEGATA	118
EUSTOMA GRANDIFLORUM	170
EVERGREEN GRAPE VINE	224
EXACUM AFFINE	136
EYELASH BEGONIA	76

F

	page
FAIRY PRIMROSE	196
FAIRY ROSE	199
FALLING STARS	112
FALSE ARALIA	128
FALSE HOLLY	179
FAN PALM	182
FATSHEDERA LIZEI	136
FATSHEDERA LIZEI VARIEGATA	136
FATSIA JAPONICA	135
FATSIA JAPONICA MOSERI	135
FATSIA JAPONICA VARIEGATA	135
FAUCARIA TIGRINA	216
FEATHER FERN	139
FEATHER PALM	181
FELICIA AMELLOIDES	136

page

FERNS 137
FEROCACTUS ACANTHODES 104
FEROCACTUS LATISPINUS 104
FICUS 142
FICUS ALI 143
FICUS AUSTRALIS 143
FICUS BENGHALENSIS 143
FICUS BENJAMINA 83, 143
FICUS BENJAMINA GOLD PRINCESS 143
FICUS BENJAMINA HAWAII 143
FICUS BENJAMINA NUDA 143
FICUS BENJAMINA STARLIGHT 143
FICUS BENJAMINA VARIEGATA 143
FICUS BUXIFOLIA 143
FICUS DELTOIDEA 142
FICUS DIVERSIFOLIA 142
FICUS ELASTICA 143
FICUS ELASTICA BLACK PRINCE 143
FICUS ELASTICA DECORA 143
FICUS ELASTICA DOESCHERI 143
FICUS ELASTICA ROBUSTA 143
FICUS ELASTICA SCHRIJVEREANA 143
FICUS ELASTICA TRICOLOR 143
FICUS ELASTICA VARIEGATA 143
FICUS LYRATA 143
FICUS PANDURATA 143
FICUS PUMILA 142
FICUS PUMILA MINIMA 142
FICUS PUMILA RIKKI 142
FICUS PUMILA SUNNY 142
FICUS PUMILA VARIEGATA 142
FICUS RADICANS 142
FICUS RADICANS VARIEGATA 142
FICUS RELIGIOSA 143
FICUS REPENS 142
FICUS RETUSA 143
FICUS RUBIGINOSA VARIEGATA 143
FICUS SAGITTATA 142
FICUS TRIANGULARIS 143
FIDDLELEAF FIG 143
FIDDLELEAF PHILODENDRON 189
FINGER ARALIA 128
FINGERNAIL PLANT 89
FIRECRACKER FLOWER 123
FIRECRACKER PLANT 170, 141
FISH HOOK CACTUS 104
FISHTAIL FERN 138
FISHTAIL PALM 182
FITTONIA ARGYRONEURA 144
FITTONIA ARGYRONEURA NANA 144
FITTONIA VERSCHAFFELTII 144
FLAME NETTLE 120
FLAME OF THE WOODS 163
FLAME VIOLET 133
FLAMING KATY 166
FLAMING SWORD 89
FLAMINGO FLOWER 66
FLAX 72
FLOWERING BANANA 173
FLOWERING INCH PLANT 221
FLOWERING MAPLE 61
FOREST LILY 100
FORGET-ME-NOT 72
FORTUNELLA MARGARITA 146
FOXTAIL FERN 69
FRAGARIA INDICA 128
FRAGARIA VESCA SEMPERVIRENS 146
FRANGIPANI 194
FRECKLE FACE 159
FREESIA HYBRIDA 98
FRENCH MARIGOLD 73
FROSTED SONERILA 209
FUCHSIA BEGONIA 79
FUCHSIA HYBRIDA 148, 149
FUCHSIA TRIPHYLLA 149
FUKIEN TEA 83

G

GALANTHUS ELWESII 95
GALANTHUS NIVALIS 95
GALTONIA CANDICANS 99
GARDENIA 83, 144
GARDENIA JASMINOIDES 144
GASTERIA MACULATA 216
GASTERIA VERRUCOSA 216
GENISTA 125
GEOGENANTHUS UNDATUS 151
GERANIUM 183, 184, 185
GERBERA JAMESONII 151
GERMAN IVY 207
GESNERIA CARDINALIS 198
GHOST PLANT 217
GLADIOLUS BO PEEP 96
GLADIOLUS COLUMBINE 96
GLADIOLUS COLVILLII 96
GLADIOLUS PRIMULINUS ROBIN 96
GLECHOMA HEDERACEA
   VARIEGATA 151
GLORIOSA ROTHSCHILDIANA 152
GLORIOSA SUPERBA 152
GLORY BOWER 117
GLORY LILY 152
GLORY OF THE SNOW 95
GLORY PEA 118
GLOXINIA 152
GOAT'S HORN CACTUS 102

page

GODETIA 72
GODETIA GRANDIFLORA 72
GOLD DUST DRACAENA 131
GOLDEN BALL CACTUS 106
GOLDEN BIRD'S NEST 204
GOLDEN EVERGREEN 65
GOLDEN LILY CACTUS 105
GOLDEN POTHOS 206
GOLDEN SEDUM 218
GOLDEN TOM THUMB CACTUS 106
GOLDEN TRUMPET 64
GOLDEN-RAYED LILY 168
GOLDFINGER 165
GOLDFISH PLANT 121
GOLDHEART IVY 155
GOODLUCK PLANT 132
GOOSEFOOT PLANT 219
GRANADILLA 186
GRAPE HYACINTH 96
GRAPE IVY 224
GRAPEFRUIT 150
GRAPTOPETALUM PACHYPHYLLUM 217
GRAPTOPETALUM PARAGUAYENSE 217
GRASS PALM 132
GREEN BRAKE FERN 140
GREEN EARTH STAR 88
GREVILLEA ROBUSTA 153
GREY-BARK ELM 82
GROUND IVY 151
GROUNDNUT 146
GUERNSEY LILY 99
GUZMANIA LINGULATA 88
GUZMANIA LINGULATA BROADWAY 88
GUZMANIA LINGULATA MINOR 88
GUZMANIA MUSAICA 88
GUZMANIA OMER MOROBE 88
GUZMANIA ZAHNII 88
GYMNOCALYCIUM MIHANOVICHII
   FRIEDRICHII 104
GYNURA AURANTIACA 153
GYNURA SARMENTOSA 153

H

HAAGEOCEREUS CHOSICENSIS 104
HAEMANTHUS ALBIFLOS 153
HAEMANTHUS KATHARINAE 153
HAMATOCACTUS SETISPINUS 104
HARE'S FOOT FERN 139, 141
HARLEQUIN FLOWER 100
HART'S TONGUE FERN 140
HAWORTHIA ATTENUATA 217
HAWORTHIA CUSPIDATA 217
HAWORTHIA FASCIATA 217
HAWORTHIA MARGARITIFERA 217
HAWORTHIA PAPILLOSA 217
HAWORTHIA REINWARDTII 217
HAWORTHIA TESSELLATA 217
HEART-LEAF PHILODENDRON 190
HEATHER 133
HEBE ANDERSONII 156
HEBE ANDERSONII VARIEGATA 156
HEDERA 154
HEDERA CANARIENSIS GLOIRE
   DE MARENGO 155
HEDERA HELIX 155
HEDERA HELIX ANNETTE 155
HEDERA HELIX CHICAGO 155
HEDERA HELIX CRISTATA 155
HEDERA HELIX EVA 155
HEDERA HELIX GLACIER 155
HEDERA HELIX GREEN RIPPLE 155
HEDERA HELIX HARALD 155
HEDERA HELIX IVALACE 155
HEDERA HELIX JUBILEE 155
HEDERA HELIX KHOLIBRA 155
HEDERA HELIX LUTZII 155
HEDERA HELIX MARMORATA 155
HEDERA HELIX MONA LISA 155
HEDERA HELIX PITTSBURGH 155
HEDERA HELIX SAGITTAEFOLIA 155
HEDERA HELIX SCUTIFOLIA 155
HEDGEHOG ALOE 214
HEDGEHOG CACTUS 103
HELICONIA ILLUSTRIS
   AUREOSTRIATA 156
HELICONIA INDICA 156
HELIOCEREUS SPECIOSUS 105
HELIOTROPE 156
HELIOTROPIUM HYBRIDUM 156
HELXINE SOLEIROLII 157
HELXINE SOLEIROLII ARGENTEA 157
HEMIGRAPHIS ALTERNATA 157
HEMIGRAPHIS COLORATA 157
HEMIGRAPHIS EXOTICA 157
HEN-AND-CHICKEN FERN 138
HENS AND CHICKENS 218
HEPTAPLEURUM 83, 157
HEPTAPLEURUM ARBORICOLA 157
HEPTAPLEURUM ARBORICOLA
   VARIEGATA 157
HERBS 147
HERRINGBONE PLANT 171
HIBISCUS 83, 158
HIBISCUS ESCULENTUS 146
HIBISCUS ROSA-SINENSIS 158
HIBISCUS ROSA-SINENSIS COOPERI 158

page

HIBISCUS SCHIZOPETALUS 158
HIBOTAN CACTUS 104
HIPPEASTRUM APPLE BLOSSOM 97
HIPPEASTRUM HYBRIDA 97
HIPPEASTRUM LUDWIG'S DAZZLER 97
HIPPEASTRUM SAFARI 97
HOLLY FERN 138
HORTENSIA 159
HOT WATER PLANT 63
HOUSE LIME 209
HOWEA BELMOREANA 181
HOWEA FORSTERIANA 181
HOYA AUSTRALIS 158
HOYA BELLA 158
HOYA CARNOSA VARIEGATA 158
HOYA MULTIFLORA 158
HYACINTHUS ORIENTALIS 92
HYACINTHUS ORIENTALIS
   ALBULUS 92
HYDRANGEA 159
HYDRANGEA MACROPHYLLA 159
HYMENOCALLIS FESTALIS 99
HYPOCYRTA GLABRA 159
HYPOCYRTA NUMMULARIA 159
HYPOESTES PHYLLOSTACHYA 159
HYPOESTES SANGUINOLENTA 159

I

IBERIS UMBELLATA 72
IMPATIENS BLITZ 161
IMPATIENS FANFARE 161
IMPATIENS HAWKERI 160, 161
IMPATIENS HOLSTII 160, 161
IMPATIENS LINEARIFOLIA 160, 161
IMPATIENS NEW GUINEA HYBRIDS 161
IMPATIENS NOVETTE STAR 161
IMPATIENS PETERSIANA 160, 161
IMPATIENS ROSETTE 161
IMPATIENS SULTANI 160, 161
IMPATIENS SULTANI
   VARIEGATA 160, 161
IMPATIENS SUPER ELFIN 161
IMPATIENS WALLERANA 161
IMPATIENS ZIG-ZAG 161
INCH PLANT 221, 222
INDIAN AZALEA 71
INDIAN PINK 126
INDIAN SHOT 98
INDIAN STRAWBERRY 128
INDOOR OAK 176
INSECT EATER 162
INSECTIVORES 162
IPHEION UNIFLORUM 99
IPOMOEA TRICOLOR 72
IRESINE HERBSTII 163
IRESINE HERBSTII
   AUREORETICULATA 163
IRIS DANFORDIAE 96
IRIS HISTRIOIDES MAJOR 96
IRIS RETICULATA 96
IRON CROSS BEGONIA 76
ITALIAN BELLFLOWER 112
IVORY PINEAPPLE 87
IVY 154, 155
IVY PEPEROMIA 188
IVY TREE 136
IVY-LEAVED GERANIUM 185
IXIA HYBRIDA 99
IXORA 83, 163
IXORA COCCINEA 163

J

JACARANDA 163
JACARANDA MIMOSIFOLIA 163
JACOBINIA CARNEA 164
JACOBINIA PAUCIFLORA 164
JACOB'S LADDER 217
JADE PLANT 83, 215
JAPANESE ARALIA 135
JAPANESE AZALEA 71, 82
JAPANESE LILY 168
JAPANESE MAPLE 82
JAPANESE SEDGE 113
JASMINE 164
JASMINUM MESNYI 164
JASMINUM OFFICINALE
   GRANDIFLORA 164
JASMINUM POLYANTHUM 164
JASMINUM PRIMULINUM 83, 164
JASMINUM REX 164
JATROPHA PODAGRICA 165
JELLY BEANS 218
JERUSALEM CHERRY 208
JESSAMINE 114
JEWEL PLANT 80
JOSEPH'S COAT 119
JUANULLOA AURANTIACA 165
JUNIPERUS CHINENSIS 82

K

KAFFIR LILY 118
KALANCHOE BEHARENSIS 217
KALANCHOE BLOSSFELDIANA 166
KALANCHOE BLOSSFELDIANA
   VESUVIUS 166
KALANCHOE DAIGREMONTIANUM 214

page

KALANCHOE MANGINII 166
KALANCHOE MANGINII WENDY 166
KALANCHOE MARMORATA 217
KALANCHOE TOMENTOSA 217
KALANCHOE TUBIFLORA 214
KANGAROO THORN 62
KANGAROO VINE 224
KANGAROO WATTLE 62
KENTIA BELMOREANA 181
KENTIA FORSTERIANA 181
KENTIA PALM 181
KING'S CROWN 164
KLEINIA ARTICULATA 217
KLEINIA TOMENTOSA 217
KOHLERIA ERIANTHA 165
KRIS PLANT 66
KUMQUAT 146

L

LACE ALOE 214
LACE ARALIA 193
LACE FERN 139
LACE FLOWER 133
LACE LEAF 144
LACHENALIA ALOIDES 166
LACHENALIA ALOIDES LUTEA 166
LACTUCA SATIVA 147
LACY TREE PHILODENDRON 190
LACYLEAF IVY 155
LADDER FERN 141
LANTANA CAMARA 167
LAPIDARIA MARGARETAE 169
LARIX KAEMPFERI 82
LATANIA BORBONICA 182
LATHYRUS ODORATUS 72
LAURUS NOBILIS 167
LAURUSTINUS 225
LEAF FLOWER 84
LEEA COCCINEA BURGUNDY 167
LEEA GUINEENSIS 167
LEMAIREOCEREUS MARGINATUS 105
LEMON 150
LEMON GERANIUM 183
LEMON-SCENTED GUM 134
LEOPARD LILY 127
LEPIDIUM SATIVUM 147
LETTUCE 147
LILIUM AURATUM 168
LILIUM CITRONELLA 168
LILIUM DESTINY 168
LILIUM EMPRESS OF CHINA 168
LILIUM FIESTA HYBRID 168
LILIUM GOLDEN SPLENDOR 168
LILIUM LONGIFLORUM 168
LILIUM MID-CENTURY HYBRID 168
LILIUM PUMILUM 168
LILIUM REGALE 168
LILIUM SPECIOSUM 168
LILY 168
LILY OF THE VALLEY 95
LILY-FLOWERED TULIP 94
LINUM GRANDIFLORUM 72
LIPSTICK VINE 63
LISIANTHUS RUSSELIANUS 170
LITHOPS BELLA 169
LITHOPS FULLERI 169
LITHOPS LESLIEI 169
LITHOPS OPTICA 169
LITHOPS PSEUDOTRUNCATELLA 169
LITHOPS SALICOLA 169
LITHOPS TURBINIFORMIS 169
LITTLE LADY PALM 182
LIVING STONES 169
LIVINGSTONE DAISY 72
LIVISTONA CHINENSIS 182
LIZARD PLANT 224
LOBELIA 72
LOBELIA ERINUS 72, 73
LOBIVIA AUREA 105
LOBIVIA FAMATIMENSIS 105
LOBIVIA HERTRICHIANA 105
LOBSTER CLAW 118
LOLLIPOP PLANT 179
LOVE-LIES-BLEEDING 67
LYCASTE 178
LYCASTE AROMATICA 178
LYCOPERSICON ESCULENTUM 145

M

MADAGASCAR DRAGON TREE 130
MADAGASCAR JASMINE 210
MADAGASCAR PERIWINKLE 113
MAGIC CARPET 205
MAHOGANY 83
MAIDENHAIR FERN 138
MAMMILLARIA BOCASANA 105
MAMMILLARIA HAHNIANA 105
MAMMILLARIA RHODANTHA 105
MAMMILLARIA WILDII 105
MANDEVILLA SPLENDENS 128
MANETTIA BICOLOR 170
MANETTIA INFLATA 170
MAPLELEAF BEGONIA 76, 77
MARANTA BICOLOR 171
MARANTA LEUCONEURA
   ERYTHROPHYLLA 171

	page
MARANTA LEUCONEURA FASCINATOR	171
MARANTA LEUCONEURA KERCHOVEANA	171
MARANTA LEUCONEURA MASSANGEANA	171
MARANTA MAKOYANA	172
MARANTA TRICOLOR	171
MARGUERITE	115
MARMALADE BUSH	211
MARTHA WASHINGTON PELARGONIUM	185
MATTHIOLA INCANA	72
MEDINILLA MAGNIFICA	170
MENTHA SPICATA	147
MERMAID VINE	224
MESEMBRYANTHEMUM CRINIFLORUM	72
METALLIC LEAF BEGONIA	76
MEXICAN SUNBALL	107
MEXICAN TREE FERN	138
MICROCOELUM WEDDELIANUM	181
MIKANIA TERNATA	173
MILK BUSH	215
MILTONIA	178
MIMOSA	62
MIMOSA PUDICA	173
MIND YOUR OWN BUSINESS	157
MING ARALIA	193
MINIATURE ROSE	199
MINIATURE WAX PLANT	158
MINT	147
MINT GERANIUM	183
MISTLETOE CACTUS	108
MISTLETOE FIG	142
MOCK ORANGE	192
MONEY TREE	215
MONKEY PLANT	200
MONSTERA DELICIOSA	174
MONSTERA DELICIOSA BORSIGIANA	174
MONSTERA DELICIOSA MINI	174
MONSTERA DELICIOSA VARIEGATA	174
MOONSTONES	217
MORNING GLORY	72
MOSES IN THE CRADLE	198
MOTH ORCHID	178
MOTHER FERN	138
MOTHER OF THOUSANDS	205
MOTHER-IN-LAW'S TONGUE	204
MUSA COCCINEA	173
MUSA VELUTINA	173
MUSCARI ARMENIACUM	96
MUSCARI BOTRYOIDES	96
MUSHROOM	146
MUSTARD	147
MYOSOTIS ALPESTRIS	72
MYRTILLOCACTUS GEOMETRIZANS	105
MYRTLE	175
MYRTUS COMMUNIS	175
MYRTUS COMMUNIS MICROPHYLLA	175

N

NAGAMI KUMQUAT	146
NARCISSUS	93
NARCISSUS CYCLAMINEUS	93
NARCISSUS HYBRIDA	93
NARCISSUS TAZETTA	93
NASTURTIUM	73
NATAL VINE	224
NEANTHE BELLA	181
NEEDLEPOINT IVY	155
NEMESIA	72
NEMESIA STRUMOSA	72
NEOREGELIA CAROLINAE MARECHALII	89
NEOREGELIA CAROLINAE TRICOLOR	89
NEOREGELIA SPECTABILIS	89
NEPENTHES COCCINEA	162
NEPETA HEDERACEA	151
NEPHROLEPIS CORDIFOLIA	139
NEPHROLEPIS EXALTATA	139
NEPHROLEPIS EXALTATA BOSTONIENSIS	139
NEPHROLEPIS EXALTATA FLUFFY RUFFLES	139
NEPHROLEPIS EXALTATA GLORIOSA	139
NEPHROLEPIS EXALTATA MAASSII	139
NEPHROLEPIS EXALTATA ROOSEVELTII	139
NEPHROLEPIS EXALTATA SCOTTII	139
NEPHROLEPIS EXALTATA SMITHII	139
NEPHROLEPIS EXALTATA WHITMANII	139
NEPHTHYTIS PODOPHYLLUM	219
NERINE FLEXUOSA	99
NERINE SARNIENSIS	99
NERIUM OLEANDER	175
NERTERA DEPRESSA	175
NET PLANT	144
NEVER NEVER PLANT	172
NEW ZEALAND TREE FERN	139
NICODEMIA DIVERSIFOLIA	176
NICOTIANA HYBRIDA	72
NIDULARIUM FULGENS	89
NIDULARIUM INNOCENTII	89
NIDULARIUM INNOCENTII STRIATUM	89

	page
NIGHT JESSAMINE	114
NOLINA TUBERCULATA	79
NORFOLK ISLAND PINE	68
NOTOCACTUS APRICUS	106
NOTOCACTUS LENINGHAUSII	106
NOTOCACTUS OTTONIS	106

O

OCIMUM BASILICUM	147
OCTOPUS TREE	205
ODONTOGLOSSUM	178
ODONTOGLOSSUM GRANDE	178
OILCLOTH FLOWER	66
OKRA	146
OLD MAN CACTUS	102
OLD MAN OF THE ANDES	107
OLEA	83
OLEANDER	175
OLIVE	83
OLIVERANTHUS ELEGANS	216
OPHIOPOGON JABURAN	176
OPHIOPOGON JABURAN VARIEGATA	176
OPHIOPOGON JAPONICUS	176
OPLISMENUS HIRTELLUS	176
OPLISMENUS HIRTELLUS VARIEGATUS	176
OPUNTIA BERGERIANA	106
OPUNTIA BRASILIENSIS	106
OPUNTIA CYLINDRICA	106
OPUNTIA MICRODASYS	106
OPUNTIA MICRODASYS ALBINOSPINA	106
OPUNTIA RUFIDA	106
ORANGE	150
ORCHID	177, 178
ORCHID CACTUS	109
OREOCEREUS CELSIANUS	107
OREOCEREUS TROLLII	107
ORGAN PIPE CACTUS	105
ORIGANUM MARJORANA	147
ORNAMENTAL FIG	142
ORNAMENTAL PEPPER	192
ORNITHOGALUM CAUDATUM	99
ORNITHOGALUM THYRSOIDES	99
OROSTACHYS SPINOSUS	217
OSMANTHUS HETEROPHYLLUS PURPUREUS	179
OSMANTHUS HETEROPHYLLUS VARIEGATUS	179
OTAHEITE ORANGE	117
OX TONGUE	216
OXALIS BOWIEI	99
OXALIS CERNUA	99
OXALIS DEPPEI	99

P

PACHYPHYTUM AMETHYSTINUM	217
PACHYPHYTUM OVIFERUM	217
PACHYSTACHYS LUTEA	179
PAINTED LADY	216
PAINTED NET LEAF	144
PAINTED TONGUE	200
PAINTER'S PALETTE	66
PALM	180
PAN-AMERICAN FRIENDSHIP PLANT	191
PANAMIGA	191
PANDA PLANT	189, 217
PANDANUS BAPTISTII	179
PANDANUS VEITCHII	179
PANDANUS VEITCHII COMPACTA	179
PANICUM VARIEGATUM	176
PANSY	73
PANSY ORCHID	178
PAPER FLOWER	80
PAPHIOPEDILUM	178
PAPHIOPEDILUM HYBRIDEN	178
PAPYRUS	125
PARADISE PALM	181
PARASOL PLANT	83, 157
PARLOUR IVY	207
PARLOUR PALM	181
PARODIA AUREISPINA	106
PARODIA CHRYSACANTHION	106
PARODIA SANGUINIFLORA	106
PARROT BILL	118
PARSLEY	147
PARSLEY IVY	155
PARTRIDGE-BREASTED ALOE	214
PASSIFLORA CAERULEA	186
PASSIFLORA QUADRANGULARIS	186
PASSION FLOWER	186
PATIENT LUCY	161
PEACE LILY	209
PEACOCK FERN	207
PEACOCK PLANT	172
PEANUT	146
PEANUT CACTUS	102
PEARL PLANT	217
PEDILANTHUS TITHYMALOIDES	217
PEDILANTHUS TITHYMALOIDES VARIEGATUS	217
PELARGONIUM CAPITATUM	183
PELARGONIUM CRISPUM	183
PELARGONIUM DOMESTICUM	185
PELARGONIUM FRAGRANS	183

	page
PELARGONIUM GRANDIFLORUM	185
PELARGONIUM GRAVEOLENS	183
PELARGONIUM GRAVEOLENS VARIEGATUM	183
PELARGONIUM HORTORUM	184
PELARGONIUM ODORATISSIMUM	183
PELARGONIUM PELTATUM	185
PELARGONIUM TOMENTOSUM	183
PELARGONIUM ZONALE	184
PELLAEA ROTUNDIFOLIA	140
PELLAEA VIRIDIS	140
PELLAEA VIRIDIS MACROPHYLLA	140
PELLIONIA DAVEAUANA	186
PELLIONIA PULCHRA	186
PEN WIPER	217
PENCIL EUPHORBIA	215
PENTAS CARNEA	186
PENTAS LANCEOLATA	186
PEPEROMIA ARGYREIA	188
PEPEROMIA CAPERATA	188
PEPEROMIA CAPERATA LITTLE FANTASY	188
PEPEROMIA CAPERATA VARIEGATA	188
PEPEROMIA CLUSIIFOLIA	188
PEPEROMIA FRASERI	188
PEPEROMIA GLABELLA	187
PEPEROMIA GREEN GOLD	188
PEPEROMIA GRISEOARGENTEA	188
PEPEROMIA HEDERAEFOLIA	188
PEPEROMIA MAGNOLIAEFOLIA	188
PEPEROMIA MAGNOLIAEFOLIA VARIEGATA	188
PEPEROMIA OBTUSIFOLIA	188
PEPEROMIA ORBA ASTRID	188
PEPEROMIA PERESKIAEFOLIA	188
PEPEROMIA PROSTRATA	187
PEPEROMIA ROTUNDIFOLIA	187
PEPEROMIA SANDERSII	188
PEPEROMIA SCANDENS VARIEGATA	187
PEPEROMIA SENSATION	188
PEPEROMIA VERTICILLATA	188
PERENNIAL SPIRAEA	70
PERESKIA ACULEATA	107
PERESKIA GODSEFFIANA	107
PERSEA AMERICANA	150
PERSIAN SHIELD	219
PETROSELINUM CRISPUM	147
PETUNIA	73
PETUNIA HYBRIDA	73
PHALAENOPSIS	178
PHALAENOPSIS HAPPY ROSE	178
PHILODENDRON ANDREANUM	189
PHILODENDRON ANGUSTISECTUM	189
PHILODENDRON BIPENNIFOLIUM	189
PHILODENDRON BIPINNATIFIDUM	190
PHILODENDRON BURGUNDY	189, 190
PHILODENDRON DOMESTICUM	189
PHILODENDRON ELEGANS	190
PHILODENDRON ERUBESCENS	189, 190
PHILODENDRON HASTATUM	189, 190
PHILODENDRON ILSEMANNII	189, 190
PHILODENDRON IMBE	190
PHILODENDRON MELANOCHRYSUM	189, 190
PHILODENDRON OXYCARDIUM	189
PHILODENDRON PANDURIFORME	189
PHILODENDRON PERTUSUM	174
PHILODENDRON RED EMERALD	189, 190
PHILODENDRON SCANDENS	189, 190
PHILODENDRON SELLOUM	190
PHILODENDRON TUXLA	190
PHLEBODIUM AUREUM	141
PHLOX DRUMMONDII	73
PHOENIX CANARIENSIS	181
PHOENIX DACTYLIFERA	150, 181
PHOENIX ROEBELENII	181
PHYLLITIS SCOLOPENDRIUM	140
PHYLLITIS SCOLOPENDRIUM CRISPUM	140
PHYLLITIS SCOLOPENDRIUM UNDULATUM	140
PIGGYBACK PLANT	220
PIGTAIL PLANT	66
PILEA BRONZE	191
PILEA CADIEREI	191
PILEA CADIEREI MINIMA	191
PILEA DEPRESSA	191
PILEA INVOLUCRATA	191
PILEA MICROPHYLLA	191
PILEA MOLLIS	191
PILEA MOON VALLEY	191
PILEA MUSCOSA	191
PILEA NORFOLK	191
PILEA NUMMULARIIFOLIA	191
PILEA REPENS	191
PILEA SILVER TREE	191
PILEA SPRUCEANA	191
PINEAPPLE	87, 150
PINEAPPLE LILY	98
PINK JASMINE	164
PINK SPOT BEGONIA	79
PINUS SYLVESTRIS	82
PIPER CROCATUM	192
PIPER ORNATUM	192
PISONIA UMBELLIFERA VARIEGATA	192
PISTACHIO	83
PISTACIA	83

	page
PITCHER PLANT	162
PITTOSPORUM TOBIRA	192
PITTOSPORUM TOBIRA VARIEGATUM	192
PLATYCERIUM ALCICORNE	140
PLATYCERIUM BIFURCATUM	140
PLATYCERIUM GRANDE	140
PLECTRANTHUS AUSTRALIS	193
PLECTRANTHUS COLEOIDES MARGINATUS	193
PLECTRANTHUS OERTENDAHLII	193
PLECTRANTHUS PARVIFLORUS	193
PLEOMELE REFLEXA VARIEGATA	131
PLUMBAGO AURICULATA	194
PLUMBAGO AURICULATA ALBA	194
PLUMBAGO CAPENSIS	194
PLUME ASPARAGUS	69
PLUME FLOWER	113
PLUMERIA RUBRA	194
PLUSH VINE	173
PODOCARPUS MACROPHYLLUS	194
PODOCARPUS MACROPHYLLUS MAKI	194
POINSETTIA	195
POISON PRIMROSE	196
POLIANTHES TUBEROSA	100
POLKA DOT PLANT	159
POLYANTHUS	196
POLYNESIAN TI	132
POLYPODIUM AUREUM	141
POLYPODIUM AUREUM MANDAIANUM	141
POLYSCIAS BALFOURIANA	193
POLYSCIAS BALFOURIANA MARGINATA	193
POLYSCIAS BALFOURIANA PENNOCKII	193
POLYSCIAS FRUTICOSA	193
POLYSCIAS GUILFOYLEI VICTORIAE	193
POLYSTICHUM AURICULATUM	141
POLYSTICHUM TSUS-SIMENSE	141
POMEGRANATE	83, 197
PONY TAIL	79
POOR MAN'S ORCHID	205
POT BEGONIA	74,75
POT CHRYSANTHEMUM	115
POT DAHLIA	126
POT MARIGOLD	72
POTHOS ARGYRAEUS	206
POWDER PUFF CACTUS	105
POWDERPUFF PLANT	111
PRAIRIE GENTIAN	170
PRAYER PLANT	171
PRICKLY PEAR	106
PRICKLY SHIELD FERN	141
PRIMROSE	196
PRIMROSE JASMINE	83, 164
PRIMULA ACAULIS	196
PRIMULA KEWENSIS	196
PRIMULA MALACOIDES	196
PRIMULA OBCONICA	196
PRIMULA SINENSIS	196
PRIMULA VARIABILIS	196
PRIMULA VULGARIS	196
PROPELLER PLANT	215
PSALLIOTA CAMPESTRIS	146
PSEUDERANTHEMUM ATROPURPUREUM	197
PSEUDERANTHEMUM ATROPURPUREUM TRICOLOR	197
PSEUDERANTHEMUM ATROPURPUREUM VARIEGATUM	197
PTERIS CRETICA	141
PTERIS CRETICA ALBOLINEATA	141
PTERIS CRETICA ALEXANDRAE	141
PTERIS CRETICA WILSONII	141
PTERIS CRETICA WIMSETTII	141
PTERIS ENSIFORMIS VICTORIAE	141
PTERIS TREMULA	141
PTERIS VITTATA	141
PUNICA GRANATUM	83, 197
PUNICA GRANATUM NANA	197
PURPLE HEART	222
PUSSY EARS	222
PYGMY DATE PALM	181
PYRACANTHA ANGUSTIFOLIA	82

Q

QUEEN'S TEARS	88
QUEENSLAND WATTLE	62

R

RABBIT'S TRACKS	171
RADERMACHERA DANIELLE	197
RADERMACHERA SINICA	197
RAINBOW STAR	88
RAT TAIL CACTUS	215
RAT'S TAIL CACTUS	102
RATTLESNAKE PLANT	172
REBUTIA KUPPERIANA	107
REBUTIA MINISCULA	107
REBUTIA MINISCULA GRANDIFLORA	107
REBUTIA MINISCULA VIOLACIFLORA	107
REBUTIA PYGMAEA	107
REBUTIA SENILIS	107

	page
RECHSTEINERIA CARDINALIS	198
RECHSTEINERIA LEUCOTRICHA	198
RED BUNNY EARS	106
RED CAP CACTUS	104
RED DRACAENA	132
RED ECHEVERIA	216
RED-HOT CATSTAIL	62
RED IVY	157
RED PINEAPPLE	87
REED PALM	180
REGAL ELKHORN FERN	140
REGAL PELARGONIUM	185
REGAL LILY	168
RESURRECTION PLANT	207
REX BEGONIA	76
RHAPIS EXCELSA	182
RHIPSALIDOPSIS GAERTNERI	109
RHIPSALIDOPSIS ROSEA	109
RHIPSALIS BURCHELLII	108
RHIPSALIS CASSUTHA	108
RHIPSALIS HOULLETIANA	108
RHIPSALIS PARADOXA	108
RHODODENDRON OBTUSUM	71
RHODODENDRON OBTUSUM REX	71
RHODODENDRON SIMSII	71
RHODODENDRON SIMSII AMBROSIA	71
RHODODENDRON SIMSII INGA	71
RHODODENDRON SIMSII OSTA	71
RHODODENDRON SIMSII STELLA MARIS	71
RHOEO DISCOLOR	198
RHOEO DISCOLOR VITTATA	198
RHOICISSUS CAPENSIS	224
RHOICISSUS RHOMBOIDEA	224
RHOICISSUS RHOMBOIDEA ELLEN DANICA	224
RHOICISSUS RHOMBOIDEA JUBILEE	224
RIBBON PLANT	131
ROCHEA COCCINEA	198
ROCHEA COCCINEA ALBA	198
ROCHEA COCCINEA BICOLOR	198
ROCHEA FALCATA	215
ROCK CACTUS	102
ROMAN HYACINTH	92
ROSA CHINENSIS MINIMA	199
ROSA ROULETTII	199
ROSARY VINE	214
ROSE CACTUS	107
ROSE GERANIUM	183
ROSE GRAPE	170
ROSE MAIDENHAIR	138
ROSE OF CHINA	158
ROSETTE CLOVER	99
RUBBER PLANT	143
RUELLIA MACRANTHA	200
RUELLIA MAKOYANA	200
RUSTY FIG	143

S

SAGE	147
SAGERETIA THEEZANS	83
SAGO PALM	182
ST. AUGUSTINE'S GRASS	210
ST. BERNARD'S LILY	114
SAINTPAULIA CONFUSA	202
SAINTPAULIA IONANTHA	202
SAINTPAULIA MAUNGENSIS	201
SALPIGLOSSIS SINUATA	200
SALVIA	73
SALVIA OFFICINALIS	147
SALVIA SPLENDENS	73
SANCHEZIA NOBILIS	200
SANCHEZIA SPECIOSA	200
SANSEVIERIA CYLINDRICA	204
SANSEVIERIA GOLDEN HAHNII	204
SANSEVIERIA GRANDIS	204
SANSEVIERIA HAHNII	204
SANSEVIERIA SILVER HAHNII	204
SANSEVIERIA TRIFASCIATA	204
SANSEVIERIA TRIFASCIATA BANTEL'S SENSATION	204
SANSEVIERIA TRIFASCIATA CRAIGII	204
SANSEVIERIA TRIFASCIATA LAURENTII	204
SANSEVIERIA TRIFASCIATA MOONSHINE	204
SANSEVIERIA ZEYLANICA	204
SARRACENIA DRUMMONDII	162
SATIN PELLIONIA	186
SAUCER PLANT	213
SAXIFRAGA SARMENTOSA	205
SAXIFRAGA SARMENTOSA TRICOLOR	205
SAXIFRAGA STOLONIFERA	205
SCARBOROUGH LILY	225
SCARLET PLUME	135
SCARLET STAR	89
SCHEFFLERA	83, 205
SCHEFFLERA ACTINOPHYLLA	205
SCHEFFLERA DIGITATA	205
SCHEFFLERA OCTOPHYLLUM	205
SCHIZANTHUS HYBRIDA	205
SCHLUMBERGERA GAERTNERI	109
SCHLUMBERGERA TRUNCATA	109
SCILLA ADLAMII	96

	page
SCILLA SIBERICA	96
SCILLA TUBERGENIANA	96
SCILLA VIOLACEA	96
SCINDAPSUS AUREUS	206
SCINDAPSUS AUREUS GOLDEN QUEEN	206
SCINDAPSUS AUREUS MARBLE QUEEN	206
SCINDAPSUS AUREUS TRICOLOR	206
SCINDAPSUS PICTUS ARGYRAEUS	206
SCINDAPSUS SIAMENSE	206
SCREW PINE	179
SEA GRAPE	121
SEA ONION	84
SEA URCHIN CACTUS	104
SEDUM ADOLPHI	218
SEDUM ALLANTOIDES	218
SEDUM BELLUM	218
SEDUM GUATEMALENSE	218
SEDUM MORGANIANUM	218
SEDUM PACHYPHYLLUM	218
SEDUM PREALTUM	218
SEDUM RUBROTINCTUM	218
SEDUM SIEBOLDII MEDIOVARIEGATUM	218
SEERSUCKER PLANT	151
SELAGINELLA APODA	207
SELAGINELLA EMMELIANA	207
SELAGINELLA KRAUSSIANA AUREA	207
SELAGINELLA LEPIDOPHYLLA	207
SELAGINELLA MARTENSII	207
SELAGINELLA MARTENSII WATSONIANA	207
SELAGINELLA UNCINATA	207
SEMPERVIVUM ARACHNOIDEUM	218
SEMPERVIVUM SOBOLIFERUM	218
SEMPERVIVUM TECTORUM	218
SENECIO ARTICULATUS	217
SENECIO CITRIFORMIS	218
SENECIO CRUENTUS	116
SENECIO CRUENTUS GRANDIFLORA	116
SENECIO CRUENTUS MULTIFLORA NANA	116
SENECIO CRUENTUS STELLATA	116
SENECIO HERREIANUS	218
SENECIO HYBRIDUS	116
SENECIO MACROGLOSSUS	207
SENECIO MACROGLOSSUS VARIEGATUS	207
SENECIO MIKANIOIDES	207
SENECIO ROWLEYANUS	218
SENSITIVE PLANT	173
SENTRY PALM	181
SETCREASEA PURPUREA	222
SETCREASEA STRIATA	222
SEVILLE ORANGE	117
SHRIMP BEGONIA	78
SHRIMP PLANT	80
SICKLETHORN	69
SIDERASIS FUSCATA	222
SILK OAK	153
SILVER CROWN	215
SILVER NET LEAF	144
SILVER TORCH CACTUS	103
SILVER VINE	206
SILVERY INCH PLANT	222
SINAPIS ALBA	147
SINGLE EARLY TULIP	94
SINGLE NARCISSUS	93
SINNINGIA SPECIOSA	152
SLIPPER FLOWER	110
SLIPPER ORCHID	178
SMALL-LEAVED BOX	90
SMILAX	69
SMITHIANTHA HYBRIDA	208
SMITHIANTHA ZEBRINA	208
SNAKE PLANT	204
SNAKESKIN PLANT	144, 204
SNAPDRAGON	72
SNOWBALL CACTUS	103
SNOWDROP	95
SOLANUM CAPSICASTRUM	208
SOLANUM MELONGENA OVIGERUM	145
SOLANUM PSEUDOCAPSICUM	208
SOLEIROLIA SOLEIROLII	157
SONERILA MARGARITACEA	209
SONG OF INDIA	131
SOUTHERN YEW	194
SPANISH BAYONET	225
SPANISH MOSS	85, 87
SPARAXIS TRICOLOR	100
SPARMANNIA AFRICANA	209
SPATHIPHYLLUM MAUNA LOA	209
SPATHIPHYLLUM WALLISII	209
SPATHIPHYLLUM WALLISII PETITE	209
SPECIES TULIP	94
SPIDER LILY	99
SPIDER PLANT	114
SPIDERWORT	222
SPINELESS YUCCA	225
SPIRAL GINGER	122
SPLEENWORT	138
SPLITLEAF PHILODENDRON	174
SPOTTED FLOWERING MAPLE	61
SPOTTED LAUREL	70
SPREADING CLUBMOSS	207
SPRING STARFLOWER	99

	page
STAGHORN FERN	140
STAPELIA GIGANTEA	210
STAPELIA VARIEGATA	210
STAR CACTUS	102
STAR OF BETHLEHEM	112
STAR WINDOW PLANT	217
STENOCACTUS	103
STENOTAPHRUM SECUNDATUM VARIEGATUM	210
STEPHANOTIS FLORIBUNDA	210
STERCULIA	83
STEREOSPERMUM SUAVEOLENS	197
STOCK	72
STRAWBERRY	146
STRAWBERRY CACTUS	104
STRELITZIA REGINAE	211
STREPTOCARPUS HYBRIDA	211
STREPTOSOLEN JAMESONII	211
STRING OF BEADS	218
STRING OF BUTTONS	215
STRING OF HEARTS	214
STRIPED INCH PLANT	222
STROBILANTHES DYERANUS	219
STROMANTHE AMABILIS	172
SUGAR ALMOND PLANT	217
SUMMER HYACINTH	96
SUN CACTUS	105
SUNDEW	162
SUNSET CACTUS	105
SWAMP LILY	123
SWEDISH IVY	193
SWEET FLAG	64
SWEET MARJORAM	147
SWEET ORANGE	117
SWEET PEA	72
SWEET PEPPER CANAPE	146
SWEET PEPPER GYPSY	146
SWEETHEART PLANT	189, 190
SWIETENIA	83
SWISS CHEESE PLANT	174
SWORD FERN	139
SYAGRUS WEDDELIANA	181
SYNGONIUM ANGUSTATUM	219
SYNGONIUM AURITUM	219
SYNGONIUM PODOPHYLLUM	219
SYNGONIUM PODOPHYLLUM EMERALD GEM	219
SYNGONIUM PODOPHYLLUM GREEN GOLD	219
SYNGONIUM PODOPHYLLUM IMPERIAL WHITE	219

T

TABLE FERN	141
TAGETES ERECTA	73
TAGETES PATULA	73
TAMARIX	83
TAZETTA NARCISSUS	93
TEDDY BEAR VINE	222
TEMPLE BELLS	208
TETRASTIGMA VOINIERIANUM	224
THREAD AGAVE	213
THUNBERGIA ALATA	220
THYME	147
THYMUS VULGARIS	147
TI CANE	129
TI PLANT	132
TI TREE	129
TIGER JAWS	216
TIGER ORCHID	178
TILLANDSIA ARGENTEA	87
TILLANDSIA CAPUT-MEDUSAE	87
TILLANDSIA CYANEA	88
TILLANDSIA IONANTHA	87
TILLANDSIA JUNCEA	87
TILLANDSIA LINDENII	88
TILLANDSIA USNEOIDES	85, 87
TOBACCO PLANT	72
TOLMIEA MENZIESII	220
TOM THUMB CACTUS	106
TOMATO FLORIDA PETIT	145
TOMATO MINIBEL	145
TOMATO TINY TIM	145
TOMATO TUMBLER	145
TORCH CACTUS	107
TORENIA FOURNIERI	220
TRACHYCARPUS FORTUNEI	182
TRADESCANTIA ALBIFLORA	221
TRADESCANTIA ALBIFLORA ALBOVITTATA	221
TRADESCANTIA ALBIFLORA AUREA	221
TRADESCANTIA ALBIFLORA TRICOLOR	221
TRADESCANTIA BLOSSFELDIANA VARIEGATA	221
TRADESCANTIA FLUMINENSIS	221
TRADESCANTIA FLUMINENSIS QUICKSILVER	221
TRADESCANTIA FLUMINENSIS VARIEGATA	221
TRAILING ABUTILON	61
TRAILING AFRICAN VIOLET	201
TRAILING CAMPANULA	112
TRAILING FIG	142
TRAILING PELARGONIUM	185

	page
TREE ALOE	214
TREE FERN	139
TREE PHILODENDRON	190
TRICHOCEREUS CANDICANS	107
TRICHOCEREUS SPACHIANUS	107
TRITONIA CROCATA	100
TROPAEOLUM MAJUS	73
TROUT BEGONIA	78
TRUE IVY	155
TSUS-SIMA HOLLY FERN	141
TUBEROSE	100
TULIP	94
TULIPA GREIGII	94
TULIPA HYBRIDA	94
TULIPA KAUFMANNIANA	94
TURKISH TEMPLE	215

U

UMBRELLA PLANT	125
UMBRELLA TREE	83, 205
URN PLANT	86

V

VALLOTA SPECIOSA	225
VANDA	178
VARIEGATED TABLE FERN	141
VARIEGATED WAX PLANT	158
VELTHEIMIA CAPENSIS	100
VELVET LEAF	217
VELVET PLANT	153
VENUS FLY TRAP	162
VERBENA	73
VERBENA HYBRIDA	73
VIBURNUM TINUS	225
VIBURNUM TINUS PURPUREUM	225
VIBURNUM TINUS VARIEGATUM	225
VINCA ROSEA	113
VINE	223
VIOLA	73
VIOLA HYBRIDA	73
VIOLA TRICOLOR	73
VITIS VOINIERIANA	224
VRIESEA CARINATA	89
VRIESEA FAVORITE	89
VRIESEA FENESTRALIS	89
VRIESEA HIEROGLYPHICA	89
VRIESEA RODIGASIANA	89
VRIESEA SPECIOSA	89
VRIESEA SPLENDENS	89
VRIESEA VULCANA	89
VUYLSTEKEARA	178

W

WAFFLE PLANT	157
WANDERING JEW	221, 222
WART PLANT	217
WASHINGTONIA FILIFERA	182
WATERMELON PELLIONIA	186
WATERMELON PEPEROMIA	188
WAX BEGONIA	79
WAX FLOWER	210
WAX PLANT	158
WAX PRIVET	187
WAX VINE	207
WEEPING CHINESE LANTERN	61
WEEPING FIG	83, 143
WHITE JASMINE	164
WHITE LILY TURF	176
WHITE PARLOUR MAPLE	61
WHORLED PEPEROMIA	188
WILD COFFEE	193
WINDMILL PALM	182
WINE FISHTAIL PALM	182
WINTER ACONITE	95
WINTER CHERRY	208
WISHBONE FLOWER	220

Y

YELLOW SAGE	167
YESTERDAY, TODAY AND TOMORROW	90
YUCCA ALOIFOLIA	225
YUCCA ELEPHANTIPES	225

Z

ZANTEDESCHIA AETHIOPICA	100
ZANTEDESCHIA ELLIOTTIANA	100
ZANTEDESCHIA REHMANNII	100
ZEBRA BASKET VINE	63
ZEBRA HAWORTHIA	217
ZEBRA PLANT	67, 172
ZEBRINA PENDULA	222
ZEBRINA PENDULA PURPUSII	222
ZEBRINA PENDULA QUADRICOLOR	222
ZELKOVA SERRATA	82
ZEPHYR LILY	100
ZEPHYRANTHES CANDIDA	100
ZEPHYRANTHES GRANDIFLORA	100
ZINNIA	73
ZINNIA ELEGANS	73
ZONAL PELARGONIUM	184
ZYGOCACTUS TRUNCATUS	109

The Experts

Acknowledgements

The author wishes to acknowledge the painstaking work of Gill Jackson, Paul Norris, Linda Fensom, Angelina Gibbs and Constance Barry. Grateful acknowledgement is also made for the help or photographs received from Joan Hessayon, Pat Brindley, Heather Angel, Harry Smith Horticultural Photographic Collection, Andrew Lawson, Syndication International, Peter Stiles, Michael Warren, Michael Brockway/Robert Harding Picture Library, Sheila Terry/Robert Harding Picture Library, Tommy Candler/The Garden Picture Library, Richard Bryant/Arcaid, Michael Dunne/EWA, Andreas von Einsiedel/EWA, Rodney Hyett/EWA, Neil Lorrimer/EWA, Jerry Tubby/EWA, Carleton Photographic, EWA, Tesco, Marks & Spencer, Van Hage's Garden Centre, Europlants UK Ltd, Pathfast Ltd, Sainsbury's Homebase, Mr & Mrs John Ainsworth of Tokonoma Bonsai Ltd and H Evans & Sons Ltd.

John Woodbridge provided both artistry and design work. The artists who contributed were Deborah Mansfield, John Dye and Derek Watson.